Jesus: Evidence and Argument or Mythicist Myths?

Jesus: Evidence and Argument or Mythicist Myths?

Maurice Casey

BLOOMSBURY

LONDON • NEW DELHI • NEW YORK • SYDNEY

Bloomsbury Academic

An imprint of Bloomsbury Publishing Plc

50 Bedford Square	1385 Broadway
London	New York
WC1B 3DP	NY 10018
UK	USA

www.bloomsbury.com

Bloomsbury is a registered trade mark of Bloomsbury Publishing Plc

First published 2014

British Library Cataloguing-in-Publication Data
A catalogue record for this book is available from the British Library.

ISBN: HB: 978-0-56729-458-6
PB: 978-0-56744-762-3
ePDF: 978-0-56759-224-8
ePub: 978-0-56701-505-1

Library of Congress Cataloging-in-Publication Data
Casey, Maurice
Jesus: Evidence and Argument or Mythicist Myths? / Maurice Casey p.cm
Includes bibliographical references and index.
ISBN 978-0-5672-9458-6 (hardcover) – ISBN 978-0-5674-4762-3 (pbk.)

Typeset by Fakenham Prepress Solutions, Fakenham, Norfolk NR21 8NN
Printed and bound in Great Britain

This book is dedicated to
Stephanie Louise Fisher,
my dearest friend who inspired me
and helped me with it from beginning to end.

CONTENTS

PREFACE

This book is a sort of sequel to *Jesus of Nazareth* (T&T Clark International, 2010). When I finished it, Stephanie Fisher persuaded me to write this as she was concerned with a growing phenomenon, enhanced by amateur blogs on the internet and inspired partly by publications by Price and Doherty, that there was no historical Jesus. Arguments against his existence were flawed, ignorant of recent scholarship or attacking it indiscriminately, and often based on out-of-date mythicist arguments written before newer advances in knowledge, she said. She felt this mythicist element was fuelled by atheism and anti-religion which attacked scholarship as religiously motivated. There was also a large element of genuinely interested and naturally sceptical people. Much of their doubt derived from the variety they perceived in historical Jesus figures and an inability to understand the historical process. She therefore persuaded me to write a book and set out the main arguments for the existence as a historical figure of Jesus in first-century Galilee. I should also explain why some people believe he was not, and refute the reasons which they put forward for their views. This book is the result. I am sorry that serious illness has delayed it, and doubly grateful to the publishers for proceeding with it all the same.

I am grateful to everyone who has helped with the composition of this book. I would especially like to thank Stephanie. After inspiring me to write it, she provided continued inspiration, did a lot of the relevant research, and helped me throughout its composition. She has also become my dearest friend. I am therefore very happy to dedicate it to her.

ABBREVIATIONS

AB	Anchor Bible
Adv. Haer.	*Adversus Haereses (Against Heresies)*
Ant.	*Antiquities of the Jews*
Apc. Mos.	Apocalypse of Moses
b.	Babylonian Talmud
b. *Pes.*	Babylonian Talmud, Tractate *Pesahim*
3 Bar.	3 Baruch
BBR	*Bulletin of Biblical Research*
Cic. *Verr.*	Cicero, *Against Verres*
Col.	Colossians
1 Cor.	1 Corinthians
2 Cor.	2 Corinthians
Dan.	Daniel
Deut.	Deuteronomy
De Vir. Ill	*De Viris Illustribus (On Illustrious Men)*
De Vit. Const.	*On the Life of Constantine*
Dial.	*Dialogue*
1 En.	1 Enoch
Ep.	*Epistles*
Eph.	Ephesians
Eus.	Eusebius
Exod.	Exodus
ExpT	*Expository Times*
H.E.	*Ecclesiastical History*

Gal.	Galatians
Gen.	Genesis
Heb.	Hebrews
Hdt.	Herodotus
HJC	*History of Joseph the Carpenter*
HThR	*Harvard Theological Review*
HTS	*Hervormde Teologiese Studies/Theological Studies*
Isa.	Isaiah
JBL	*Journal of Biblical Literature*
Jer.	Jeremiah
Jer.	Jerome
Jn	John
Jos.	Josephus
JSNT	*Journal for the Study of the New Testament*
Jub.	Jubilees
Judg.	Judges
1 Kgdms	1 Kingdoms (Septuagint of 1 Samuel)
Leg.	*Legatio (Embassy)*
Lev.	Leviticus
Lk.	Luke
LNTS	Library of New Testament Studies
LXX	Septuagint
Mk	Mark
Mt.	Matthew
Neof. 1	Neofiti 1
NTS	*New Testament Studies*
Num.	Numbers
p.	Palestinian Talmud
p. Keth.	Palestinian Talmud, Tractate Kethubhim
1 Pet.	1 Peter

Phil.	Philippians
Prov.	Proverbs
Ps.	Psalm
Rab. Perd.	Cicero, *Pro Rabellio Perduellionis*
RBL	*Review of Biblical Literature*
Rom.	Romans
1 Sam.	1 Samuel
Sir.	Sirach
SNTSMS	Society of New Testament Studies Monograph Series
Strom.	*Stromateis*
Tac.	Tacitus
Tg.	Targum
Tg. Ps-J	Targum Pseudo-Jonathan
1 Thess.	1 Thessalonians
2 Thess.	2 Thessalonians
2 Tim.	2 Timothy
WCG	Worldwide Church of God
Wsd.	Wisdom
Wsd. Sol.	Wisdom of Solomon
Zech.	Zechariah

1

Introduction: From fundamentalism to mythicism. Issues, 'scholars' and bloggers

Issues

One of the most remarkable features of public discussion of Jesus of Nazareth in the twenty-first century has been a massive upsurge in the view that this important historical figure did not even exist. This view became respectable during the formative period of critical scholarship in the nineteenth century, when it was no longer possible for Christian opinions to be taken for granted among educated European scholars. It became known as part of the work of the *Religionsgeschichtliche Schule*, learned men who were mostly from Germany. Because of its scholarly presentation, with as much evidence and argument as could reasonably be expected at that time, this view was much discussed by other learned people. Some way into the twentieth century, competent New Testament scholars believed that it had been decisively refuted in a small number of readily available books, supported in scholarly research by commentaries and many occasional comments in scholarly books.[1]

I do not formally discuss in this book the work of scholars of the *Religionsgeschichtliche Schule*, which is now regarded as out of date. They were learned men who did their best to advance knowledge in their own times, and who, after much learned and lengthy discussion, are known a good century later to have been significantly mistaken. I do discuss all

---

[1]The major generally available books were S. J. Case, *The Historicity of Jesus: A Criticism of the Contention that Jesus Never Lived, a Statement of the Evidence for His Existence, an Estimate of His Relation to Christianity* (Chicago: University of Chicago Press, 1912; 2nd edn, 1928); M. Goguel, *Jesus the Nazarene: Myth or History?* (1925. Trans. F. Stevens. London: Unwin and New York: Appleton, 1926. With a new introduction by R. Joseph Hoffmann, Amherst, New York: Prometheus, 2006).

those arguments that are still being put forward. Their work was taken up in England in the second half of the twentieth century by G. A. Wells, a professor of German at Birkbeck College, London. As a genuinely learned professor of German, Wells was thoroughly familiar with the work of the *Religionsgeschichtliche Schule,* the main points of which he repeated. He was also naturally familiar with the work of radical Christian scholars in Germany, such as Bultmann. After his retirement, he became gradually more and more learned in other New Testament scholarship. New Testament scholars, however, did not generally discuss his work, because it was not considered to be original, and all his main points were thought to have been refuted long ago, for reasons which were very well known. I do discuss his work to some extent in this book, because he has been influential in the recent presentation of the view that Jesus did not exist.

The presentation of this view has changed radically in recent years, led by unlearned but regrettably influential people in the United States. As far as I can tell, as we live through this change, it has three major features. One is rebellion against traditional Christianity, especially in the form of American fundamentalism. It is very striking that the majority of people who write books claiming that Jesus did not exist, and who give their past history, are effectively former American fundamentalists, though not all are ethnically American. Of these, only Robert Price can be regarded as a qualified New Testament scholar. After early involvement in a fundamentalist Baptist church, Price went on to become a leader in the Montclair State College chapter of the Inter-Varsity Christian Fellowship. He eventually received his Ph.D. in New Testament from Drew University in 1993. He has been listed as Professor of Theology and Scriptural Studies at Coleman Theological Seminary and Professor of Biblical Criticism at the Center for Inquiry Institute, as well as a fellow of the Committee for the Scientific Examination of Religion and the Jesus Seminar.

The second major feature of recent presentations of the view that Jesus did not exist is the massive contribution of the internet. Unlike published scholarly work, the internet is uncontrolled and apparently uncontrollable, making it a perfect forum for people with negative views about critical scholarship. It is therefore important that two of the most influential writers of published work advocating the mythicist view – that is, the view that Jesus was not a historical figure, but rather a myth – appeal directly to an audience on the internet.

A third major feature is drastic reliance on work which is out of date, most of which was of questionable quality when it was written, mostly in the nineteenth and early twentieth centuries. This level of incompetence is rare in conventional scholarship.

In *Jesus: Neither God Nor Man,* Earl Doherty, perhaps the most influential of all the mythicists, commented:

The advent of the Internet has introduced an unprecedented "lay" element of scholarship to the field ... the absence of peer pressure and constraints of academic tenure, has meant that the study of Christian origins is undergoing a quantum leap in the hands of a much wider constituency than traditional academia...

Commenting further on his website and his previous book, he added,

The primary purpose of both site and book was to reach the open-minded "lay" audience...[2]

We shall see that this is as inaccurate as possible. The internet audience is 'lay', but most of it is not open-minded. It has both the 'Christian apologists' whom mythicists love to hate, and atheists who are determinedly anti-Christian. Both groups consist largely of people with closed minds who are impervious to evidence and argument, a quite different world from the critical scholars among whom I am happy to have spent most of my life, whether they were Christian, Jewish or irreligious. These wonderful people were not concerned by 'peer pressure' or the 'constraints of academic tenure', except that we were united by an absolute determination to oppose any threat to the academic freedom of people in our universities, regardless of status, colour, race, religion or creed. I have of course worked entirely in England, except for two years in Scotland and a few weeks in Germany, with conferences for very short periods in different countries abroad, and there is every reason to believe that that is a crucial difference from mythicists, who largely stem from the USA. While I have profited greatly from discussion with a small number of the best American scholars at SNTS, notably Chilton, Fitzmyer and Sanders, the majority of the most helpful discussions that I have had have been with colleagues from Germany, Holland and Scandinavia, and to a lesser extent (because there are fewer of them) Israel, Australia and New Zealand. None of these people had significant connections with fundamentalists or mythicists.

It is at this point that Doherty's reference to 'the absence of peer pressure and constraints of academic tenure' appears to be specifically American. I left the Christian faith in 1962, and as I qualified with a doctorate, obtained appointments at the universities of St Andrews and Nottingham, was appointed to membership of SNTS and obtained major research awards, I had massive support from most of my peers despite the controversial nature of some of my opinions. Peer review behind the scenes did lead to massive delay in the publication of *From Jewish Prophet to Gentile God*, and, more

---

[2]E. Doherty, *Jesus: Neither God Nor Man: The Case for a Mythical Jesus* (Ottawa: Age of Reason, 2009), pp. vii, viii, referring back to http://jesuspuzzle.humanists.net/Critiquesrefut1. htm [last accessed 12 February 2012], and E. Doherty, *The Jesus Puzzle: Did Christianity Begin with a Mythical Christ?* (Ottawa: Canadian Humanist Publications, 1999).

recently, to *Is John's Gospel True?* being largely ignored.[3] Precisely because of this, however, peer support and academic tenure were of central positive importance. The fact that I had tenure at an independent British university meant that no significant measures could be taken against me. Their threats were of no effect precisely because amidst this revolting 'peer pressure', I had *massive peer support* and *academic tenure*. The peer support was entirely based on appreciation of the quality of my scholarship, and not on agreement with my opinions.

This is quite different from American institutions, where so-called 'tenure' sometimes depends on holding certain opinions. For example, as I commented in *Jesus of Nazareth* on an attack on critical scholarship in general:

> Witherington, whose PhD qualified him to teach at an independent university, wrote these comments when he taught at Ashland Theological Seminary, whose 'Core Values' include the belief that the Old and New Testaments are 'God's infallible message for the church and the world', and whose 'Statement of Faith' calls them 'the infallible record of the perfect, final and authoritative revelation of his work and will'. In 1995, he was appointed as 'Amos Professor of New Testament for Doctoral Studies' at Asbury Theological Seminary, whose 'Statement of Faith' describes the Old and New Testaments as 'the only Word of God, without error in all that it affirms ... the only infallible rule of faith and practice'. Its trappings of scholarship can be seen at the inauguration of Dr Timothy C. Tennent as its eighth President on 9 November 2009, replete with lots of distinguished-looking academic gowns. All these statements illustrate the hollowness of the trappings, because they ensure that independent critical thought is not allowed. Witherington illustrated this especially well in 2009 when he made an attack on the Department of Biblical Studies at the University of Sheffield. When the department was threatened with the closure of its undergraduate department, and being turned into a 'research centre', which did not seem likely to work, its students protested, and the university received a massive quantity of letters of support for the department from all over the world. The situation was rapidly reviewed, the department was saved from this drastic damage, and it was promised that new staff would be appointed. Witherington, however, was quoted in *Christianity Today*:
>
> > Other faculty [at Sheffield] were 'bent on the deconstruction of the Bible, and indeed of their students' faith,' according to Ben Witherington, a New Testament scholar at Asbury Theological Seminary.

---

[3]P. M. Casey, *From Jewish Prophet to Gentile God: The Origins and Development of New Testament Christology* (The Cadbury Lectures at the University of Birmingham, 1985–6. Cambridge: James Clarke and Louisville: WJK, 1991); Maurice Casey, *Is John's Gospel True?* (London: Routledge, 1996).

Apart from its unacademic use of the technical term 'deconstruction', this accusation is false. In the subsequent debate on blogs, Witherington further alleged: 'Sheffield has deliberately avoided hiring people of faith.' This allegation is false too.[4] Unlike American theological seminaries, independent British universities like Sheffield do not discriminate on grounds of religion, any more than race, gender or colour, when making appointments. Independent critical thought is encouraged, whether from a Christian perspective or not. Witherington thus demonstrated not only that he does not understand independent British universities, but that, he does not always tell the truth, the most fundamental requirement of independent critical scholarship.[5]

From the perspective of an independent British university, this means that members of staff of such institutions do not have anything that we would recognize as 'academic tenure' at all.

There are moreover umpteen other American examples of the same thing. For example, Montreat College has a statement of faith which begins like this:

Montreat College is a Christ-centered institution of higher learning, grounded in the Presbyterian (Reformed) tradition. While students are welcomed regardless of religious affiliation, all of our trustees, faculty, and staff support the following faith statement:
1. *We believe the Triune God is sovereign in all matters of creation, life, salvation, and eternity.*
2. *We believe that Scripture is the inspired, authoritative, and completely truthful Word of God, and should govern the conduct of Christians in every aspect of their lives.*
3. *We believe Jesus Christ is God the Son, whom God the Father sent into the world to become a man, to die for sin, and to rise from the dead on the third day for our salvation. Thus, Jesus Christ is the only way to be reconciled to God.*
4. *We believe that, after the ascension of Jesus Christ, the Holy Spirit was sent to believers to enable them to walk in obedience to the Word of God as set forth once and for all in the Scriptures.*

The Associate Professor of Biblical and Religious Studies is Dr Paul L. Owen. In an article published with Shepherd in 2001, he attempted to refute some of my work on the Son of Man problem. In a response

---

[4]An account of the debate by Stephanie Fisher, with subsequent comments by others, was posted at http://dunedinschool.wordpress.com/ on 12 November 2009 and can be found here; http://dunedinschool.wordpress.com/2009/11/12/bewithering-is-becoming-bewildering/ [last accessed 7 February 2013].
[5]Maurice Casey, *Jesus of Nazareth: An Independent Historian's Account of His Life and Teaching* (London: T&T Clark International, 2010), pp. 22–3.

published in 2002, I pointed out his incompetence and attachment to his own traditions and scholarship which was out of date.[6] Owen did not reply, but later made a vigorous and misleading attack on my book *The Solution to the 'Son of Man' Problem*.[7] The importance of these points has nothing particular to do with him or me, or even the Son of man problem: it is rather that his faults are characteristic of American fundamentalists, and consequently inherited and continued by mythicists who used to be fundamentalists. This is at the heart of a proper explanation of why all their most important ideas are false.

The most important points are the following. First, serious misrepresentation. For example, Owen declares that 'Mark 2:10 is reduced to an original assertion that God has given some people the power to heal psychosomatic illnesses'. Owen is unable or unwilling to understand the Aramaic idiom which is unavoidable if the saying is reconstructed. He declares all the reconstructions 'highly speculative', without saying what is uncertain about them, and declares that I 'must sometimes put absurd statements on the lips of Jesus to recover his *ipsissima verba*'.[8] This is an example, but it is not what I wrote. Some of my comments in my conclusion to a complex discussion include this:

> The Son of man saying comes at the climax of the story. It is the standard idiom of a general statement which refers especially to the speaker. The general level of meaning assumes that Jesus' power was at least potentially available to other human beings. At the same time it was a real reference to himself in particular, and it was he who actually exercised the power to heal.[9]

In a lengthy discussion of the healing of psychosomatic illnesses in general, and paralysis in particular, all based on the most recent research and including very recent discussion of this story, I gave reasons for *my* view that this man's paralysis was of psychosomatic origin, like some of the other illnesses which Jesus healed. I did not attribute this view to Jesus, who would not have heard of it, and in this case, but not in general, he used the biblical model of illness caused by sin because it was appropriate.

---

[6]P. Owen and D. Shepherd, 'Speaking up for Qumran, Dalman and the Son of Man: Was *Bar Enasha* a Common Term for "Man" in the Time of Jesus?', *JSNT* 81 (2001), pp. 81–122; Maurice Casey, 'Aramaic Idiom and the Son of Man Problem: A Response to Owen and Shepherd', *JSNT* 25 (2002), pp. 3–32.
[7]P. L. Owen, review of Maurice Casey, *The Solution to the 'Son of Man' Problem* (LNTS 343. London/New York: T&T Clark International, 2007), *RBL* 2/9/2009. On 15 December 2010, *RBL* published a more accurate and therefore more informative review by Panayotis Coutsoumpos. I regret that the online reviews, which I quote, have no page numbers: I cite by the page numbers of my printout, so there may be slight variations in other people's printouts.
[8]Owen, review of Casey, *Solution to the 'Son of Man' Problem*, p. 4.
[9]Casey, *Solution to the 'Son of Man' Problem*, p. 167.

Again, in a one-line judgement, Owen declares that 'The "son of man" sayings in the Gospel of John are set aside... (pp. 274–313)'.[10] It should be obvious that a 39-page discussion did a little more than set them aside. I not only discussed the important point that they cannot be reconstructed in Aramaic, the language spoken by the Jesus of history, I interpreted all of them as part of the theology of the Johannine community in Ephesus towards the end of the first century CE. This was intended to be a positive contribution to scholarly understanding of the Fourth Gospel, its environment, and of the development of early Christian Christology. All Owen can see is that it does not fit with the fundamentalist view that Jesus himself made all the speeches in the Fourth Gospel. For the Son of man sayings, this has led Owen to depend on the work of Dalman.[11]

I have argued elsewhere that Dalman's work is out of date. Owen, however, accuses me of leaving it out, and declares that 'Since Dalman is arguably the most accomplished Aramaist *of the nineteenth century* [my italics], the omission is curious, especially since he spends some eight pages giving detailed attention to the "son of man" question, offering conclusions very much at odds with Casey's assertions.'[12] In fact, however, after discussing Dalman's unsatisfactory contribution in *Aramaic Sources of Mark's Gospel*, where I also discussed other scholars whom Owen accuses me of leaving out,[13] I commented fully in my response to Owen and Shepherd, beginning like this (except that the Aramaic was in the original script): 'we must discuss the regrettable frame of reference used by Owen and Shepherd to consider the earlier examples of *br 'nsh'*. They take this from Dalman about a century ago, before the publication of the Dead Sea Scrolls and other Aramaic documents. Two major points that they quote are verifiably false in the light of these discoveries:

The singular number *bar 'nash* was not in use; its appearance being due to imitation of the Hebrew text...

---

[10] Owen, review of Casey, *Solution to the 'Son of Man' Problem*, p. 5.
[11] Gustav Dalman, *Die Worte Jesu mit Berücksichtigung des nachkanonischen jüdischen Schrifttums und der aramäischen Sprache. 1. Einleitung und wichtige Begriffe* (Leipzig: J. C. Hinrichs, 1898. 2nd edn, 1930. There was no second volume); *The Words of Jesus, Considered in the Light of Post-biblical Jewish Writings and the Aramaic Language. 1. Introduction and Fundamental Ideas* (Trans. D. M. Kay. Edinburgh: T&T Clark International, 1902).
[12] Owen, review of Casey, *Solution to the 'Son of Man' Problem*, p. 2.
[13] Maurice Casey, *Aramaic Sources of Mark's Gospel* (SNTSMS 102. Cambridge: Cambridge University Press, 1998), pp. 16–19, together with pp. 29–33, 40–1 on Black, pp. 51–2 on Jeremias, and 52–4 on Fitzmyer, all scholars whose work I have discussed intermittently elsewhere. I have also discussed the most important work of Hurtado, which was hardly relevant to presenting a *new* solution to the Son of man problem: Maurice Casey, 'Lord Jesus Christ: A Response to Professor Hurtado', *JSNT* 27.1 (2004), pp. 83–96; Larry W. Hurtado, 'Devotion to Jesus and Historical Investigation: A Grateful, Clarifying and Critical Response to Professor Casey', *JSNT* 27.1 (2004), pp. 97–104.

We now know that the singular *br 'nsh* was in use, because apart from Dan. 7.13, we have four examples extant. The earliest is at *Sefire* 3.16',[14] which is centuries before the time of Jesus. I had noted previously that Dalman's conjecture of a Hebrew original for Dan. 7.13 was without foundation.[15]

The importance of Owen's mistakes is that he has employed the same methodology as mythicists. First, he has again misrepresented me, accusing me of omitting scholarship which I discussed elsewhere, discussions which I did not think should be repeated in my presentation of a *new* solution to a very difficult problem. Second, he has preferred scholarship which is out of date to recent research. Third, he has done so because scholarship which is out of date supports the tradition to which he has intellectually arbitrary adherence. Fourth, we should note that he is just one short step away from accusing me of 'suppressing' old scholarship that I did not see fit to reproduce in a book presenting new research.

All these points are central to the mythicist case. Owen had a very difficult childhood. His mother brought him up in difficult conditions, but died of cancer when he was 13. He then went through seven different foster homes.[16] According to the Montreat College website, he was converted at the age of 15 in an evangelical foster family, and spent his formative Christian years within the Pentecostal community. When studying in Scotland, he fell for the Presbyterian tradition, and he and his wife were confirmed into the Anglican Church in 2005. It is entirely understandable that anyone from such a difficult background should accept the religion of genuinely welcoming environments in which he found himself, and that he should change lots of details as part of his pilgrimage through life. I do not normally see fit to discuss the social background of scholars, whether distinguished or otherwise, but in this case it is important to consider what could happen if Owen had another conversion experience, this time to mythicism.

There are two reasons why this is of real importance in this particular case. Firstly, Owen, as a fundamentalist Christian, already has the most important faults of mythicists, and he would simply need to continue with them. To begin with, he could be said to misrepresent scholarship which does not belong to his tradition, as they do. Moreover, he holds recent research by people more learned than he in complete contempt, and prefers nineteenth-century scholarship which is out of date. All he would need to do is to replace Dalman with Massey, Higgins and co. It is also just a short step from declaring that I have 'omitted' scholars whose work I have discussed in books he is not discussing to announcing, as mythicists do, that

---

[14]Casey, 'Response to Owen and Shepherd', p. 27, quoting Owen and Shepherd, 'Speaking up for Dalman and the Son of Man', p. 106, quoting Dalman, *Words of Jesus*, p. 237.

[15]Casey, *Aramaic Sources of Mark's Gospel*, p. 17.

[16]For his version of the story, P. Owen, *The Long Winter: One Man's Journey through the Darkness of Foster Care* (Indiana: AuthorHouse, 2010).

scholars have 'suppressed' incompetent work which we no longer generally discuss because it was inaccurate when it was written, and is now also out of date. All this is despite the fact that he has a doctorate from a respected British institution.

Second, we can now put Doherty's comments on scholars into their cultural context of American fundamentalism. I have noted his preference for an internet audience with his comment that 'the absence of peer pressure and constraints of academic tenure, has meant that the study of Christian origins is undergoing a quantum leap in the hands of a much wider constituency than traditional academia…'.[17] If Owen were to convert to mythicism, he would immediately encounter a massive amount of 'peer pressure' to do nothing of the kind, it would be highly likely that he would lose his job in Montreat College, where members of staff have to agree to the college's 'faith statement'. This is why, from the point of view of an independent British university, his position is based on certain conditions and is accordingly not quite the same as what we regard 'tenure' to be. This is why it is completely untrue to say that 'the study of Christian origins is undergoing a quantum leap in the hands of a much wider constituency than traditional academia…'.[18] What might properly be called 'traditional academia' – that is to say, decent independent universities in several different countries, with scholars of different opinions and many of us with genuinely open minds – did, and still does, far better than the fundamentalists and atheists on the internet. Doherty has simply preferred an audience of people who will more easily agree with him.

Among bloggers, Doherty refers especially to Steven Carr,[19] to some of whose comments I shall accordingly refer. Doherty cites him as if he might be some kind of expert on Josephus, which he is not. This is because Doherty is discussing Josephus, *Ant.* XX, 197–203, where Josephus relates how King Agrippa removed from office the high priest, whom he calls Ananus son of Ananus. His father is better known to most people as Annas, high priest 6–15 CE, and father-in-law of Joseph Caiaphas, who was responsible for handing Jesus of Nazareth over to Pilate for execution. It is therefore entirely coherent that, as Josephus relates, the younger Ananus took advantage of the death of Festus, the Roman procurator, and arrested Jacob, brother of Jesus, usually known in English as James. Before the new procurator, Albinus, could travel to Israel from Rome, the younger Ananus arrested Jacob and some others, brought them before a Sanhedrin of judges, and had them stoned. This led to many objections, and the deposition of the younger Ananus.

---

[17] Doherty, *Jesus: Neither God Nor Man*, p. vii.
[18] Doherty, *Jesus: Neither God Nor Man*, p. vii.
[19] Doherty, *Jesus: Neither God Nor Man* p. 571 with p. 771n. 221, referring to Carr commenting on Josephus on his own blog at http://www.bowness.demon.co.uk/marston2.htm [last accessed 7 February 2013].

Josephus describes Jacob as 'the brother of Jesus called Christ, Jacob his name' *Ant.* XX, 200, which is as clear as could be. Mythicists, however, do not wish to believe this. This is why Doherty calls upon a blog post by Carr to argue that Josephus could not have written this passage as it stands. This is a standard ploy by mythicists. They cannot cope with the evidence as it stands, and constantly seek to alter it by positing interpolations. For this purpose they frequently repeat, often without references, very old scholarship written before the study of ancient texts had settled down in modern scholarship.

Carr is also catalogued by Dorothy Murdock. She is another influential mythicist, who cites him as an expert on New Testament textual criticism.[20] This is because she has noticed that the mss of the NT are not inerrant, as every textual critic knows. Neither she nor Carr, however, offers a proper critical disucssion, nor demonstrates a convincing grasp of critical scholarship. In Murdock's case, we know that she was converted to a form of fundamentalism for a time.[21]

Information about the background of Carr is not generally available. We do, however, know that Carr often comments on the blog of Neil Godfrey, a former member of the Worldwide Church of God, an American fundamentalist cult, now split into several pieces and generally known in its largest recent incarnation as Grace Communion International. I shall therefore make most use of Blogger Carr and Blogger Godfrey as examples of the audience for whom mythicists write, while referring occasionally to other mythicist bloggers and commentators who are no better. It is only fair to add, however, that Blogger Carr's blog has many entries which show that he knows more about early Christianity than anyone could guess from such entries. He shows no sign, however, of any significant knowledge of Aramaic.

'Scholars'

I introduce here the most influential mythicists who claim to be 'scholars', though I would question their competence and qualifications.

Acharya, S.

Acharya, S. is a pseudonym for Dorothy Murdock, q.v.

---

[20] D. M. Murdock, *Who Was Jesus?: Fingerprints of the Christ* (Seattle: Stellar House Publishing, 2007), p. 224, with p. 268, referring to Carr, 'Textual Reliability of the New Testament', on Carr's own blog at www.bowness.demon.co.uk/reli2.htm [last accessed 7 February 2013].

[21] See pp. 21–2.

Barker, Dan

Dan Barker is well known for one book, which is important for this chapter: *Godless: How an Evangelical Preacher Became One of America's Leading Atheists.*[22] This gives details of his pilgrimage from an American fundamentalist to an American atheist.

Dan Barker was born in 1949 into a fundamentalist Christian family in California. At the age of 15, he felt he underwent a conversion experience to be an evangelist, and went out to preach. He took part in 'healing' meetings, and converted people, including on mission in Mexico. From 1968–72, he attended Azusa Pacific College. This is now Azusa Pacific University, and its statement of faith includes the following:

> We believe the Bible to be the inspired, the only infallible, authoritative word of God.
>
> We believe that there is one God, creator of heaven and earth, eternally existent in three persons—Father, Son, and Holy Spirit.
>
> We believe in the deity of our Lord Jesus Christ, in His virgin birth, in His sinless life, in His miracles, in His vicarious and atoning death through His shed blood, in His bodily resurrection, and in His ascension to the right hand of the Father, and in His personal return to power and glory.[23]

This means that, after a fundamentalist upbringing, Barker was further processed in American fundamentalism, not seriously different from what I have noted at Ashland Theological Seminary, Asbury Theological Seminary, and Montreat College.

He did not graduate, but carried on preaching. He was ordained in 1975, and published some religious songs and worked in Hollywood, as well as carrying on in his ministry.

Barker's first tiny step away from fundamentalism seems quite extraordinary to those of us who have not been fundamentalists. In 1979, he went to a church and actually found committed Christians who did not believe that Adam and Eve were historical people! He was shocked and comments: 'I was shocked by this kind of talk. Liberal talk. The fundamentalist mindset does not allow this latitude.'[24] This is of course true, and important in understanding how some ex-fundamentalists end up with equally strong counter-convictions. He imagines that 'I made the leap, not to atheism, but to the commitment to follow reason and evidence wherever they might

[22] Dan Barker, *Godless: How an Evangelical Preacher Became One of America's Leading Atheists* (Berkeley: Ulysses Press, 2008).
[23] http://www.apu.edu/about/faith/ [last accessed 7 February 2013].
[24] Barker, *Godless*, p. 33.

lead...'.[25] It is highly regrettable that he does not appear to have been able to follow this excellent principle.

Barker next did a number of extremely sensible things. For example, 'I read some liberal and neo-conservative theologians, such as Tillich and Bultmann'.[26] It is entirely reasonable that he was not convinced, any more than I was. What is so amazing it that he has ended up in such a vigorous anti-Christian version of atheism, without apparently realizing that he has at least read, even if he has not met, as I have, perfectly decent and reasonable Christians. By the end of 1983, he had effectively left the Christian faith, after going through an awful period of feeling like a hypocrite, because he was landed with his daily life as a Christian minister, as he gradually came not to believe in it. In January, 1984, he wrote and told lots of people he was no longer a Christian.

Reactions were very varied, and some of them were appalling. For example, two former friends told him that he would go to Hell.[27] It is hardly surprising that he should be more affected by that than by liberal Christians, of whom he seems to have seen little, and who do not believe anything of the kind.

Barker then became an atheist debater, which was in his case in effect an atheist preacher, so his behaviour was not very different from his behaviour as an evangelist, except that he was preaching a different message. Such experiences naturally confirmed his faith that Christians are appalling conservative Christians, because these are the sort of people with whom he was confronted.

Most of the rest of Barker's book is devoted to refuting a hopelessly fundamentalist view of Christianity. In my view, he is largely correct in his arguments, so I do not offer any detailed discussion here, but it is regrettable that he has completely failed to recognize that this version of Christianity is not accepted by decent liberal Christians. At this level, he has not changed since he was a fundamentalist.

Chapter 15, however, is devoted to the important question, central to this book, 'Did Jesus Exist?' This chapter has a naive fundamentalist adherence to the prejudices of American atheism, and contains nothing new. I therefore simply illustrate this. Barker claims to have found out that 'The New Testament stories are internally contradictory'.[28] All this means is that the New Testament is not inerrant, as critical scholars have known for years. It is regrettable that Barker has taken no notice of us. Again, 'The miracle reports make the story unhistorical'. This shows a total lack of discrimination, based on Barker's fundamentalist views of what miracles are. For example, recent work, some of it available to him, has shown that

---

[25] Barker, *Godless*, p. 36.
[26] Barker, *Godless*, p. 37.
[27] Barker, *Godless*, p. 55.
[28] Barker, *Godless*, p. 252.

many of the reports of Jesus' exorcisms and other healings are perfectly plausible in the light of modern knowledge of psychosomatics and the anthropology of religion. Equally, critical scholars have not believed for years that stories of Jesus doing things such as walk on the sea, or raise Lazarus from the dead, are literally true.[29] It is regrettable that Barker has taken no notice of such work, which shows again that he has not liberated himself from his fundamentalist view of life, the world and the universe. As the most outstanding blogger, also a proper scholar of a decent cricketing nation, said of another atheist, 'Once a fundie always a fundie. He's just batting for the other side now.'[30]

Barker then takes a number of questionable comments from mythicist tradition, only sometimes offering documentation. For example, he comments: 'The early years of the Roman Republic is one of the most historically documented times in history.' This is not the case, and it is important that first-century rural Galilee is not remotely as well documented as, for example, a normal province in the British Empire in the nineteenth or twentieth centuries. He continues correctly: 'One of the writers alive during the time of Jesus was Philo-Judaeus (sometimes known as Philo of Alexandria).' Philo is correctly so known, because he lived in Alexandria. Barker, however, then follows wholly inaccurate mythicist tradition, taking a typical mythicist path of quoting a scholar who was no good when he wrote long ago, as well as out of date now. Barker quotes Remsburg in 1909: 'Philo ... was living in or near Jerusalem when Christ's miraculous birth and the Herodian massacre occurred.' Critical scholars have known for years that these stories are not literally true. Philo is, however, quite irrelevant, as he was nowhere near Jerusalem when these events did not occur in Bethlehem or Jerusalem or anywhere else, except that Jesus was born, probably in Nazareth. Barker continues quoting Remsburg: 'He was there when Christ made his triumphal entry into Jerusalem. He was there when the crucifixion with its attendant earthquake, supernatural darkness and resurrection of the dead took place...'[31] This is a gross mixture of

---

[29] See especially J. Keir Howard, *Disease and Healing in the New Testament: an Analysis and Interpretation* (Lanham: University Press of America, 2001); the works of Roger Aus, e.g. R. D. Aus, *Samuel, Saul and Jesus: Three Early Palestinian Jewish Christian Gospel Haggadoth* (Atlanta: Scholars, 1994), ch. 3, esp. pp. 134–57; *'Caught in the Act', Walking on the Sea, and the Release of Barabbas Revisited* (Atlanta: Scholars, 1998), pp. 51–133; *The Stilling of the Storm: Studies in Early Palestinian Judaic Traditions* (New York: Binghamton University, 2000), pp. 1–87; Casey, *Is John's Gospel True?*, pp. 55–7, 208–11, all of which were available to Barker, had he chosen to read such things. More recently, cf. Casey, *Jesus of Nazareth* (2010).

[30] N. T. Wrong, on a blog available at http://ntwrong.wordpress.com/2008/08/05/hector-avalos-blogs/#comment–632 [last accessed 7 February 2013].

[31] Barker, *Godless*, p. 253, quoting J. E. Remsburg, *The Christ: a critical review and analysis of the evidence of his existence* (New York: Truth Seeker Company, 1909), without proper reference.

events which did happen (triumphal entry, crucifixion), and events which did not happen. Philo was nowhere near at the time, and had no reason to hear of the events that did happen, let alone report on an increasingly Gentile version of Judaism.

Barker makes no further important points, so I do not discuss his work in the body of this book. His book is important to this discussion for one reason only: it can be taken to show the damaging effect of the fundamentalist mindset upon attempts at critical enquiry, that it can result in a merely different kind of preaching, which still takes notice only of its own traditions.

Carrier, Richard

Carrier was born in the USA in 1969. He describes his parents as 'freethinking Methodists (mother was church secretary)'.[32] He says he went to Sunday School, and to church on holy days. He became a Philosophical Taoist at the age of 15, and an Atheist (Secular 'Humanist') at the age of 21. He gained a B.A. History (minor in Classical Civilization), at UC Berkeley (1997), followed by an M.A. Ancient History, at Columbia University, New York (1998). He was then awarded an M.Phil. Ancient History, at Columbia University (2000) for a thesis on Herod the Great and the administration of the Roman Empire. Carrier subsequently wrote about it online, in a way that reveals his obsession with the Bible not being inerrant, arguing that: 'Christian apologists ... can argue from "Herod was the procurator of Syria" to "Luke and Matthew *don't* contradict each other on the year of Christ's birth, contrary to what all you mean atheist harpies keep saying".' All critical scholars, the majority of whom have been Christians, not 'mean atheist harpies', have known for years that the birth stories in Matthew and Luke are not only inconsistent with each other, but none of them is literally true. They have said so quite clearly in many publications.[33] Carrier is guilty of the fault, common among American atheists, of confusing Christians with American fundamentalists. Many Christians the world over are not like that at all. If we read Carrier's thesis, we are supposed to 'learn some stuff about various languages, Roman provincial administration, and how Herod the Great and Emperor Augustus were such party buds I'd bet a sawbuck they high-fived over a shared a [sic] hooker or two. (Not literally, of course; sure, everyone knows double-teaming hookers was invented in 1891 B.C., but the high-five is a 20th century invention; so, whatever the ancient Roman equivalent was.) Yeah, I'd risk a tenner on that. Stranger

---

[32] This information is taken from his 'brief biography' at www.infidels.org/library/modern/ richard_carrier/bio.html [last accessed 7 February 2013].
[33] I have provided a summary account for the general reader: Casey, *Jesus of Nazareth*, pp. 145–58, with basic bibliography.

shit has supposedly happened.'[34] I cannot see any point in unscholarly writing like this.

Mercifully, some of Carrier's work is better than this, but he is inclined to descend to this level whenever he discusses what he thinks of as Christian scholarship. For example, in an interview with Luke Muehlhauser on 2 January 2011, he commented on the work of Doherty and his critics: 'It's the kind of thing that most Jesus historians have never read "The Ascension of Isaiah," and I don't blame them because it's a massive long document. It's incredibly dull ... And it is considered apocryphal. Who cares? It's not canonical, right? ... Even secular historians will give that "Oh, it's not canonical, so it can't be relevant." ... But nonetheless, it's like they're trying to make their lives easier by not reading all these incredibly boring, tedious things.'

These comments bear no relationship to the reality of the work done by decent critical scholars, with whose work Carrier is evidently unfamiliar. Nor can I agree that The Ascension of Isaiah is 'a massive long document', let alone that such documents are in any way dull. When he got to Doherty, Carrier added: 'Doherty's been criticized for even the underlying background fact of there being demons of the air and for this to even be plausible. I know a lot of Jesus historians who know nothing about it. Some of them profess not to know anything about it. Some of them will insist that that's absurd, that that's not the belief, knowing nothing whatsoever about it. So one of the things I do in my book is I provide extensive documentation – not just from primary evidence but also other actual scholars – demonstrating that, yes, this is a widespread view. It's clearly a fundamental view in early Christianity.'[35] Carrier does not, however, say who these ignorant 'Jesus historians' are. We shall see, however, that there are good reasons not to believe that this is the correct background for understanding early Christianity.[36]

In 2008, Carrier was awarded a Ph.D. at Columbia University for a Dissertation entitled 'Attitudes Toward the Natural Philosopher in the Early Roman Empire (100 B.C. to 313 A.D.)'. I have seen no sign of this being published. He has, however, published other material, notably *Sense and Goodness without God: A.D.fense of Metaphysical Naturalism* (AuthorHouse, 2005), and his apologetic work *Not the Impossible Faith, Why Christianity Didn't Need a Miracle to Succeed* (Lulu, 2009), as well as some essays in R. M. Price and J. J. Lowder (eds), *The Empty Tomb: Jesus Beyond The Grave* (New York: Prometheus, 2005). His most recent book is *Proving History: Bayes's Theorem and the Quest for the Historical*

---

[34] This is now available at http://freethoughtblogs.com/carrier/archives/132, written on 6 January, 2012 [last accessed 7 February 2013].
[35] Carrier's interview with Luke Muehlhauser on 2 January, available for download at http://commonsenseatheism.com/?p=10150 [last accessed 7 February 2013].
[36] See pp. 118–31, 142–50, 169–201.

Jesus, (Amherst, New York: Prometheus, 2012). He has another one in preparation: *On the Historicity of Jesus Christ*. At present, he gives talks, and has public debates with very conservative Christians.

Doherty, Earl

Information about Earl Doherty is not readily available. The following account is based on information in the preface to *Jesus: Neither God Nor Man*, p. ix, on an undated entry on his website www.jesuspuzzle. humanists.net/, and on an interview with Blogger Godfrey.[37] Doherty was born in Canada in 1941. He was brought up as a Catholic. He comments, 'I became an atheist at the age of 19 ... It was largely an intellectual conversion, as too many things about the Catholic faith I grew up in were no longer acceptable ... Religion ... does not deserve a privileged position immune to criticism, as it largely enjoyed when I was young.' In the world as a whole, religion did not enjoy 'a privileged position immune to criticism'. This was after the *Religionsgeschichtliche Schule*, years after the advent of Bertrand Russell, and in the heyday of A. J. Ayer! This shows that, while Doherty differs from some mythicists in not being brought up as an American Protestant fundamentalist, he was nonetheless brought up in an authoritarian environment. As a Catholic of that kind, he would also necessarily be brought up to believe in the importance of the truth to be found in orthodox Church Fathers such as Augustine and later Aquinas, as well as the authority of orthodox scholars, not modernists. It is not surprising that on leaving such an authoritarian and dogmatic tradition, he should come to believe in the importance of ancient apocrypha, and the modern atheist tradition.

Doherty also claims to hold a B.A. with Distinction in Ancient History and Classical Languages, which he says gave him 'a working knowledge of Greek and Latin, which I have supplemented with the basics of Hebrew and Syriac.' He states that health reasons forced him to suspend an M.A. program, and that he did something 'very different' for some years.

This does not explain his inability to read texts correctly. For example, he says that according to Luke 2.21, Jesus was circumcised 'in the Temple eight days after his birth'.[38] Even Luke's creative story does not say this. On the contrary, it has Jesus circumcised when Luke presumably imagined he was still in Bethlehem (Lk. 2.21), and subsequently 'they went up to Jerusalem to present him to the Lord' (Lk. 2.22–4). We shall have to discuss many examples of Doherty's inability to understand ancient texts.

---

[37] http://vridar.wordpress.com/2011/04/02/interview-with-earl-doherty/ [last accessed 7 February 2013].
[38] Doherty, *Jesus: Neither God Nor Man*, p. 59.

Ehrman, Bart

Bart Ehrman has been an outstanding scholar. He is justly famous for his outstanding monograph *The Orthodox Corruption of Scripture: The Effect of Early Christological Controversies on the Text of the New Testament* (Oxford: OUP, 1996). He also revised the important textbook on textual criticism originally written by Bruce Metzger: Metzger, Bruce M. and Ehrman, Bart, *The Text of the New Testament: Its Transmission, Corruption, and Restoration* (OUP USA, 4th edn, 2005). He wrote another perfectly reasonable book, *Jesus: Apocalyptic Prophet of the New Millennium* (Oxford: Oxford University Press, 1999).

Ehrman has, however, remained in a narrow environment in the USA, and this has had a regrettable effect on some of his subsequent work. He made a bold attempt to write *Did Jesus Exist? The Historical Argument for Jesus of Nazareth* (New York: HarperCollins, 2012). This contained a number of good points, but also a small number of regrettable mistakes, grossly exaggerated by mythicists, with much regrettable creativity and contempt of critical scholarship. I have therefore not attempted to discuss it, but have chosen rather to tackle the main points of mythicist falsehood.

Freke, N. T. and Gandy, L. P.

It has been difficult to find accurate information about Freke and Gandy. Their book, *The Jesus Mysteries*[39] provides only a very slight amount of information. According to this, Freke has an honours degree in Philosophy, but I do not know at which institution. There is also a website by Freke.[40] Here we learn that 'Tim has spent years exploring and learning from the ancient Mystery School traditions. His Mystery Experience retreats offer an opportunity to participate in a twenty-first-century expression of this tradition, which is an evolution of the perennial Gnostic wisdom into a radically new and immediately accessible form.' 'The Mystery Experience cannot be captured by words, but people have said things such as … limitless love … enlightenment … gnosis … pure bliss … self-knowledge … exquisite oneness … deep peace … connection with all … the Christ within … better than sex … buddha-nature … the thing I've been searching for all my life …'. This puts Freke and Gandy in their place as vague New Age imitators and developers of those parts of ancient Gnosticism that appeal to them.

This is even clearer in their book, *The Laughing Jesus: Religious Lies*

[39] Freke, N. T. and Gandy, L. P., *The Jesus Mysteries: Was the 'Original Jesus' a Pagan God?* (London: Thorsons, 1999).
[40] http://www.themysteryexperience.com/ [last accessed 7 February 2013].

and Gnostic Wisdom.[41] Robert Price is quoted by Copac describing this as a 'manifesto for Gnostic mysticism', as he does on the inside cover. They themselves declare programmatically: 'This book is a damning indictment of Literalist religion and a passionate affirmation of Gnostic spirituality.'[42] Their description of 'Literalist religion' is, however, basically a reflection of fundamentalism, and has not emerged from careful research into early Christianity. It is especially important that the whole idea than Gnosticism is older than Literalist religion is based on inaccurate dating and misinterpretation of relatively early documents, major features of mythicism which will occupy a large proportion of this book.

In Chapter 3, they launch a slashing attack on the Old Testament. Their standard of judgement is whether it is literally true, which most of it is not. They do not acknowledge the massive role played by critical scholarship in enabling the results which they use to be achieved. Chapter 4 is a slashing attack on the New Testament, alleging for example that Jesus is a myth, not a historical figure at all. Most of this is conventional and unoriginal mythicist fantasy. For example, they allege that, in the myth of the Pagan Godman, 'He is born in a cave or humble cowshed on the twenty-fifth of December in front of shepherds.' We shall see that this is not part of any such myth, and critical scholars have known for years that such stories are not literally true of Jesus either. Again, 'He surrounds himself with twelve disciples'.[43] The historical Jesus really did do this. We shall, however, see that it was never part of a myth of a Pagan Godman. It is a conveniently false description of the occasional presence of the twelve signs of the Zodiac. This does not explain the origin of the story that Jesus had twelve disciples, which was really due to a historical first-century Jewish prophet preparing for the restoration of Israel.

Another of Freke and Gandy's books, *The gospel of the Second Coming: Jesus is back – and this time he's funny!*[44] is actually a novel! It would have been better if the authors had confessed that everything they write about Jesus is fictional.

This is ultimately due to quite gross hostility to Christianity, read back into the ancient world. This is most obvious in another of their contributions to fiction and falsehood: *Jesus and the Lost Goddess: The Secret Teachings of the Original Christians.*[45] The 'Product Description' begins,

---

[41] Freke, N. T. and Gandy, L. P., *The Laughing Jesus: Religious Lies and Gnostic Wisdom* (New York: Harmony, 2005).

[42] Freke and Gandy, *The Laughing Jesus,* p. 5.

[43] Freke and Gandy, *The Laughing Jesus,* p. 53.

[44] Freke, N. T. and Gandy, L. P., *The gospel of the Second Coming: Jesus is back – and this time he's funny!* (Alexandria, NSW and London: Hay House, 2007).

[45] Freke, N. T. and Gandy, L. P., *Jesus and the Lost Goddess: The Secret Teachings of the Original Christians* (London: Thorsons and New York: Harmony, 2001).

'Why Were the Teachings of the Original Christians Brutally Suppressed by the Roman Church?

'Because they portray Jesus and Mary Magdalene as mythic figures based on the Pagan Godman and Goddess
'Because they show that the gospel story is a spiritual allegory encapsulating a profound philosophy that leads to mythical enlightenment
'Because they have the power to turn the world inside out and transform life into an exploration of consciousness'.

We shall see that this is wrong from beginning to end. It attributes to the Roman church a power which it did not possess until some time after Constantine took over the empire in the fourth century CE. By this time a number of the teachings of the first Christians were written in the synoptic Gospels, Pauline epistles and Acts. Freke and Gandy's view is parasitic upon their false belief that the original Christians were Gnostics. The earliest Christians did not believe either that Jesus was a 'Godman', or that Mary Magdalene was anything resembling a 'Goddess'. It might be useful to know the experience of authoritarian religion which led Freke and Gandy to take such an inaccurate view of Christianity in the ancient world.

Gandy is said to have an M.A. in Classical Civilization from London University. *The Jesus Mysteries* refers to another website for more information, but I was not able to access it. He is said online to be British, to have a degree in philosophy, and to be a 'mysterious recluse'.

The Jesus Mysteries has on its cover an amulet which is an excellent symbol of their work. It purports to be a portrayal of Bacchus/Orpheus being crucified. Mythicists love this sort of thing, because it helps them to imagine that Jesus was a mythical figure, who was supposed to have been crucified in imitation of the fate of pagan deities. There are two things wrong with this. Firstly, as Freke and Gandy knew perfectly well, it was dated in the third or even fourth century CE, so it could not possibly have been relevant to the question as to whether a real, historical Jesus suffered the Roman penalty of crucifixion in the first century CE. Secondly, it was well known to be a much later forgery, as they at least should have known perfectly well.[46]

Harpur, T.

Tom Harpur was born of Irish immigrant parents in Scarborough, Ontario, in 1929. He was brought up as a fundamentalist Christian. He was awarded an Honours B.A. in 1951 at the University College, University of Toronto,

[46] In English, cf. e.g. W. K. C. Guthrie, *Orpheus and Greek Religion: a Study of the Orphic Movement* (London: Methuen, 2nd edn, 1952), p. 265 and note on p. 278.

where he won several awards in Classics. He studied Greats at Oxford from 1951 to 1954. He graduated in 1954 with the B.A and received the M.A. two years later. Between 1954 and 1956 he studied theology at Wycliffe College, University of Toronto.

Harpur was ordained priest in the Anglican Church of Canada in 1956, in accordance with his father's wishes and demands. He served as Curate at St. John's York Mills, Toronto in 1956–7. In 1962–3 he spent a year at Oriel College, Oxford, doing postgraduate research in Patristics and New Testament. From 1964 to 1971, Harpur was Assistant Professor and then full Professor of New Testament and New Testament Greek at Wycliffe College, University of Toronto. He is best known for his work with the *Toronto Star* where he worked as a journalist 1954–84. Since then he has continued to contribute a column on religious and ethical issues, and he has written a number of books on religion and theology. In his early career he was a fundamentalist.

It is evident that Harpur ceased to function as a (fundamentalist) Anglican priest long ago, and leaving that sort of post gives him one of the main qualifications for being a mythicist. However, he does not feel that he has left the Christian faith, however bizarre his views of it. On the basis of the above evidence, I suppose he could just about claim to be a qualified scholar. The title of his most recent book tells us half the story: *Born Again: My Journey from Fundamentalism to Freedom*.[47] His version of what he calls 'freedom' is his view that aspects of Christianity were derived from Egypt, that none of it is literally true, but the ancient myths on which it was supposedly based are very profound, and we all ought to live by them. This view was put forward in his most famous book, *The Pagan Christ*.[48] This is based on very old scholarship, which was of shocking quality when it was written, and which is now also hopelessly out of date. He has been rightly criticized for not giving proper references to the Egyptian material, making it hard for anyone realistically to take him seriously.

Hawkins, Rook

See Verenna, Thomas.

Leidner, Harold

Leidner was born in New York in 1916 of Polish-Jewish parentage, and died in 2008. He was not a qualified New Testament scholar. He studied Law,

---

[47]T. Harpur, *Born Again: My Journey from Fundamentalism to Freedom* (Toronto: Thomas Allen, 2011).
[48]T. Harpur, *The Pagan Christ: Recovering the Lost Light* (Toronto: Thomas Allen, 2004).

and was registered as a patent attorney in 1956, but he did not practice as such. His book, *The Fabrication of the Christ Myth* was published in 1999. It purports to give 'the Jewish leaders' 'their day in court, to which they are fully entitled'.[49] It consists of a massive outpouring of Jewish anti-Christian prejudice, the historical methodology of which is appalling. Leidner showed no more knowledge of Second Temple Judaism than understanding of the Gospels. It is regrettable that it is necessary to discuss some of his points, which show some knowledge of the mythicist debate.

Lemche, Niels Peter

Lemche is an Old Testament scholar at the University of Copenhagen. He is a minimalist, who has sought to transfer his commitment to the New Testament notably in support of his Copenhagen colleague T. L. Thompson. For example, in response to an attack on Thompson that I made in *Bible and Interpretation*, Lemche declared, 'As to Prof. Casey's review, I checked a few informations about Prof. Casey and saw something he said about the OT which is relatively out of tune with present day OT scholarship (on Jews and monotheism in Antiquity). Just to make my case clear.' This is not clear at all. Lemche does not give any reference for what I said, so no one can tell what I said. Secondly he gives no date, so no one can tell whether I am supposed to be simply wrong, or wrote something years ago which has not proved to be enduring. Thirdly, he does not say which 'present day OT scholarship'. Does he really mean I was not a minimalist? The last thing this comment does is make anything clear.

Murdock, Dorothy M., alias Acharya S.

Dorothy Murdock, who writes also under the name of Acharya Sanning, claims to have received a B.A. degree in Classics, Greek Civilization, from Franklin and Marshall College, after which she completed postgraduate studies at the American School of Classical Studies at Athens.[50] She also claims to have been brought up as a liberal Christian in the Congregationalist Church, which she found very dull, and which she more or less left at the grand old age of 12. She has also claimed to have been a born-again Christian for a short time a few years later, and to regard evangelicals as impossible to debate with. Perhaps this has something to do with the fact that her work is not only very hostile to Christianity as such, but she is

---

[49] H. Leidner, *The Fabrication of the Christ Myth* (Tampa: Survey Books, 1999), p. 14.

[50] As well as the information on her books, she has a blog, which includes 'Who is Acharya S?'. Truth Be Known. http://truthbeknown.com/author.htm [last accessed 7 February 2013].

liable to attack a fundamentalist version of Christianity rather than critical scholarship, of which she seems to be largely unaware.

The major faults in Murdock's work include her anti-Christian outlook, a lack of any proper sense of reality, failure to give adequate references, inability to interpret primary sources correctly, and dependence on inaccurate out-of-date secondary sources rather than primary evidence. The first three faults are well illustrated by her comments on the Council of Nicaea in 325 CE. This was a major council of Christian bishops, but Murdock alleges that it was also attended by 'the leaders of many other cults, sects and religions, including those of Apollo, Demeter/Ceres, Dionysus/Bacchus/Iasios, Janus, Jupiter/Zeus, Oannes/Dagon, Osiris and Isis...'[51] For this amazing assertion, she gives no evidence whatever!

Murphy, Derek

Murphy was born in Portland, Oregon. He was brought up as an Episcopalian Christian. In 1998, he went to Malta, where he studied art history and classical languages, then philosophy and theology. At some stage he became a committed atheist, the perspective from which he now writes. He went on to study art in Florence. He moved to Taiwan in 2003, where he works as a surrealist artist, and as a writer. He also gained an M.A. in Foreign Languages and Literature from National Cheng Kung University, and he is said to be studying for a Ph.D. at National Taiwan University.

Murphy is now well known for one book: *Jesus Potter Harry Christ* (Portland, OR: Holy Blasphemy, 2011).

Pfoh, Emanuel

Emanuel Pfoh did his doctorate at the University of Buenos Aires, and now teaches in the Department of History at the University of La Plata, Argentina. He does not appear to have any qualifications in New Testament Studies. He correctly describes himself as 'an outsider to the field of New Testament studies' (Thompson and Verenna, p. 79). He is a follower of Thompson, who imagines that only 'theological necessity' gives anyone a reason for believing in the historical Jesus. He omits the Jewish environment of Jesus, and does not mention Aramaisms in the synoptic Gospels. He commented on N. T. Wright, 'I am happy to say I never read him', which puts the *determined* ignorance of mythicists in a nutshell.[52]

---

[51] Acharya S., *The Christ Conspiracy: The Greatest Story Ever Sold* (Kempton, Illinois: Adventures Unlimited, 1999), p. 340.
[52] http://vridar.wordpress.com/2012/09/02/why-historical-knowledge-of-jesus-is-impossible-is-this-not-the-carpenter-chapter–5/#more–31457, comment by Emanuel Pfoh 2012/09/02 at 10.26 p.m. [last accessed 7 February 2013].

Price, Robert M.

Price was born in Mississippi in 1954. After early involvement in a fundamentalist Baptist church, he went on to become a leader in the Montclair
State College chapter of the Inter-Varsity Christian Fellowship. He was
trained at Gordon Conwell Theological Seminary. Its statement of faith and
mission statement include the following:

Statement of faith

I.   The sixty-six canonical books of the Bible as originally written were
     inspired of God, hence free from error. They constitute the only
     infallible guide in faith and practice.

II. There is one God, the Creator and Preserver of all things, infinite
     in being and perfection. He exists eternally in three Persons; the
     Father, the Son and the Holy Spirit, who are of one substance and
     equal in power and glory.

IV. The eternally pre-existent Son became incarnate without human
     father, by being born of the virgin Mary. Thus in the Lord Jesus
     Christ divine and human natures were united in one Person, both
     natures being whole, perfect and distinct. To effect salvation, He lived
     a sinless life and died on the cross as the sinner's substitute, shedding
     His blood for the remission of sins. On the third day He rose from
     the dead in the body which had been laid in the tomb. He ascended
     to the right hand of the Father, where He performs the ministry of
     intercession. He shall come again, personally and visibly, to complete
     His saving work and to consummate the eternal plan of God.

Mission and purpose

Gordon-Conwell Theological Seminary is an educational institution
serving the Lord and His Church. Its mission is ... to serve the Church
in the following ways:

**Article 1: To encourage students to become knowledgeable of God's inerrant
Word, competent in its interpretation, proclamation and application in the
contemporary world.** Because the teaching of God's Word is indispensable
to the well-being and vitality of God's people, the seminary has a fundamental responsibility to encourage in its students a love for Scripture.

It follows that after a fundamentalist upbringing, Price was also processed
in a fundamentalist institution where critical scholarship takes second
place to statements of belief. It was therefore not seriously different from
what I have noted at Ashland Theological Seminary, Asbury Theological

Seminary, Montreat College, and Azusa Pacific College. Price went on to do a Ph.D. in Systematic Theology at Drew University in Madison, New Jersey, awarded in 1981. He went on to read for a Ph.D. in New Testament, also at Drew University, and this was awarded in 1993. He was listed as Professor of Theology and Scriptural Studies at Coleman Theological Seminary and Professor of Biblical Criticism at the Center for Inquiry Institute, as well as a fellow of the Committee for the Scientific Examination of Religion and the Jesus Seminar.

Price is alone among mythicists in that there is no doubt that he was more or less a qualified New Testament scholar. It is, however, enough for him to bear a heavy responsibility for the views which he has promoted. Perhaps his most important book is *The Incredible Shrinking Son of Man*.[53] What is important about it is that it lends an air of scholarship to his personal opinions, opinions which I consider to be utter falsehoods. Price has in common with other mythicists a central point: he was a fundamentalist whose background does much to explain his genuine inability to come to terms with critical scholarship.

Thompson, Thomas L.

Thomas L. Thompson was an American Catholic born in 1939 in Detroit. He was awarded a B.A. at Duquesne University, a Catholic university in Pittsburgh, USA, in 1962, and a Ph.D. at Temple University, Philadelphia, Pennsylvania, in 1976. After several appointments, mostly in the USA, including the post of associate professor at Marquette University, a Jesuit, Roman Catholic university in Milwaukee, Wisconsin (1989–93), he was Professor of Theology at the University of Copenhagen from 1993–2009. His early work, which is thought to have successfully refuted the attempts of Albright and others to defend the historicity of the most ancient parts of biblical literature history, is said to have negatively affected his future job prospects.

Verenna, Thomas

Verenna was originally an American Catholic. He began his atheist outpourings under the pseudonym of Rook Hawkins, when he was still in his teens, continuing while an undergraduate at Rutgers University. He is co-editor with Thomas L. Thompson of the recent book *Is This Not the Carpenter? The Question of the Historicity* (Sheffield: Equinox, 2012).

---

[53]R. M. Price, *The Incredible Shrinking Son of Man: How Reliable is the Gospel Tradition?* (Amherst, NY: Prometheus, 2003).

Wells, G. A.

Wells was born in London in 1926. He studied at the universities of London and Bern, and obtained degrees in German, philosophy and natural science. He taught German at the University of London from 1949 onwards, and became Professor of German at Birkbeck College, University of London, in 1968. He was a genuinely learned professor of German, and his major works included *Goethe and the Development of Science, 1750–1900* (Alphen aan den Rijn: Sijthoff and Noordhoff, 1978).

As a student of German culture, Wells naturally took an interest in the *Religionsgeschichtliche Schule*. He was also naturally familiar with the work of radical Christian scholars in Germany, such as Bultmann. When he became an emeritus professor, he became gradually more and more learned in other New Testament scholarship. He was convinced that there was no historical Jesus, and wrote more than one book to this effect. More recently, he modified his views, especially in the light of relatively recent work on what many scholars call 'Q'. I discuss his work from time to time, because he has become more and more influential as the view that Jesus did not exist has become more common.

Zindler, F. R.

Frank Zindler was born into a Christian family.[54] Both his parents were members of a Wisconsin-Synod Evangelical Lutheran Church, which he describes as 'an extremely conservative, reactionary form of Lutheranism'. He nonetheless describes them as not very religious, compared with himself. By his own account, he was a very religious child. Between the ages of 13 and 18, however, he began to read the Bible thoroughly from beginning to end. That worried him, and his Lutheran minister's explanations of the image of God which emerged from the biblical text were not at all satisfying to him. When he was due to be taught about evolution in his biology classes, his mother suggested that he read Darwin, *On the Origin of Species*. He comments, 'By the time I finished reading Darwin, I was an evolutionist.' He went to Kalamazoo College, and after a while atheist students completed his conversion to atheism.

Eventually, Zindler completed a scientific education, and became Professor of Biology and Geology and Chairman of the Division of Science at Fulton-Montgomery Community College (SUNY-Johnstown). Here his attempts to do things in the name of atheism, such as removing 'In God We Trust' from U.S. currency, led the Fulton County Board of Supervisors to take measures against him, which led to his departure. Again, in British

---

[54] Much of this information comes from an interview with Zindler, posted by Marilyn Westfall on 20 August, 2007.

terms, these circumstances mean that he did not have anything that we would recognize as 'academic tenure', and illustrate the cultural context of the problems expounded by Doherty.

In 1982, he moved to a post with a scientific publisher in Ohio. He has also been the editor of American Atheist Press. He has published one well-known book, *The Jesus the Jews Never Knew*, which I discussed in *Jesus of Nazareth*,[55] I pointed out that it is completely misleading, because he fails to engage with New Testament Studies. He ignored all Jews who became Christians, thus omitting Matthew, Paul and others. I do not repeat this discussion here. He has also published a number of papers claiming that various places such as Nazareth and Capernaum did not exist at the time of Jesus. I discuss such claims in Chapter 7.

Bloggers

The purpose of this section is not to cast any aspersions on excellent scholarly blogs. Some scholarly blogs are very helpful to scholars and students, because of the large amount of useful information that they provide. Such a blog is that of Mark Goodacre, a fine scholar who is Associate Professor in New Testament in the Department of Religion at Duke University, North Carolina, USA.[56] Perhaps the most entertaining of blogs was that of N. T. Wrong, a deliberate pun on N. T. Wright, a very learned blog by a genuinely learned scholar, full of entertaining and sometimes somewhat naughty comments.[57] Another very helpful blog is that of Jim West, who has done a lot to publicize decent scholarship, in biblical as well as theological studies.[58] A more general blog with a lot of culturally interesting material is that of R. Joseph Hoffmann.[59] Other blogs are less frequent, but equally helpful. These include the blogs of the Sheffield University Department of Biblical Studies, and until recently the Dunedin School, which has now ceased.[60] Once in a while, a blog turns up written by someone previously unknown, making a number of important points. For example, an Irish Australian called Tim O'Neill produced a fine and incisive review of D. Fitzgerald, *Nailed: Ten Christian Myths That Show Jesus Never Existed at All.*[61]

---

[55] F. R. Zindler, *The Jesus the Jews Never Knew: Sepher Toldoth Jeshu and the Quest of the Historical Jesus in Jewish Sources* (Cranford, NJ: American Atheist Press, 2003), discussed in Casey, *Jesus of Nazareth*, pp. 38–43.
[56] See http://ntweblog.blogspot.com [blog last accessed, and active, 7 February 2013].
[57] Cf. http://ntwrong.wordpress.com/ [last accessed February 2013]. This blog was written between April 2008 and January 2009.
[58] http://zwingliusredivivus.wordpress.com/ [accessed 7 February 2013].
[59] http://rjosephhoffmann.wordpress.com [accessed 23 October 2013].
[60] http://www.sheffield.ac.uk/bibs; http://dunedinschool.wordpress.com [accessed 23 October 2013].
[61] http://armariummagnus.blogspot.com/2011/05/nailed-ten-christian-myths-that-show.html [last accessed 14 May 2013], reviewing D. Fitzgerald, Nailed: Ten Christian Myths That Show Jesus Never Existed at All (Lulu.com, 2010).

Unfortunately, however, many blogs are ignorant, opinionated, rude and malicious. They are written by people who do not understand scholarship, and who love to misrepresent scholars, especially by portraying us as ignorant, and this applies to most people who comment on them as well. We must recall at this point that Doherty appeals deliberately to his internet audience, and that both Doherty and Murdock cite Blogger Carr as an authority, which he is not.[62] I therefore consider next something of what is known of Blogger Carr and Blogger Godfrey, on whose blogs Carr often comments on New Testament subjects. I should note first that Blogger Carr and Blogger Godfrey appear to have especial contempt for myself, James Crossley, my last successful Ph.D. student at Nottingham University, now Professor of Biblical Studies at the University of Sheffield, and Stephanie Fisher, who is working to complete her doctoral thesis with me. This appears to be because all three of us are what are politely called 'secularists' or 'secular scholars' (though bloggers and their commentators are known to call us both 'atheists' and 'Christian apologists'), and we all believe in the existence of the historical Jesus. There are good reasons for this, which have not needed to be restated until lately, and which are presented in the rest of this book. Since Joseph R. Hoffmann joined with Stephanie and me to write preliminary essays about mythicism, they have attacked him too.

Blogger Carr

Steven Carr lives in Birkenhead, England, where he gives private tuition in mathematics. There is a phenomenally brief 'Brief Biography of Steven Carr' on the *Secular Web*, as well as an online advertisement for private tuition in mathematics. His 'brief biography' has him born on 19 July, 1957, so he should now be 56 years old, and after gaining a Class 1 B.A. in Natural Sciences at the University of Cambridge, he became a 'Computer Consultant'. This goes some way to explain his unusual views. At Cambridge, he could easily have gone to Tyndale House, and picked up the ideas central to his debates, such as that 'real' Christianity is hopelessly conservative, and the only form of Christianity worth debating with, because it can be refuted. As a computer expert as opposed to a humanities scholar, he could also have picked up all sorts of dogmatic and ignorant assumptions, such as that arguments 'from silence' are either always valid or invalid, whereas any decent ancient historian knows perfectly well that each such argument has to be assessed on its merits,

---

[62] See p. 9 above, with Doherty referring to Carr commenting on Josephus on Carr's own blog at http://www.bowness.demon.co.uk/marston2.html and Murdock referring to Carr, 'Textual Reliability of the New Testament', on Carr's blog at www.bowness.demon.co.uk/reli2.htm [both last accessed 7 February 2013].

especially if it is only part of a lengthy argument of cumulative weight. A first class degree and a career in a scientific subject like this would also explain his ability to argue his case with confidence, regardless of whether it is correct or not.

I first encountered Blogger Carr because he comments on the blog of Neil Godfrey, who follows, but he has his own blog as well.[63] Carr describes it as 'The UK's Leading Atheist Page'. In it, he shows more knowledge of the New Testament than one might expect from his comments on Blogger Godfrey's blog, but it is a quite specific form of 'knowledge'. It is the kind of 'knowledge' of the text to be expected of a fundamentalist, complete with grossly overliteral interpretation and an assumption that, even when so interpreted, it somehow ought to be inerrant, so he finds it very important that it is not inerrant. It is also evident that he is dependent on English translations, not on the Greek text, and that he includes conservative Christian tradition as well as the text of the New Testament.

For example, he has a whole section headed 'Mark was not by Mark!' All these arguments are directed at supposing that the author of Mark's Gospel was not Jewish. This could not possibly mean that this Gospel was not written by an unknown Christian called 'Marcus'. Blogger Carr is of course right to suppose that Mark was not a companion of Peter as Christian tradition has inferred from Papias. He writes as if he is really opposed to the idea that Mark's Gospel was written in accordance with very conservative tradition by John Mark, who lived in Jerusalem and would have been Jewish himself and have had a profound knowledge of Judaism, including the geography of Israel.

Some of Blogger Carr's arguments are moreover not valid at all, and none of them shows that Mark was not Jewish. For example, he compares Mark 7.10, 'For Moses said, "Honour your father..."' with Mt. 15.4, 'For God said, "Honour father..."', and comments 'Matthew, a Jew, would never have attributed the 10 commandments to Moses. It was God who said them, as all Jews will tell you.' And which Jews did Blogger Carr consult? Did he do a tour of first-century Galilean Judaism to see how Aramaic-speaking Jewish people spoke to each other? Of course not! He has simply consulted some modern Jews, and reported those who told him what he wanted to hear. Blogger Carr does not discuss at this point passages such as Mt. 19.7, where Pharisees say to Jesus, 'Why then did Moses command...'.

Again, Carr declares that Mark 14.12 confuses Nisan 15 with Nisan 14, because he interprets the phrase 'On the first day of unleavened breads' to mean literally the first day of the official feast of Unleavened Bread, Nisan

[63] http://www.bowness.demon.co.uk/marston2.htm [last accessed 7 February 2013].

15 (cf. Lev. 23.3). We should not interpret Mark like this.[64] In fact, leavened
bread had to be destroyed on the morning of Nisan 14, so later that day
only unleavened bread could be eaten. It was therefore entirely reasonable
of Mark to describe that as 'on the first day of unleavened breads', and
then to specify more precisely 'when they were sacrificing the Passover
(victim)', which puts Jesus and his disciples in the Temple that afternoon.
Hence the next thing they asked him was 'where do you want us to go
and prepare that you may eat the Passover?'. Carr imagined that Matthew
dropped the phrase which he translates 'when they sacrificed the Passover'
to correct Mark in accordance with Jewish custom. He does not notice
that Matthew's very abbreviated account removes all trace of Jesus and the
disciples being in the Temple, and alters the story in various other ways to
what Matthew preferred, so that, for example, Jesus eats the Passover with
only the Twelve (Mt. 26.20).

Blogger Carr has also conducted debates on New Testament topics.
These are all arguments with very conservative or fundamentalist
Christians, such as for example Stephen Motyer of London Bible College.
At this stage, Carr seems to have been happy to contemplate in public the
Aramaic level of traditions about Jesus. For example, he comments: 'It is
generally agreed that Luke struggled with the Aramaic language ... How
could Luke have spoken to eyewitnesses of Jesus if he could not cope
with Aramaic? If he had spent much time talking with eyewitnesses, how
could he not have picked up more Aramaic?' It is therefore remarkable
that in subsequent comments on Blogger Godfrey's blog, Carr is vigorously and rudely opposed to any idea that Mark's Gospel could have
used Aramaic sources. For example, he comments: 'Never underestimate
the psychic abilities of independent historians. They can read Aramaic
documents nobody has seen better than people who speak Aramaic as
their mother tongue and who have actually seen the documents. And they
can tell that people would have revised a previous work. This all puts
Paul the psychic octopus into the shade.'[65] This is typical of the way in
which Carr dismisses all possibility of Aramaic sources in the synoptic
Gospels without considering any of the evidence on which they are based,
because he cannot understand a word of it. Nor does he discuss the earlier
work of scholars such as Meyer, Wellhausen and Black, who attempted
what reconstruction of Aramaic sources seemed possible when much less
Aramaic was available.[66]

Carr's basic rejection of scholarly argument is shown for example in
his comment: 'Long arguments are always wrong. If an argument has 10

[64] For a brief explanation for the general reader see Casey, *Jesus of Nazareth*, pp. 429–30,
referring for detailed scholarly discussion to Casey, *Aramaic Sources of Mark's Gospel*, ch. 6.
[65] http://vridar.wordpress.com/2010/11/10/make-a-path-evidence-of-an-aramaic-source-for-
marks-gospel-or-creative-fiction/#comment–12430/ [last accessed 7 February 2013].
[66] See Casey, *Aramaic Sources*, pp. 12–15, 26, 29–33.

steps in it, and each step has a 95 per cent chance of being right, then what is the chance of the argument being correct?'[67] This shows that Carr cannot contemplate the possibility of a proper scholarly argument being valid. He should apply this to his own 'arguments' most of which have no chance, rather than a 95 per cent chance, of being correct. Another example is his comment on one of Blogger Godfrey's criticisms of James Crossley's arguments about the cultural background of Mark 7.1–23 noted below,

> I guess the readers of Mark would skim through all 16 pages as it was all stuff that Mark could assume people knew – all 16 pages of it...
> If it takes 16 pages of detailed background knowledge to explain things, how can we assume that readers of Mark were au fait with this background knowledge?
> Or does Crossley not assume it, and show that Mark's readers were familiar with the details that it takes him 16 pages to document?[68]

This shows firstly that Blogger Carr had not read Crossley's book when he commented on it. This is par for the course among ignorant bloggers. Secondly, it shows a total lack of understanding of what is required for modern scholars to reconstruct the details of an ancient culture which is not like ours. Of course Jesus and his disciples did not need 16 pages of detailed argument to understand an aspect of their daily lives. It is us who need the detailed arguments, because we do not live in the world of first-century Judaism. Mark took it for granted that when his Gospel was read in churches, many people would understand what he meant. He will have known that someone would explain what his text meant for the benefit of those who did not understand it.

Blogger Godfrey

Neil Godfrey is apparently Australian. He seems to have been born about 1950, since he wrote a post in 1998 saying that he was 48, so he should now be about 63 years old.[69] He was divorced, with two sons. He was brought up in a Methodist family. He was, however, a baptized member of the Worldwide Church of God for no less than 22 years. He says: 'I had my personal Martin Luther transforming experience when I believed

---

[67] http://vridar.wordpress.com/2010/04/29/biblical-historians-make-detectives-look-silly/#comment–9089/ [last accessed 7 February 2013].
[68] http://vridar.wordpress.com/2010/05/20/okay-just-one-more-early-dating-of-mark-critique-but-quickly/#comment–9342 [last accessed 7 February 2013].
[69] Much of the information which follows was taken from Non-Believer Former Members of the Worldwide Church of God, http://ironwolf.dangerousgames.com/exwcg/archives/4home page [last accessed 7 February 2013].

I had been unconditionally accepted by God. It was a real "born again" experience – I felt more at peace, joyful, accepting of others and incredibly blessed. I even discovered that I could speak in tongues once someone showed me how – and if I wanted to.' This means that he spent much of his life being converted to religious views, in total contempt for critical scholarship.

He converted to 'atheism' later, but he has offered much less detail about this. Its importance is that he has had *two conversion experiences*, and this means that his contempt for evidence and argument as means of reaching decisions about important matters is central to his life.

A number of Godfrey's comments on himself when he was a member of the Worldwide Church of God are sufficiently similar to his comments on scholars as to give the impression that not only has he no clue about critical scholars, which is obvious from many of his comments, but that he is basically expressing rejection of his former self. For example, he comments: 'Only by lazy assumptions about their sources can biblical "historians" declare Jesus' crucifixion a "fact of history"...'[70] Godfrey, however, comments on his previous self: 'As a fundamentalist WCG believer I believed I had all the big answers to the big questions of life. I simply shut my mind to any idea that questioned those answers.' In a little more detail, he comments on his movement out of the Worldwide Church of God in the 1980s, 'So I seriously studied the origins and nature of the Bible for the first time in my life. Strange (or just lazy or cowardly or both?) that I had spent my whole life studying its content (as passed on through a particular set of translations and manuscripts with dubious histories) but all that time I never before thought to study in any real depth, and with true open-minded honesty, the origins of that content.' I do not doubt that these are fair comments on Blogger Godfrey, but that is no excuse for him to attribute similar habits to critical scholars.

Godfrey has stated, defending himself from having a prejudice against the Jewishness of Jesus, that members of the WCG followed Jewish observances. In a subsequent post, replying to comments by Stephanie which he erroneously applied to himself, Godfrey gave a rather different account of his time in the Worldwide Church of God. This stressed the Jewish observances which members had to follow in those days. I can no longer find this post. It is of course true that, given the dates when Godfrey belonged to the Worldwide Church of God, he will have followed Armstrong's instructions to observe for example the feast of Tabernacles, despite making no attempt to observe Judaism as a whole, or attend a synagogue. It is all the more notable that this has left Godfrey with no understanding of Judaism at the time of Jesus, let alone of Jesus as a Jewish figure.

---

[70] *Comments by Neil Godfrey* http://vridar.wordpress.com/2010/05/03/evidence-for-the-unhistorical-fact-of-jesus-death/ [last accessed 7 February 2013].

Godfrey also claims to have 'a BA and post graduate Bachelor of Educational Studies, both at the University of Queensland, and a post graduate Diploma in Arts (Library and Information Science) from Charles Sturt University near Canberra, Australia'.[71] He has worked as a librarian. For example, he was Bibliographic Consultant at National Library Board Singapore 2009–11. He moved back to a post at Melbourne in his native Australia, and the most recent news I have of him is that he has moved to a post in Darwin, on which he commented at the end of June, 2011,

> I have recently moved (again) to take up a better position, still in the field of making research publications, cultural and other resources available online to the widest target audiences possible or appropriate into the long-term future, this time at the top end of Australia ... My job is one of those new fangled types that can never be really explained to those not in the know, and I have been very lucky to have been in the right place at the right time, and to have met the right people, to have a forefront seat in the way everything is moving with digitized research and cultural collections globally. And some exciting directions are being initiated up north here in Australia.[72]

Godfrey's contempt for scholarship is shown in many comments on scholars in general, as well as on particular scholars and particular arguments. For example, he condemns biblical scholars as no better than 'silly detectives'. In a post dated 29 April, 2010, and headed Biblical historians make detectives look silly, he did not give proper references, and referred back later to his post like this:

> Only by lazy assumptions about their sources can biblical "historians" declare Jesus' crucifixion a "fact of history"...
>   In other words, Paula Fredriksen is but one of a host of biblical "historians" who "do history" according to the analogy of the silly detectives in my earlier post.[73]

Godfrey's earlier post said that Fredriksen 'is one scholar who did "respond" to something Doherty had written, but her response demonstrated that she at no point attempted to read Doherty's piece seriously. I would even compare her responses to those like a naughty schoolgirl who has no interest in the content of the lesson, believing the teacher to be a real dolt, and who accordingly seeks to impress her giggly "know-it-all" classmates by interjecting the teacher with smart alec rejoinders at any opportunity.'

[71] http://vridar.wordpress.com/about/ [last accessed 7 February 2013].
[72] http://vridar.wordpress.com/2011/06/27/unsettled-settling/ [last accessed 7 February 2013].
[73] http://vridar.wordpress.com/2010/05/03/evidence-for-the-unhistorical-fact-of-jesus-death/#more–6799 [last accessed 14 May 2013].

When my final postgraduate student pointed out that this is rude, Blogger Godfrey wrote, 'Hoo boy, Steph. For you to complain about rudeness is like a vampire declaring an outrage if someone shows it the sign of the cross.'[74]

Godfrey is particularly rude about James McGrath (Dr James F. McGrath, Clarence L. Goodwin Chair in New Testament Language and Literature at Butler University, Indianapolis), and pillories him as 'McDaft'. For example, in a post headed 'Category Cloud (50 only) Biblical historian McDaft admits to relying on hearsay and uncorroborated reports',[75] Godfrey's comments include the following:

> But we can't simply think there 'might be' a unicorn or pixie under the mushrooms in the garden despite never having seen them. No one has seen the teacup and saucer orbiting Saturn yet, but that doesn't mean it might not be there. It might be, and theologian James McGrath's exploringourmatrix fantasies might be real. Aliens might have brought life to earth as an experiment of some kind. Maybe we really are all just a dream of Buddha and all will end when he wakes up.[76]

As Steph pointed out in response, 'No one has of course suggested anything remotely like Godfrey's fantasy. This is rude because it is fantastical and inaccurate.'

Godfrey's comments on this book, which he had obviously not seen, include a number of other points which manifest a complete rejection of the nature of scholarly research. For example, when Steph pointed out that I was writing it, and that it would probably take about two years, Blogger Godfrey commented: 'Can you imagine a student getting something wrong in a test, being failed, and when asking why he was failed, the teacher telling him, "It would take a book to explain why you got it wrong. Wait 2 years till one is published and then you will know what is wrong with your answer."'[77] This completely misleading analogy is typical of Godfrey's misrepresentation of scholars. It is one of many comments which show that he does not understand scholars at all. In particular, he does not seem to understand that we spend a long time doing research to ensure that our results are correct, or as near correct as we can make them. We do not fire

---

[74] http://vridar.wordpress.com/2010/05/27/how-and-why-scholars-fail-to-rebut-earl-doherty/ [last accessed 14 May 2013].

[75] http://vridar.wordpress.com/2010/07/05/biblical-historian-mcdaft-admits-to-relying-on-hearsay-and-uncorroborated-reports/ [last accessed 14 May 2013].

[76] http://vridar.wordpress.com/2010/11/21/caseys-historical-method–2-aramaic-plausibility/ [last accessed 14 May 2013]. The reference is to Professor McGrath's previous blog at exploringourmatrix.blogspot.com/. His current address is: http://www.patheos.com/community/exploringourmatrix/.

[77] http://vridar.wordpress.com/2010/05/27/how-and-why-scholars-fail-to-rebut-earl-doherty/# comments, 2010/05/29 at 11.19 a.m. [last accessed 7 February 2013].

off immediate judgements in accordance with fantasies in the back of our heads, as many bloggers seem to do all the time.

Godfrey is also, incapable of correctly summarizing genuinely learned arguments. Instead, he replaces them with simple summaries. For example, he commented in another response to Steph, 'Your repeated assertion that Mark made certain assumptions and that this explains certain features of his text is not a fact, but an interpretation. It needs to be supported with evidence to persuade others. But Crossley and Casey, from what I have read, use circular reasoning to argue that this was his assumption. It is circular to say that we know X is true because Y is true, and Y is true because X is true.'[78] As Steph pointed out,

> This simple syllogism is blindingly obvious, but it has nothing to do with the arguments of Casey or Crossley, which are not circular at all. Godfrey's claim that they are circular depends entirely on his replacement of their arguments, which he is not learned enough to understand, with his simple syllogisms. In the same post, he replaces Crossley's complex arguments of cumulative weight like this: 'The maths proves it: 0+0+0=3'. Neither Crossley nor anyone else is stupid enough to believe that.

Again, Blogger Godfrey commented on part of James Crossley's *Date of Mark,*

> Crossley writes about 16 pages of small print arguing the point that Mark was actually addressing the tradition of handwashing, and not Levitical food laws, in Mark 7:1–23. (A recent commenter was dead right when he noted I was "labouring" with Crossley.) It is tempting to say that Crossley won this point of his argument from its unrelenting pressure to exhaust any reader with pointless minutiae. I say pointless because I know of a cult that argues exactly the same thing in one twentieth of the number of words. I was once a member of it. So I have no problem agreeing with his argument that Mark may indeed have been addressing handwashing throughout, and not necessarily Levitical food laws.[79]

This illustrates the fact that Blogger Godfrey, like Blogger Carr, prefers to replace complex scholarly arguments with short summaries which are easier to understand. In this case, he has taken his short summary from the fundamentalist dogma of the Worldwide Church of God.

---

[78] http://vridar.wordpress.com/2010/04/29/biblical-historians-make-detectives-look-silly/ comment from 'neilgodfrey' at 8.43 a.m. [last accessed 7 February 2013].
[79] http://vridar.wordpress.com/2010/05/20/okay-just-one-more-early-dating-of-mark-critique-but-quickly/ [last accessed 7 February 2013].

Given Godfrey's outspoken views, it was almost inevitable that some scholar, despite always being polite to decent colleagues, would reciprocate. Godfrey commented on him, 'So these are the "honeys" adored by the likes of Maurice Casey's fans. Charming.'[80] There is no excuse for this description, and his removal from Godfrey's blog, like the removal of Stephanie, is totally hypocritical.

Blogger Widowfield

Blogger Widowfield used to comment on Blogger Godfrey's blog, but he has recently taken over a half share in doing this blog, and he has confessed that he 'grew up in a very strict fundamentalist Protestant denomination called The Church of the Nazarene. We shunned "worldly" things like going to the movies, playing cards, dancing, smoking, etc. We were, literally, "holy-rollers" – believing in a distinct, second work of grace after conversion. First you're converted; then you're sanctified by the Holy Spirit. We took the Bible very literally and accepted it as the living Word of God.'[81]

Blogger Widowfield proceeds to draw a picture of his miserable life of fear: for example, 'My greatest fear was accidentally committing "Holy Spirit Thought Crime." I was continually afraid I would accidentally blaspheme the Holy Spirit in my mind and be damned for eternity.' This bears no reasonable relationship to the life of Sarah, the only member of the Church of the Nazarene with whom I have knowingly worked. She seemed very happy, and when we went out from a seminar on the use of the Old Testament in the New, she came to the pub with me. As far as I remember, I bought orange juice for her while I got cider for myself, but I can't see anything wrong with that, she certainly was not living a life of fear, and she was well able to take part in academic debates.

Blogger Widowfield also misrepresents my explanation of how mythicists like Blogger Godfrey have changed sides. He does so under a large heading of his third myth about mythicists, '*Myth #3: When a fundamentalist stops believing, he becomes a "village atheist" – "Once an extremist, always an extremist."*' I have never maintained any such thing, for the very good reason that many fundamentalists become more moderate Christians. He comments further, 'I'm reminded of Casey's calumny: "One example is blogger Neil Godfrey, an Australian who was a baptized member of the Worldwide Church of God for 22 years, so he belonged to a hopelessly fundamentalist organization which holds critical scholarship in contempt. He converted to 'atheism' later, so he has had *two conversion experiences*,

---

[80] https://vridar.wordpress.com/2011/04/25/highly-esteemed-friends-and-supporters-of-steph-and-mauric-casey/ [last accessed 7 February 2013].
[81] http://vridar.wordpress.com/2012/07/05/how-i-escaped-fundamentalism–5-myths-about-ex-fundies/ [last accessed 7 February 2013].

and this means that his contempt for evidence and argument as means of reaching decisions about important matters is doubly central to his life."

'What Casey is trying to say in his own, smug, puerile way is that when fundamentalists become unbelievers, it's like changing the polarity of a magnet. He thinks we have all remained intensely dogmatic, but we've flipped sides.' I have never commented like this on what happens when fundamentalists become unbelievers. I put the term 'atheism' in inverted commas because it was Blogger Godfrey's term, not mine, and in context it should have been obvious that I was discussing the conversion of ineducable unqualified people from fundamentalism to mythicism. People who simply realize that fundamentalism is seriously wrong take all sorts of different turns, including adhering to more reasonable forms of Christianity as well as reasonable forms of not believing in God. Lester Grabbe is a good example of this.

Blogger Widowfield next puts one of the major mythicist illusions in a nutshell: 'So when Casey talks about "contempt for evidence and argument," he has no idea what he's talking about. From my experience we ex-fundies continually check and re-check the evidence. Are we letting our presuppositions color our conclusions? Are we cherry-picking evidence to get the answers we want? We now know firsthand how easy it is to fall into that trap, and we don't want to make that mistake again.' This is, however, the mistake which mythicists make repeatedly, and they do so because they cannot even realize that their notion that Jesus of Nazareth was not a historical figure is a product of their present faith, not of historical research.

The Author of this Book

After all this information about other people involved in this sort of work, I thought I ought to tell readers my qualifications, especially as some bloggers, led by Blogger Godfrey and Blogger Carr, have poured scorn on them. For example, Blogger Godfrey, being some sort of librarian, nonetheless evidently could not look up my qualifications given in my published books. He commented, 'And why does he appear to be so coy about the details of his qualifications?' This appears to mean that Blogger Godfrey could not find them instantaneously on the internet, since my most important scholarly qualifications are readily available on the dust jackets and in the prefaces of my published books. After the publication of *Jesus of Nazareth: An Independent Historian's Account of His Life and Teaching* (T&T Clark, 2010), some people commenting on blogs made very unfavourable comments on the subtitle. For example, Blogger Widowfield commented on Blogger Godfrey's blog, 'Yes, he is a "Lecturer in Theology" who earned a Ph.D. But in what? It would be presumptuous (not to say damning) for us to say it's a Ph.D. in Theology, since the self-appellation of "historian" would be dishonest, or at least greatly misleading.'[82] This is typical of the malice and spite of bloggers, and people who comment on blogs. Widowfield could of course have looked up my doctoral thesis, and/or the resulting published book, if he cared to take the trouble, which seems to be quite beyond bloggers and their commentators. There is, however, a much more important point here. I have spent the whole of my life as a scholar trying to tell the truth. Widowfield has, however, decided that, to call myself an 'independent historian', I should have an *elementary* qualification in *modern* history. We shall see in Chapter 2 that this is important to mythicists, because it enables them to *assume* standards of attestation for Jesus and the Gospels which are completely inappropriate to the ancient world.

I have also recently been accused by bloggers of being elitist and all sorts of alien things, and my life has been quite misrepresented by bloggers, so I have given many more details of my ordinary life here than I did in the original draft of this book. I was born in 1942, in the middle of an air raid in Sunderland. My father was the Anglican vicar of Wheatley Hill, a mining village some seven miles outside Durham, as he had been for a long time (since the First World War, I think). My mother was his second wife, and a local woman. My grandfather was in charge of the electricity in the mine, where my uncle Jack was a miner. My uncle Sep ran the local Co-op. I was very happy among local people, and very happy being educated at the local infants' school. After my father's death, my mother returned to school-teaching, beginning in the Suffolk country village of Chevington, where I was educated at the local primary school. I was very happy among local people there too. Many of them were not very well educated by modern standards either.

I was then sent away to boarding school at the Sanctuary School, Walsingham, and a minor public school, which I was not happy about at all. I did, however, begin to learn Latin, Greek and French. I began serious scholarship by reading for a degree in Theology at the University of Durham, beginning in the autumn of 1961, and expecting to train for the Anglican priesthood. However, after being exposed to quite outstanding critical scholarship, I left the Christian faith early in 1962. I completed my degree in Theology nonetheless. What kept me going was the outstanding scholarly quality of our teachers in the Department of Theology, and fellow students, many of whom were quite happy to have endless debates with me about all the most profound things in life, including naturally the existence of God, and all aspects of the life and teaching of Jesus. Contrary to the prejudices of Blogger Godfrey and his commentators, this meant that I received a quite outstanding elementary training in historical methods, notably from Kingsley Barrett in New Testament, and to a lesser

---

[82] http://vridar.wordpress.com/2010/12/15/open-invitation-to-dr-maurice-casey/ comment by Tim Widowfield, 2010/12/18, at 8.22 a.m. [last accessed 14 May 2013].

extent Hewie Turner in the history of doctrine, and even a forgettable lecturer in church history. What mattered was the cumulative effect of their approaches, which had significant points in common. Following Kingsley Barrett's brilliant first year lectures on the Gospel of Mark, I took a second and third year optional course in Aramaic and Syriac. He convinced me that this might hold a key to understanding what the historical Jesus originally said and meant, and the whole of my life's work has in my view shown that he was right.

I then read a degree in Classical and General Literature. This naturally included a proper elementary training in *Ancient* History, which is more directly relevant to understanding the origins of Christianity than modern history, which rightly has different standards for basic points such as how well events and people are attested. I especially benefited from elementary instruction in Greek History from Peter Rhodes. He is now Emeritus Professor of Ancient History, and at the time he was already becoming the world's leading authority on the Athenian *Boulē*: he duly became famous for his book *The Athenian Boule* (Oxford: Clarendon, 1972, rev. edn, 1985). His many subsequent works include *A History of the Classical Greek World: 478 – 323 B.C.*[83] I cannot imagine how I could have been more fortunate than to obtain such an outstanding elementary education in Ancient History. I was also taught Roman History by Mr Wright, who, while not remotely as outstanding a scholar, was an effective specialist in Roman Britain. This led me to go to archaeological sites, and that enabled me to see what was clearly lacking in New Testament archaeology. The Professor of Latin was a complete atheist, and the Professor of Greek was a very committed Christian. This caused no trouble to any of us. They were not hostile to each other, nor to any of us.

I then taught Classics, including Ancient History, at Spalding High School for Girls, from 1967–71. This was a very great delight, and I am especially grateful to Les Churchill, Head of the Department of Classics, for effectively teaching me to teach. I also learnt a lot from working on the Cambridge Schools Classics Project.

It slowly dawned on me that, if I did not strive mightily to tell the truth about Jesus, no one else would. I was therefore very delighted to be accepted to read for a Ph.D. back at the University of Durham under Kingsley Barrett. I told him I wanted to solve the Son of man problem, because I thought it was technically the most difficult problem preventing scholars from recovering the Jesus of history. He kindly and politely told me that this was too big for a doctoral thesis, so we narrowed it down. My doctoral degree was eventually awarded in 1977, for a thesis entitled 'The Interpretation and Influence of Daniel vii in Jewish and Patristic Literature

---

[83] *A History of the Classical Greek World: 478 – 323 B.C.* (Chichester: Wiley-Blackwell, 2006. 2nd edn, 2010).

and in the New Testament: an Approach to the Son of Man Problem'. The scope was much broader than originally intended, which is why it took so long to do. This is because in the course of doing the research, I realized the importance of studying the interpretation of Daniel in the Syriac-speaking church and in mediaeval Jewish sources, in both of which the original inter-pretations of the authors were to some extent preserved, a fact not known before. In the meantime, I held a one year temporary post at Darlington College of Education, teaching New Testament, Church History and the like, and spent six weeks on a scholarship at the University of Tübingen. A much shortened version of the thesis (100,000 words rather than 180,000) was published in 1980.[84] By this stage I had worked for two years at the University of St Andrews, one year substituting for Matthew Black, who was on study leave, and one year working under him, which was very fruitful and very instructive. In 1979, I was appointed to a permanent post at the University of Nottingham, which was necessary to keep a wife and two young children, but which unfortunately meant I had to turn down a Research Fellowship which I was awarded at the University of Münster, where I could have learnt more, and would have become fluent in German.

In those days it was difficult to work at the University of Nottingham – the library facilities were poor, and the Head of the Theology Department was a Pro-Vice Chancellor who did not understand the needs of scholarly research. The first ray of light was being invited by the Department of Theology at the University of Birmingham, and Michael Goulder in the Department of Adult Education, to deliver the Cadbury Lectures. I properly thanked them in the preface for 'their invitation, their warm hospitality, and their enthusiasm for scholarship. This was very refreshing and I enjoyed myself no end.' It should be noted that most members of staff were Christians, Michael was a self-declared 'non-aggressive atheist', and I was already well known as a New Testament scholar who was completely irreli-gious. This caused no trouble at all, and led to interesting debates after the final lecture. A revised version of the lectures was accepted for publication by T&T Clark, but later turned down by Geoffrey Green, who was in charge. It has been suggested to me privately that this may have been due to Christian prejudice under the guise of peer review, including the comment 'Maurice's work is sometimes anti-Christian'. Consequently, the resulting book was not published until 1991.[85]

The next rays of light were fundamental changes at the University of Nottingham. The first was the appointment of Sir Colin Campbell as Vice-Chancellor in 1988. He set up a new and outstanding management

[84] Maurice Casey, Son of Man. The Interpretation and Influence of Daniel 7 (London: SPCK, 1980).
[85] Maurice Casey, From Jewish Prophet to Gentile God: The Origins and Development of New Testament Christology (Cambridge: James Clarke and Louisville: Westminster/John Knox, 1991).

group, and they did a massive amount to improve our working conditions. The second was the replacement of the Head of Department by Tony
Thiselton in 1992. Tony was well known to us as a committed evangelical
Christian, but his leadership of the Department was impeccably academic,
as he sought vigorously to foster the work of *all* members of the Department,
regardless of status, colour, race, religion or creed. Shortly afterwards, I was
appointed to a Readership in the University, and from 1994–6, I held a
British Academy Research Readership. This resulted in two books, one on
Aramaic sources of Mark's Gospel, and the other on an Aramaic Approach
to the Double Tradition, the material which Matthew and Luke have in
common but which is not in Mark's Gospel. They were somewhat held up
for the very good reason that the publication of the second set of Aramaic
Dead Sea Scrolls enabled me to do more fruitful work than I had originally
planned, and for the regrettable reason that by this stage of my 'career', I
had to undertake more administrative duties.[86]

In due course, I was also appointed to a personal chair for excellence
in research, and then to a Leverhulme Major Research Fellowship, which
I held from 2001–4. This enabled me to write *The Solution to the 'Son of
Man' Problem*, which was not, however, published until 2007.[87] This was
due to serious illness, on account of which I took early retirement. For the
same reason, I have not completed the second monograph, which was to be
a more extensive treatment of the 'son of man' passages in the Similitudes
of Enoch, a task made more difficult as the first part of the work showed
clearly the need for study of the oldest Ethiopic manuscripts, which are not
generally in the public domain.[88]

Since then, I have also written a life of Jesus. This was first drafted
several years ago, but it too was turned down, and again there was a regrettable but this time verifiable report that one of the very hostile reports to
the publisher also declared, as a reason for an independent publisher not to
publish it, 'Maurice's work is sometimes anti-Christian'. It finally saw the
light of day, in a much revised form, on the basis of subsequent research,
especially on the Aramaic sources of the synoptic Gospels, as *Jesus of
Nazareth: An Independent Historian's Account of His Life and Teaching*
(T&T Clark, 2010).

I hope it is clear from all this that I described myself as a historian because
I have spent my life doing historical research. This should underline the fact
that, after their elementary training, independent scholars take charge of

---

[86]P. M. Casey, *Aramaic Sources of Mark's Gospel* (SNTSMS 102. Cambridge: Cambridge
University Press, 1998); *An Aramaic Approach to Q: Sources for the Gospels of Matthew and
Luke* (SNTSMS 122. Cambridge: Cambridge University Press, 2002).
[87]P. M. Casey, *The Solution to the 'Son of Man' Problem* (LNTS 343. London: T&T Clark
International, 2007).
[88]For a preliminary treatment, based on the evidence which was available, see Casey, *The
Solution to the 'Son of Man' Problem*, ch. 3, esp. pp. 91–111.

their own learning. In consequence, they should be judged by their results, not by the elementary training which they had when they were young.

Conclusion

I hope this introduction is sufficient to make clear the appalling state of the pseudo-scholarship which has dominated the whole notion that Jesus of Nazareth was not a historical figure. The rest of this book is devoted to demonstrating that he was. In Chapter 2, I turn to historical method, which is fundamental to the major mistakes made by mythicists.

2

Historical method

Introduction

The purpose of this chapter is to discuss historical method. In my view, this is one of the most serious weaknesses of the whole mythicist movement. Mythicists have not the foggiest notion of historical method, and they do have a massive amount of bias and prejudice to put in its place. One of their major illusions is that New Testament scholars are completely ignorant of historical method. Blogger Godfrey has said this with the greatest clarity. For example, he commented:

> Casey and Crossley demonstrate no more awareness of historical methodology than any of their American counterparts. They demonstrate perfectly McKnight's point about ignorance of historiography among biblical 'historians'.

Stephanie Fisher correctly replied:

> This is completely inaccurate and probably reflects your 'embarrassing failure' to read the sources you claim to refute. See the essays by Crossley in J. G. Crossley and C. Karner, *Writing History, Constructing Religion* (Ashgate, 2005), published papers from a conference of the same name, especially the one on 'Defining History' (pp. 9–29). Because of Crossley's work published here, Casey makes much briefer reference to the same debates among 'historians and people who may or may not be thought of as philosophers of history' in the opening of his contribution to the same conference, 'Who's Afraid of Jesus Christ? Some comments on Attempts to Write a Life of Jesus' (pp. 129–46), referring briefly to R. J. Evans, *In Defence of History* (Granta, 1997) and C. B. McCullagh, *The Truth of History* (Routledge, 1998) for more detailed discussion. Decent European scholars do not share the need of second-rate semi-learned American 'scholars' to 'demonstrate... awareness' of all their knowledge every time they write about anything.[1]

---

[1]http://vridar.wordpress.com/2010/04/29/biblical-historians-make-detectives-look-silly/ Comment by neilgodfrey – 2010/05/01 @ 4:41 p.m. and by steph – 2010/05/02 at 12:07 a.m. [last accessed 14 May 2013].

This should have been quite sufficient to indicate that Blogger Godfrey was simply wrong to announce that Crossley and I were unaware of historical methodology, and doubly so if this 'librarian' had actually taken the trouble to *read the book* to which Stephanie referred. A decent honest person, let alone someone with pretensions to scholarship, would have apologised and withdrawn, since the book makes it absolutely clear to any unbiased observer that we had gathered at a conference to discuss historical methodology and its significance for the study of religion. The notion that any of us knew nothing about this beforehand, and knew no more after the conference than we did before it, would not occur to any unbiased observer. Blogger Godfrey sidestepped the question, commenting:

> The essays by Crossley are about ideology and the nature of history. That is all fine and good. Nothing wrong with discussing that. But there is something far more basic to the historian's practice and craft that is not the topic of Crossley's essays, and that is discussed by the likes of Carr, Elton and, yes, Hobsbawm...

Steph added, quite correctly: 'This still means that they are not ignorant, though of course they don't agree with you, which they obviously don't.'

This also highlights Godfrey's bossy declarations of how biblical scholars somehow ought to follow his selected quotations from 'historians', most of whom did good work when they were alive, but all of whom are seriously out of date. This preference for old 'authorities' over against recent research is a serious fault normal among mythicists, as it is among the Christian fundamentalists whom they used to be. That Crossley's essays did not discuss what Godfrey decided afterwards he should have discussed does not mean that either he or I have no awareness of historical methodology. This should have been even more obvious since Evans, in the work cited, briefly put Ranke, Carr and Elton in their historical contexts.[2]

I discuss next the historians whom Godfrey most sees fit to quote. The earliest is Leopold Ranke. Ranke, later von Ranke, should not be described as a 'secular historian'. He was born into Lutheran Christianity in 1795, into a family most of whose men had been Lutheran ministers, and he maintained this faith all his life.[3] He argued that history recognizes 'in every being, something eternal, coming from God, and this is its vital principle'. Again, 'In all of history, God dwells, can be recognized ... Let us do our part to unveil this holy hieroglyph! In this way we serve God, we are also

---

[2]Cf. further now J. G. Crossley, 'Writing about the Historical Jesus: Historical Explanation and "the Big *Why* Questions", or Antiquarian Explanation and Victorian Tomes?' *JSNT* 7, 2009, pp. 63–90.

[3]For an up-to-date account of main points, see now L. Von Ranke, *The Theory and Practice of History*, edited with an introduction by G. G. Iggers (London and New York: Routledge, rev. edn, 2011).

priests and teachers.'[4] He studied Lutheran Theology and Classics at the University of Leipzig, and taught history at the University of Berlin. He wrote a massive history of the papacy in the Middle Ages, as well as other works of history.[5] Godfrey declares in 'The Gospels and Acts as Historical Sources', 'These are not primary sources of Jesus or the founding of the church since they are not preserved in a condition that physically goes back to those times.' Again, 'Primary evidence, by the way, is according to the language of historiography ever since the father of modern history, Leopold von Ranke, evidence that is physically situated at the time and place of the event or person in question. The Gospels that we have are not primary but secondary evidence – their physical existence can be traced no further back than the second and third and fourth centuries.'[6] This makes nonsense of Godfrey's comment that 'An early or late date for the gospels does not, of itself, make any difference to the arguments for or against the historicity of Jesus.' On the contrary, ludicrously late dates for the Gospels are central to the assumptions of mythicists that they are not, and did not incorporate, primary sources.

Continuing with his inaccurate criticisms of Crossley and me, Blogger Godfrey added: 'Pity, since Carr and Elton who wrote landmark publications on the nature and practice of history as a discipline were both British.'[7] E. H. Carr (1892–1982) read a degree in Classics at Cambridge University, and went into politics, joining the Foreign Office in 1916, and remaining there until 1936. He became increasingly interested in the Soviet Union when he worked there. In 1936, he became Woodrow Wilson Professor of International Politics at the University of Wales in Aberystwyth. He spent a lot of this time writing as a journalist, being an Assistant Editor of *The Times* from 1941–6, during which time he wrote many leading articles. While he had been very favourable towards appeasement to Germany, he became increasingly left-wing. After running into trouble in Aberystwyth, because of his political opinions, for which he could not of course be sacked because British universities have genuine academic tenure, he was removed from his post in 1947, because he began to live with Joyce Forde, who remained his common law wife until 1964. In 1966, he left Joyce Forde, and married the historian Betty Behrens. He became increasingly Marxist. When he worked in Oxford and then Cambridge from the 1950s onwards, he was well known as a supporter of the Soviet Union. When he wrote

---

[4]Von Ranke, *Theory and Practice of History*, pp. xxviii, 4.

[5]L. Von Ranke, *History of the Popes, Their Church and State, and Especially of their Conflict with Protestantism in the Sixteenth and Seventeenth Centuries* (3 vols. 1840. Trans. S. Austin. London: Murray, 1901).

[6]http://vridar.wordpress.com/2010/04/29/biblical-historians-make-detectives-look-silly/ Comment by neilgodfrey – 2010/05/01 at 4:41 p.m. [last accessed 14 May 2013].

[7]http://vridar.wordpress.com/2010/04/29/biblical-historians-make-detectives-look-silly/ Comment by neilgodfrey – 2010/05/01 at 4:41 p.m. [last accessed 14 May 2013].

his major historical work, *History of Soviet Russia*, it would be entirely reasonable to describe him as a dogmatic politician rather than a historian.[8]

Carr is nonetheless famous for his book *What is History?* (1961).[9] Evans begins his introduction by saying that Carr 'was not a professional historian in any sense of the term that would be acceptable today'! His book is famous for grappling with the very serious problems which confront any historian trying to tell the truth, a virtue much more important to Carr and Elton than to Doherty, Murdock, Blogger Godfrey and other mythicists, none of whom has any proper sense of historical reality, and a fact which should be recognized even as we notice that Carr and Elton were seriously biased and are seriously out of date. Carr was already heavily involved in debates about major points such as determinism with his friend Isaiah Berlin, when he was invited to deliver the Trevelyan lectures, first published in *The Listener*, and later as *What is History?*

These lectures were controversial at the time and have provoked discussion ever since. One of Berlin's major criticisms was of Carr's inadequate approach to cause and effect. Evans incisively comments that this was because Carr spent his formative intellectual years 'in the practical world of the diplomatic service and the Foreign Office, where nothing was of direct interest unless it made a contribution to the formation of policy'.[10] It is ironical that academic historians have been better at proper explanations of cause and effect precisely because they are involved in academic research which does not have to have that kind of practical effect.

Another major debate concerned historical objectivity. Carr's definition again shows that he was hardly a historian at all. He supposed that when 'we' 'praise a historian for being objective', 'we mean that he (*sic!*) has the capacity to project his vision into the future in such a way as to give him a more profound and more lasting insight into the past than can be attained by those historians whose outline is entirely bounded by their own immediate situation'.[11] It was obvious to Carr's critics that the last thing this involved was being 'objective' in any normal sense of that word. Moreover, as Evans put it mildly, 'it was more than likely that the historian's vision of the future would be falsified by events, as Carr's own vision of a future organized along the lines of a Soviet-style planned economy ... has so far proved to be'.[12] Trevor-Roper was blunter, as so often:

'objectivity' means, not being 'objective' in the hitherto accepted sense

---

[8]E. H. Carr, *History of Soviet Russia* (London: Macmillan, 14 vols, 1950–78).

[9]E. H. Carr, *What is History?* (London: Macmillan, 1961); see further 2nd edn, with a New Introduction by Richard J. Evans (Basingstoke: Palgrave, 2001), with bibliography to Carr's life and work.

[10]Evans, in Carr, *What is History?* 2nd edn, pp. xxiii–xxiv.

[11]Carr, *What is History?* 2nd edn, p. 117.

[12]Evans, in Carr, *What is History?* 2nd edn, pp. xxvii–xxviii.

of the word – i.e. being uncommitted, dispassionate, fair – but the exact opposite, being committed to that side which is going to win: to the big battalions...

Trevor-Roper further declared that Carr's 'vulgar worship of success' had been evident in the 1930s in his championing of the appeasement of Hitler's Germany; now he had transferred it to Stalin's Russia.[13]

I hope this is sufficient to show that, however well Carr may be thought to have done in 1961, he is now hopelessly out of date. We had no reason to discuss his work in particular when we met in the twenty-first century to discuss *Writing History, Constructing Religion,* and it is quite ridiculous of Blogger Godfrey to judge the proceedings of the conference by whether its participants 'showed knowledge' of work which was so seriously out of date and methodologically flawed.

Gottfried Rudolf Ehrenberg was born in Tübingen to Jewish parents in 1921. In 1929, the Ehrenbergs moved to Prague, where Gottfried's father was Professor of Classics. In February 1939, they fled to Britain. Ehrenberg continued his education at Rydal School, a Methodist school in Wales, where he became assistant master in Maths, History and German. He also took correspondence courses at London University, and graduated with a degree in Ancient History in 1943. Ehrenberg enlisted in the British Army in 1943. During military service in the British Army against the Third Reich, it was not convenient for him to have a German name, and he changed it to Geoffrey Rudolph Elton. After the war, Elton studied early modern history at the University of London, graduating with a Ph.D. in 1949. He took British citizenship in 1947.

From 1949 onwards, Elton taught at Cambridge University, where he was Regius Professor of Modern History from 1983 to 1988. He was politically right-wing as well as academically conservative, vigorously opposed to Marxist historians, and to attempts to use the insights of anthropology and sociology in historical research. His classic book, *The Practice of History,* was not primarily a response to Carr, though it did respond to some of his main points.[14] For example, as a leading specialist on British history in the Tudor period, Elton naturally and rightly objected to Carr's dismissal of mediaeval history as unknowable and irrelevant. For the future, however, it was more important that Elton became embroiled in disputes about what ought to be taught as history, and how. This is how he became out of date, even in his own lifetime. This was especially because of his opposition to interdisciplinary research, and because, like Carr, he imagined that politics

---

[13] H. R. Trevor-Roper, 'E. H. Carr's Success Story', *Encounter* (May, 1962), as quoted and referred to by Evans, in Carr, *What is History?* 2nd edn, pp. xxviii–xxix, with p. xlv n. 40.

[14] G. R. Elton, *The Practice of History* (Sydney: Sydney University Press and London: Methuen, 1967). See now especially G. R. Elton, *The Practice of History*; afterword by Richard. J. Evans (Oxford: Blackwell, 2nd edn, 2002), with some bibliography and references.

was more important than any other aspect of history. His comments on causation in history have not stood the test of time either. He was also opposed to the use of history in education. Evans commented correctly: 'Even in *The Practice of History* Elton declared that history should not be taught in schools because it depended on a knowledge of life that school-children simply did not have – a point of view that can only be described as frankly absurd.'[15]

Eric Hobsbawm was born of Jewish parents, Leopold Percy Obstbaum and Nelly Grün, in Alexandria in 1917. He grew up in Vienna and Berlin, and moved to London in 1933 with the relatives who adopted him after the death of his parents. He read history at Cambridge University, and after war service in the British Army, he completed his Ph.D. on the Fabian Society in 1949. He worked for the most part at Birkbeck College in the University of London, where he became a lecturer in history in 1947, Professor in 1970, and Emeritus Professor of History in 1982. He is famous/notorious as a long-standing Marxist and member of Communist organizations. He wrote extensively on social banditry in the relatively modern world, but not on the Gospels, and Blogger Godfrey's attempts to use him to distort the Gospels should not be accepted.[16]

I hope this brief account is sufficient to explain why, when we gathered to discuss 'Writing History, Constructing Religion' in the twenty-first century, we had far more to say about postmodernism and people who denied that there are any historical facts than about Ranke, Carr, Elton and Hobsbawm. To infer from the published papers that any of us knew nothing about historical method is the kind of creative fiction which Blogger Godfrey excels in. We did of course discuss previous historical work when that seemed appropriate. For example, I drew attention to Nazi attempts to present a non-Jewish Jesus, because these had been overlooked by New Testament scholars who did not want to know about them.[17]

Assumptions taken from modern historians

The views of modern historians, perfectly correct in their original contexts, are incorporated in the work of mythicists as a set of assumptions which are completely misapplied. This affects most drastically the date of the synoptic

---

[15] Evans, in Elton, *Practice of History*, 2nd edn, p. 190.

[16] Cf. e.g. https://vridar.wordpress.com/2011/08/16/how-modern-historians-use-myths-as-hist orical-sources-or-can-hobsbawm-recover-the-historical-robin-hood/ [last accessed 14 May 2013].

[17] P. M. Casey, 'Who's Afraid of Jesus Christ? Some comments on Attempts to Write a Life of Jesus', in Crossley and Karner, *Writing History, Constructing Religion*, pp. 130–1.

Gospels, and, with this, the question as to whether they may reasonably be described as 'primary sources'.

For example, Murdock declares that '*all* of the canonical gospels seem to emerge at the same time – first receiving their names and number by Irenaeus around 180 AD/CE ... If the canonical texts *as we have them* existed anywhere previously, they were unknown, which makes it likely that they were not composed until that time or shortly before, based on earlier texts.'[18] The criterion of not being mentioned in other texts is an important mythicist weapon, and we shall see that it embodies the fundamentalist assumption that the Gospels somehow should have become sacred texts immediately, and therefore quoted by all extant Christian authors as fundamentalists quote the New Testament. They really are not so quoted, whereas the Old Testament is, from which mythicists draw their conclusion that the canonical Gospels were unknown. It also presupposes that the attestation of the Gospels somehow ought to be similar to the attestation of modern documents written in cultures where writing is normal, and books are printed.

This is why, as mythicists try to date the Gospels as late as possible, one of the reasons they use is the date of surviving manuscripts. In doing this, however, they show no understanding of the nature of ancient documents and their transmission, which was very different from the writing of books in the modern world.[19] There are in fact far more copies of the Gospels surviving from relatively soon after they were written than is the case of most works from the Graeco-Roman world, or ancient Judaism. The reasons why fewer survive than might have done in the stories which mythicists invent are twofold: relatively few copies were made of any writing before the invention of printing in the mediaeval period, and there were a number of disasters in the destruction of books when libraries were destroyed, and in the Christian case, in persecutions by the Roman state.

For example, when the emperor Constantine sought to make a real splash by commissioning *lots* of copies of the Bible, he commissioned a *grand total of 50* (Eus., *De Vit. Const.* IV, 36)! Where would that leave a modern publisher? Not in serious business! This is one major reason why what mythicists regard as very few copies of the New Testament and other early Christian works survive. It is accordingly useful to compare the preservation of the earliest manuscripts of highly regarded classical works. For example, the earliest fragment of the text of the Greek historian Thucydides (c. 455–395 BCE) is one tiny piece dated to the third century BCE, and the earliest complete manuscript is from the tenth century CE. This is a bigger gap than for Christian documents, and a much bigger gap for complete

---

[18] Murdock, *Who Was Jesus?*, p. 82.
[19] See especially H. Y. Gamble, *Books and Readers in the Early Church: A History of Early Christian Texts* (New Haven: Yale University Press, 1995); A. R. Millard, *Reading and Writing in the Time of Jesus* (Sheffield: Sheffield Academic, 2000).

manuscripts, and no one is mad enough to suggest that Thucydides should therefore be dated later than the fifth century BCE. It follows that we should not attempt to date any ancient work by the date of the earliest fragments of it, let alone the earliest complete manuscript.

The second major factor is the destruction of manuscripts in disasters. For example, Eusebius helped to build up a wonderful library in Caesarea.[20] It took off from the personal library of Origen. There should be no doubt that Eusebius had there a copy of the work of Papias, bishop of Hierapolis in the early second century, *An Exposition of the Lord's Oracles (Logia)*, because he quotes important information from it (Eus., *H.E.* III, 39, 1–7, 14–17). Jerome describes it as 'the library of Origen and Pamphilus' (*De vir. Ill.*112). Jerome also notes that under Eusebius' successors Acacius (340–66) and Euzoius (369–76), an effort was made to preserve the holdings of the library by transcribing them from papyrus onto more durable parchment (Jer. *Ep.* 34.1; *De vir. Ill.*113). The library was, however, destroyed. The last reliable mention of it is by Jerome, though it may not have been destroyed until the Arab invasion in the seventh century. In a world where there were not many copies of old books, this destruction was a major disaster, and there should be no doubt that many Christian books were lost in this way. We should contrast the creative fiction of Acharya, who comments on the disappearance of Papias' work: 'It is inexplicable that such a monumental work by an early Christian father was "lost", except that it had to be destroyed because it revealed the Savior as absolutely non-historical.'[21] This comment has no connection with the reality of the ancient world, and Acharya's 'reason' for its destruction is nothing better than malicious invention.

The other major kind of disaster for the preservation of specifically Christian books was the destruction of them in persecutions by the Romans before the time of Constantine. For example, at the beginning of the fourth century, Diocletian aimed his first edict at the confiscation and destruction of Christian books (Eus., *H.E.*, VIII, 2, 4). The effect of this is graphically illustrated in the *Gesta apud Zenophilum*, which gives an account of the resulting events in Cirta, capital of Numidia in North Africa. For example, the mayor ordered people, 'bring out the scriptures so that we can obey the orders and commands of the emperors', which were to have them destroyed. The subdeacon Catullinus then produced one very large volume, and despite the obvious reluctance of Christians to bring forward their sacred texts for destruction, a number of other volumes were found and handed over to the Roman authorities.[22] This is *how* so many early

---

[20] See Gamble, *Books and Readers in the Early Church*, pp. 155–60.
[21] Acharya, *Christ Conspiracy*, p. 227.
[22] Cf. W. H. C. Frend, *Martyrdom and Persecution in the Early Church* (Oxford: Blackwell, 1965), pp. 351–92.

Christian documents were destroyed.[23] I have already pointed out that no scholar dates classical works by the date of their surviving manuscripts; the known destruction of Christian manuscripts in persecutions makes even more nonsense of the whole idea of dating Christian documents by the date of surviving manuscripts.

All this shows that the date of extant manuscripts is not a satisfactory criterion for dating any ancient documents, including the Gospels. It also explains why there are fewer ancient copies of the Gospels than mythicists expect, because they are ignorant of the production of books in the ancient world. This is especially strange in the case of Doherty and Murdock, both of whom claim to have qualifications in Classics. They should therefore have known about the production and preservation of ancient documents, and how to date them. I turn next to the internal criteria for dating the Gospels.

Dating the synoptic Gospels

The criteria for dating the synoptic Gospels are necessarily not quite the same as for the dating of all ancient historical documents, and certainly quite different from the criteria for dating recent documents. It is important to be clear about the reasons for this, and to justify the need for valid criteria, which are quite different from the fundamentalist outpourings which mythicists are given to repeating from their past, and correctly rejecting, without apparently realizing that they are not the criteria used by critical scholars. There are two main points. The first is that Jesus lived in first-century Galilee, which was a primarily oral culture with a very important written text, very roughly equivalent to our modern Old Testament, with some Apocrypha and Pseudepigrapha. This was a quite different environment both from those dealt with by modern historians, and from the figures from ancient history whom mythicists choose to mention. For example, Blogger Godfrey comments that historians 'have primary evidence for Julius Caesar, his nephew Augustus, the Roman empire, the Senate. Coins, epigraphical evidence, archaeological remains'.[24] This is obvious in itself, and as usual, what is wrong is that it should not be applied in Godfrey's simplistic fashion to the evidence about Jesus. He was not a Roman emperor, nor a major institution such as the Senate, let alone the whole empire! This is why he did not mint coins or leave epigraphical evidence, and a first-century Jewish prophet from Galilee

---

[23] Cf. Gamble, *Books and Readers in the Early Church*, pp. 145–51, and more generally Frend, *Martyrdom and Persecution in the Early Church*.
[24] http://vridar.wordpress.com/2010/06/29/kafkas-biblical-historians-outdo-alice-in-wonderlands-trial/ [last accessed 14 May 2013].

cannot reasonably be expected to have done so. It follows that the absence of such evidence is not evidence of his absence. It also follows that the evidence for his existence in first-century Galilee should not be expected to be the same as evidence conventional among modern historians for our knowledge of people in the modern world, nor for our knowledge of Roman emperors.

The next main point is that the synoptic Gospels are quite clearly set within first-century Judaism. This is a major problem for the mythicist view, because mythicists generally wish to present early Christianity as a Hellenistic cult, and never offer any proper explanation of the major Jewish elements in the synoptic Gospels. I discuss details more fully in Chapter 3, but two main points which mythicists ignore and do not understand are of central importance here. First, the synoptic Gospels contain a number of features of Judaism which simply would not be there if Christianity originated as a Hellenistic cult, or as anything outside Judaism. For example, Jesus is said to have headed for his final visit to Jerusalem. The day after his arrival, he did what we politely call 'cleansed the Temple', a completely Jewish event in which he made appropriate and authoritative quotations from Scripture (Mk 11.15–17).[25] This story does not make any sense as an invention by Gentiles, nor by anyone long after the destruction of the Temple in 70 CE.

After a few days, Jesus took rather complicated measures to ensure that he could celebrate his final Passover with his disciples. This was because the chief priests and others objected to his action in the Temple, which also led one of the Twelve to undertake to betray him. Jesus succeeded in celebrating this Passover.[26] None of this story makes any sense as part of a novel composed by members of a Gentile community long after the destruction of the Temple.

Our earliest source, the Gospel of Mark, is also full of peculiarities which are due to his use of sources which were written in Aramaic, the language of Jesus and of all his earliest followers. For example, when Jesus healed a synagogue leader's daughter, Mark relates that he grasped her hand and said: 'Talitha koum', which is in translation, 'little girl, I tell you, get up!' (Mk 5.41). The first two words, Talitha koum, are Aramaic for 'little girl, get up', so Mark has correctly translated them into Greek for his Greek-speaking audiences, adding the explicitative comment 'I tell you', as translators sometimes do. Moreover, I have followed the reading of the oldest and best manuscripts. The majority of manuscripts read the technically correct written feminine form koumi, but there is good reason to believe that the feminine ending 'i' was not pronounced. It follows that Talitha koum is exactly what Jesus said.

---

[25] For discussion for the general reader, see Casey, *Jesus of Nazareth*, pp. 411–15.
[26] For discussion for the general reader, see Casey, *Jesus of Nazareth*, pp. 415–37.

Again, at the beginning of a healing narrative, some old manuscripts have Mark say that Jesus 'was angry' (*orgistheis*), which makes no sense at all. Most manuscripts of Mark accordingly read 'had compassion' (*splanchnistheis*), which is what copyists would much have preferred to read. Matthew and Luke both leave the word out, which makes good sense only if they both read *orgistheis* too. The Aramaic *rᵉgaz*, however, means both 'be angry' and 'be deeply moved', which makes perfect sense. It follows that this is a mistake typical of bilingual translators, who suffer from interference. This is one of many pieces of evidence that parts of Mark's Gospel were translated from Aramaic sources.

Some differences in the Double Tradition are of the same kind. There are examples of this at Luke 11.42:

> But woe to you Pharisees, for you tithe mint and rue and every herb and pass over justice and the love of God. It was necessary to do the latter and not pass over the former.

If we did not have Matthew's version of the herbs to be tithed (Mt. 23.23), we would be puzzled by 'rue and every herb'. Since, however, Matthew has 'dill and cumin', we can see what has gone wrong. The Aramaic for dill was four letters written as *sh- b- th- ā*: Luke misread it as *sh- b- r- ā*, 'rue', i.e. Syrian rue (*peganum harmala*). This is just one letter different, an easy mistake to make if he was reading a wax tablet or a single sheet of papyrus. Luke then replaced 'and cumin' with 'and every herb'. Also, Matthew has 'mercy and faith', where Luke has the otherwise plausible 'the love of God'. Consequently, we can see that Matthew correctly translated *rḥmthā*, 'mercy', which Luke misread as *rḥmyā*, 'love', and that is what he edited.[27]

The response of mythicists to arguments of this kind is appallingly ignorant even by their own standards. Writing in 2007, when many examples had been in the public domain for years, Acharya simply dismissed the whole question without considering *any* examples. She commented,

> It is also claimed that the mythicists make too much of the Pagan origins and ignore the Jewish aspects of the Gospel tale. The Jewish elements, argue historicizers, must be historical and, therefore, Jesus existed.

Here again, Acharya gives *no references*. To whose arguments does she imagine that she is referring? She continued,

> Specious and sophistic though it may be, since anyone can interpolate quasi-historical details into a fictional story...this historicizer argument

---

has conveniently allowed for the dismissal of the entire mythicist school...[28]

Acharya does not, however, discuss *one single example*. What is quite wrong about this argument is the *quality and nature* of some of the Jewish material in the synoptic Gospels. This is what I have illustrated above, and this is why it is so important that Acharya does not discuss a single example from either the primary sources or the secondary literature.[29]

What is, and is not, in the Epistles

Another major problem is created by mythicists from what is *not* said in the New Testament epistles, of which the most important at this point are those of Paul. Having dated the synoptic Gospels ludicrously late, some mythicists turn Paul's genuine epistles into our earliest sources for the life and teaching of Jesus. If Paul is taken to be a real Christian writing relatively early, this may seem at first sight to be a major problem, because his epistles say very little about Jesus.

There are several things wrong with this. One is that the social context of many scholars, especially Americans, is a low context society, in which a lot of both important and mundane information needs to be constantly repeated. This is one major reason why some scholars grossly misinterpret what Paul does not say, and imagine that it reflects what neither he nor his converts believed. The term 'low context' society was introduced into scholarship by the anthropologist E. T. Hall.[30] Hall was concerned to discuss the modern world, and the application of some of his insights to the ancient world requires great care, but his discussion of modern American society can be applied directly to mythicists without much trouble or risk of distortion.

He comments: 'Although no culture exists exclusively at one end of the scale, some are high while others are low. American culture, while not at the bottom, is toward the lower end of the scale.'[31] This is blindingly obvious, and partly explains why Americans and their followers imagine that ancient sources should have given far more information about Jesus than they do. It does matter that Hall also comments: 'We are still considerably above the German-Swiss, the Germans, and the Scandinavians in the amount of contexting needed in daily life.' The reason why this matters is that it partly explains why scholars from these countries have also expected so much

---

[28] Acharya, *Christ Conspiracy*, p. 22.
[29] See further many more examples at *passim*, esp 66–80, 82, 87–90, 90–2, 94–6, 103–4, 105–7, 117–18, 121–8 below, with my response to other comments by other mythicists.
[30] E. T. Hall, *Beyond Culture* (New York: Anchor, 1976).
[31] Hall, *Beyond Culture*, p. 91.

more information from our primary sources about Jesus, even when this is not what they were really about. It is not, however, the only point. The other main point is that New Testament scholars have traditionally been mostly Christians, and have for this reason also imagined that Paul should have said far more about the historical Jesus.

The position of both Jesus and Paul was different from this, and their situation is more complicated to describe. It is possible that when Jesus worked among, and preached to, his fellow Jews in Galilee, he effectively lived in a high context society. Similarly, it is possible that when Paul founded churches, he effectively produced another high context society. In each case, this would mean that a lot of things did not need to be explicitly stated, because they were well known to everyone.

There is, however, a more complex possibility also to be taken into account, '"situational dialects" which are used in specific situational frames'.[32] For example, some years ago, before attempts were made to make railway travel 'cheaper' and more 'efficient' by getting people to travel at off-peak times, I could have gone to the desk in the railway station at Nottingham and said 'Exeter, two returns, please'. I would have been given two second-class tickets to leave that day, and return when we liked during a considerable period. There was no need to say that they were railway tickets, or that they were second-class, or that we wanted to leave that day, or exactly when we needed to come back.[33] People who live in low context societies behave in such specific circumstances like people who live in high context societies, and do not say more than is strictly necessary. It is perfectly possible that the circumstances in which Jesus or Paul said less than modern scholars expect were due to their situational contexts, rather than to Jesus belonging to, or Paul forming, a high context society.

For example, when Paul wrote to a Corinthian church which he knew only too well, he commented, 'we preach Christ crucified, a stumbling-block to Jews but foolishness to Greeks, but to those who are called, both Jews and Greeks, Christ power of God and wisdom of God' (1 Cor. 1. 23–4). This did need saying, because of problems in the Corinthian church, which was largely Gentile, because of the rejection of Paul's message by the Jewish community, and which Paul thought was obsessed by its own wisdom. Paul had, however, no need whatever to write anything such as, 'We preach Christ crucified on earth outside the walls of Jerusalem a few years ago, after being betrayed by Judah of Kerioth, and handed over to the chief priests, scribes and elders, because he cleansed the Temple, and then handed over by them to Pontius Pilatus, the governor of Judaea at the time, to be flogged and crucified.' That is because many people in the Christian

---

[32] Hall, *Beyond Culture*, p. 132.
[33] Cf. Hall, *Beyond Culture*, pp. 132–3, on the basis of which I have made my own English example.

church in Corinth would know this already, and if new members turned up to a church meeting and did not know enough about the death of the historical Jesus, there would always be someone there to explain to them what they did not know.

All this would be exacerbated by the problems of writing, another major aspect of the situational context in which the epistles were written. For this letter to be written at all, someone, whether Paul, Sosthenes, or more likely a scribe such as Tertius (Rom. 16.22), who was in effect a professional writer, indicated by the fact that Paul merely added a greeting in 'my hand' (1 Cor. 16.21), would have to dip a stylus repeatedly in a disgusting black substance which we normally dignify with the name of 'ink', and scrawl with that on papyrus sheets. This was a difficult and time-consuming process, and another good reason for Paul not to write unnecessary information in his epistles.

Two New Testament passages are especially illuminating in considering the situational context of the Pauline epistles: Gal. 2 and Acts 18.24–8. Both are important because they show both that Christianity at this stage was a definite subgroup within Judaism, our main concern at the moment, and that Paul's Gospel was not identical with that of Jesus' earliest followers in the Jerusalem church, a matter to which we must return.

In Galatians 2, Paul tells the story of how he went to Jerusalem with Barnabas and Titus 'after 14 years', long after he began to preach his Gospel. Titus was a Gentile, and it was important to Paul that he did not have to be circumcised, despite demands to this effect from people described by Paul as 'false brethren' (Gal. 2.4–5). The leaders of the Jerusalem church, of whom Paul mentions Jacob, Cephas/Peter and John, however, 'gave me and Barnabas the right hand of fellowship, so that we to the Gentiles, but they to the circumcision' (Gal. 2.9). Here it is evident that the people whom Paul calls 'false brethren' were Jewish Christians who argued that Gentiles who became followers of Jesus should be circumcised. This was the difference between Paul's Gospel and what the members of the Jerusalem church had always believed, and this is why it was so important to him that they 'gave me and Barnabas the right hand of fellowship', so that they would carry on repeating and doubtless developing the teaching of Jesus for his Jewish followers, while Paul preached salvation for Gentiles without their having to do the works of the Jewish Law. There is not a breath of a suggestion anywhere in Paul's epistles or in Acts that he ever thought otherwise. It follows that Paul accepted the teaching of Jesus, though not that it was the centre of his Gospel.

The next part of Galatians 2 is very revealing about the position of Simeon the Rock, provided that we can see past Paul's polemic to what was really going on. Paul notes, surely correctly, that when Cephas went to Antioch, he ate with Gentiles, so Gentile Christians. This was very good of him, and may well have been due to a vision which Luke reports him having when he went to visit Cornelius the centurion, another Gentile

Christian (Acts 10.9–48), even though this has been written up later. Paul, however, comments on Peter's behaviour, surely correctly in his facts, and quite wrongly on his motivation:

> But when Cephas came to Antioch, I opposed him to his face, because he was condemned. For before some (people) came from Jacob he used to eat with the Gentiles, but when they came, he withdrew and separated himself, fearing those of the circumcision. And the rest of the Jews joined in hypocrisy with him, so that Barnabas too was led away with their hypocrisy. But when I saw that they were not acting rightly to the truth of the Gospel, I said to Cephas in front of everyone, 'If you, being a Jew, live like a Gentile and not like a Jew, why do you compel the Gentiles to Judaize?' (Gal. 2.11–14).

Here it should be clear that Simeon the Rock ate with Gentile Christians in Antioch, and did not keep strictly to Jewish food laws because they were fellow Christians. Paul's misrepresentation of him centres on fear, hypocrisy, and compelling them to Judaize. It should be clear that the men from Jacob were people from the Jerusalem church whom Simeon knew well, and for all we know, they may have included people from the historic ministry of Jesus. Of course Simeon wanted to eat with them! This did not require 'fear' or 'hypocrisy', and the whole idea that this would compel anyone to 'Judaize' presupposes that Gentile Christians would have to eat Jewish food with the men from Jacob, which they do not appear to have done. Moreover, for them to 'Judaize' in any serious sense, they would have had to undertake circumcision and keep the dietary and other laws, which they more obviously did not do, as Paul knew perfectly well.

At Acts 18.24–8, Luke tells the story of Apollos going to Ephesus. He describes him as 'skilled in the scriptures' and says that he taught 'accurately the things concerning Jesus, knowing only the baptism of John'. So 'Priscilla and Aquila took him on one side, and explained the way of God more accurately'. This reflects a similar situation to that shown in Gal. 2. Apollos evidently knew a Gospel similar to that of the Jerusalem church, including the life and teaching of Jesus. We should note that no one tried to stop him from repeating material about the historical Jesus, so it should not be surprising that Pauline churches were places where the teaching of Jesus was preserved, and later rewritten. However, Priscilla and Aquila taught him also about salvation for the Gentiles without their having to keep the works of the Law. This was the centre of Paul's Gospel, which eventually enabled what we call Christianity to emerge from the Jewish diaspora in the Greek world.

Cultural context

The next point is the need, well known to all historians of the ancient world, to set our sources in their original cultural context. Mythicists will not do this, and, as so often, Blogger Godfrey expresses the crassest mistakes with clarity. Describing his departure from Christianity, he comments:

> I had always swallowed the teaching that the Bible is like a jig-saw puzzle, that the only way we could 'understand' the writings of Paul, for example, was to refer, say, to what James said in a letter addressed to someone else while discussing a different theme! What I wanted to do for a change was to study thoroughly each of the Bible books in isolation from one another to explore the mind of the writer of each book and understand its meaning to its original audience. That sounded a more intellectually honest approach so I expected it to verify afresh 'the truths of God' that I had been taught. What happened, however, was that when I let Romans alone interpret Romans my confidence in all I had been taught by the WCG began to be shaken. Peter warned of those who twisted the writings of Paul, but surely the ones twisting Paul were those who forced isolated texts to fit with books written in different cultures and times to different audiences for different purposes and with different theologies![34]

The first mistake in this paragraph is one normally made not only by fundamentalists, but by conservative and orthodox Christians of all kinds. Blogger Godfrey was taught to understand the epistles of Paul firstly in the light of the rest of the New Testament, and, as is clear from the final sentence, in the light of 'books written in different cultures and times', so the rest of the tradition in which he allowed himself to be mindlessly processed. Blogger Godfrey's reaction was, however, equally remote from historical reality: 'to study thoroughly each of the Bible books in isolation from one another'. The trouble with this is that, in practice, it involves interpreting these books in isolation not just from each other, but from their original cultural context: the 'original audience' disappears completely from view. This sets authors free, not just from fundamentalism, but also from the cultural context of biblical authors. Doherty's interpretation of Paul, which Blogger Godfrey is so enthusiastic about, is only an outstanding example of this. His view of Christ crucified up there in the sublunar realms would not have been recognized by Paul or by Christians in the churches.[35]

Two other points are again of central importance at this point. One is

---

[34] http://ironwolf.dangerousgames.com/exwcg/archives/date/1998/02 [last accessed 14 May 2013], posted on Sunday, 22 February 1998 at 12:34 p.m.
[35] On Doherty's view of Paul, see pp. 174–200.

the genre of the epistles. Not only are they not our earliest sources for the life and teaching of Jesus, they are not sources for his life and teaching at all. Secondly, the life and teaching of Jesus were central for the view of Judaism taken by people in the Jerusalem church, as they doubtless were for other members of the Twelve who presumably continued as faithful Jews in Galilee, and had nothing to do with the mission to the Gentiles either. It follows that Paul did not normally have reason to mention anything much to do with the life and teaching of Jesus. This is the main reason why he did not generally do so. It does not follow that he, or his Gentile converts, knew nothing about it.

Conclusions

We must conclude that one major element in the mythicist case is total contempt for sound historical method. Mythicists refuse to make any serious attempt to understand New Testament documents in their original cultural context. The most straightforward reason for this is that they begin with their conclusions, and fit the evidence into them. As we saw in Chapter 1, they are by and large former fundamentalist Christians, who begin with their faith, and fit the evidence into it. They have had a conversion experience away from Christianity, and they are no more sympathetic to critical scholarship now than they were before. In particular, as ignorant Christians they rejected Jesus' Jewish culture, and they still do.

As fundamentalist Christians, this was part of their completely uncritical belief in Jesus as the second person of the Trinity walking on this earth performing miracles, including of course the miracles as well as all the speeches found only in the Fourth Gospel, in which his opponents are often 'the Jews'. At that stage they could not cope with his Jewishness, and now they cannot cope with his existence at all, and like to claim that early Christianity was a Hellenistic cult. The real historical Jesus, however, was a first-century Jewish prophet, as I have pointed out elsewhere.[36] To establish this, we must consider next the overwhelming evidence for the early date of the Gospels of Mark and Matthew, and the reliability of parts of all three of the synoptic Gospels.

---

[36] Casey, *Jesus of Nazareth*.

3

The date and reliability of the canonical Gospels

Introduction

We have seen that one of the most extraordinary features of the mythicist position is the attempt to date all four canonical Gospels much too late. I have noted that Murdock declares that '*all* of the canonical gospels seem to emerge at the same time – first receiving their names and number by Irenaeus around 180 AD/CE ... If the canonical texts *as we have them* existed anywhere previously, they were unknown, which makes it likely that they were not composed until that time or shortly before, based on earlier texts.'[1] As we saw in Chapter 2, this criterion is remote from the reality of the composition and preservation of ancient documents.

The New Testament canon was not formed until much later, and Irenaeus' dogmatic and uncritical view as to why there are four Gospels, 'since there are four zones of the world in which we live, and four principal winds' (*Adv. Haer.* III, 11, 8), c. 177 CE, is an early step down that road. It did not prevent a massive quarrel as to whether the Fourth Gospel should be accepted, not least because it is so obviously different from the other three which did make it into the canon, because they were the first to be written and widely treasured in the churches. Later Gospels, such as those of Thomas, Mary and Judas, which some mythicists like to date earlier than they should be dated, were written later and treasured by relatively small Christian subgroups, not by the churches as a whole.

Freke and Gandy say of the four canonical Gospels: 'These books are traditionally said to be eyewitness accounts of the life of Jesus written by his disciples.'[2] By whom? In accordance with mythicist custom, Freke and Gandy give no references, and fundamentalists are surely the vast majority of such people known to them. For example, at www.Paul-Timothy.net

---

[1]Murdock, *Who Was Jesus?*, p. 82.
[2]Freke and Gandy, *Jesus Mysteries*, p. 170.

we are told by someone who calls themselves Paul-Timothy – Shepherd's Study – Bible, #37:

> The Holy Spirit has given to us four witnesses to the Life and teachings of Jesus: Mark, Matthew, Luke and John, the compilers and writers of the four Gospels. Each of the four Gospel writers lived while Jesus was on earth. Three of them knew him well, and Luke investigated the facts about Jesus (Luke 1:1–3). Thus, the four gospels are 'eye-witness' accounts, the strongest kind. All four writers included in their Gospel some of the same accounts about Jesus, and each one adds some accounts that the others left out. Yet all agree; the four Gospels form a single true story.

This is fundamentalist falsehood from beginning to end. None of the Gospel writers knew Jesus well, none of them were 'eye-witnesses', and critical scholarship has demonstrated abundantly that they do not 'form a single true story'.

As so often, mythicists are firing at fundamentalists in total disregard of critical scholarship, even though Freke and Gandy acknowledge elsewhere that critical scholars have shown that the Gospel of John was nothing like an eyewitness account, and that there are various historical problems with the other Gospels.[3] They present obvious disagreements between the Gospels, which do indeed show that they are not four eyewitness accounts of the ministry, but not that Jesus did not exist, and not even that no *parts* of *any* Gospels really were based on such accounts. Freke and Gandy, however, declare, 'The Gnostic sages authored a huge number of gospels and spiritual treatises', which is true, 'including of course the original version of the story of Jesus which became the Gospel of Mark.'[4] They give no references for this amazing comment either, presumably assuming that all readers will remember their brief comments on the *Secret Gospel of Mark,*[5] which was a forgery by Morton Smith.

Another problem is what mythicists make of the date of NT manuscripts. They have produced too many falsehoods to enumerate here, but I give the most important points. Firstly, Acharya cites Walker for the view that 'no extant manuscript can be dated earlier than the 4th century A.D.'.[6] This is misleading in itself, because it is true only of major mss of more or less the whole New Testament, which were obviously not produced until after the formation of the New Testament Canon. Many were commissioned in the

---

[3]Freke and Gandy, *Jesus Mysteries*, e.g. pp. 168–200.
[4]Freke and Gandy, *Jesus Mysteries*, pp. 266–7.
[5]Freke and Gandy, *Jesus Mysteries*, pp. 120–2, cf. 134.
[6]Acharya, *Christ Conspiracy*, p. 26, quoting B. Walker, *The Woman's Encyclopedia of Myths and Secrets* (San Francisco: HarperCollins, 1983), p. 469.

fourth century by the Emperor Constantine, whom mythicists also love to hate, not without some reason. Secondly, it is clear that P[45] originally contained all four Gospels and Acts. Metzger and Ehrman correctly report the editors dating it 'in the first half of the third century', a date which should be accepted.[7] P[52] has only a small fragment of the Fourth Gospel, but it is important that it must be dated in the first half of the second century.[8] We now have also P[4], P[64] and P[67]. These papyrus fragments are now known to have been part of a codex of all four Gospels which the most recent study dates to the late second century.[9] P[66], which should not be dated later than c. 200 CE, contains significant parts of the Fourth Gospel. P[75], which should be dated in the late second or early third century, contains the Gospels of Luke and John.[10]

All this illustrates the fact that Acharya is too anti-Christian to be relied on even for apparently objective information. She frequently relies on scholarship which is out of date. For example, she further bolsters the claim that there are no copies of the Gospels from before 325 CE by citing Waite, who wrote in the nineteenth century.[11] More recent and more reliable information is available from contemporary scholarship! It is of course more important that, as we have seen in Chapter 2, the date of the extant mss of ancient works is not a satisfactory criterion for dating the documents themselves.

The final problem to be considered here is the obvious fact that all the earliest evidence for the existence of Jesus is Christian. Some mythicists have used this as an argument for pouring scorn on the methods normally used by New Testament scholars who have attempted to reconstruct the figure of Jesus in history, and to suggest that this is a decisive argument against his existence. Perhaps the clearest presentation of this view is that of Blogger Godfrey, because, as an unregulated blogger, he seems happiest to be rudest about New Testament scholars. For example:

It is not true that these Jesus historians use the same starting assumptions and methods as nonbiblical historians...We have primary evidence — that is, physically contemporary evidence, for the existence of other

---

[7] B. M. Metzger and B. D. Ehrman, *The Text of the New Testament: Its Transmission, Corruption, and Restoration* (4th edn, Oxford: Oxford University Press, 4th edn, 2005), p. 54.
[8] Metzger and Ehrman, *Text of the New Testament*, pp. 55–6.
[9] Metzger and Ehrman, *Text of the New Testament*, p. 53.
[10] Metzger and Ehrman, *Text of the New Testament*, pp. 56–7, 58–9.
[11] Acharya, *Christ Conspiracy*, p. 26, citing C. Waite, *History of the Christian Religion to the Year Two Hundred*, p. 461. Acharya's bibliography lists this as published by Caroll Bierblower in 1992; it was in fact published in 1881, and this illustrates that her bibliography cannot be trusted. My own copy is correctly attributed to Charles Burlinghame Waite, published by General Books in 2009, but correctly dated to 1881. Its page references have no reasonable relation to reality. The earliest copy that I have seen was that of the second edition (Chicago: Waite & Co., 1881), in the British Library.

persons from ancient times (e.g. Julius Caesar, Alexander the Great...) Primary evidence, by the way, is according to the language of historiography ever since the father of modern history, Leopold von Ranke, evidence that is physically situated at the time and place of the event or person in question. The Gospels that we have are not primary but secondary evidence — their physical existence can be traced no further back than the second and third and fourth centuries... The Gospels are NOT primary evidence. They are secondary sources. Only if you use the term "primary evidence" loosely in lay language can the term be justified for the Gospels. Anyone seriously doing history as a scholarly enterprise ought to have some basic grasp of the terminology and philosophy of history and historiography. Biblical historians, as McKnight himself notes, are rarely aware of the nature of the study they claim to be doing. Few have any idea of landmark publications on the nature of history by von Ranke, Collingwood, Carr, Elton, or even the postmodernists... Casey and Crossley demonstrate no more awareness of historical methodology than any of their American counterparts.[12]

There are several important points here, apart from the unlearned bossiness throughout and the creative fiction reflected at the end, exposed above in Chapter 2.[13] Firstly, why is all the earliest evidence for the existence of Jesus of Nazareth found in Christian sources? Secondly, to what extent are the methods of 'Jesus historians' different from those of other historians, and to what extent is that difference justifiable? It is notable that Blogger Godfrey simply assumes, here as often, that comments made by supposedly secular historians long ago should simply be taken out of their original context and reapplied to the Quest of the Historical Jesus without question, in accordance with his instructions. The purpose of this chapter is to address these and all the other questions raised in this introduction.

Why are all our earliest primary sources Christian?

It will be noted that I have not followed Blogger Godfrey's orders to use the terminology which he ascribes to Von Ranke as if this committed Christian scholar, who made important contributions to knowledge in the nineteenth century, had written Holy Scripture the authority of which we should all accept, as reapplied by Blogger Godfrey. There is a good reason for this.

---

[12] http://vridar.wordpress.com/2010/05/30/in-brief-dates-q-aramaic-heavenly-or-earthly-they-make-no-difference-to-the-mythical-jesus-view/ [last accessed 14 May 2013], and other similar posts and comments.
[13] See pp. 43–8 above.

One of the major problems of working and teaching in New Testament Studies is that a lot of interested people belong to Christian subgroups and believe, without much question, the books written by scholars who belong to the same social subgroup. So when a significant book was edited by Bob Funk, or an introductory textbook written by Howard Marshall, they were more or less guaranteed an uncritical audience of American ex-fundamentalists, or evangelicals from anywhere, respectively.[14] Consequently, many of us use 'primary sources' to refer to the synoptic or canonical Gospels when studying Jesus, and Paul's epistles when studying Paul, while we use 'secondary literature' to refer to the works of Funk, Marshall and all other modern scholars. This terminology is clear as long as it is understood, and Blogger Godfrey has no excuse for ordering us to use his interpretation of Von Ranke's comments instead.

The major reasons why all our earliest primary sources for the Life and Teaching of Jesus are Christian is that Jesus was a first-century prophet who lived in a primarily oral Jewish culture, not a significant politician in the Graeco-Roman world. By contrast, for example, Julius Caesar was an important political and literary figure in the highly literate culture of the Romans. It is therefore natural that he should have written literary works which have survived, and that other surviving literary sources have written about him. It is equally natural that coins minted on his orders survive, as well as inscriptions about him, and busts and statues of him. It is entirely right that these resources should be properly used by historians writing about the events in which he was involved, and by people who also, quite rightly, consider it worthwhile writing books about him.[15]

Jesus of Nazareth left no literary works at all, and he had no reason to write any. He lived in a primarily oral culture, except for the sanctity and central importance of its sacred texts, which approximate to our Hebrew Bible. A variety of works now thought of as Apocrypha (e.g. Sirach) or Pseudepigrapha (e.g. 1 Enoch) were held equally sacred by some Jewish people, and could equally well be learnt and repeated by people who did not possess the then-difficult skill of writing. Almost all our surviving primary sources about Jesus are Christian because most people who had any interest in writing about him were his followers, and the few relatively early comments by other writers such as Josephus and Tacitus are largely due to special circumstances, such as the judicial murder of Jesus' brother

---

[14] Cf. e.g. R. W. Funk, R. W. Hoover and the Jesus Seminar, *The Five Gospels: The Search for the Authentic Words of Jesus* (New York: Macmillan, 1993); I. H. Marshall, *The Acts of the Apostles: an introduction and commentary* (Tyndale New Testament Commentaries. Leicester: IVP and Grand Rapids: Eerdmans, 1980).

[15] Cf. e.g. R. Garland, *Julius Caesar* (Bristol: Bristol Phoenix, 2003); L. Canfora, *Julius Caesar: the People's Dictator* (1999. Trans. M. Hill and K. Windle. Edinburgh: Edinburgh University Press, 2007); M. Griffin (ed.), *A Companion to Julius Caesar* (Malden and Chichester: Wiley-Blackwell, 2009).

Jacob (Jos. *Ant.* XX, 200), or the great fire of Rome (Tac. *Annals* XI, 44). We shall see that mythicists love to declare these passages interpolations for quite spurious reasons, so that they can imagine that there are *no* rather than few non-Christian sources which mention Jesus.

Jesus also minted no coins, and he was not the kind of political figure who might be featured on coins or inscriptions either. It follows that the criteria reasonably used by historians writing about important political figures such as Julius Caesar need modification in dealing with the historicity of Jesus. In itself, this does not tell us whether he existed or not. It merely means that the surviving sources need careful critical assessment, using methods which are in fact very similar to those used by secular historians dealing with other literary sources. We must therefore consider how decent critical scholars deal with the historicity of the life and teaching of Jesus. This is in no way undermined by the obvious fact that a lot of people behave quite differently and order us to believe by faith in the literal historicity of all four canonical Gospels.

Dating the Gospels

We have seen that mythicists try to date the Gospels as late as possible, and one of the reasons they use is the date of surviving manuscripts. This criterion is completely faulty, for mythicists show no understanding of the nature of ancient documents and their transmission, which was completely different from the writing of books in the modern world.[16] The dating of ancient documents requires us to use quite different criteria.

The most important single criterion in dating the Gospels is what scholars call their *Sitz im Leben,* a German term which basically refers to the cultural context in which they were originally written, and which has been reasonably translated into English as 'Setting in Life'. This term is also used to refer to the culture of the historical Jesus himself, which is significantly different from the culture(s) in which the Gospels were written. The most up-to-date term for discussing the culture of the historical Jesus is the criterion of Historical Plausibility, helpfully put forward by Theissen and Winter.[17] This is indispensable for discussing the dates of the Gospels, because the synoptic Gospels – Mark above all because he is the earliest, but also those of Matthew and Luke – seriously reflect the environment of the historical Jesus in first-century Aramaic-speaking Judaism in Galilee, as well as their own (somewhat later) Christian environments, for which they wrote in Greek. We must therefore consider carefully both Semitisms,

---

[16] See pp. 43–8 and Chapter 30 above.
[17] G. Theissen and D. Winter, *The Quest for the Plausible Jesus: The Question of Criteria* (1997. Trans. M. E. Boring. Louisville: Westminster John Knox, 2002).

reflections in the Gospels of Aramaic sources on which they were partly dependent, and features of first-century Judaism which would not be found in fictional documents written entirely by Greek-speaking Christians.

This is a brief summary of Theissen and Winter's proposal:

> What Jesus intended and said must be compatible with the Judaism of the first half of the first century in Galilee ... What Jesus intended and did must be recognizable as that of an individual figure within the framework of the Judaism of that time ... What we know of Jesus as a whole must allow him to be recognized within his contemporary Jewish context and must be compatible with the Christian (canonical and noncanonical) history of his effects.[18]

All these points are of central importance. Our early primary sources are unanimous and unambiguous in placing Jesus within a context of first-century Judaism. It follows that our picture of Jesus should be comprehensible within that cultural framework, and further, when a piece of information about Jesus or those present during the historic ministry fits *only* there, that is a strong argument in favour of its historicity.

For example, after Jesus had performed an exorcism in a Capernaum synagogue one sabbath (Mk 1.23–7) and healed Peter's mother-in-law of a fever (Mk 1.30–1), Mark records this:

> Now when evening came, when the sun had set, (people) brought to him all those who were ill and those who were possessed of demons ... (Mk 1.32)

Carrying burdens on the sabbath was against the Law (Jer. 17.21–2), and anyone who has tried to carry a sick person should understand that the person is so heavy and difficult to carry that bringing this under the prohibition of carrying burdens is almost inevitable. This is why Mark's note of time is so careful. The sabbath ended when darkness fell. 'When evening came' might not be clear enough: 'when the sun had set' settles it – his audiences would know that people carried other people only when the sabbath was over, so as not to violate the written Law. It follows that this report cannot be the work of the early church, who were not interested in such matters: it must go back to a real report transmitted during the historic ministry, when this observance of the written Law mattered, and everyone took this so much for granted that the careful note of time was sufficient to bring it to mind. It is also therefore powerful evidence of Jesus' successful ministry of exorcism and healing.

This further illustrates that our picture of Jesus 'must be recognizable as

---

[18] Theissen and Winter, *Plausible Jesus*, pp. 211–12.

that of an *individual* figure within the framework of the Judaism of that time'.[19] Placing him within ancient Judaism does not mean turning him into an ordinary or average first-century Jew. I have argued elsewhere that Jesus was by far the most successful exorcist and healer of his time.[20] That judgement is based on a massive amount of evidence in our oldest primary sources, critically assessed within the criterion of historical plausibility. The rest of *Jesus of Nazareth* was further devoted to allowing the emergence of a quite unique figure, yet a figure seen within his historical context in first-century Judaism. Within this framework, I was also able to interpret the opposition to Jesus, and how it led to his crucifixion.

This is where the Aramaic criterion should be fitted in. First, despite the Gospels being written in Greek, they attribute some Aramaic words to Jesus, and those in Mark, our oldest source, are found in narratives which satisfy the rest of the criterion of historical plausibility too. For example, when Jesus healed a synagogue leader's daughter, Mark relates that he grasped her hand and said: *Talitha koum*, which is in translation, little girl, I tell you, get up! (Mk 5.41).

The first two words, *Talitha koum*, are Aramaic for 'little girl, get up', so Mark has correctly translated them into Greek for his Greek-speaking audiences, adding the explicitative comment 'I tell you', as translators sometimes do. Moreover, I have followed the reading of the oldest and best manuscripts. The majority of manuscripts read the technically correct written feminine form *koumi*, but there is good reason to believe that the feminine ending '*i*' was not pronounced. It follows that *Talitha koum* is *exactly* what Jesus said.[21] I have given reasons elsewhere for supposing that the whole of this healing narrative is literally true, and that it is dependent ultimately on an eyewitness account by one of the inner circle of three of the Twelve, who were present throughout, and who accordingly *heard and transmitted exactly* what Jesus said.[22]

I deliberately put the use of Aramaic under the general heading of historical plausibility, because fiction could be composed in Aramaic as well as in any other language, and Aramaic or Hebrew words could be placed in a Greek story by a storyteller seeking a reality effect. For example, at Jn 4.25, the Samaritan woman says to Jesus 'I know that Messiah (*Messias*) is coming, who is called Christ (*Christos*).' Here the word *Messias* is an obvious attempt to put into Greek letters the Aramaic *meshīḥā*, which means 'anointed' or 'Messiah' (equivalent to the Hebrew (*ha*) *mashīaḥ*). The Samaritan woman then supplies the Greek equivalent *Christos*. The Samaritans, however, did not call the figure whom they expected 'anointed'

---

[19]Theissen and Winter, *Plausible Jesus*, p. 211 (my selective emphasis).

[20]Casey, *Jesus of Nazareth*, ch. 7.

[21]For more technical discussion, see P. M. Casey, 'Aramaic Idiom and the Son of Man Problem: A Response to Owen and Shepherd', *JSNT* 25 (2002), pp. 3–32 (9–10).

[22]Casey, *Jesus of Nazareth*, ch. 7, pp. 268–9.

or 'Messiah'. They called him *Taheb*, which means 'Restorer'. Accordingly, this use of *Messias* has no historical plausibility at all. Nor does her use of the Christian term *Christos*, nor do some specifically Johannine features of the story, such as Jesus' ability to give her living water and eternal life (Jn 4.10–14). These two examples illustrate how important it is to use Aramaic as part of the criterion of historical plausibility. We must not imagine that the *mere occurrence* of one or two Aramaic words is sufficient evidence of historical authenticity. We must always look for the historical plausibility of the narratives in which Aramaic words are embedded. We shall see that this criterion is satisfied in Mark's stories, and I argue that this is because our oldest Gospel is partly dependent on eyewitness accounts by Aramaic-speaking disciples.

Secondly, the Gospels, especially Mark, have various peculiarities in Greek which can be explained by their use of Aramaic sources. The simplest examples are mistakes. For example at Mk 2.23, Mark begins a story of Jesus' disciples going through the fields on the sabbath plucking ears of corn. Poor people were entitled to take *Peah*, the grain left for them at the edge of fields (Lev. 23.22), and for this purpose they naturally had to *go along* the paths in between other people's fields. Hence the Pharisees do not complain at them doing so. Mark, however, says that they began to *make* a path. This is due to a simple misreading of his Aramaic source. Mark's Aramaic source will have read *lema'ebhar*, so they began 'to go along' a path, which everyone was perfectly entitled to do on the sabbath, and this has been slightly misread as *lema'ebhadh*, 'to make', with 'd' rather than 'r' as the final letter. In Aramaic, the letters 'r' and 'd' are always similar, now conventionally printed as r and d, which are obviously alike, and in the Dead Sea Scrolls they are often indistinguishable. Moreover, this mistake occurs in a story which in all other respects satisfies the criterion of historical plausibility, and this applies to all other examples of such mistakes in Mark's Gospel.

Similar mistakes in Luke's Gospel would be more difficult to uncover if we did not have Matthew's much more accurate version of some of the so-called 'Q' material. There are outstanding examples of this at Lk. 11.42:

> But woe to you Pharisees, for you tithe mint and rue and every herb and pass over justice and the love of God. It was necessary to do the latter and not pass over the former.

If we did not have Matthew's version of the herbs to be tithed (Mt. 23.23), we would be puzzled by 'rue and every herb'. Since, however, Matthew has 'dill and cumin', we can see what has gone wrong. The Aramaic for dill was four letters written as *sh-b-th-ā*: Luke misread it as *sh-b-r-ā*, 'rue', i.e. Syrian rue (*peganum harmala*). This is just one letter different, an easy mistake to make if he was reading a wax tablet or a single sheet of papyrus. Luke then replaced 'and cumin' with 'and every herb'. Also, Matthew has 'mercy and faith', where Luke has the otherwise plausible 'the love of God'. Consequently, we can see that Matthew correctly translated *rḥmthā*, 'mercy', which Luke misread as *rḥmyā*, 'love', and that is what he edited.

In both these examples, my use of Aramaic has been carefully controlled. In each case there is a mistake in the text, 'make' at Mk 2.23, and 'rue' at Lk. 11.42, and Mt. 23.23–4 forms a control over the understanding of Lk. 11.42. We must not, however, alter the meaning of texts at the hand of Aramaic conjectures, an error of method widespread in the history of scholarship Misreadings and mistranslations of Aramaic sources should be proposed only in cases where they are at least part of an argument of cumulative weight for supposing that a document was partly based on one or more Aramaic sources. Secondly, the proposed Aramaic must be realistic, and so must any proposed misreading or mistranslation.

As well as simple mistakes, there are cases where Mark's Greek is unidiomatic, because Mark was suffering from interference from an Aramaic source in front of him, as translators often do. For example, Mark transmits John the Baptist's prediction of his successor in a form which may be literally translated as follows: 'The one stronger than me is coming after me, of whom I am not worthy to bend down and undo the latchet of the sandals of him' (Mk 1.7). Here the meaning is unambiguous and correct, but 'of whom' followed by 'of him' is no more idiomatic in Greek than it is in English. The relative particle in Aramaic (*de* or *di*), the equivalent of the English 'who', 'what', etc., has to be picked up by another particle later in the sentence, in this case *delēh*, the equivalent of 'of him'. In Greek, this is not the case, just as in English, and once Mark had correctly put 'of whom', there was no need for him to put 'of him' at the end of the sentence. He did so because he had *delēh* at the end of the sentence in the text in front of him. This is very valuable evidence, because it shows that Mark was translating a written Aramaic source. There are more unidiomatic features of this kind in Mark's Gospel than in any of the others. Matthew and Luke have a natural tendency to alter such features in their attempts to write better Greek. In this case, Matthew has so many differences from Mark that it is difficult to know whether he was altering Mark, or shifting already to another source from which he took the end of John the Baptist's prediction (Mt. 3.11–12, cf. Lk. 3.17). Luke, however, despite making some minor alterations, left 'of whom … of him' unchanged.

The Fourth Gospel has only one comparable example: 'Among you stands one whom you do not know, the one who comes after me, of whom I am not worthy to undo of him the latchet of the sandal' (Jn 1.26–7). This same peculiarity, 'of whom … of him' is straightforward evidence that the Johannine community possessed Mark's Gospel, as is to be expected of a Christian community at the end of the first century CE. At the same time, they have rewritten the whole context so as to ensure that John bears unambiguous witness to Jesus, 'the lamb of God who takes away the sin of the world' (Jn 1.29). This is reflected at the end of Jn 1.26, an addition to Mark in which the words 'one whom *you* do not know' reflect John the Baptist's knowledge of Jesus, which he is about to reveal, clean contrary to the synoptic Gospels and historical reality.

This indicates again how careful we must be to fit evidence of Aramaic sources into historical plausibility as a whole. The peculiarity of the Greek of Mk 1.7 shows that he was translating an Aramaic source, and fits into the evidence of the historicity of the whole of Mark's Aramaic source. The same peculiarity in the Greek of Jn 1.27 indicates that the Johannine community inherited Markan tradition, and is found in a context in which they have rewritten history in accordance with their own needs.

The phenomenon of interference also affects single words. A bilingual translator may use a word in an unfamiliar sense, because he is so used to using it as equivalent to a word in his source. There is an example of this, 'being angry' (*orgistheis*) used of Jesus at Mk 1.41 when he healed, or perhaps pronounced clean, a man with a skin disease. Here again Mark's Greek is perfectly comprehensible as a literal and unrevised translation of an Aramaic source which gave a perfectly accurate albeit very brief account of an incident which really took place. The Aramaic source will have read *regaz*. This word often does mean 'be angry', which is why Mark translated it like this. But it has a wider range of meaning than this, including 'tremble' and 'be deeply moved'. Accordingly, Mark did not mean that Jesus was angry. He was suffering from interference, as all bilinguals do, especially when they are translating. In Mark's mind, the Greek word for being angry also meant 'tremble' or 'be deeply moved', because this was the range of meaning of the normally equivalent Aramaic word in front of him.

Translation also affects the frequency with which words are used. For example, Mark uses the Greek word for 'begin' 26 times, far more than one would expect in a Greek document, and Matthew and Luke have a very strong tendency to remove it, though they have other examples of their own. The word for 'begin' (*archomai*) is as normal in Greek as it is in English, but the Aramaic equivalent (*sheri*) is often used when to us it means nothing very much, and this is what Matthew in particular seems not to have liked. He kept only six of Mark's 26 examples, and he has only 13 altogether. Examples include Mk 2.23, where the disciples 'began to make a path'. I have discussed 'make', and I pointed out that this is a mistake due to Mark's misreading of an Aramaic source.[23] There should be no doubt that in this instance Mark has translated *sheri* literally from his Aramaic source. Matthew omitted the incorrect 'make a path' and edited the narrative to read 'began to pluck the ears' (Mt. 12.1), while Luke omitted 'began to make a path' altogether. Mark's 26 examples should be attributed

---

[23] See pp. 69–70.

to his use of Aramaic sources. This is part of an argument of cumulative weight for the dependence of our oldest Gospel on written Aramaic sources.

Sometimes, a Greek word in a saying of Jesus can represent only one particular Aramaic word, which has a different meaning which fits much better into the criterion of historical plausibility. For example, some Pharisees are said to have warned Jesus that Herod Antipas wanted to kill him (Lk. 13.31). Jesus is said to have replied, 'Go and tell this fox, Look! I am casting out demons and performing healings to-day and tomorrow, and on the third I am perfected' (Lk. 13.32). Jesus' apparent reference to Herod Antipas as a fox (Greek *alōpēx*) has led many scholars to describe Antipas as cunning, for foxes were commonly thought of in the Greek world as cunning.[24] This does not, however, make good historical sense, since Herod Antipas is not otherwise known to have been particularly cunning. Moreover, Jesus' Aramaic word can only have been *ta'alā*, which also means 'jackal' (*canis aureus*), and there seem to have been more jackals than foxes in Israel. Luke's translation of *ta'alā* with *alōpēx* was, however, virtually inevitable, because *ta'alā* does mean 'fox', whereas there was no standard Greek word for 'jackal', because there were no jackals in Greece.[25] We may therefore conclude that Jesus described Antipas as a jackal. That makes perfect polemical sense! The jackal was a noisy, unclean nuisance of an animal, a predator which hunted in packs. This is a beautiful description of one member of the pack of Herods, none of them genuinely observant Jews, some of them ruthless rulers who worked with packs of supporters to hunt down their opponents and kill them, as Antipas had hunted down and killed John the Baptist and was now hunting down Jesus himself. Thus the recovery of Jesus' original word *ta'alā* helps to fit this saying more accurately into its original cultural context.

One of the problems encountered by all translators is that words in their sources may have idiomatic meanings which do not have the same connotations in their target language. Many translators respond by translating literally. Lk. 13.32 has two examples of this as well. One is the last word, 'I am perfected'. In Aramaic, this word (*sheʲlam*) was used idiomatically with reference to death, so here Jesus referred idiomatically to his forthcoming death. The other idiomatic usages in this verse are the indications of time. Jesus' declaration that he was continuing his ministry of exorcism and healing 'to-day and to-morrow', more literally in Aramaic 'this day and another day', and that he would die 'on the third', are not to be taken literally. They refer to short intervals of time, as was normal in Aramaic but not in Greek.

---

[24] E.g. M. H. Jensen, *Herod Antipas in Galilee* (WUNT 2, 115. Tübingen: Mohr Siebeck, 2006), pp. 116–17, not mentioning the Aramaic reconstruction and discussion of Lk. 13.31–3 in Casey, *Aramaic Sources of Mark's Gospel*, pp. 188–9.

[25] For scholarly discussion, see Casey, *Solution to the 'Son of Man' Problem*, pp. 170–2, with bibliography to foxes and jackals.

The most striking Aramaic idiom in the whole of the Gospels is the use of two words, *bar* (*ᵉ*)*nāsh*(*ā*), literally 'son of man'. I argue that Jesus used these words of himself in a particular Aramaic idiom, in which a speaker used a somewhat general statement to refer to himself, or himself and other people made obvious by the context.[26] These words were, however, difficult to translate, because there is no such idiom in Greek, so the translators adopted a strategy. They decided to render *bar* (*ᵉ*)*nāsh*(*ā*) with the Greek *ho huios tou anthrōpou*, literally 'the son of (the) man', whenever it referred to Jesus, and to use other terms whenever it did not. In this way they produced a major Christological title, which we call 'the Son of man' in English. Mark found this term in Scripture at Dan. 7.13, where the term is *kᵉbhar ᵉnāsh*, 'one like a son of man', the same two words 'son' and 'man', but preceded by 'like' (*kᵉ*), and not used in the same idiom. Mark also rewrote one of Jesus' major predictions of his death and Resurrection, and used it in different forms more than once. Matthew and Luke followed him in this. They also inherited sayings from the 'Q' material, and they were so happy with the Greek term *ho huios tou anthrōpou* as a Christological title that they used it in new sayings of their own.

This has left a very complex problem for modern scholars, and given that most New Testament professors cannot read the language Jesus spoke, it has been exceptionally difficult to solve. Every time that the Greek term *ho huios tou anthrōpou* occurs, it is an obvious Aramaism. Yet such was the delight of the Gospel writers in this new Christological title that it does not follow that all the 'Son of man' sayings are authentic sayings of Jesus – some are creations of the evangelists. The Aramaic criterion can still be used, but using it is very complicated.

I discuss here briefly the particular Aramaic idiom, in which a speaker used a somewhat general statement to refer to himself, or himself and other people made obvious by the context. About a dozen examples of this idiom can be reconstructed from sayings of Jesus found in the Gospels, and all of them should be regarded as genuine. For example, at his final Passover meal with his disciples, Jesus made the following comment on his forthcoming betrayal:

A/The son of man goes as it is written concerning him, and woe to that man by whose hand a/the son of man is betrayed/handed over. (Mk 14.21)

Here the idiomatic Aramaic *bar ’nāsh*(*ā*), literally 'son of man', cannot lose its level of generality, though this is not the main point of the saying. Jesus was in no doubt that he was going to suffer a humiliating death, and that this was to have a fundamental redemptive function. He therefore

---

[26] See further for full scholarly discussion, Casey, *Solution to the 'Son of Man' Problem*.

had good reason to state the prediction of his death in Scripture, and the doom awaiting the traitor, by means of general statements. The Aramaic word 'goes' (*ªzal*) was a normal metaphor for 'dies', as the Greek word for 'goes' was not, so this is further evidence that Mark was translating an Aramaic source. Despite the general level of meaning, no one will have been left in doubt that Jesus' own death was primarily referred to. The doom pronounced on the traitor also has a general level of meaning, which helped to make it acceptable. There should therefore be no doubt that this saying is genuine, and the same goes for all the other examples of this idiom that can be reconstructed from sayings of Jesus in the synoptic Gospels. All of them fit perfectly into the life and teaching of Jesus. Moreover, sayings in which Jesus uses this idiom are found in Mark, in the 'Q' material, and one of them is found in Luke's special material (Lk. 22.48), so this also satisfies the criterion of multiple attestation by source. While these examples are found in our oldest sources, there are no examples in the Fourth Gospel. This distribution is consistent with everything we know about the historical reliability of the Gospels.

There is here a massive complex of evidence for the historicity of some parts of the synoptic tradition. However, as I noted in Chapter 2, Acharya, writing as late as 2007, simply dismisses the whole question without considering any examples. She comments:

> It is also claimed that the mythicists make too much of the Pagan origins and ignore the Jewish aspects of the Gospel tale. The Jewish elements, argue historicizers, must be historical and, therefore, Jesus existed.

Here again, Acharya gives *no references*. To whose arguments does she imagine that she is referring? She continues:

> Specious and sophistic though it may be, since anyone can interpolate quasi-historical details into a fictional story...this historicizer argument has conveniently allowed for the dismissal of the entire mythicist school...[27]

Acharya does not, however, discuss *one single example*. What is quite wrong with this argument is the *quality and nature* of some of the Jewish material in the synoptic Gospels. This is what I have illustrated above, and this is why it is so important that Acharya does not discuss a single example from either the primary sources or the secondary literature.

For example, in the first article which I published on this material as long ago as 1988, I offered a complete Aramaic reconstruction of Mark

---

[27] Acharya, *Christ Conspiracy*, p. 22.

2.23–8.[28] As I noted above, there is a mistake in v. 23, where Mark says that the disciples began to 'make' a path, which would have been against the Law, rather than 'go along' it, which the story requires them to do to make proper sense. This is easy to explain as a mistake made by Mark because of a slight misreading of an Aramaic source. Is it really feasible to regard this as explained by the general statement that 'anyone can interpolate quasi-historical details into a fictional story'? This detail is *not* 'quasi-historical': it is a mistake. Again, Jesus' first argument in response to the Pharisees' complaint has often been thought to be illogical, because the incident which he cites, in which David ate the shewbread and gave it to his followers, is not said in Mark's account to have taken place on the sabbath, whereas Mark says explicitly that the incident in the Life of Jesus took place on the sabbath. I pointed out that, since the priest in the story of 1 Sam. 21.1–6, said that the shewbread was the only bread which he had available, Jesus and the Pharisees would all assume that this was the sabbath, since this was the day on which the shewbread was changed, and no one was allowed to bake more bread because this was regarded as work, which was prohibited on the sabbath. Is this detail really there because 'anyone can interpolate quasi-historical details into a fictional story'? Surely not. It is not a 'quasi-historical detail'. It requires knowledge of Jewish culture, which Mark could take for granted because he used Jewish sources which were written in Aramaic, and which were written in a high context culture, in which culturally universal details could be taken for granted. Mark likewise wrote in a high context culture, so he could take what I called 'cultural assumptions' for granted too. Jesus' argument in support of his disciples does not make sense as an interpolation, a main plank of mythicist arguments, at all.

I also pointed out the importance of Mark 2.27–8. Here Jesus' second argument in defence of his followers begins with a general statement, 'the sabbath was made for man, and not man for the sabbath'. This was so unwelcome to Matthew and Luke that they both left it out. Consequently, when they edited Mk 2.28, the term 'Son of man' appeared to them as an authoritative Christian title, so 'the Son of man is Lord of the sabbath' declares Jesus' massive authority, and has nothing to do with the conveniently omitted Mk 2.27. In its original context, however, Mk 2.27–8 makes sense only in Aramaic. The general statement that 'the sabbath was made for man' belongs to Jesus' interpretation of God's purposes at creation. Mark 2.28 then follows from this, using an Aramaic idiom which was not known in Greek, and declaring Jesus' authority over sabbath halakhah only by assuming the authority of all faithful Jews as well. Is this the interpolation of 'quasi-historical details into a fictional story'? No, it makes no sense as such.

---

[28] See P. M. Casey, 'Culture and Historicity: The Plucking of the Grain (Mk 2.23–8)', *NTS* 34 (1988), pp. 1–23. See further Casey, *Aramaic Sources of Mark's Gospel*, ch. 4.

Acharya concludes with a general statement from a lecture by Massey published in 1887, before the discovery of many of our important Aramaic sources, and before modern critical scholarship on the historical Jesus was written, though her bibliography gives its date as 1985, the date of a modern reprint.[29] Massey was not a qualified scholar even by the standards of 1887, and all his published work is hopelessly incompetent and biased, so his declaration that Jesus did not exist, and that 'Christianity pre-existed without the Personal Christ' is not relevant to assessing learned scholarship written since.[30] Acharya has allowed her anti-Christian convictions to colour her arguments and make her reject scholarly research. This illustrates the massive extent to which she depends on a readership that is unfamiliar with critical scholarship.

Blogger Godfrey and his commentators have rejected all these points. For example, in his introduction to a number of mistakes by his commentators, Godfrey commented on part of my recent book:

> Maurice Casey (and his colleague James Crossley in *The Date of Mark's Gospel*) insist that the disciples would never really have "made a path" through the corn fields, since that would have been breaking the sabbath, and Jesus would never have permitted that. Both insist, rather, that what the disciples were really doing was taking their entitlement, according to Leviticus 19:9–10... Casey (and Crossley) assume that this Levitical law dominated the cultural and religious landscape in Galilee (a landscape well removed from the purview of Pharisees and Temple priesthood) in the early decades of the first century.[31]

Here, the term 'assume' is quite wrong. Crossley and I put forward these opinions with argument based on evidence, a fact more obvious in our own academically rigorous publications.[32] We did not argue that 'this Levitical law dominated the cultural and religious landscape in Galilee', but that many Jews were observant. Those who were not fully observant included 'tax collectors and sinners', who were distinctive for that reason, and Jesus was criticised for eating and drinking with them (Mt. 11.19/Lk 7.34, cf. Mk

---

[29] Acharya, *Christ Conspiracy*, pp. 22, with p. 23n. 12 and p. 420, quoting G. Massey, *Gnostic and Historic Christianity*, one of G. Massey's lectures, published in London in 1887, as republished by Sure Fire Press, 1985.

[30] See further pp. 204–6, 221.

[31] http://vridar.wordpress.com/2010/11/10/make-a-path-evidence-of-an-aramaic-source-for-marks-gospel-or-creative-fiction/ [last accessed 14 May 2013].

[32] J. G. Crossley, *The Date of Mark's Gospel: Insight from the Law in Earliest Christianity* (JSNTSup 266. London: T&T Clark International, 2004), especially ch. 4, 'Jesus' Torah Observance in the synoptic Gospels', and pp. 160–72, 'Sabbath: Dating Mark through Mk 2.23–8 and Parallels'. I am grateful to Professor Crossley for giving me a copy of this book. Casey, *Aramaic Sources of Mark's Gospel*, esp. ch. 4, 'Two sabbath controversies: Mark 2.23–3.6'.

2.14–17). We do not know how many people in charge of fields left *Peah*, but the idea that none of them did so is out of synch with everything that we know about first-century Galilee. Observant Jews did not need Pharisees or the Temple priesthood to keep them observant then any more than they do now.

In the following 'discussion', Godfrey and his commentators depended entirely on English translations of Mark's Greek, and elementary Greek dictionaries, because they are not learned enough to understand anything else. For example,

Mark 2:23
And it came to pass, that he went through the corn fields on the sabbath day; and his disciples began, as they went, to pluck the ears of corn.

as they went
odon poiein
ὁδὸν ποιεῖν

While the discussion is fascinating, we start with Maurice Casey cherry-picking a translation without explanation. *odon poiein* — A little checking indicates "as they went" as a simpler and more accurate translation. Even Rotherdam has "began to be going forward" so the Young's-Casey translation looks to be the aberration.[33]

Avery appears to be a fundamentalist Christian, as Godfrey used to be. He is associated with a website which is 'for believers in Jesus Christ'. It is 'an independent Christian research and apologetics ministry', and openly declares 'The Bible Alone is the Word of God'.[34] He relies on the two most literal translations he can find, not on the Greek text.[35] The idea that I was 'cherry-picking a translation without explanation' is the kind of misleading fabrication I have come to expect from fundamentalists and mythicists alike. I was not 'cherry-picking' Young's or anyone else's translation: I translated the Greek text, as I said. I offered more learned discussion elsewhere, but in a book written for scholars I did not need to say more than that Mark's *hodon poiein* 'is notoriously unsatisfactory Greek'.[36] For

---

[33] http://vridar.wordpress.com/2010/11/10/make-a-path-evidence-of-an-aramaic-source-for-marks-gospel-or-creative-fiction/ Comment by Steven Avery – 2010/11/12 @ 12:49 a.m. [last accessed 14 May 2013].
[34] www.seekgod.ca [last accessed 14 May 2013].
[35] New World Bible Translation Committee, *New World Translation of the Holy Scriptures* (New York: Watchtower Bible and Tract Society, 5th edn, 1961); R. Young, *The Holy Bible: consisting of the old and new covenants:* translated by Robert Young (1862); now available both online (the 3rd edn of Young, 1898), and e.g. R. Young, *Young's Literal Translation of the Bible* (3rd edn. Greater Truth Publishers, 2005).
[36] E.g. Casey, *Aramaic Sources of Mark's Gospel*, p. 140.

example, Allen, supposing that the text should mean that the disciples 'began to go forward', correctly said that 'We should expect *poieisthai*' and regarded Judg. 17.8 as 'a doubtful parallel'. Taylor noted that *hodon poiein* 'means literally "to make" (build) a way', adding that 'it is probably used in the sense of *iter facere* = *hodon poieisthai* 'to journey', as in Judg. xvii.8... It would be possible to translate the Greek in the sense "they began to make a road by plucking the ears of corn" (so Bacon *BGS*. 30f)... The MS. tradition shows how difficult copyists found Mark's words...' Marcus notes that 'Although *hodon poiein* can mean "to make one's way, to journey" (cf. Judg. 17:8 LXX), it usually signifies "to create a road".' Witherington follows my proposals.[37] Competent serious scholars have been unanimous because the trouble with Mark's Greek is obvious to anyone competent in both Greek and Second Temple Judaism.

Judges 17.8 is significant, because it has a similar mistake.[38] It is possible that Mark knew this text in Greek, and that it influenced him in his translation.

Blogger Godfrey uses the work of Kelber in an incompetent piece of creative fiction. He comments on the quotation of Isa. 40.3 at Mk 1.3: 'An interlinear translation shows that the words used here for "way" and "make" are the same as we read in Mark 2:23 where the disciples of Jesus are said to "make a way" or path!' Blogger Godfrey uses an interlinear translation because he is not learned enough to understand the Greek text. His comments are quite misleading. The word *hodon* ('way', 'path') is the same in both texts, and I have not suggested there is anything wrong with it at Mk 2.23. What is wrong is that Mark's Greek should mean that the disciples were building a path on the sabbath. This would have been against the Law, but it does not feature in the following dispute with hostile Pharisees at all. Mark 1.3 has nothing to do with the sabbath, nor with building paths. It urges people to *prepare* the way (*hodon*) of the Lord, and make *straight* (*eutheias poieite*) his *paths* (*tribous*). In its context, this is treated as a prophecy of the ministry of John the Baptist in the wilderness: it has nothing to do with building paths. He adds: 'I suggest that when the author of the Gospel of Mark opened his gospel with "make a path for the Lord!" and subsequently depicted the disciples of that Lord "making a path", presumably for Jesus, their Lord, as they plucked ears of corn to eat, this author was consciously linking the action of the disciples with the call of John the Baptist and the earlier prophets to "make a path" for their Lord!' This is completely remote from the Jewish environment of this incident. The dispute is about eating when you are hungry, which fits poor

---

[37] W. C. Allen, *The Gospel According to Saint Mark* (London: Rivingtons, 1915), p. 71; V. Taylor, *The Gospel According to St. Mark* (London: Macmillan, 1959), p. 215; J. Marcus, *Mark 1–8* (AB 27. New York: Doubleday, 1999), p. 239; B. Witherington III, *The Gospel of Mark. A Socio-Rhetorical Commentary* (Michigan: Eerdmans, 2001), pp. 128–32.

[38] Casey, *Aramaic Sources of Mark's Gospel*, p. 140.

people taking *Peah*, not disciples making a path for their Lord, who will not particularly have needed one.[39]

Blogger Godfrey has no sympathy for the idea of *Peah* at all. For example, he comments:

> I once on this blog questioned another "independent scholar" who coincidentally believes the same explanation for why the Pharisees were cross only with the disciples and not Jesus. I found it difficult to understand how close associates of Jesus, particularly one who had been a tax collector and was able to entertain a houseful of people, others who owned a house in Capernaum and had a fishing business behind them, could go so hungry that they were forced to eat on the spot raw grain picked with their hands. Had they not just been to the local synagogue on the sabbath day, and if so, weren't they in the vicinity of other well-wishers who would be happy to invite them to share a little bread on their holy day? Or could not the disciples even ask a few to lend them a little morsel so they did not have to go out famished into the fields to pick a few grains? And what was the more well-to-do Jesus doing all this time? Refusing to share his packed lunch with them? The "independent scholar" questioned whether I had any idea how destitute and poor some people could be.[40]

This is a reference back to comments by Stephanie Fisher on a previous post, accompanied by absolute determination to take no notice of a first-century Jewish environment. Stephanie's comments included this:

> Of course we do not eat raw grain, none of us is that poor! Peah, the grain left at the edges of the field for the poor, was for people who had no house at all, let alone one with a loaf of bread in it. This is why Matthew retells a story of Jesus in which 'the king' says, on behalf of others, "I was hungry and you gave me to eat...I was naked and you clothed me" (Matt. 25.35, 36), and Luke retold a story of Jesus in which Lazar (short for Eleazar) "had been thrown down at his [the rich man's] gate and longed to be filled from what fell from the rich man's table." Have you no idea how poor people can be, and were in Galilee at the time of Jesus? Some of them had no house, clothing or food. That's what Jewish people were urged to give alms for![41]

---

[39] http://vridar.wordpress.com/2010/11/10/make-a-path-evidence-of-an-aramaic-source-for-marks-gospel-or-creative-fiction/ [last accessed 14 May 2013]. Comment by neilgodfrey – 2010/05/30 at 12:02 p.m., making some use of W. H. Kelber's elementary lectures for Lent, 1978, *Mark's Story of Jesus* (Philadelphia: Fortress, 1979).

[40] http://vridar.wordpress.com/2010/04/29/biblical-historians-make-detectives-look-silly/#comment–9130 [last accessed 14 May 2013].

[41] http://vridar.wordpress.com/2010/04/29/biblical-historians-make-detectives-look-

All Blogger Godfrey's comments are remote from this environment. These were Jesus' poor disciples, not his 'close associates'. They obviously did not include 'one who had been a tax collector and was able to entertain a houseful of people', nor 'others who owned a house in Capernaum and had a fishing business behind them', none of whom would have been entitled to take *Peah,* and would not wish to eat raw grain anyway. They had not 'just been to the local synagogue on the sabbath day', and they were not 'in the vicinity of other well-wishers who would be happy to invite them to share a little bread on their holy day'. The idea that Jesus had a 'packed lunch' is taken from our culture, not theirs.

Blogger Godfrey also has no sympathy for the translation process. He argues that without a massive set of assumptions, his misrepresentation of my detailed arguments, 'it is very hard to imagine a translator of Aramaic in this context making such a silly mistake so that he erroneously wrote that Jesus allowed his disciples to "make a path", thus breaking the sabbath! Did the alternative and more natural reading of "go along a path" never occur to him as he must have wondered whether he was reading a resh 7 or a dalet 7.' This is not what Mark did at all. Translators are not inerrant, and confusion between *resh* (not final *kaph,* printed erroneously by Godfrey here) and *daleth,* which looked more alike at Qumran than they do in our square script, was natural, and not confined to Judges 17.8. Mark was suffering from the very common phenomenon of interference, not making a 'silly mistake' at all. Consequently, he meant that the disciples were going along a path, certainly not that they were building the path, let alone breaking the sabbath. I have discussed Translation Studies in general and interference in particular in detail elsewhere, with bibliography.[42]

The dates of the synoptic Gospels: The Gospel according to Marcus

We must therefore consider next the dates of the synoptic Gospels, beginning with the oldest, the Gospel according to Mark, or rather Marcus, the commonest male name in the Graeco-Roman world. I have already pointed out that the dates proposed for the Gospels by mythicists are seriously awry. Unfortunately, conventional dates for the synoptic Gospels are not altogether satisfactory either. Like the dates proposed by mythicists for all the canonical Gospels, the conventional dates for the Gospels of Mark and Matthew are too late, and do not make proper sense of these evangelists' environments.

silly/#comment–9130 [last accessed 14 May 2013]. Comment by steph – 2010/05/05 at 4.35 a.m.
[42] Casey, *Aramaic Sources of Mark's Gospel,* pp. 55–7, 93–107.

There are *two different conventional* dates for the Gospel of Mark in more or less mainstream scholarship, apart from the hopelessly late dates proposed by mythicists. Some scholars, especially in Europe, date it c. 65–9 CE, not long before the destruction of Jerusalem by the Romans in 70 CE, whereas others, especially in the USA, date it c. 75 CE, not long after the same event. A consequence of such late dates is, necessarily, even later dates for the Gospels of Matthew and Luke. Earlier dates have occasionally been suggested, but mostly by scholars whose conservative convictions were strong enough to damage the plausibility of their arguments. All this should now be changed in the light of the brilliant book by James Crossley, *The Date of Mark's Gospel*.[43] Crossley has proposed a date c. 40 CE. I therefore examine the basic arguments for each of these dates.

The later conventional dates are based primarily on the witness of some Church Fathers, and on a possible interpretation of the predictions in Mark 13. The earliest piece of evidence from the Church Fathers is a quotation attributed to Papias, bishop of Hierapolis, in Asia Minor, in the early second century. All his writings have disappeared, but fragments of his work are preserved in the Ecclesiastical History written by Eusebius, bishop of Caesarea in the early fourth century. Papias claimed to have met not the first disciples from the historic ministry, but the next generation of Christians, including the mysterious figure of John the Elder, sometimes identified as the author of the Johannine epistles, and even as the author of the Fourth Gospel. Eusebius quotes Papias attributing the following comments to John the Elder:

> Mark, having become an interpreter of Peter, wrote down accurately whatever he remembered, what was said or done by the Lord, not however in order. For he neither heard the Lord nor followed him, but later, as I said, (he followed) Peter.
>
> (Eus., *H.E.* III, 39, 15)

Papias goes on to explain that Mark heard Peter teaching, which is why the material is not in order, and he stresses that Mark's writing of this was very accurate, to the point where it is not clear whether some of his comments are due to John the Elder or not. The term 'later' is not defined by Papias, and would make perfect sense if Mark had heard Peter teach at any date.

The same kind of connection between Mark and Peter is indicated by Justin Martyr, writing in the middle of the second century. Justin refers not to the Gospel according to Mark, but to the *apomnēmoneumata* of Peter. The Greek word *apomnēmoneumata* is usually translated 'memoirs' in Justin, whether or not they are said to be 'of Peter', 'of the apostles', or 'of

[43] Crossley, *The Date of Mark's Gospel*. My discussion here is based on my earlier discussion in *Jesus of Nazareth*, pp. 62–78.

his apostles and their followers'. It has, however, a somewhat wider range of meaning, and does not necessarily carry the connotation of the person having written the *apomnēmoneumata* himself. One reference to Peter's 'memoirs' has the sons of Zebedee called 'Boanerges, which is "sons of thunder"' (*Dial.* 106). The word 'Boanerges' is known only from Mk 3.17, where Mark says that Jesus gave Jacob and John, the sons of Zebedee, 'the name "Boanērges", which is "sons of thunder"'. This reference is not merely unique. The term 'Boanerges' is a *mistaken* attempt to transliterate into Greek letters the Aramaic words *benē re'em*, which mean 'sons of thunder'. It is not surprising that both Matthew and Luke left it out! The possibility that two independent sources made *almost identical mistakes* in the transliteration of these words is negligible. It follows that by 'the memoirs of Peter' Justin meant the Gospel of Mark. He does not say anything to indicate when Mark wrote his Gospel, nor how much of it was derived from Peter.

Papias' comments have frequently been interpreted in the light of later church traditions. The next one to have survived is the so-called anti-Marcionite prologue, which must be dated c. 160–180 CE. This repeats that Mark was an interpreter of Peter, and adds that he wrote his Gospel after Peter's death, in the regions of Italy. According to early and apparently accurate church tradition, Peter was martyred in Rome in 64 CE, during the persecution of Christians instigated by the emperor Nero. Irenaeus, bishop of Lugdunum in Gaul, now Lyons in France, repeated all this c. 177 CE, in terms which imply that Mark wrote in Rome (*Adv. Haer.* III, 1, 1). Thus the dominant church tradition was established by the end of the second century, and since Mark is supposed to have written after Peter's death in 64 CE, the earliest possible date for his Gospel is 65 CE.

Some aspects of this tradition must be true, but not all of them. First, the author was certainly Mark. Our name Mark is the Greek *Markos* without its ending, and this is the Greek form of the Latin *Marcus*, one of the commonest names in the Roman Empire. Secondly, Papias must be right in supposing that Marcus 'neither heard nor followed the Lord'. The early church would not have attributed its first Gospel to someone called simply Marcus, who was not a follower of Jesus, unless both points were known facts.

Problems arise with Papias' use of the tradition that Mark heard Peter teach to establish the accuracy of the whole Gospel, despite the fact that it is not in the order of a historical outline. This indeed it is not, apart from the Cleansing of the Temple and the Passion narrative at the end. An undue proportion of conflict stories are placed together (Mk 2.1–3.6). A high proportion of parables are placed together in ch. 4, complete with the quite unconvincing theory that they were told to conceal the mystery of the kingdom of God (Mk 4.10–12), a view contrary to the nature of Jesus' ministry, but one which has an excellent setting in the life of Christians who found the parables difficult to understand. This wondrous theory is immediately followed by a secondary allegorical interpretation of the parable of the sower (Mk 4.14–20), which cannot possibly have been derived from the teaching of Peter. A high proportion of Mark's eschatological teaching is collected in ch. 13, and some of that is evidently secondary too. Moreover, I have noted a small part of the evidence that some parts of Mark's Gospel are unrevised translations of written Aramaic sources.[44] These parts cannot be due to Mark hearing Peter teach.

It follows that Papias drastically overplayed his hand. While Mark may well have heard Peter teach, and this may have been the source of some of some of his perfectly accurate material, the *whole* of his Gospel cannot possibly have been derived from this source. Papias has produced a legitimating tradition. Faced with the fact that this Gospel was written by an unknown man called Marcus who never encountered the historical Jesus, he has sought to legitimate the accuracy of the whole of Mark's Gospel by associating it as closely as he could with the leader of the Twelve during the historic ministry.

Nor has Papias provided a sound explanation as to *why* Mark's material is not in a convincing historical order. Suppose that Mark heard Peter teach often enough for this to be his main source for the life and teaching of Jesus in his Gospel, why did he never ask Peter to provide him with the chronological outline which his Gospel so obviously lacks? Even if he did not actually write his Gospel until after Peter was martyred, anyone knowing that he had some intention of producing the first Gospel would surely have asked for any information that he did not possess, provided only that he saw a lot of Peter, and did not just hear him once or twice before he had decided to write. The associated tradition that Mark wrote in the centre of the Roman Empire shows every sign of being secondary too. By the time of Irenaeus, the authenticity of 1 Peter was accepted, and at its end Peter, be this originally the famous apostle himself or a pseudonym, sends greetings from people in 'Babylon', a cipher for Rome, and from 'Mark my son' (1 Pet. 5.13). How easy it is to add in some details from the increasing witness of the Church Fathers! It is possible that this was a major cause of the tradition known to us from Papias. According to Eusebius, it was quoted by Origen in the third century, in support of his view that Mark wrote in accordance with Peter's instructions (Eus. *H.E.* VI, 25, 5).

It has naturally been tempting to identify Mark the Evangelist in other New Testament references as well, so much so that Taylor commented in 1959, 'Today this view is held almost with complete unanimity and it may be accepted as sound.'[45] A critical review of the evidence demonstrates otherwise. At Acts 12.12, Peter goes to the house of Mary, 'the mother of John, also named Marcus'. This associates Peter and Mark, but if this

---

[44] See further Casey, *Aramaic Sources of Mark's Gospel.*
[45] Taylor, *Gospel According to St. Mark,* p. 26.

is Mark the Evangelist, it is surprising that church tradition does not call him John Mark. While John was a common enough Jewish name, the double name John Mark is far more distinctive than the simple Marcus. At Acts 12.25, where Barnabas and Saul take him with them to Jerusalem, he is again called 'John, also named Marcus'. At Acts 13.5, where he still accompanies Barnabas and Saul, he is simply referred to as 'John', as also at Acts 13.13, where he leaves 'those around Paul' and returns to Jerusalem. This incident led to subsequent disagreement between Barnabas, who again wanted to take 'John, called Marcus' (Acts 15.37), which Paul refused to do, so they parted company and Barnabas took him, now for the only time in Acts simply called 'Marcus' (Acts 15.39), to Cyprus. It is therefore probable that he is the same person as is referred to by Paul/Timothy as 'Marcus, the cousin of Barnabas' (Col. 4.10), where 'the cousin of Barnabas' tells us which Marcus is meant. At Philemon 24, someone simply called 'Marcus' is among Paul's co-workers whose greetings he sends, and at 2 Tim. 4.11, which is to be regarded as pseudonymous, Paul asks for 'Marcus' to be brought to him. It is by no means clear that these last two passages refer to the same person. All the other references make quite clear which Mark is being referred to. It is even less probable that all these references mean Mark the Evangelist, since Luke nowhere mentions him composing a Gospel, let alone the one which provided him with so much material, and the earliest traditions in Papias and others do not mention his being the well-known John Mark, cousin of Barnabas.

Nor should we believe the alternative tradition among other Church Fathers, according to which Mark wrote during Peter's lifetime, and either wrote in, or at least went to, Alexandria. According to Eusebius, he preached the Gospel, which he had already written, in Egypt and founded churches in Alexandria, and Eusebius could be understood to mean that Mark was bishop there (*H.E.* II, xv, 1; xxiv, 1). At the end of the fourth century, John Chrysostom says that he actually wrote the Gospel in Alexandria (*Homily 1 on Matthew*, 7). By the time of Jerome in the early fifth century, Mark the Evangelist clearly is the first bishop of Alexandria (*Commentary on Matthew*, Prooemium 6). This tradition is too late and too poorly attested to be taken seriously as historical fact.

We must therefore treat the witness of the Church Fathers with caution. The evidence of Papias shows that the Gospel of Mark was written by an unknown Christian called Marcus, who was not present during the historic ministry of Jesus. It is probable that Marcus heard Peter preach, but it is most improbable that he heard him often, and out of the question that he knew him well. We cannot tell from the evidence of the Fathers when or where Marcus wrote his Gospel, because the relatively early external evidence consists of unreliable legitimating traditions.

The evidence provided by Mark 13 is not straightforward either. Here Jesus predicts the destruction of the Temple, declaring that 'there shall not be left here a stone upon a stone that shall not be destroyed' (Mk 13.2).

The destruction of the Temple in 70 CE was an event of such importance that it is understandable that Christians have interpreted it as a fulfilment of Jesus' prophecy. When people believe predictions like this, they tolerate a certain degree of difference between the prophecy and its fulfilment. If, however, we are to treat Mark 13 as a pseudo-prophecy written after the destruction of Jerusalem, it becomes important that such differences cannot be explained. It is not literally true that not one stone was left standing upon another: some stones are *still* standing, and they are famous as the 'Wailing Wall', where observant Jews still worship. Moreover, one of the most famous aspects of the destruction of the Temple was that it was burnt down (Jos. *War* VI, 250–84). It is accordingly inconceivable that a pseudo-prophecy written *after* these dramatic events should make an incorrect statement about the stones and omit the centre of the drama, the burning down of the whole Temple.

Furthermore, Mark predicts that they will see 'the abomination of desolation standing where (he/it) should not' (Mk 13.14): there was no such event in 70 CE. When this non-event happens, Jesus urges them to flee to the mountains, which did not happen either. It follows from all this that Mark 13 was not written *after* the events of 70 CE: it is a genuine prediction written *before* them, though not a prediction made by the historical Jesus.

This is sufficient to exclude the latest dates proposed for the composition of Mark's Gospel, but it does not tell us *how long* before 70 CE it was written. At this point it becomes important that a quite different event might have inspired these predictions: the Caligula crisis of 39 CE. At that time, the emperor Gaius, often known by his nickname Caligula, 'little boots', ordered that a statue of himself should be set up in the Temple in Jerusalem. From a Jewish perspective, that would have been idolatry in the centre of the Jewish faith, strongly reminiscent of the Maccabaean crisis, when the Greek king Antiochus Epiphanes set up a statue of himself in the Temple. It was this event which led to the pseudo-prophecy of the book of Daniel, which says of Antiochus' persecution: 'He shall make a strong covenant with many for one week, and for half of the week he shall make sacrifice and offering cease: and on a wing shall be an abomination that desolates, until the decreed end is poured out upon the desolator' (Dan. 9.27).

Here the 'abomination that desolates' is the statue of Antiochus Epiphanes in the Temple. The prediction that the persecution would end after 'one week', i.e. one week of years = seven years, that the cessation of the sacrifice and offering would last half of the week = three and a half years, and that the 'decreed end' would be 'poured out upon the desolator', all this is genuine prediction, and many interpreters, including in due course the whole of the Syriac-speaking church, saw this fulfilled in the defeat of Antiochus and the rededication of the Temple.

Most interpreters in the West, however, have continually pushed it forwards as a prophecy of the future, and it is to this tradition that Mark belonged.[46] This is why Mk 13.14 runs as it does: 'Now when you see the "abomination of desolation" standing where (he/it) ought not (let the reader understand), then let those in Judaea flee to the mountains...' Here the 'abomination of desolation' is a reference back to the prophecy of Dan. 9.27 (referred to also in the prophecies of Dan. 11.31, 12.11: at 12.11, the LXX has the exact phrase used by Mark). This reference was inspired by Caligula's instructions to have a statue of himself placed in the Temple, which would have been seen as a fulfilment of that prophecy. This also explains a peculiarity in Mark's Greek. The Greek word for 'abomination' (*bdelugma*) is neuter, but the word for 'standing' (*hestēkota*) is masculine, whereas in grammatically correct Greek it would be neuter, because it refers to the 'abomination'. It is masculine because it refers to a masculine person (Caligula), and the Greek word for statue (*andrias*) used for Caligula's statue by both Philo (*Leg. ad Gaium* 188, 203, etc.) and Josephus (*Ant.* XVIII, 261, 269, etc.) is masculine too. The stage direction 'let the reader understand' refers to the situation when Mark's Gospel would be read at Christian meetings, and the person who read it out would explain what it meant, including the reference back to Dan. 9.27 and to Caligula's threat to put his statue in the Temple in Jerusalem, and to the normally incorrect Greek grammar. It follows that this prophecy originated during the Caligula crisis, c. 40 CE. Moreover, it makes much better sense then than at any other time, because as far as we know this threat was not repeated subsequently.

This also explains the editing of the prophecy by the other synoptic evangelists. Matthew, writing not very much later, clarified the prediction, but corrected the grammar: 'When therefore you see the "abomination of desolation" spoken of through Daniel the prophet standing in a holy place (let the reader understand)...' (Mt. 24.15). Luke, however, genuinely writing after the fall of Jerusalem, altered it completely: 'Now when you see Jerusalem surrounded by armies, then know that its desolation is at hand' (Lk. 21.20). Of course, as Matthew shows, once the prophecy was written it might be repeated even if there was no specific threat from the current emperor, and the Roman historian Tacitus confirms continued Jewish fears that a later Roman emperor would repeat Caligula's threat (*Annals* XII, 54). Nonetheless, the Caligula crisis makes by far the best sense of the origins of the prophecy, and the whole of Mark 13, secondary as much of it is, makes excellent sense at this time too. The prophecy of the destruction of the Temple (Mk 13.2) takes off from Jesus' preaching on Jeremiah 7 in the Temple.[47] Mark quotes 'den of robbers' from Jer. 7.11 (Mk 11.17), and the Jeremiah context is also important. Criticizing sinful people who worshipped in the Temple, Jeremiah has God threaten to do to the Temple

---

[46] For detailed discussion of these exegetical traditions see P. M. Casey, *Son of Man: The Interpretation and Influence of Daniel 7* (London: SPCK, 1980), chs 3–4.

[47] Cf. Casey, *Jesus of Nazareth*, pp. 411–15.

'as I did to Shiloh' (Jer. 7.14). Everyone believed that God had destroyed Shiloh (Ps. 78.60, cf. Jer. 7.12), so this means that Jesus made a conditional threat of the destruction of the Temple too. This was naturally remembered, and will have seemed especially real when the Caligula crisis loomed. It was therefore rewritten into the definite prediction of the destruction of the Temple with which Mark's eschatological discourse begins.

With the destruction of the Temple set up at the beginning of Mark 13, Mark moves Jesus and his disciples from the Temple across to the Mount of Olives, a traditional eschatological site. He brings forward the inner group of three, Peter, Jacob and John, together with Andrew, Peter's brother and another member of the Twelve, to ask the vital question: 'When will these things be, and what (will be) the sign when all these things are about to be completed?' (Mk 13.3–4). The resulting discourse has numerous indications of the influence of the early church, as for example the reference to persecutions with the central piece of information: 'And first the Gospel must be preached to all the nations' (Mk 13.10). The climax is entirely based on scriptural passages. Some of them are difficult to identify, but there is no doubt about the centre of the hope of the early church: 'And then they shall see the Son of man coming in clouds with much power and glory' (Mk 13.26). This is a clear reference to the second coming of Jesus seen as predicted at Dan. 7.13. It does not fit into the teaching of the historical Jesus, for he hoped that God would establish his kingdom without Jesus having to die first.[48] Jesus' second coming was, however, central to the hopes of the early church. They searched the Scriptures to find it, and the climax of Mark's eschatological discourse is a result of this. Hence for example the gathering of the elect at Mark 13.27, part of traditional Jewish expectation found in scriptural passages such as Deut. 30.4 and Zech. 2.10 (LXX). This makes the discourse later than the time of Jesus, but not necessarily *much* later. The spread of the Gospel to the Gentiles and the hope for Jesus' second coming were both well established features of early Christianity by the time of the Caligula crisis. The whole discourse could therefore have been written at the time of the Caligula crisis, when the threat of his statue being set up in the Temple was a real one, Jewish opposition to it might well lead to the destruction of the Temple, and Christians hoped that Jesus would return in triumph.

Mark's view of the Law fits in perfectly with such a date. He makes a number of comments which *presuppose* knowledge of Jewish Law perfectly possible at a relatively early stage of the Gentile mission, and increasingly improbable as time went on. I have noted the dispute between Jesus and some Pharisees at Mk 2.23–8, arising from the disciples going through other people's fields plucking grain on the sabbath.[49] Mark takes it for

---

[48] Cf. Casey, *Jesus of Nazareth*, pp. 214–24, 435–9.
[49] Cf. pp. 75–80.

granted that his audience will know that the disciples must have been poor people taking *Peah*, the grain left for poor people at the edges of every field, in accordance with Lev. 23.22, and that if anyone at a church meeting did not know this, a reader would be able to explain it. Similarly, when Jesus had performed an exorcism in the synagogue at Capernaum one sabbath, and healed Simeon Peter's mother-in-law at home, people brought other sick people and demoniacs to Jesus so that he could heal them (Mk 1.21–34). Mark's note of the time at which they did so is very precise: 'in the evening, when the sun had set'. This presupposes the knowledge that the Law prohibits the carrying of burdens on the sabbath (Jer. 17.21–2), which ends when darkness falls, as well as the obvious fact that sick people who have to be carried are heavy enough to be burdens.

The dispute at the beginning of Mark 7 has been more controversial, and it is more difficult to sort out.[50] It differs from the two previous examples in that Mark does explain the situation, and it has often been suggested that he did not do so correctly because he was out of touch with Jewish customs. This dispute was begun by Pharisees and some scribes from Jerusalem, who wanted to know why Jesus' disciples ate food with their hands not in a state of purity, that is to say, without washing them first, as Mark correctly explains. They asked: 'Why do your disciples not walk according to the tradition of the elders, but eat food with profane hands?' (Mk 7.5). Accordingly, what the disciples violated was not the written Torah, but an oral tradition of orthodox Jews, and this is why Mark has felt it necessary to explain the situation.

Mark's further explanation has often been thought to be partly wrong:

> For the Pharisees and all the Jews, unless they wash their hands with a fistful [of water] do not eat, adhering to the tradition of the elders, and [when they come] from the market-place, they do not eat without immersing, and there are many other [traditions] which they have received to adhere to, immersions of cups and pots and bronze kettles and dining couches. (Mk 7.3–4)

This is a perfectly accurate account of the behaviour of Pharisees and other orthodox Jews, who adhered to many expansions of the written Torah. It is full of technical terminology, including the basic terminology for the handing down and receiving of traditions, as well as details on account of which I have added some bracketed words so that it makes sense in normal English. One point is exaggerated, the attribution of these customs to 'all the Jews'. This exaggeration is, however, more characteristic of observant Jews being hopeful about what Jews ought to do, than of Gentiles who do not understand Jewish customs. For example, the *Letter of Aristeas* says

---

[50] Cf. Casey, *Jesus of Nazareth*, pp. 326–31.

of the Jewish people involved in translating the Hebrew Bible into Greek, 'following the custom of *all the Jews*, they washed their hands in the sea in the course of their prayers to God' (*Aristeas* 305). Handwashing among Jews during prayers was not universal in the second century BCE, but this unimpeachably knowledgeable Jewish author would like us to imagine that it was, and this is the same kind of exaggeration as we find in Mark. We must therefore conclude that Mark has accurately described the oral Law of orthodox Jews in considerable detail, which is easier to envisage when Christianity was still partly a Jewish movement, than later when Greek-speaking churches were more and more Gentile.

After his account of Jesus' response to the scribes and Pharisees, Mark concludes by attributing further teaching to Jesus, some of which is of doubtful authenticity. The first saying is at Mk 7.15: 'There is nothing outside a man going into him which can make him unclean, but the (things which) come out of a man are what make the man unclean.' Mark has that addressed to 'the crowd', and gives Jesus' subsequent attempt to explain this to the disciples in 'the house away from the crowd', which is often suspected to be a deliberate indication that this is a secondary explanation for the benefit of the church. Be that as it may, it is clearly accompanied by Mark's own comment: 'Do you not understand that everything outside going into a man cannot make him unclean, because it does not go into his heart but into his stomach and goes out into the latrine (cleansing all foods)...' (Mk 7.18–19).

Here the comments attributed to Jesus himself make perfect sense in the original context of Jewish purity law. In the first place, and central to the original dispute, whatever is on your hands when you have not washed them will not make you unclean when you pick up food in your hands to eat it, because nothing outside a person can make that person unclean when it enters them, that is, when they eat or drink it. Since you might have touched all sorts of unclean things with your hands before you picked up your food to eat it, Jesus expressed himself in this very general way: 'There is nothing outside a man going into him which can make him unclean...' Secondly, the Torah says very clearly, forcefully and repeatedly, that God has forbidden his people to eat unclean food. For example: 'These you shall detest among the birds; they shall not be eaten, they are an abomination: the eagle and the vulture and the osprey and the kite and the falcon of every kind, every raven of any kind...' (Lev. 11.13–15). Since you do not eat unclean animals, Jesus could make the very general statement that 'There is nothing outside a man going into him which can make him unclean...'

It was different with all sorts of bodily discharges, which do make you unclean. The Torah defines these, and gives instructions for dealing with them. For example: 'If a man lies with a woman and has an emission of semen, they shall bathe in water and be unclean until the evening' (Lev. 15.18). Hence the second part of Jesus' saying at Mk 7.15: 'the things which come out of a man are what make the man unclean'. The second version at Mk 7.18–19 is more dubious as a saying of Jesus, because its rationale would allow the eating of unclean foods, since what goes into your stomach and out into the latrine brings to mind food rather than dirt or any sort of uncleanness on your hands. Mark's gloss is accordingly reasonable: 'cleansing all foods'. Some scholars are also right to see here Gentile influence, but it does not follow that Mark was personally Gentile or that his Gospel is to be dated later than c. 40 CE. The Gentile mission began early. St Paul retained his Jewish identity, but he considered it right in principle to eat unclean food, and qualified this only through concern for weaker brethren, especially if food was known to have been sacrificed to idols (e.g. Rom. 14.1–4, 14–21; 1 Cor. 8). This was a necessary part of a successful Gentile mission, the only possible context for a Gospel written for Greek-speaking Christians. Mk 7.18–19 locates Mark in that cultural context, but it does not tell us whether he was personally Gentile, nor does it imply a late date for the composition of his Gospel. I therefore conclude that Crossley is right: Mark's Gospel was written c. 40 CE.

The dates of the synoptic Gospels: The Gospel attributed to Matthew

The Gospel of Matthew is usually dated c. 75–85 CE, and its author is considered to be unknown. I have proposed that it should be dated c. 50–60 CE, and that its author was an unknown Jewish Christian, who may or may not have been called *Mattai* or the like, a standard Jewish name of this period.[51] Church tradition has for centuries held that the author of 'the Gospel According to Matthew' was the apostle Matthew, who is found in Mark's list of the Twelve (Mk 3.18). It has also been considered significant that whereas Mark relates the call of a tax collector whom he names Levi, son of Alphaeus (Mk 2.14), Matthew, in copying the story, names him 'Matthew' instead, and adds 'the tax collector' as a description of Matthew in his list of the Twelve (Mt. 9.9, 10.3). The church tradition has often been traced back to Papias, quoted by Eusebius continuing the passage about the authorship of Mark (Eus. *H.E.* III, 39, 15–16).[52] Papias records a traditional view that 'Matthew compiled the sayings/oracles (*logia*) in a Hebrew language', which could mean either Hebrew or Aramaic, and certainly did not mean Greek. Papias also says that everyone 'translated/ interpreted (*hērmēneusen*)' them as well as they were able. The way this was understood by later Church Fathers is already clear in the comments of Irenaeus c. 177 CE, as quoted by Eusebius: 'Now Matthew published among the Hebrews in their language a writing of a Gospel, while Peter

---

[51] Casey, *Jesus of Nazareth*, pp. 86–93.
[52] Cf. pp. 81–4.

and Paul were in Rome evangelizing and founding the church' (Iren. *Adv. Haer.* III, 1, 1, quoted by Eus. *H.E.* V, 8, 1). Later Church Fathers repeat this tradition and amplify it.

When applied to our Gospel of Matthew, this tradition is complete nonsense, as most scholars have recognized. Our Gospel is not only written in perfectly decent Greek, it was partly written by an author who was revising our Greek Mark into better Greek, including the removal of a number of features of Mark's Aramaic sources. It was therefore written in Greek. Moreover, one of the Twelve would not have had reason to copy Mark's outline in this way. On the contrary, he would have had very good reason to replace it with an accurate outline which included the length of the ministry.

The origin of this tradition naturally proved difficult to fathom. How could such a grossly confused view of our Gospel of Matthew have arisen? It has often been suggested that the transmission of the so-called 'Q' material was a source of the confusion, and this should be accepted.[53] A significant part of the Double Tradition consists of perfectly accurate material about Jesus, almost all of it sayings, and all of it within the slightly wider range of the Greek word *logia*. It is entirely reasonable to suppose that one of the Twelve wrote at least some of it. The Gospel writer's view of the apostle Matthew was that he was a tax collector (Mt. 9.9, altering Mk 2.14; Mt. 10.3, expanding Mk 3.18), and he is most unlikely to have added this view to his Markan tradition, unless he had a good source for it. We should therefore accept this. As a tax collector, the apostle Matthew would be very experienced in writing information accurately and legibly on wax tablets, an unusual and highly valuable skill in a primarily oral culture. It is entirely natural that one of the Twelve, who was a tax collector, selected himself to write down material about Jesus during the historic ministry.

Some of this Gospel's 'Q' material and some of the material unique to it resulted from Matthew the tax collector's material being transmitted accurately and translated and interpreted in accordance with the original Jewish tradition. On its way to Luke, however, some of the material transmitted in Aramaic was translated and interpreted as well as someone else was able, not very accurately and in accordance with the needs of Gentile Christian congregations. I have noted Mt. 23.23–24/Lk. 11.42, which provides excellent examples of these points. Mt. 23.23–24 was translated as accurately as possible, though Matthew used the Greek word *barūtera*, literally 'heavier', in a novel sense, because the best he could do with the Aramaic technical term *ḥōmerayā* was to translate it literally. Luke, however, dropped it, misread the Aramaic *sh-b-th-ā*, 'dill', as *sh-b-r-ā*,

---

[53] See for example the influential discussion of T. W. Manson, *The Sayings of Jesus* (London: Nicholson and Watson, 1937, as Part II of H. D. A. Major et al. (eds), *The Mission and Message of Jesus*. Reprinted separately, London: SCM, 1949), pp. 17–20.

'rue', so he has one of the herbs wrong, and misread the Aramaic *rḥmthā*, 'mercy', as *rḥmyā*, 'love', so he has another word wrong. While some of the differences between Matthew and Luke are due to Luke's editing for his Gentile congregations, it is clear that Matthew the Gospel writer made, or had available to him, a much better translation than that used by Luke.

It follows that this is what Papias meant! It is genuinely true that the apostle Matthew 'compiled the sayings/oracles in a Hebrew language, but each (person) translated/interpreted them as he was able'. Moreover, the Greek word *logia*, which I have translated 'sayings/oracles', has a somewhat broader range of meaning than this, and could well be used of collections which consisted mostly, but not entirely, of sayings. It would not, however, have been a sensible word to use of the whole Gospel of Matthew. It was later Church Fathers who confused Matthew's collections of sayings of Jesus with our Greek Gospel of Matthew.

I suggest that a second source of the confusion lay with the real author of this Gospel. One possibility is that he was also called Matthias or Matthew. These were common enough Jewish names, and different forms were similar enough to cause confusion, as identical forms more obviously could. There is accordingly nothing in the least improbable or peculiar in the author of one synoptic Gospel having more or less the same name as one of the Twelve. Alternatively, we must bear in mind the nature of authorship in Second Temple Judaism. Composite authorship was common, and so was the attribution of documents to the fountainheads of traditions. So, for example, the final authors of the book of Isaiah were quite happy to leave the impression that it was the work of Isaiah of Jerusalem, even though they included the work of another major prophet (Isa. 40–55), who is consequently known to us only as Second Isaiah. They also included several other prophetic pieces, and they endeavoured to unify this massive compilation with their own editorial work. Similarly, when the authors of the book of Jubilees rewrote part of the Pentateuch, they attributed it to the angel of the presence, speaking on behalf of God to Moses on Mount Sinai. Whatever the personal name of the final editor of our Greek Gospel of Matthew, he may have been absolutely delighted to have his completed work known as the Gospel according to (the apostle) Matthew, a highly desirable designation in churches which already knew the Gospel of Marcus. Second only to Jesus himself, the apostle Matthew was the fountainhead of many authentic traditions now part of this Gospel. How many people translated and edited these traditions, we do not know. The final editor used their work, and included other material, such as the birth narratives.[54]

Thus our Greek Gospel of Matthew is of composite authorship in the same sense as many ancient Jewish works, such as the books of Isaiah and Jubilees. Most Christians would notice that, in accordance with ancient

---

[54]On these stories, cf. pp. 114–15, 208–9.

custom, the author of the Greek Gospel of Matthew made extensive use of the Gospel of Marcus, the only written Gospel previously available in Greek. He will have been very happy for everyone to know that significant portions of his other material had been transmitted directly from Matthew the tax collector, one of the Twelve. At this stage there would be no risk of confusion, because ancient Jewish habits of authorship were pervasive in Jewish communities. The title of this Gospel, though not included in the text of the work and known to us only from much later manuscripts, is likely to have been generally known when the work was first composed, and to have been written at the beginning or end of the first copies.

The third source of eventual confusion was that it was extremely helpful to the early church to imagine that the Gospel which it most loved was written by one of the Twelve. This is the overwhelming force which drove the mistakes of the Church Fathers from Irenaeus onwards. It will have been helped by assumptions about authorship normal in the Graeco-Roman world. However much sources were used by authors such as Livy, the pre-eminent Roman historian, and Plutarch, who wrote lives of Julius Caesar, Augustus and many other people in Greek, they each claimed the authorship of what they saw as their own work. When later Church Fathers inherited the tradition which we know from Papias, it would be natural for them to conclude that the apostle Matthew wrote our Gospel of Matthew. Hence the quite confused tradition that it was originally written in Aramaic or even Hebrew.

This explains both the real nature of this Gospel and the confusion of church tradition about it. That some of the so-called 'Q' material and some material special to Matthew was written by one of the Twelve explains the presence of perfectly accurate material. Confusion between two men called Matthew or the like, the fact that one of them was one of the Twelve, and the need to believe in the apostolic authority of Gospels, is one possible explanation of how the early church tradition became confused. Equally, the final editor of the Gospel may have released it under the name of Matthew, because the apostle Matthew was his major source, apart from Mark. That the material transmitted in Aramaic was translated by several different people explains both the evidence which requires a chaotic model of the so-called 'Q' material, and the inaccuracies detectable in Lukan tradition.

I consider next the date of this Gospel. Apart from the extraordinarily late dates proposed by mythicists, the traditional scholarly date c. 75–85 CE is largely dependent on conventionally late dates for Mark, plus the perfectly correct view that Matthew copied Mark. It has several unsatisfactory features, the most important of which are Matthew's eschatology and his position within Judaism.

Mark already believed that the kingdom was at hand. Matthew often makes this clearer, whereas Luke was concerned to distance himself from any idea that the kingdom had been expected to come long ago. For example, Mark has Jesus predict 'that there are some of those standing here who will not taste death until they have seen the kingdom of God come in power' (Mk 9.1). Matthew edited this so that Jesus predicted that they would not taste death 'until they have seen the Son of man coming in his kingdom' (Mt. 16.28). This makes absolutely clear the church's view that Jesus predicted his own second coming. Matthew has, however, retained the notion that some of the people present with Jesus at the time would see the event which Jesus predicted. This makes much better sense c. 50–60 CE, when eschatological expectation was extremely vigorous, than after the fall of Jerusalem, when most of the people present during the historic ministry were dead. Matthew retains features of the prediction of the destruction of the Temple which did not come true. So he retains the prediction that 'there will not be left here a stone upon a stone which will not be thrown down' (Mt. 24.2, from Mk 13.2), and does not mention the Temple being burnt down. He not only retains, but also clarifies the reference to 'the abomination of desolation … standing in a holy place' (Mt. 24.15, editing Mk 13.14). He retains the instruction to flee to the mountains, and adds to Mark's instruction to pray that this may not happen in winter (Mk 13.18) 'or on a sabbath' (Mt. 24.20). All this entails a date before 70 CE, and makes perfect sense c. 50 CE.

When he edited Mark's prediction of the destruction of the Temple, Matthew added the instruction to pray that the flight of 'those in Judaea' (Mt. 24.16) might not happen 'on a Sabbath' (Mt. 24.20). This shows great concern for, and understanding of, the observance of Jewish Law. While mainstream Jews believed that saving life overrides the sabbath, some Jews did not. Indeed, the first known need to promulgate a decision to fight when attacked on the sabbath (1 Macc. 2.41) arose from an incident when 1,000 Jews died because they refused to profane the sabbath in order to save their lives. Matthew knew that if 'those in Judaea' had to 'flee to the mountains' on the sabbath, some would refuse, and all of them would be unable to observe the sabbath and would feel bad about it. His concern could be found only within Judaism.

Matthew was of course very much in favour of the Gentile mission. His concluding Resurrection appearance puts this in a nutshell, for Jesus instructs the Eleven left of the Twelve: 'Go therefore and make disciples of all the nations, baptizing them in the name of the Father and the Son and the Holy Spirit, teaching them to keep everything which I have commanded you' (Mt. 28.19–20). This is a beautifully condensed presentation of the needs of Christian churches as Matthew saw them. It begins with the Gentile mission, and continues with the central initiation rite of both Jewish and Gentile Christians. But we must consider the implications of 'teaching them to keep *everything* which I have commanded you'. This Gospel writer's ideal Christian was a 'scribe discipled for the kingdom of Heaven' (Mt. 13.52). His introduction to the Sermon on the Mount, his own edited collection of teachings attributed to Jesus, comments on the permanent validity of the Law: 'So whoever sets on one side one of the least of these commandments and teaches people thus, shall be called least in the kingdom of Heaven, but whoever does and teaches (them), he shall be called great in the kingdom of Heaven' (Mt. 5.19). It follows that Gentile Christians who do not take on the observance of the Law will still be saved, but that this position is not to be approved of. Rather, they ought to take on the observance of the Law when they are converted to Christianity. This is not feasible after the fall of Jerusalem either, and the later we date Matthew after c. 50 CE, the more difficult it becomes.

Matthew's profoundly Jewish understanding of the Law is all of a piece with this. For example, in editing Jesus' dispute with scribes and Pharisees in Mark 7, Matthew drops Mark's comment that Jesus 'cleanses all foods' (Mk 7.19), and adds his own conclusion, 'but eating with unwashed hands does not defile a man' (Mt. 15.20b). This editing makes certain that we keep this dispute within its original cultural context as a dispute about whether to follow the recent tradition of scribes and Pharisees who washed their hands before meals, and that we do not draw from it the exaggerated conclusion favoured by Mark.[55]

In view of all this, it is natural that some perfectly accurate material which presupposes Jesus in his original Jewish context is to be found in Matthew's Gospel only. For example, Matthew's Sermon on the Mount contains this:

> So whenever you do almsgiving, do not sound a trumpet before you, as the actors do in the synagogues and in the streets, so that they may be glorified by men. Amen, I'm telling you, they have their reward. But you, when you do almsgiving, do not let your left hand know what your right hand is doing, so that your almsgiving may be in secret. And your Father who sees in secret will reward you. (Mt. 6.2–4)

This has an excellent setting in the life of Jesus, and several characteristics of his teaching. In the first place, almsgiving was a major feature of Judaism at the time, the nearest thing there was to social security for the very poor. It was therefore of great importance to the community that the rich gave alms abundantly. Secondly, Jesus was very opposed to rich people in general, and loved to attack them, as he does here.[56] His description of them as 'actors', using the Greek word *hupokritai*, is especially polemical, because almsgiving was a Jewish custom, and actors were a Greek phenomenon to be found in Greek theatres. His description of them as sounding a trumpet before them in synagogues and on street corners is equally polemical. Jesus'

---

[55] Cf. pp. 144–7.
[56] Casey, *Jesus of Nazareth*, pp. 305–8.

instructions presuppose his concern for the poor, and his description of God as simply 'your Father' reflects a major aspect of his teaching.

It follows that material special to Matthew always requires independent assessment. While he was perfectly capable of secondary editing, he also preserved original material, and it should never be considered secondary only because it is attested just once. At this point, the brief comment of Papias is again important. When Matthew wrote his Gospel, Luke had not yet written his, so there could not be any difference between what we may think of as 'Q' material, which Luke used, and special Matthaean material which Luke did not use. Passages such as Mt. 6.2–4 may have been written down accurately in Aramaic on a wax tablet by Matthew, the apostle and tax collector.

I conclude that the Gospel of Matthew is a major source for our knowledge of the life and teaching of Jesus, written c. 50–60 CE.

The dates of the synoptic Gospels: The Gospel according to Luke

The Gospel According to Luke has major features in common with Matthew, as well as significant differences. Like Matthew, Luke made significant use of Mark and of the so-called 'Q' material. Luke was, however, a highly educated Greek-speaking Gentile Christian, who wrote primarily for Gentile churches. The conventional date for the writing of his Gospel is c. 80–90 CE, sometime after the fall of Jerusalem, and this date is entirely reasonable. Early church tradition is unanimous in supposing that this Gospel was written by Luke, a companion of Paul, who was not present during the historical ministry of Jesus. This part of church tradition should be accepted, because it is soundly based in the primary source material. Other aspects of later church tradition, such as that Luke came from Antioch, or that he was a constant companion of Paul and transmitted the Gospel which Paul preached, are full of imaginative conjectures, and are no more reliable than other legends and legitimating traditions.

The prologue to the Gospel contains important information about its author, though it does not name him. It is written in excellent Hellenistic Greek, as is the Gospel as a whole, by someone who was familiar with the tradition of writing prologues to literary Greek works, so the author was a highly educated Greek:

> Since many (people) have set their hand to compiling an orderly account concerning the events which have been fulfilled among us, as the eyewitnesses from the beginning and those who became ministers of the Word handed down to us, it seemed good to me too, after following through

everything from the beginning, to write it down for you accurately and in order, most excellent Theophilos, so that you might know the certainty of those things about which you were instructed. (Lk. 1.1–4)

The opening of this prologue tells us that Luke had read several attempts to give some account of at least part of the ministry of Jesus. It distinguishes the author clearly from the eyewitnesses of the ministry, and from the next people who handed the material down. It follows that important material from this early period has been lost. The prologue also rules out any possibility of an early date for the completion of this Gospel. Since Matthew completed his Gospel c. 50–60 CE, he was much the most conspicuous person to have written 'an orderly account concerning the events which have been fulfilled among us', using material 'handed down to us', including that from Matthew the apostle and tax collector, one of 'the eyewitnesses from the beginning'. We should therefore infer that Luke had read our Greek Gospel According to Matthew, as well as the Gospel of Marcus, which he copied and edited.

Secondly, the dedication of this educated work to 'most excellent Theophilos' shows that Luke had a rich, distinguished and well-educated Christian patron, who could be relied upon to provide for his needs. These might include for example scrolls of the Septuagint, the major translation of the Hebrew Bible into Greek. Between this and his membership of at least one major Greek Christian community, Luke will also have had access to such assistants as he may have needed. We should envisage them travelling to other churches and synagogues to collect information, reading source material to him, and copying his Gospel out as he dictated it. Communication between different churches and synagogues, though slow by our standards, was effective and frequent. An author of Luke's education and determination could have gained access to more material than we can envisage, and to oral sources as well as written ones. Moreover, if he were educated somewhere like Corinth or Thessalonica and did not know Aramaic, Luke could have gained access to people who would have translated Aramaic sources for him. How well they would do so is another matter, and he might have been able to control the suitability of the results for Gentile Christians, but not the degree of accuracy. Equally, if he really came from somewhere like Antioch, he may well have known some Aramaic and Hebrew, and have done some of this work himself.

After writing his Gospel, Luke wrote Acts, which is also dedicated to his patron Theophilos. It would be good if we knew who this person was. Murdock tells her own stories, according to which this was Theophilos, bishop of Antioch in 169–177 CE, which gives her the late date which she seeks.[57] Following grossly out-of-date scholarship, she firstly assumes

---

[57] Acharya, *Christ Conspiracy*, pp. 36–7; Murdock, *Who Was Jesus?*, pp. 70–7.

that we must have an independent record of Luke's Theophilos, so that only men called Theophilos and whose records survive from the first two centuries CE can be referred to. Since the only earlier Theophilos she can find was a Jewish high priest 37–41 CE (Jos. *Ant* XVIII, 123; XIX, 297), and he really is not likely to have been Luke's Theophilos, she concludes that Luke's Theophilos must have been the bishop of Antioch, 169–77 CE. There are in fact two more men called Theophilos in Josephus alone. One was the father of the high priest Matthias, who was appointed by Herod the Great (Jos. *Ant.* XVII, 78). The other was a writer, mentioned by Josephus as witnessing to the antiquity of the Jews (Jos. *Apion* I, 216), possibly identical with a writer Theophilos quoted by Alexander Polyhistor (Eus. *Praep. Ev.* IX, 34, 19). What this should underline is the fact that Theophilos was a normal Greek name, found of both Jews and Gentiles, in literature, inscriptions and papyri from the third century BCE onwards. It is therefore quite unremarkable that Luke's patron should bear this name, and unrealistic to expect independent historical attestation of him.

Murdock proceeds to misinterpret even later patristic sources which comment on the Lukan prologue. Luke himself wrote this in a highly literary style characteristic of Hellenistic literary prologues, and this must be borne in mind in interpreting it. It begins, 'Since many have tried to set in order an account of the things which were fulfilled among us...' (Lk. 1.1). Murdock interprets this as Luke already having access to many successful documents which we would regard as completed Gospels. This should not be accepted. Luke had access to the completed Gospels of Mark and Matthew, as well as many other sources, amounting together to a lot of material which includes what we often label the Double Tradition and Luke's special material. This is quite sufficient to explain his literary description in the above terms.

Murdock further claims that Church Fathers named books from second century authors on whom Luke was dependent. She begins with part of the opening of Origen's first homily on Luke, claiming to quote the original Latin, and noting a variant in the 'Greek edition'.[58] It is well known that Origen wrote these homilies in Greek, which survives only in fragments, which are very probably genuine, whereas we have a complete translation of surviving homilies in a Latin translation by Jerome.[59] This is further evidence that Murdock is not learned enough to discuss these sources with

---

[58] Murdock, *Who Was Jesus?*, p. 74.
[59] The major scholarly editions are M. Rauer (ed.), *Die homilien zu Lukas in der Übersetzung des Hieronymus und die Griechischen Reste der homilien und des Lukas-Kommentars* (2nd edn. GCS 49. Berlin: Akademie-Verlag, 1959); Origéne, *Homélies sur S. Luc: texte latin et fragments grec de M.Rauer: introduction, traduction et notes par H. Crouzel, F. Fournier et P. Périchon* (SC 87. Paris: Cerf, 1962. 2nd edn, 1998). For an English translation from Jerome's Latin, see Origen, *Homilies on Luke: Fragments on Luke* (Trans. J. T. Lienhard. Fathers of the Church, vol. 94. Washington: Catholic University of America, 1996).

any semblance of accuracy. The part which Murdock chooses to quote in Jerome's Latin translation may be translated into English as follows:

The church has four gospels, heresy (has) many, from which a certain one is written 'according to Egyptians' another according to 'the Twelve apostles' [Jerome's 'apostles' is absent from the Greek fragment of this]. And Basilides dared to write a gospel and to entitle it with his own name.

Origen does *not* say that these heretical Gospels were written before that of Luke and were being referred to by him. On the contrary, he says later in the prologue (I, 6):

The Apostle praises him deservedly when he says, 'He is praised for his Gospel throughout all the churches' (2 Cor. 8.18). This is said of no-one else but it is handed on as said of Luke only.

This means that Origen interpreted Paul's comment at 2 Cor. 8.18 as a reference to Luke's written Gospel, which dates it during Paul's lifetime, not in the second century after the heretical Gospels to which Origen refers. He has simply inferred from Luke's prologue that Luke in his own day knew other regrettable attempts to 'try' to write a Gospel.

Murdock also quotes Waite in 1881 (listed in her bibliography as 1992, the date of a reprint), discussing a passage of Jerome:

Jerome admits that not only the Gospel of Basilides, composed about A.D. 125, and other gospels, admitted to have been published in the second century, were written before that of Luke, but even the Gospel of Apelles also, which was written not earlier than A.D. 160.[60]

She seems to be referring to Jerome's Preface to his commentary on Matthew, which she partially quotes and misinterprets in her subsequent book, again citing Waite.[61] Jerome dictated his commentary on Matthew in great haste in Bethlehem in March, 398. He does clearly refer to these various Gospels, but he does *not* say that they were written before the Gospel of Luke. For example, he comments: 'That there were many who wrote gospels, both Luke the evangelist testifies...and the literary

---

[60] Acharya, *Christ Conspiracy*, p. 36, quoting C. Waite, *History of the Christian Religion to the Year Two Hundred* (Caroll Bierblower, 1992), p. 80.
[61] Murdock, *Who Was Jesus?*, pp. 76–7, citing Waite, *History of the Christian Religion*, p. 385. The Latin text has been readily available for years: S. Hieronymi presbyteri opera. Pars 1. Opera exegetica. 7, *Commentariorum in Matheum libri IV*, cura et studio D. Hurst et M. Adriaen (CCSL 77. Turnholt: Brepols, 1969). There is now a complete English translation: St. Jerome, *Commentary on Matthew* (Trans. T. P. Scheck. Washington: Catholic University of America Press, 2008).

monuments which, published by various authors, have been the beginning of various heresies.' He mentions the Gospels according to the Egyptians, and Thomas and Matthias and Bartholomew, so these are clearly in the second group of Gospels which have been the beginning of heresies, not in the first group of Gospels known to Luke. Then Jerome adds that there is also a Gospel of the Twelve Apostles and of Basilides and of Apelles, and of others whom it would take too long to list. It follows that he does not suggest that the Gospels of Basilides and of Apelles were written before that of Luke.

In the second section of his prologue, Jerome says that the church's Gospels are Matthew, Mark, Luke 'a disciple of the apostle Paul', and the fourth is John whom he treats as a disciple of Jesus during his earthly ministry. It follows that he followed the conventional assumption that Luke wrote in the first century CE. It was therefore quite wrong of Murdock to declare that 'Jerome dropped a bombshell which might have shaken the foundations of the Church but which has apparently been ignored'. Jerome's commentary on Matthew has not been ignored at all. That Waite's gross misinterpretation of a selected part of Jerome's prologue to Matthew in his incompetent 1881 book has not excited much scholarly comment is natural. Murdock further suggests that her interpretation of Jerome's remarks was supported by the even later witness of Bede, again citing Waite.[62] This is wrong too. Bede follows Jerome, and does not in any way imply that Luke wrote later than Basilides, Apelles and Marcion.

For more fruitful work on the date of Luke, we must turn to his second volume, generally known as the Acts of the Apostles. The second part of Acts gives an account of the Gentile mission led by St Paul, and this contains the famous 'we' passages. These begin when Paul was in Troas, a Roman *colonia*, that is, a city which had been settled with veterans from the Roman army. Troas was in the north-west of Asia Minor, and there Paul had a vision of a man of Macedonia urging him 'come across into Macedonia and help us' (Acts 16.9). Luke's account continues:

> Now when he had seen the vision, we immediately sought to go out to Macedonia, concluding that God had called us to evangelize them. Having set sail from Troas, we made a straight run to Samothrace, and on the next day to Neapolis, and from there to Philippi, which is a leading city of a district of Macedonia, a colonia. Now we stayed in this city for some days. (Acts 16.10–12)

---

[62] Murdock, *Who Was Jesus?*, p. 77, again citing Waite, *History of the Christian Religion*, p. 386. For the text, she cites Giles in 1844. See now the more recent standard edition, *Bedae venerabilis opera. Pars II. Opera exegetica 3. In Lucae evangelium expositio: in Marci evangelium expositio.* Cura et studio D. Hurst (CCSL CXX. Turnholt: Brepols, 1960). I am not, however, aware of a recent English translation.

This gets Luke in Paul's party at a major centre of the Pauline mission, c. 49 CE.

This narrative 'we' stops when Paul and Silvanus were arrested and subsequently thrown out of the city, so Luke presumably stayed there for some time preaching the Gospel. The narrative 'we' resumes after a matter of years, c. 57 CE, when Paul and named Christians including Timothy 'went ahead and waited for us in Troas, but we sailed out from Philippi after the days of Unleavened Bread, and in five days we came to them in Troas, where we stayed for seven days' (Acts 20.5–6). This presupposes that Luke and others were still in Philippi, and now went to join Paul and his party in Troas.

Most scholars infer that, except for this story when 'we' went out to join Paul and others in Troas, Luke was with Paul's party when his narrative uses 'we', and not the rest of the time. This is an entirely natural interpretation of a major primary source written by an intermittent eyewitness.

Paul also mentions Luke at the close of two or three letters. At the end of the epistle to Philemon, written in the name of Paul and Timothy when Paul was in prison, so probably c. 62 CE from Rome, he sends greetings from Luke, with Mark, Aristarchus and Demas, referring to them as 'my co-workers'. At Col. 4.14, also written in the name of Paul and Timothy when Paul was in prison, so again probably c. 62 CE from Rome, he sends greetings from 'Luke the beloved physician' and Demas, in a context of many greetings, including those from 'Aristarchus my fellow-prisoner and Mark the cousin of Barnabas', who are described as 'of the circumcision' (Col. 4.10–11), so Luke is assumed to be Gentile. Luke's presence in Rome c. 62 CE is consistent with the narrative of Acts, in which the 'we' passages end with Paul's journey to Rome, when 'we came into Rome' (Acts 28.14–16). Luke is also mentioned at 2 Tim. 4.11, which is written in Paul's name to Timothy, but which is almost certainly pseudonymous, and probably should be dated in the second century. For what it is worth, this says 'Luke alone is with me' (2 Tim. 4.11), though he is not among those from whom 'Paul' sends greetings, except under the general term 'all the brethren' (2 Tim. 4.21).

All this evidence is interlocking in a consistent manner. When Luke wrote his Gospel, he had been a committed Gentile Christian for over 30 years. He sometimes worked as an evangelist and missionary, and some of this work was done in specifically Pauline churches. While he was not one of Paul's closest co-workers like Timothy and Silvanus, he travelled round different Christian churches. Churches where he stayed for some considerable time included those in Philippi and in Rome, and Christian centres which he visited included Jerusalem. This put him in an ideal position to collect information for his Gospel, as well as for parts of Acts. He knew both Jewish and Gentile Christians, and was evidently capable of journeys which he has not told us about, to collect information from such people. For this purpose, he could use the contacts already traditional between different churches and indeed synagogues, and he could gain access to people who spoke Aramaic, and/or transmitted sources in Aramaic, as well as in Greek.

All this is consistent with the evidence of Luke's Gospel itself that it was written at a relatively late date, by conventional standards for the synoptic Gospels, though not of course by mythicist standards, so c. 80–90 CE. Here its eschatology is of prime importance. I have discussed the eschatological discourses of Mark 13 and Matthew 24, and we have seen that they could not possibly have been written after the fall of Jerusalem, and that a much earlier date, c. 40 CE for Mark and c. 50–60 CE for Matthew, is to be preferred. Luke's discourse is significantly different. His most important change to Mark's eschatological discourse was to replace the prediction of the abomination of desolation, a prediction which was known not to have been fulfilled, with a different prediction:

> But when you see Jerusalem surrounded by armies, then know that her desolation is at hand ... there will be great distress on the land and wrath against this people, and they will fall by the edge of the sword and be taken captive to all the nations, and Jerusalem will be trampled on by Gentiles, until the times of the Gentiles are fulfilled. (Lk. 21.20, 23–4)

Here Mark's predictions have been rewritten in the light of the fall of Jerusalem, and the subsequent taking of prisoners who were sold into slavery elsewhere. This is sufficient to date Luke's Gospel some time after the destruction of Jerusalem in 70 CE. The reference to the 'times of the Gentiles' being fulfilled is not precise, but this is evidently supposed to be some time before the coming of the Son of man in a cloud (Lk. 21.27). Again, Luke altered Mark's prediction that 'there are some of those standing here who will not taste death until they have seen the kingdom of God come in power' (Mk 9.1). Luke dropped Mark's expression 'in power', so that any display of the kingship, or authority, of God could be seen as a fulfilment of this prediction. He then altered the immediately following introduction to the Transfiguration to read: 'Now it came to pass about eight days after these words...' (Lk. 9.27–8). Thus the prediction could be seen to have been fulfilled in the Transfiguration, and the original notion of the final coming of the kingdom has been removed, so that the prediction could no longer be seen to be false.

In addition to alterations removing predictions which had been falsified, Luke added pieces which made clear that the coming of the kingdom should never have been expected at an earlier time. For example, Luke introduces a *very* edited version of an earlier saying with an explicit piece of his own, fired at some of Jesus' most vigorous opponents:

> Now being asked by the Pharisees when the kingdom of God would

come, he answered them and said, 'The kingdom of God does not come with watching, nor will they say "Look here!", or "There!", for behold!, the kingdom of God is among you'. (Lk. 17.20–1, cf. Mt. 24.23, Mk 13.21)

This makes it absolutely clear that any notion of the kingdom of God coming long ago was the province of Jesus' opponents, not part of Jesus' expectations.

All this evidence is completely consistent. As a culmination of many years' work as a committed Christian evangelist and inveterate collector of traditions about Jesus, Luke, with much help from other Christians, finally completed his Gospel c. 80–90 CE.

It remains to note that, as an outstanding historian by ancient standards, Luke found some material about Jesus which does not turn up in other ancient Gospel sources. Perhaps the most outstanding example is Lk. 13.31–3. It contains several Aramaisms, and I offer here a translation of Luke's (literally translated) Aramaic source:

In that hour Pharisees went and said to him, 'Get out and go away from here, for Herod wants to kill you.' And he said to them, 'Go tell that jackal, "Look! I am casting out demons and performing healings to-day and to-morrow, and on the third (day) I am perfected. But I am going to proceed to-day and to-morrow and on the following day, for it would not be fitting for a prophet to perish outside Jerusalem."'

Scholars have been extraordinarily reluctant to see this as a historical result of Mk 2.23–3.6, where some Pharisees took counsel with 'Herodians', followers of Herod Antipas, to have Jesus put to death, when he had merely defended poor disciples who were plucking grain on the sabbath, and healed a man with a paralyzed arm on the sabbath. They took counsel with Herodians because they could not get two violations of their own expansions of the Law to stand up in a normal court so as to obtain a conviction, whereas Herod had had John the Baptist executed, so he was a convenient choice as the powerful secular arm. Pharisees as such, however, were merely orthodox Jews, so it is entirely reasonable that some of them should have considered this action wicked, and a potential violation of the sixth commandment, 'You shall do no murder'. They may well have considered that to do this to a second prophet, who also brought normal Jews back to the Lord himself, was doubly wicked and clean contrary to the will of God.

Thus this is a perfect example of authentic material, literally translated from Aramaic, transmitted to us by Luke alone. Who originally wrote it down we do not know, but it was someone who had access to authentic material which they wrote down briefly, so in any given instance, a passage like this might have been written down in Aramaic by the apostle

Matthew.[63] It follows that, however much we have to dismiss some items attested by Luke alone c. 80–90 CE, we must never dismiss any piece of tradition only on the ground that it is transmitted by Luke alone. As noted above, he was an outstanding historian by ancient standards, and he had access to a wide variety of sources, so we must assess independently each piece of tradition attested by Luke alone.

I therefore conclude that the Gospel of Luke, like that of Matthew, is a major source for our knowledge of the life and teaching of Jesus. We should follow the conventional date of it c. 80–90 CE, not the later dates proposed by mythicists.

Anachronisms

Mythicists allege that the Gospels contain a number of anachronisms, points which demonstrate a later date, and sometimes a different environment, from Galilee c. 30 CE. If true, this would be important. It is the opposite of the major argument which I have used in this chapter for the early date and authenticity of many aspects of the synoptic tradition, which make sense only in Aramaic-speaking Judaism of approximately the proposed date.

For example, Murdock cites in this respect '"synagogue" as concerns a place of prayer'. She dates this after 70 CE. She does not, however, discuss primary sources or archaeological evidence, but simply cites the Jewish scholar Friedlander in 1911.[64] Friedlander's comments were extremely brief and inadequate, even in 1911. Doherty announces that Mark contains 'many anachronisms. It is generally agreed, for example, that there is no evidence for synagogues (in which Jesus is regularly said to preach) in Galilee forty years prior to the Jewish War nor much of a Pharisee presence there... Both are the mark of the post–70 dispersion following the fall of Jerusalem...'[65] Doherty does not, however, give any sources for this 'general agreement', nor does he discuss what a 'synagogue' might reasonably be, or be called, c. 30 CE, nor does he discuss what kind of evidence might reasonably be expected from Galilee.

There has in fact been vigorous scholarly debate in recent years as to whether Jewish meetings would be in a building, whether it would be a separate building set apart for such meetings, or a room in a house, and, in the case of the synagogue in Capernaum, whether the base of the building has been found by archaeologists. Some years ago, some scholars

---

[63] On the apostle Matthew (not to be confused with the evangelist referred to as 'Matthew') as a source for Jesus traditions, see pp. 90–2.
[64] Murdock, *Who Was Jesus?*, p. 80, citing G. Friedlander, *The Jewish Sources of the Sermon on the Mount* (New York: KTAV, 1969), and acknowledging that this is a reprint of a 1911 book.
[65] Doherty, *Jesus: Neither God Nor Man*, p. 413.

were prepared to argue that there were no synagogue buildings in Israel before the fall of the Temple in 70 CE or even later.[66] Colleagues who saw through this position immediately included Sanders, in a book published already in 1990,[67] and this view is not held by serious scholars any longer, as far as I am aware. Decisive evidence includes the archaeological remains of synagogues at Gamla, Herodium and Masada, and the Theodotus inscription (*CIJ* ii, 1404) which records the building of a synagogue in Jerusalem, probably during the Herodian period. It has Theodotus, who built the synagogue, be a priest and synagogue leader, and both son and grandson of a synagogue leader. It specifies the function of the building as the reading of the Law and the teaching of the commandments, as well as more general social functions, including putting up people from abroad.

There is also significant literary evidence from Josephus. For example, in *Ant.* XIX, 300, he discusses a synagogue in the city of Dora on the coast of Israel. This is clearly a building, Josephus calls it a synagogue, and a significant incident took place there in 41 CE, which shows it being treated as a sacred place. At this date, however, an appropriate Jewish building could be referred to as a *proseuchē*, literally perhaps a prayer-house, as often in Philo. The most dramatic literary example is Josephus' discussion of events at the synagogue in Tiberias, which Herod Antipas had made his capital in Galilee. He calls it a *proseuchē*, and describes it as 'a very large building, and capable of accommodating a very large crowd' (Jos. *Life*, 276). The events there do include prayer, but are much more concerned with political events at the beginning of the Roman war. This 'very large building' must have been constructed in Galilee some considerable time previously.

Archaeological evidence from Capernaum itself, a major centre of the historic ministry, is inconclusive. The massive synagogue building which can be seen there now is of much later date. The remains of a basalt structure beneath it may have been the foundations of a first-century synagogue, whether it was a separate building only for such purposes, or not.

We should infer that Jesus often went to Jewish meetings on the sabbath, but we do not know how many of such meetings were in a separate building for this purpose. In Capernaum, we do not know whether the building in which meetings were held was beneath the present synagogue, nor whether it was a separate building for services and other Jewish meetings. We should completely reject the mythicist view that the mention of synagogues in the Gospels is anachronistic. That Murdock and Doherty should publish their views in 2007 and 2009, without any recognition of scholarship published

---

[66] See especially H. C. Kee, 'The Transformation of the Synagogue after 70 C.E.: Its Import for Early Christianity', *NTS* 36 (1990), pp. 1–24; for a summary of the debate, with bibliography, e.g. J. S. Kloppenborg, 'The Theodotos Synagogue Inscription and the Problem of First-Century Synagogue Buildings' in J. H. Charlesworth (ed.), *Jesus and Archaeology* (Grand Rapids: Eerdmans, 2006), pp. 236–82.

[67] Sanders, *Jewish Law From Jesus to the Mishnah*, pp. 341–3nn. 28–9.

in the immediately previous years, illustrates yet again that they may often simply repeat selected opinions in which they wish to believe.

Doherty's view that there was 'not much of a Pharisee presence' in Galilee at the time of Jesus is more complicated.[68] We do not have sufficient non-Christian Jewish evidence about the presence of Pharisees in Galilee to tell us whether this is true or false. That is one reason why it is important that the Pharisees and some of the scribes who are said to have started the dispute at the beginning of Mark 7 are said to have 'come from Jerusalem'. We have no idea of the extent to which Pharisees lived in Galilee normally, nor as to the origin of all Jesus' Pharisaic opponents when they turn up in the Gospels. Accordingly, we should not imagine that all the disputes are anachronistic, especially since the subjects of the disputes do have an excellent setting in first-century Judaism.

Murdock suggests that the expression 'disciples of the Pharisees' (Mk 2.18, cf. Lk. 5.33) is anachronistic, but her reasons are unconvincing. She comments: 'Since the Pharisees were technically not "priests" *per se* but pious unlearned laymen, it would be unusual for them to have "disciples" in the clerical sense. The phrase may not have come into use until after the destruction of the temple in 70 AD/CE...'[69] It was not priests who had 'disciples' in anything like a 'clerical sense': it was rabbis who had 'disciples', and at the time of Jesus people who could properly be called 'rabbis' were generally identified as Pharisees, who were much the most prominent orthodox Jewish group who remained living within the Jewish community. So, for example, Josephus describes Hyrcanus as 'a disciple' of the Pharisees, before he changed sides and became a Sadducee (Jos. *Ant.* XIII, 288–9, cf. 290–98). This was perfectly feasible in the late second century BCE, when the Pharisees were a powerful party. It is not feasible after 70 CE, when prominent Pharisees such as Gamaliel II ceased to self-identify as Pharisees, because they gathered together as rabbis who were no longer in any sense 'separated', but who sought to legislate for the welfare of all Israel. All our evidence also indicates that Pharisees were learned in the Law, not unlearned at all.

Most proposed 'anachronisms' in the synoptic Gospels involve errors of method. For example, Murdock proposes '"Gehenna" (Hell) as a place of punishment', again citing only Friedlander in 1911.[70] The equivalent Hebrew is used in the Hebrew Bible for a valley at the south of Jerusalem, as for example at Jer. 7.32, where *gy' ben hinnōm*, the actual place where children were burnt as sacrifices, is to be renamed *gy' haḥᵃrēgāh,* 'the valley of slaughter'. This is the origin of the Aramaic word *gyhnm* or *ghynm*,

---

[68] Doherty, *Jesus: Neither God Nor Man*, p. 413.

[69] Murdock, *Who Was Jesus?*, pp. 80–1, with a misleading citation of Meier, *Marginal Jew*, vol. II, pp. 442–3, to which should be added his caveats on p. 499n. 198 to p. 443.

[70] Murdock, *Who Was Jesus?*, p. 80, citing Friedlander, *Jewish Sources of the Sermon on the Mount*.

which lies behind the Gospel *geena*, and which is abundantly attested later (e.g. Tg. Isa. 66.24; Tg. Neof. I Gen. 3.24). The idea of this being a fiery hell is attested dated well before the time of Jesus, as for example at 1 En. 90.26, where blinded sheep, a cipher for renegade Jews, are to be cast into 'this fiery abyss, and they burned; now this abyss was on the south of that house'. This refers to Hell in the valley of Gehinnom, to the south of Jerusalem. It follows that the fact that the Aramaic word *geena* is first attested in the Gospels is due to the meagre attestation of Aramaic as early as this, not that it is any kind of anachronism.

Quite how vulnerable this kind of argument is to the vagaries of the survival of texts is especially well illustrated by another of Murdock's examples, '"mammon" as meaning "money"', which is found at Luke 16.9, 11 and Mt. 6.24/Lk 16.13. For this she again cites only Friedlander in 1911.[71] When Friedlander wrote, this word was abundantly attested in Aramaic in the Yerushalmi, or Palestinian Talmud, as well as in later Hebrew, but not as early as the Gospels. It is now clearly attested in Hebrew before the time of Jesus, e.g. as *mmōnō* at 1Q27 frg 1 col 2 line 5. For this reason, it is entirely reasonable to restore it in Aramaic as [*m*]*m*[*ōn*]*h* at 11QTg Job XI, 8, and as [*mm*]*ōn* at 4Q550 5.5. From a methodological point of view, the lack of attestation of any word in Aramaic before the time of Jesus should never be regarded as evidence that its occurrence in the Gospels is anachronistic. This is because Aramaic was a very stable language, which survives only in part from earlier periods.

Conclusions

I therefore propose the following conclusions. The very late dates for the canonical Gospels proposed by mythicists should be uniformly rejected. In the first place, the whole idea of dating them by the date of the earliest extant manuscripts should be rejected, even when we have correct dates for them, as mythicists frequently do not. This is partly because few copies of books were made, and partly because they were destroyed. In the case of early Christian documents, persecution by Roman authorities was a major source of damage. The destruction of libraries added in due course to this. For similar reasons, no decent historian has argued that classical Greek or Roman works should be dated in such a way.

Secondly, we should not imagine that Jesus did not exist because there are no coins or inscriptions about him, nor any busts or statues of him. This is because he was not an important political figure in the Graeco-Roman world. Nor did he leave any literary works. He had no reason to do so.

---

[71] Murdock, *Who Was Jesus?*, p. 80, citing Friedlander, *Jewish Sources of the Sermon on the Mount*.

Apart from the sacred texts which now approximate to our Hebrew Bible, he lived in an oral culture.

For these reasons, we have to rely on internal evidence for the dating of the Gospels. For this purpose, we should consider carefully both Aramaisms which survive in the Gospels as they stand, evidence of misunderstandings which have led to mistakes, and passages where Jewish assumptions, which would be alien to a Gentile Christ cult, are clear. I have put forward examples of all these points, and I have noted the extraordinary extent to which mythicists dismiss these points with general statements, but without considering detailed examples.

I next discussed the dates of the individual synoptic Gospels. I followed Crossley in dating Mark c. 40 CE, and proposed a date c. 50–60 CE for the Gospel attributed to Matthew. I followed the conventional date c. 80–90 CE for the Gospel of Luke. I refuted Murdock's particular reasons for dating this Gospel towards the end of the second century, and showed that she repeatedly misinterpreted patristic texts. Throughout these discussions, I continued to exemplify the evidence of Aramaisms and Jewish assumptions which provide an argument of cumulative weight for the authenticity of some of the traditions in these Gospels, as well as for these relatively early dates for these three completed documents.

Finally, I discussed some of the proposed anachronisms in the synoptic Gospels, and showed that these are spurious.

It follows from these points that there was a historical Jesus, and that we have a significant amount of information about him. I turn next to what the Gospels do *not* say, another matter which has assumed too much importance in the work of the mythicists.

4

What is not in the Gospels,
or not in 'Q'

Introduction

One of the major arguments of mythicists is that, if there had been a historical Jesus, various things would have been written in New Testament documents, and since they are not found there, Jesus cannot have existed. This is a massive argument from silence, applied to a high context situation, and I propose to argue that it is entirely false. I shall deal in detail in Chapter 5 with the traditional form of this argument, associated especially with G. A. Wells, that the Pauline epistles do not contain enough, or any, material about the historical Jesus. In this chapter, I discuss the new forms of the argument, found especially in the work of Murdock and Doherty. This argues generally that some things would be found in the Gospels as a whole, or more particularly, in one of them. The most extraordinary form of this argument goes in from what is not found in 'Q', or even in a given 'layer' of 'Q'. For this purpose, Doherty has taken over Kloppenborg's version of these entirely hypothetical documents, so he has drawn dramatic conclusions from the absence of things from 'documents' which did not exist until modern scholars invented them.

What is not in the Gospels

The most basic point is made by Harpur, when he says that the Gospels 'are not biographies at all', in terms which mean in effect that they are not modern biographies, as critical scholars have known for years.[1] Early twentieth-century scholars already argued that the Gospels are not biographies. Bultmann was conspicuous and influential. He commented, for

---

[1] Harpur, *Pagan Christ*, p. 144.

example: 'There is no historical-biographical interest in the Gospels, and that is why they have nothing to say about Jesus' human personality, his appearance and character, his origin, education and development ...'[2] All this shows, however, is that the Gospels are not biographies in the modern sense. More recent scholarship has, however, considered them in the light of ancient lives (*Bioi*, or *vitae*) of people, and the complete appropriateness of this has been established by the outstanding work of Richard Burridge.[3] Burridge has shown that all four canonical Gospels fit within the rather broad parameters of ancient lives of people. Harpur fails to take account of the most relevant primary sources and secondary literature.

Acharya's arguments are equally flawed. Noting the lack of Gospel evidence of Jesus' appearance, she comments: 'It is beyond belief that had Jesus existed and been seen by "the multitudes", no-one would remember what he looked like. The authors of the gospels, pretending to be apostles, professed to remember Jesus's exact deeds and words, verbatim, yet they couldn't recall what he looked like.'[4] Everything is wrong with this. We have already seen that the authors of the Gospels were not apostles, and did not pretend to be apostles. Nor did they profess to remember Jesus' exact deeds and words verbatim, a view to be found only among fundamentalists, and demonstrably false, not least in the use of Mark's Gospel made by 'Matthew' and Luke.

Of course some people in Galilee will have remembered what Jesus looked like, as would his brother Jacob and the inner group of three, Peter, Jacob and John in Jerusalem. The fact that this is not what the Gospels tell us does not mean otherwise. The authors of the Gospels did not see him. To tell us what he looked like, they would have needed someone to tell them, and they would have needed to be interested enough to tell us. This is where the genre of the Gospels is important at two levels. Firstly, as we have them, they fall within the broad parameters of *ancient* lives, which were not always interested in people's appearance either. Secondly, they are *Gospels*. What does Jesus' appearance have to do with, for example, the validity of Jesus' atoning death, or salvation for Gentiles? Nothing. These two points explain why the Gospels do not describe Jesus' appearance. Murdock has assumed that everyone in the ancient world somehow should have had an attitude to Jesus characteristic of Christian piety centuries later. This is also evident in her assertion that they 'professed to remember Jesus's exact deeds and words, verbatim', which is derived from American fundamentalism, not from the Gospel writers.

---

[2] Bultmann, *History of the Synoptic Tradition*, p. 372.
[3] R. Burridge, *What Are the Gospels? A Comparison with Graeco-Roman Biography* (SNTSMS 70. Cambridge: Cambridge University Press, 1992. Grand Rapids: Eerdmans, 2nd edn, 2004). I am grateful to Prof. Burridge for many illuminating discussions, and for giving me a copy of his book.
[4] Acharya, *Christ Conspiracy*, p. 78.

Acharya makes fun of much later attempts to portray Jesus, which are naturally not consistent with each other, and in which he may be thought to look like various other characters. These are all much later in date, and consequently quite irrelevant. Criticizing one, in which Christ is supposed to have been represented as a 'graceful youth', she comments: 'According to the Gospel story, Jesus disappeared between the ages of around 12 and 29 before he began his ministry, so this depiction of him at "about fifteen to eighteen years of age" certainly would be odd, since his followers never saw him at this age.'[5] This is completely untrue. No Gospel says that 'Jesus disappeared between the ages of around 12 and 29', and we have no reason to believe that, before the beginning of his ministry, any people could reasonably be called his 'followers'. This is creative fiction by Acharya. Mark's Gospel does not start until the ministry of John the Baptist, followed immediately by the baptism of Jesus and his ministry. Matthew and Luke added birth stories, and Luke says that, at the beginning of the ministry, Jesus was about thirty years old (Lk. 3.23). At the end of his birth stories, Luke adds a story of Jesus going to Jerusalem for Passover when he was twelve years old (Lk. 2.41–51). No source says that he 'disappeared' in the meantime. For what it is worth, Luke says the obvious about the intervening period: 'And Jesus advanced in wisdom and stature/age and favour with God and people' (Lk. 2.52).

Doherty expressed with clarity the presuppositions which appear to underlie all arguments of this kind. He comments firstly on the epistles, 'important fundamentals of doctrine and background, which almost two millennia of Christian tradition would lead us to expect, are entirely missing.'[6] This is clean contrary to the nature of historical research. The last thing we should expect to find in first-century documents is the deposit of centuries of later Christian tradition. This is the same mistake that Acharya has made.

What is not written in a particular Gospel

Some arguments of this general kind concentrate on what mythicists think one particular Gospel should have said. The most outstanding examples are given by Doherty, in accordance with his presupposition noted in the

---

[5]Acharya, *Christ Conspiracy*, p. 78. This is quite ludicrous regardless of which picture of him, if any, she has in mind. She refers only to T. W. Doane, *Bible Myths and their Parallels in Other Religions* (New York: Bouton, 1882), p. 502, who refers only to J. P. Lundy, *Monumental Christianity, or the Art and Symbolism of the Primitive Church as Witness and Teachers of the One Catholic Faith and Practice* (New York: Bouton, 1876), p. 231. Acharya dates Doane's book wrongly in 1985, the date of a reprint by Health Research. I used a reprint by Forgotten Books, published in 2010.
[6]Doherty, *Jesus: Neither God Nor Man*, p. 15.

previous paragraph. Doherty believes in Kloppenborg's 'Q', as we shall see in the next section. In support of this view he rejects the view of Goodacre and others that Luke used Matthew, and argues that Luke would have copied various parts of Matthew if he had known them. It is at such points that this mythicist, once a very conservative American Catholic, argues like a fundamentalist.

One such passage is Matthew 16.17–19, where Matthew's Greek may reasonably be translated as follows:

> Blessed are you, Simon Bar Jona, because flesh and blood did not reveal (this) to you, but my Father who (is) in the heavens. And I tell you that you are Peter (*Petros*), and on this rock (*petra*) I will build my church (*ekklēsia*), and (the) gates of Hades will not prevail against it. I will give you the keys of the kingdom of the heavens, and whatever you bind on the earth will be bound in the heavens, and whatever you release on the earth will be released in the heavens.

It has been very difficult for scholars to sort this out. As so often, the most important obstacles are in the later world. This passage was used by Catholics to legitimate authoritarian and often corrupt popes centred in Rome, which the passage does not mention, not least because they had not yet been thought of. This was naturally objected to by Protestants, and it has given some Protestant scholars an undue sense of certainty that Jesus cannot have said any of it. Aspects of the Matthaean tradition imply an Aramaic background. Jesus addresses him as 'Simon Bar Iōna', a Greek version of the Semitic 'Simeon' followed by the Aramaic for 'son of Jonah'. 'Flesh and blood' is a Semitic expression, though it is one which was known to Greek-speaking Jews. More important is the Aramaic original for the central declaration. In Matthew's Greek, there is a pun between Peter (*Petros*) and the rock (*petra*). This pun, however, works in no less than three languages. We have seen that in Aramaic Jesus called him *Kēphā*, which means 'rock'. Thus the pun works perfectly well in Aramaic too, and that is not likely to be a coincidence. It is more of a coincidence that it works in American English, as American students in St Andrews pointed out to us in most entertaining fashion, citing American students called Rock, which even more obviously means 'rock'. I have argued that it is possible to reconstruct something which Jesus is likely to have said.[7]

That is not, however, what Luke read in the Gospel of Matthew. He read Mt. 16.17–19, and it should be obvious that he would not like it! In the first place, it was not in Mark. Luke will have known that Mark was the first Gospel to be written, and he chose to follow Mark, with many alterations of his own, when he could have chosen to follow Matthew.

[7]Casey, *Jesus of Nazareth*, pp. 187–9.

He certainly visited Jerusalem, and he might well have known that this is where Mt. 16.17–19 originated. He was intermittently a companion of Paul and worked in Pauline churches, where the idea that Peter was the rock on which the whole church was built might seem quite foolish. Moreover, Luke not only visited Jerusalem, but whereas Peter may seem in Acts to be in charge of the Jerusalem church soon after Jesus' death and Resurrection, Jesus' brother Jacob was clearly in charge later. A clear example is the so-called Apostolic Council in Acts 15, where speeches were given by Peter, Barnabas and Paul, and the decisive speech was given by Jesus' brother Jacob, who properly referred to 'Peter' by his real name, Simeon (Acts 15.14). Then the apostles and elders and the whole church (of Jerusalem) acted on Jacob's advice. At this point it does not matter how far Luke wrote up this story after the event. The story was obviously not written by someone who believed that Peter was the rock on which Jesus built the church.

We must remember also that when Luke wrote, the story that Peter founded the church at Rome had probably not yet been invented. Moreover, Luke travelled to Rome with Paul. If the story that Peter founded 'the' Roman church had been invented, Luke will have known that it was not true. And 'I will give you the keys of the kingdom of the heavens...' Really? Would a missionary companion of Paul find that remotely plausible? Surely not.

There are several other aspects of Matthew's Gospel that would not appear plausible to a Gentile Christian who had spent years in the mission field. For example,

> Amen I'm telling you, until heaven and earth pass away, not one iota or hook will pass away from the Law, until all things are fulfilled. [19]*Therefore*, whoever undoes one of the least of these commandments and teaches people thus, shall be called least in the kingdom of the heavens. But whoever does and teaches (them), he shall be called great in the kingdom of the heavens. [20] For I'm telling you, unless your righteousness exceeds that of the scribes and Pharisees, you will *certainly not enter* the kingdom of the heavens. (Mt. 5.18–20)

Where does that leave Paul? He gets into the kingdom, but he will be least when he gets there! No wonder Luke preferred those sources which Matthew rewrote, and Luke also found, to Matthew's Sermon on the Mount. Luke did include, 'it is easier for heaven and earth to pass away than for one hook to fall from the Law' (Lk. 16.17). What effect does that have on the Gentile mission? As Paul put it, 'and I became as a Jew to the Jews, so that I might gain Jews' (1 Cor. 9.20). If only Jews observed the Law, and if Jewish Christians observed the Law with appropriate adjustments for Gentiles, there is no harm to the Gentile mission in Luke 16.17 at all. This is quite different from Matthew's rewriting of selected portions of the teaching of Jesus, with additions of his own, in the Sermon on the Mount. Luke must have read it, but he had very sound reasons for not copying it, and for not even returning to it too often.

Doherty discusses briefly a few other passages which he cannot imagine Luke omitting if he knew them. For example, he quotes R. H. Stein, Senior Professor of New Testament Interpretation at Southern Baptist Theological Seminary, a major centre of American fundamentalism, who could not possibly imagine Luke finding anything uncongenial in Matthew, and who is in any case bound by his ideological commitments to harmonize the two:

> Why would Luke have omitted such material as the coming of the wise men? Would not the presence of such Gentiles at the birth of Jesus have been meaningful for Luke's Gentile-oriented Gospel? Why would he have omitted the flight to Egypt and return to Nazareth; the story of the guards at the tomb and their report; the unique Matthean material concerning the resurrection; and so on? Added to this is the observation that if Luke had before him Matthew's birth account and genealogy, one wonders if he would not have sought in some way to 'harmonize' the one we have in his Gospel with the Matthean version.[8]

It should be obvious that this has nothing to do with critical scholarship or historical research. Luke was a highly educated Greek Christian. He did not read about 'wise men' being 'Gentiles' at the birth of Jesus. He read about '*magoi* from the East' (Mt. 2.1). From his point of view they were something like magicians or astrologers, and the notion that 'we saw his star in the East' (Mt. 2.2) probably seemed silly enough, before he got to 'Behold, the star which they saw in the East, went before them, until it came and stood over the place where the child was' (Mt. 2.9). Luke will have known perfectly well that not only did such things not happen, but magicians/astrologers told untrue stories in which such things did happen. He was writing for churches in the Graeco-Roman world, and he will have known that starting like that would not have been attractive to the sort of people he knew well.

The most chronic comment is the last one. It is fundamentalists who 'harmonize' their sacred texts. Luke had good reason not to believe that an 'angel of the Lord' appeared to Joseph and *not* to Mary! What's more, Joseph found out that she was preggers and needed the vision to stop him divorcing her! (Mt. 1.18–25). Matthew was not Scripture in a canonical New Testament. It was a Gospel written by one of 'many (people)' who 'set their hand to compiling an orderly account concerning the events which

---

[8]Doherty, *Jesus: Neither God Nor Man*, pp. 316–17, quoting R. H. Stein, *The Synoptic Problem: An Introduction* (Grand Rapids: Baker Book House, 1984), p. 102. I have not otherwise noted a copy published before 1987; 2nd edn, 2001.

have been fulfilled among us' (Lk. 1.1), and one which was too Jewish for Luke. Why 'harmonize' it with anything? Why not prefer a different story or write his own? The result is infinitely better for educated Greek Christian readers. There are no astrologers, and no doubt by Joseph about Mary's pregnancy, let alone a threat to divorce her. Instead, we have the birth of John the Baptist as well as Jesus, with the angel of the Lord appearing to John's father as well as to Mary, the Magnificat and the Nunc Dimittis. Why harmonize that with Matthew? It's far better on its own!

Moreover, Matthew does *not* have 'the flight to Egypt and *return* to Nazareth', a view which presupposes the traditional harmonization of the birth narratives favoured by fundamentalists. On the contrary, Matthew assumes that Mary and Joseph lived in Bethlehem. There is no indication that they were anywhere else before 'Jesus was born in Bethlehem of Judaea' (Mt. 2.1), and the *magoi* found him 'when they went to the house' (Mt. 2.10). No story about an inn, a stable or a cave! The story about the 'flight to Egypt' is not convincing, and Luke will have known that the story of Herod killing all male children under two in the whole region was false. Joseph then needed *two* dreams to get him to Nazareth. The angel of the Lord told him in the first one to take the family 'to the land of Israel… for those seeking the child's life are dead' (Mt. 2.20). Then Joseph was afraid when he heard that Archelaus was ruling Judaea in place of his father Herod: so, 'being directed in a dream, he took refuge in the region of Galilee, and went and lived in a city called Nazareth' (Mt. 2.22–3). This means that he had not lived there before.

Luke knew all that was wrong. When he made up or inherited his birth stories, he had the angel Gabriel sent 'to a city of Galilee, the name of which was Nazareth' (Lk. 1.26). At least that has them in the right place. His story getting them to Bethlehem is no more accurate than Matthew's stories, but if it took a non-existent census to get Joseph and Mary to Bethlehem (Lk. 2.1–7), at least they are supposed to have left the place where they lived. Luke does not even record their return to Nazareth, treating that as so obvious that he does not even record where Jesus was circumcised, and has the next event being the journey to Jerusalem for purification after child-birth (Lk. 2.22–4). After this they genuinely '*returned* to Galilee, to *their* city Nazareth' (Lk. 2.39).

Matthew's stories about the Resurrection also contain things that Luke will not have liked either. Why ever should Luke have repeated the story that guards at the tomb were bribed to say that the disciples had stolen Jesus' body? Matthew evidently felt he had better do so because the story was circulating 'among Jews' in his own time (Mt. 28.15). It is not true, so it will not have circulated in Gentile churches in Luke's day, so he was much better off without it. And what about Matthew's one major Resurrection appearance to the Eleven (Mt. 28.16–20)? When they saw the risen Jesus, 'some doubted'. Really? Is that what Luke would appreciate and write for his Gentile churches? Surely not. By this stage, however, Matthew's Gospel was circulating in the churches, so Luke sought to neutralize this tale. When Cleopas and his companion returned to the Eleven and those with them in Jerusalem, Jesus appeared to them all, and to show that he was not a spirit, he showed them his hands/wrists and feet. 'And when they were disbelieving because of joy and being amazed...' (Lk. 24.41). So that's all right then! Not *real* disbelief after all.

Matthew's Resurrection appearance also ends with ringing commands to the Eleven: 'Go, therefore, make disciples of all the nations, baptizing them in the name of the Father and the Son and the Holy Spirit...' (Mt. 28.19). This was not what Luke needed either. He worked in the Pauline mission, where it was especially obvious that it was not the Eleven who made disciples of all the nations. So Luke replaced the tradition of Resurrection appearances in Galilee with his own tradition of appearances in Jerusalem. Here Luke tells a significantly larger number of disciples that it was written that 'repentance for forgiveness of sins would be preached in his [Christ's] name to all the nations, beginning from Jerusalem' (Lk. 24.47). This was perfectly true, as well as in accordance with Luke's narrative in Acts. This begins with a final appearance in Jerusalem, a speech by Peter and the election of Matthias in place of Judas, when Luke has 'women' and Mary, Jesus' mother, and his brothers all still together in Jerusalem. Then he narrates the dramatic event of Pentecost. After that, apart from Peter, Jacob and John, there is just the occasional mention of 'the apostles' and one extraordinary story about Philip. Then the Eleven just disappear from the narrative, and Paul and his helpers take over the Gentile mission. The true story will have been more complicated, but perhaps not much more complicated, and the important point is that most of the Eleven played no significant part in the Gentile mission. From Luke's point of view, therefore, Matthew's Resurrection appearance was not what he needed.

In the context of Doherty's argument, all this is simply intended to dispute the whole idea that Luke used Matthew, because Doherty has an uncritical adherence to Kloppenborg's view of 'Q'. This is so that he can use it, complete with layers, to argue that what was not written in 'Q' or even in a given layer of 'Q', did not happen, or was said by someone other than Jesus. He thus uses Kloppenborg's 'Q' to marshal one of his major arguments against the existence of Jesus. We must therefore turn next to 'Q'.

What is not written in 'Q', or in a layer of 'Q'

The so-called 'Q' hypothesis has a long history. It is basically a hypothesis caused by the problems found by scholars in understanding the relationship between the Gospels of Matthew, Mark and Luke. When the priority of Mark was being established, it was obvious that Matthew and Luke had a lot of material in common which is not found in Mark. Much of the early work on this was done in Germany in the second half of the nineteenth century, and this led to it being labelled 'Q', an abbreviation of the German word *Quelle*, which simply means 'Source'. Some scholars now regard the view that this was a *single Greek document* as the dominant theory, and some of them believe that John Kloppenborg has shown that it is correct.[9] This is the view which Doherty has uncritically absorbed.

The mainstream version of this view, represented by Kloppenborg, has one general problem, namely that the disappearance of 'Q' is difficult to explain. More extreme forms of this hypothesis, all American, regard 'Q' as the first Gospel, the product of a 'Q Community', who were often located in Galilee, and sometimes viewed as sort of cynic philosophers, and/or as not really Christian at all.[10] However, the more vigorous the community for which the 'first Gospel' is supposed to have been written, the more impossible it is to explain its disappearance. Moreover, if 'Q' is regarded as cynic and hardly Christian, it becomes difficult to explain why Matthew and Luke had anything to do with it, let alone copied some of it with exceptional accuracy, as the verbally identical parts of 'Q' show that they must have done. It is also difficult to connect it with Jesus in his original environment.

Other scholars believe that the 'Q' material was not source material used independently by Matthew and Luke, but that Luke copied parts of Matthew, editing as he went along. This is generally known as the 'Mark without Q' hypothesis, since its adherents believe in the priority of Mark but not in the existence of 'Q'. This is the hypothesis of Goodacre and others which Doherty was so concerned to criticize, because it would leave him without a document from which major aspects of the life and teaching of Jesus were missing.

Some scholars are not convinced that all of the 'Q' material was a single document, nor that all of this material was transmitted to Matthew and Luke in Greek rather than in Aramaic, nor that Luke's use of Matthew provides a feasible explanation of most of the material which they have in common. I have therefore proposed what I call a 'chaotic model of "Q"', according to which it was nothing like a single document. It is rather a convenient term for the material used by both Matthew and Luke which is not found in Mark. Some of it was written in Greek, but it should not

---

[9] J. S. Kloppenborg, *The Formation of Q. Trajectories in Ancient Wisdom* (Philadelphia: Fortress, 1987); J. S. Kloppenborg Verbin, *Excavating Q. The History and Setting of the Sayings Gospel* (Minneapolis: Fortress and Edinburgh: T&T Clark International, 2000).

[10] For the most important American variations, see A. D. Jacobson, *The First Gospel: An Introduction to Q* (Sonoma: Polebridge, 1992); B. L. Mack, *The Lost Gospel: The Book of Q and Christian Origins* (San Francisco: HarperCollins and Shaftesbury: Element, 1993); and L. E. Vaage, *Galilean Upstarts: Jesus' First Followers According to Q* (Valley Forge: Trinity Press International, 1994).

be regarded as a single document because it was not in common order. Some of it was written in Aramaic and translated twice, and none of this material is in common order at all. This model used to be implicit in the work of outstanding scholars who took seriously the Aramaic dimension of 'Q', but who did not write whole books devoted to establishing this model.[11] In 2002, I contributed *An Aramaic Approach to Q*, in which I examined in detail a small number of passages (Mt. 23.23–6/Lk. 11.39–51; Mt. 11.2–19/Lk. 7.18–35; Mk 3.20–30; Mt. 12.22–32; Lk 11.14–23 and 12.10), and argued that only a relatively chaotic model of the 'Q' material could explain all the varied evidence which it provides.[12] Doherty omits all such work. He is not learned enough to read it with understanding, let alone offer a scholarly assessment of it. Repeating Kloppenborg's criticisms of Goodacre is no substitute for learned scholarship.

It follows that all Doherty's work on 'Q' is based on a completely insecure foundation. He suggests that scholarly adherence to it 'does not serve any theological self-interest' because it does not refer to Jesus' death and Resurrection.[13] This is completely misleading. It would be entirely reasonable to describe the idea of it as a Gospel rather than as source material as 'anti-theological', and just as full of self-interest and bias as American fundamentalists. In a profound sense, the Westar Jesus seminar was the predecessor of mythicists. Its most important members were to a large extent former American fundamentalists, or at least very conservative American Christians, as were most of the mythicists. For example, Burton Mack, author of *The Lost Gospel*, his description of the 'Q' material, is said to have been brought up as a conservative Christian and to have become a minister in the Church of the Nazarene, which is very conservative though it has not embraced inerrancy.[14] Accordingly, Mack's declaration that 'The remarkable thing about the people of Q is that they were not Christians'[15] is in no way unbiased or lacking in self-interest – it is simply that his bias and self-interest is anti-Christian, rather than theological.

Doherty follows suggestions that 'the Q community' was centred in Galilee, because it mentions Capernaum, Bethsaida and Chorazin.[16] He does not, however, explain why a 'Q' community which had no knowledge of the historical Jesus should produce sayings so critical of 'their' cities. He

---

[11] E.g. C. K. Barrett, 'Q: A Re-examination', *ExpT* 54 (1942–3), pp. 320–3; M. Black, 'The Aramaic Dimension in Q with Notes on Luke 17.22 and Matthew 24.26 (Luke 17.23)', *JSNT* 40 (1990), pp. 33–41.

[12] See now Casey, *Jesus of Nazareth*, pp. 78–86, looking forward to the doctoral thesis of Stephanie Fisher, who should establish the chaotic model of the Double Tradition.

[13] Doherty, *Jesus: Neither God Nor Man*, p. 314.

[14] P. Jenkins, *Hidden Gospels: How the Search for Jesus Lost its Way* (Oxford: Oxford University Press, 2002), p. 168. It is regrettable that accurate information of this kind is difficult to find, and therefore not generally known.

[15] Mack, *The Lost Gospel*, p. 4.

[16] Doherty, *Jesus: Neither God Nor Man*, p. 325.

announces that Galilee was a land of 'mixed peoples', relying on American work which is out of date, rather than on the most recent scholarship, in which it has been clearly shown that the environment of Jesus was not of this kind: extreme Hellenization was found in Scythopolis, the Decapolis and Samaria, not in Nazareth or Capernaum.[17]

Doherty proceeds to declare that 'In all of Q1 there is scarcely a specific Jewish idea to be found.'[18] It would not matter if this was true, because Q1 is a modern scholarly construct, not a document which ever existed, and it should be obvious that Jesus' teaching did indeed contain some features which have parallels outside Judaism. However, Doherty's statement is false. For example, he includes in Q1, 'Blessed are the poor, for theirs is the kingdom of God', which has been reconstructed from Mt. 5.3 and Lk. 6.20. This is perfectly Jewish, and vague comments about 'cynics and popular philosophy', with *no references at all*, are not sufficient to upset this obvious point.[19] Again, he quotes what he calls 'Q 6:33-4' conveniently following Luke's 'sinners', whereas Mt. 5.47 has the naturally Jewish 'Gentiles', which Luke would obviously need to change. Perhaps Jesus said, and 'Q' reported, this: 'And if you greet your brethren only, what good is it to you? the Gentiles do the same.' This is obviously Jewish! Doherty asks: 'Why do we find a void on all things specifically Jewish?'[20] We don't, not even in the scholarly construct Q1. Doherty does manage to find one sound principle amid all his mistakes: 'We can only make postulations on the basis of the evidence we *do* have...'[21] It is regrettable that his appreciation of evidence does not stretch to the presentation of a Jewish Jesus in the Gospels of Matthew, Mark and Luke, which we do have, and concentrates instead on Q1, which we do not have. He concludes that his interpretation of 'Q1' against the quite faulty background of Cynicism, 'best makes sense in the *absence* of a founder figure'.[22] This does not follow even from Doherty's misinterpretation of a 'document' which never existed until modern scholars made it up.

Moreover, Doherty seems to have *no* model for the transmission of sayings in anything shorter than a document which is at one and the same time quite a short source such as Q1, yet long enough for him to draw dramatic conclusions from what is absent from it. For example he comments on the Lord's Prayer: 'not even this had come to Q attached to a specific setting in Jesus' career'. From such phenomena in his 'Q1' and 'Q2',

---

[17] See especially M. Chancey, *The Myth of a Gentile Galilee* (SNTSMS 118. Cambridge: Cambridge University Press, 2002); *Greco-Roman Culture and the Galilee of Jesus* (SNTSMS 134. Cambridge: Cambridge University Press, 2005).
[18] Doherty, *Jesus: Neither God Nor Man*, p. 327.
[19] Doherty, *Jesus: Neither God Nor Man*, pp. 327, 331.
[20] Doherty, *Jesus: Neither God Nor Man*, p. 328.
[21] Doherty, *Jesus: Neither God Nor Man*, p. 332.
[22] Doherty, *Jesus: Neither God Nor Man*, p. 334.

he concludes that 'Q, in these early strata, was simply a list of sayings, with no associations made to a Jesus or his ministry.'[23] It does not seem to have occurred to him that the Lord's Prayer might have been written down on a wax tablet by Matthew the apostle and tax collector, and translated into Greek by a Christian who made copies of it on single sheets of papyrus, two of which were transmitted in due course to Matthew and Luke. This is the kind of model of the transmission of the so-called 'Q' material which makes perfect sense from a historical and cultural perspective. It is quite wrong to infer from this that these sayings had no association with Jesus, when they are clearly attributed to him in our surviving sources.

Having decided, on the basis of a reconstructed 'document' divorced from its cultural context, that sayings in 'Q1' are not attributed to Jesus, Doherty finds an exception, which he labels 'Q 9:57-62', following American scholarship according to which it 'is assigned to Q1'.[24]

He classifies them as 'A Set of Three *Chreiai*', in accordance with American custom, apparently following Kloppenborg as usual. I criticized this as long ago as 2002:

> ...when he discusses Matt. 8.19–20//Luke 9.57–8, he declares it the first of three chriae. Subsequently, he avers that Q contains several chriae, 'a form which is not indigenous to Jewish (or Near Eastern) collections, but very common in Greek circles'.[25] This, together with the supposed 'very fact' that Q was composed in Greek, not in Hebrew or Aramaic, is supposed to make it likely that resonances with Greek material will be found. At no point does Kloppenborg consider an Aramaic reconstruction of Matt. 8.19–20//Luke 9.57–8.[26] Yet it is precisely this which shows that it is not of Greek origin, because an Aramaic reconstruction falls properly into place in the culture of Jesus with a meaning which could not entirely be suspected by monoglot speakers of Greek. It follows that the loose definition of chriae has let in under this head sayings which were originally Jewish and transmitted in Aramaic, and which were not originally examples of Greek chriae. We thus end where we began: one of Kloppenborg's major weaknesses is that he is not expert in the language Jesus spoke.[27]

It appears that Doherty has not read this, which could explain why he does not answer it.

Instead, Doherty turns to the Gospel of Thomas saying 68, the only one of the three sayings reproduced there. He proposes that its version is earlier,

---

[23] Doherty, *Jesus: Neither God Nor Man*, p. 337.
[24] Doherty, *Jesus: Neither God Nor Man*, p. 337.
[25] Kloppenborg, *Formation of Q*, pp. 190–2, 263.
[26] For detailed discussion, see Casey, 'Jackals', published in 1985.
[27] Casey, *Aramaic Approach to Q*, p. 31.

because it is simpler, being introduced simply 'Jesus said', without the lead-in remarks and without any parallel to Luke 9.59–62. This criterion is completely unsatisfactory. The Gospel of Thomas was produced by a Gnosticizing Christian subgroup, who began their Gospel:

> These are the secret words which the living Jesus spoke, and Judas, who (is) also (called) Thomas, wrote. And he said, 'Whoever finds the interpretation of these words will not taste death.'

This is the crucial evidence that this Gospel was never intended for most Christians in the churches, which is one reason why it never ended up in the church's canon. Looking through the Gospel as a whole, and comparing it with the Gospels of Matthew, Mark and Luke, it is clear that it omits Jewish material. The last thing its compilers would want is the introduction: 'A scribe said to him, "Rabbi, I will follow you wherever you go"' (cf. Mt. 8.19). Moreover, most of the sayings of Jesus in the Gospel of Thomas are introduced simply 'Jesus said'. This will have facilitated the Thomasine community transmitting its own interpretations of those sayings which it chose to transmit, without undue disturbance from first-century Judaism.

Moreover, Doherty follows a translation of 'Q 9:57–62' based on Luke, which conveniently reduces the number of mentions of Jesus from two to one, and on this sort of basis he announces that the one example is 'a later construction' so that 'the name "Jesus" (or a founder by any name) was entirely absent from the original Q1 stratum.'[28]

All this is entirely spurious. I offer a translation of a much more probable version of what Jesus said at Mt. 8.19–22/Lk. 9.57–60, based more on Matthew, whose version is more clearly anchored in Second Temple Judaism, whereas Luke has clearly modified it in favour of his lengthy journey in which he placed lots of the Double Tradition. I also take into account the Aramaic idiom in the original version of Mt. 8.20/Lk. 9.58:

> A scribe said to him, 'Rabbi, I will follow you wherever you go.' And Jesus said to him, 'Jackals/foxes have holes, and the birds of heaven/ the sky have roosts, but a/the son of man has nowhere to lay his head.' Another of the disciples said to him, 'Master, Let me first go back and bury my father'. And Jesus said to him, 'Follow me, and leave the dead to bury their dead.'

These sayings have a perfect setting in the ministry of Jesus. The first has a natural setting in the migratory phase of Jesus' ministry, when he moved through the towns and villages of Galilee.[29] A scribe would normally sit

---

[28] Doherty, *Jesus: Neither God Nor Man*, pp. 337–8.
[29] See further Casey, *Solution to the 'Son of Man' Problem*, pp. 168–78.

at the feet of his teacher in a reasonably comfortable building, so this one took a major step when he undertook to follow Jesus wherever he went. The saying contrasts the divine provision of natural haunts for animals with the lack of such provision for people, who have to build houses to live in. It is therefore important that the birds have 'roosts', not the traditional 'nests', which Doherty uses in the translation which he follows, and which nature does not provide. Neither Matthew nor Luke has 'nests' (for which the straightforward Greek word would be *nossias*). Both have a general word for dwelling-places (*kataskēnōseis*), so Jesus will have used an equally general Aramaic word (e.g. *mishkenīn*). At this point, the behavioural patterns of birds in Israel are important. Palestine was a major flyway for centuries before and after the time of Jesus. Most of the birds seen there were migratory – they stopped on their way over to roost, not to build nests and rear their young. Moreover, among the many species native to Israel, Cansdale noted the Lesser Kestrel, which 'travels in large flocks and roosts in hundreds, in such conspicuous places as the trees round Capernaum'.[30] Thus the places which the birds had to stay for as long as they needed were provided for them by God in the ordinary course of nature, and they were provided for them as they moved about the countryside.

Equally, 'holes' are places where both foxes and jackals lay up in the daytime, they are not 'dens' which they may or may not have to dig out to rear their young (both animals take over existing holes even for this purpose, sometimes made by other animals, when these are available). Both Matthew and Luke have 'foxes' (Greek *alōpekes*) rather than 'jackals', but Jesus can only have used the Aramaic *ta'alāyā*. Tristram commented on the related Hebrew *shū'al*:

> The Hebrew word undoubtedly includes the jackal (*Canis aureus*) as well as the fox (*Vulpes vulgaris*). Indeed, in most of the passages where it occurs, the jackal rather than the fox is intended, as may be seen from the context. The Hebrew *shu'al*, Arabic *jakal*, the Persian *shagul*, and the English *jackal*, are all the same word ... But the two animals are commonly confounded by the natives of Syria, though they are perfectly aware of their distinctness ... The natives of the East discriminate very little between the two animals, or rather look on the fox as a small and inferior species of jackal. Indeed their appearance to a cursory observer is very similar, the jackal having its fur of paler colour, or yellowish rather than reddish in hue.[31]

This was probably true in the ancient period as well. Both Matthew and Luke virtually had to specify 'foxes' because the Greek 'foxes' (*alōpekes*)

---

[30] F. S. Cansdale, *Animals of Bible Lands* (Exeter: Paternoster, 1970), p. 140.
[31] H. B. Tristram, *The Natural History of the Bible* (London: Christian Knowledge Society, 1867, 10th edn, 1911), pp. 85, 110.

is a perfectly correct translation of the Aramaic *ta'alāyā*, and there was no normal Greek word for 'jackal' because there were no jackals in Greece.

We can now see the general level of meaning which cannot be avoided in the original Aramaic. The reference will have been in the first place to Jesus himself, for he had nowhere to go as he moved about, and he could not provide for his disciples. This would be a humiliating thing to say, and consequently Jesus used an indirect way of saying it. The general level of the saying also takes in his followers, especially the one who had just declared that he would follow Jesus wherever he went (Mt. 8.19/Lk. 9.57). Doherty has misinterpreted the saying, removing it from its original setting in the ministry of Jesus and giving it a different setting in which it does not make proper sense.

The next saying is equally Jewish.[32] In Judaism, burying the dead was a pious duty. This saying takes for granted Jesus' preaching of the imminence of the coming of the kingdom of God. If this assumption is removed, the man's request to bury his father 'first' is unmotivated. Jesus' answer does not make proper sense in any other context either, since without the centrality of his ministry and the imminence of the kingdom there is no rationale in his refusal, nor any reason for his description of live people who would carry out the funeral as 'the dead'. Doherty's assumption that this saying could have been created for a Greek cult without any proper setting makes no sense at all.

Doherty proceeds to get Gentiles into Q1 by means of his technique of imagining what would have been there if it had been Jewish. Regardless of its short length, and of the fact that it is a scholarly construct, he thinks Q1 should have said something explicit about Jesus' teaching on the Jewish dietary Laws. He then declares that 'in fact, they are noticeably excluded from consideration in its mission statement', quoting only part of Luke 10.7, and omitting Luke 10.6, which says of the house 'if a son of peace lives there'.[33] A reasonable translation of this part of Luke 10.7 would be: 'Stay in that house, eating and drinking what they have, for the worker is worthy of his pay.' Luke has defined where they go as 'into every town and place where he was intending to go' (Lk. 10.1). Matthew has 'Do not go away into the way of the Gentiles, and do not enter a town of Samaritans, but go rather to the lost sheep of the house of Israel' (Mt. 10.5–6). Both evangelists follow shortly with the instruction that 'the kingdom of God/ heaven is at hand' (Mt. 10.7/Lk. 10.9). It was therefore obvious to both evangelists, in accordance with all our evidence of Jesus' historic ministry, that the disciples were sent to go to Jewish homes, that they were told to eat and drink what they were given so that they should have no inhibitions

---

[32] For summary discussion, with bibliography, see Casey, *Jesus of Nazareth*, pp. 309–10.
[33] Doherty, *Jesus: Neither God Nor Man*, p. 341.

about accepting the whole of this hospitality, and that only kosher food would be available.

Doherty replaces this with his own invented situation: 'No thought is given to whether the host is Jewish or Gentile (an option to be expected in Galilee and Syria), or whether his food is kosher or not, nor are the missionaries reminded of Jesus' liberal teachings on the subject.'[34] This is not true of Galilee, and it should be obvious that the disciples were not being sent into Syria, which is not mentioned, Doherty's usual criterion for excluding reference to anything taken for granted. Moreover, as we shall see, Jesus and his disciples kept the dietary laws, and everyone else around them did the same.[35]

Doherty proceeds to declare: 'Similarly, no mention is made of the issue of circumcision; if Gentiles were approached, what is to be the rule on this traditional requirement?'[36] This question again results entirely from Doherty removing the teaching of Jesus from its original Jewish environment and plonking chunks of it in a Gentile environment instead. There is no mention of circumcision in the Double Tradition because it was of no relevance there, because most of the Double Tradition comes from the ministry of Jesus in first-century Galilee, not from a Hellenistic cult invented by Doherty and his ilk. In this high context culture, nothing as obvious as circumcision needed to be mentioned unless there was a special reason for doing so.

Doherty proceeds to Q2, which he again appears to have taken over uncritically from Kloppenborg. He begins by declaring: 'On entering Q2, one encounters a startling change of atmosphere.' He then quotes sayings about judgement, which are indeed different from those put into Q1, and comments: 'It is difficult if not impossible to regard the same community, the same people – not to mention the same man – as having produced the two sets of sayings...'[37] What Doherty has not realized is that this impression has been produced by the scholarly isolation of Q1 and Q2, neither of which is a genuine feature of the primary source material. Moreover, Doherty considers it important that sayings in both 'layers' do not always have the same context, and that in incorporating them into their Gospels, Matthew and Luke placed them 'at different points in their Gospel story'.[38] Doherty likes this information because it enables him to imagine that these sayings were not originally attributed to Jesus. It is accordingly regrettable that he does not seem to have noticed that this is one of the most important arguments against the whole idea that 'Q' was a single Greek document, whether it was formed from 'layers' or not. He

---

34 Doherty, *Jesus: Neither God Nor Man*, p. 341.
35 See pp. 144–7.
36 Doherty, *Jesus: Neither God Nor Man*, p. 341.
37 Doherty, *Jesus: Neither God Nor Man*, p. 342.
38 Doherty, *Jesus: Neither God Nor Man*, p. 344.

might have noticed at this point also the massive variation in the level of verbal agreement in passages which modern scholars ascribe to 'Q'. Both points are a natural result of Matthew and Luke inheriting a large number of small pieces of tradition, whereas large volumes of 'Q' scholarship have still not produced a convincing explanation of Matthew and /or Luke changing the supposedly fixed order in which these sayings were placed in this wondrously reconstructed 'document'.

Doherty's comments on the Double Tradition about John the Baptist are even more extraordinary. Here, in discussing what sayings in 'Q' meant, he *presupposes* that the 'Q' community were *creating* sayings *so fictional* that it would have made a reference to Jesus in the first ones clearer if *it* imagined that it was the coming of Jesus to which they referred. He comments on his English translation of Mk 1.7 followed by material from the Double Tradition, which in my opinion is so inadequate that I repeat my own translation before reproducing his comments:

One stronger than I is coming after me, of whom I am not worthy/sufficient to bend down to undo the latchet of the sandals of him. I baptize you in/with water, and he will baptize you in/with holy spirit and fire, whose winnowing shovel is in his hand, and he will cleanse his threshing floor, and he will gather his wheat into the storehouse, but the chaff he will burn with unquenchable fire. (Mk. 1.7, continued at Mt. 3.11–12/ Lk. 3.16–17)[39]

Doherty comments: 'it would seem that *the community* knew *no founding figure* in its background, for if it did, *it* would not have *created* for John a saying which shows no knowledge of such a figure' (my italics).[40] But the mythical 'Q community' did not create this saying. It is a genuine saying of John the Baptist, as is clear from his uncertain question, in which he sent disciples to ask Jesus whether he was in fact the figure whom John had predicted, or whether they should expect another (Mt. 11.2–3/Lk. 7.18–19). Doherty, however, comments: 'to maintain that the saying may actually have been authentic to John and faithfully preserved would be alarmingly naïve'.[41]

When he gets to John's question and Jesus' answer under the heading 'Introducing Jesus to Q', Doherty offers a confused discussion based on the work of Kloppenborg and other scholars.[42] In 2002, I offered a detailed discussion of this passage. I sorted out authentic traditions from secondary development and evangelists' editing, and offered a complete reconstruction

[39] Casey, *Jesus of Nazareth*, p. 175.
[40] Doherty, *Jesus: Neither God Nor Man*, p. 346, after an inaccurate quotation from Kloppenborg, *Formation of Q*, p. 104, from which the word 'not' has dropped out!
[41] Doherty, *Jesus: Neither God Nor Man*, p. 747n. 128 from p. 346.
[42] Doherty, *Jesus: Neither God Nor Man*, pp. 369–75.

of authentic sayings in Aramaic. I also discussed the serious effect which this has on the interpretation of some aspects of some parts of these passages, especially Mt. 11.19/Lk. 7.34. I also offered a reconstruction of the Greek source used by Matthew and Luke.[43] Doherty fails to address this topic.

I begin by repeating my English translation of my reconstruction of an Aramaic source which was translated into Greek to form a Greek source used by both Matthew and Luke at Mt. 11.2–6/Lk. 7.18–23. I follow Matthew's verse divisions, because I argue that in this passage he made fewer editorial alterations than Luke did:

> [2]And John sent by the hand of his disciples [3]and said to him, 'Are you him coming, or shall we wait for another?' [4]And he answered and said to them, 'Go inform John of what (people) see and hear: [5]blind (people) see and lame (people) walk, people-with-skin-diseases are cleansed and deaf (people) hear, and dead (people) are raised and poor (people) have good news preached to them. [6]And blessed is whoever does not stumble over me.'

It should be obvious that the passage as a whole is a collection of sayings about John the Baptist and Jesus, and that we should not assume that they were all given on the same occasion, or that all or none of them are genuine. This first part, however, is a unified whole.

Doherty begins with a set of assumptions which he appears to have taken from Kloppenborg (he cites passages in accordance with the conventional versification of Luke, because this is in accordance with the habits of devotees of the mythical document 'Q'). He begins by quoting this judgement from Kloppenborg: 'It is more than likely that the entire pronouncement story (7:18–23) is a post-Easter creation.'[44] Neither of them offers sufficient evidence for any such view. Kloppenborg announces that the story 'invokes Baptist expectations in its use of the title "the Coming One", but infuses the title with specifically Christian content.'[45] It obviously does invoke his prediction at Mk. 1.7, but Kloppenborg does not offer evidence that it was a title, let alone a title as early as Matthew. As I pointed out, however, in work available to Doherty but not to Kloppenborg, 'it is not a known title, either in Judaism at the time of Jesus or in the early church', and I suggested it was a translation of the Aramaic *hu' 'thh* which is not a title.[46] It could not be the translation of an Aramaic title, but Kloppenborg and Doherty avoid that problem by treating the passage entirely in Greek (Kloppenborg) or English (Doherty). Moreover, as I pointed out, John the

---

[43] Casey, *Aramaic Approach to Q*, pp. 105–45.

[44] Doherty, *Jesus: Neither God Nor Man*, p. 370, quoting from Kloppenborg, *Formation of Q*, p. 107, omitting the word 'however' and Kloppenborg's comment on Bultmann.

[45] Kloppenborg, *Formation of Q*, p. 107.

[46] Casey, *Aramaic Approach to Q*, pp. 108, 110.

Baptist's 'question has no *Sitz im Leben* in the early church...nor did they have reason to invent the notion that John was uncertain as to whether Jesus was the figure whose coming John had predicted'.[47]

Both Kloppenborg and Doherty see a problem in the difference between John the Baptist's original prediction and Jesus' later answer to his question. But this is surely the point of both John's question and Jesus' answer. Jesus was a reasonable candidate for the fulfilment of John's prophecy because he had been baptized by John and was in the middle of a dramatically successful prophetic ministry to Israel. At the same time, he had achieved more repentance and less judgement than John expected, as well as a successful ministry of exorcism and healing. Hence he replied in largely scriptural terms, with indirect references to the favourable parts of Isa. 29.18-19; 35.5-6; 61.1, omitting references to their comments on judgement, adding reference to Isa. 8.14-15 in the concluding beatitude. All this has a perfect setting in the ministry of Jesus, whereas it was not in the church's interest to invent the question.[48]

Doherty is so ignorant of Second Temple Judaism that he cannot see that Jesus answered John's question at all. Noting, not *very* inaccurately, that John warned of the 'coming apocalyptic judge', Doherty glosses 'in 'Q's eyes the Son of Man'. This Greek Christological title is quite absent from all reports of John the Baptist's preaching, and there is no excuse for introducing it here. Doherty then declares that 'John is "answered" by Jesus' performance of miracles – on the spot of some handy blind, sick and lame, a lame device seemingly of Luke's invention...' This is indeed an insertion by Luke, and Doherty should not have included Luke 7.21 in his NEB translation supposedly of 'Q'. It does not belong in the Double Tradition, as scholars have known for a long time.[49]

Doherty continues:

Matthew simply has Jesus refer to past miracles. Yet there had been no thought of the Coming One being due to perform miracles in the earlier Baptist prophecy, thereby making him now recognizable by John. The contradictions between the two passages are too great to think that that Dialogue is anything other than a clumsy editorial construction serving the immediate purpose of clarifying John's relationship to Jesus when

---

[47] Casey, *Aramaic Approach to Q*, p. 110.

[48] For detailed discussion, see Casey, *Aramaic Approach to Q*, pp. 108-15.

[49] E.g. Casey, *Aramaic Approach to Q*, p. 111, noting among previous scholars taking the same view W. G. Kümmel, *Jesu Antwort an Johannes den Täufer: ein Beispiel zum Methodenproblem in der Jesusforschung* (Wiesbaden: Steiner, 1974), p. 149; G. Häfner, *Der verheißene Vorläufer. Redaktionskritische Untersuchung zur Darstellung Johannes des Täufers im Matthäusevangelium* (SBB 27. Stuttgart: Katholisches Bibelwerk, 1994), pp. 164-6. Doherty shows no sign of reading, or indeed of being able to read, such scholarly work.

the latter was introduced to Q. Had a Q Jesus been on the scene from the beginning, the opening Baptist passage would have reflected that situation.

Everything is wrong with this. It is not only Matthew who refers to past events, which Doherty regards as 'miracles'. Mt. 11.4–6/Lk.7. 22–3 is *verbally identical* in Matthew and Luke, which proves beyond reasonable doubt that it belonged to one of the parts of the Double Tradition written in Greek, unlike Luke 7.21. Secondly, the description of past events as 'miracles' is, in Doherty's hands, prejudicial, because he regards miracles as events only possible by the direct intervention of God. As a conservative American Catholic, he presumably used to believe in the literal truth of all biblical and some ecclesiastical miracles (though not in any pagan ones), but he now no longer believes in the truth of any story which he can label a miracle. He shows no sign of knowing the work of Vermes, Sanders and Keir Howard, whose discussions show that most of the events referred to by Jesus in his ministry here are perfectly possible in the work of traditional healers, unlike the large quantity of suddenly convenient healings in the summary produced by Luke at Lk. 7.21.[50]

Jesus' ministry of exorcism and healing was different from John the Baptist's prediction of one stronger than he coming after him. How Doherty imagines he could 'baptize you in/with holy spirit and fire', 'cleanse his threshing floor' and so on without performing miracles in the strictest sense, that is without direct divine intervention, is not clear. His opinion that there are serious 'contradictions' between the two passages is simply wrong. The differences between John's prediction and Jesus' ministry led him to send messengers with a perfectly proper question, which Jesus answered. Doherty concludes, however: 'Had a Q Jesus been on the scene from the beginning, the opening Baptist passage would have reflected that situation.' This is again dependent on Doherty's view of 'Q'. The only editors of the tradition known to us, Mark followed by Matthew and Luke, did present Jesus as the fulfilment of John's prophecy. Doherty has simply invented a mythical Q editor, who did not exist, and whom Doherty presents as a kind of creative novelist who would have done what Doherty imagines. It is difficult to imagine a weaker argument.

Stephanie Fisher pointed out Doherty's uncritical use of Kloppenborg's work on 'Q'.

Blogger Godfrey commented:

---

[50] See G. Vermes, *Jesus the Jew: A Historian's Reading of the Gospels* (London: Collins, 1973), pp. 69–78; E. P. Sanders, *The Historical Figure of Jesus* (London: Penguin, 1993), ch. 10; J. Keir Howard, *Disease and Healing in the New Testament: an Analysis and Interpretation* (Lanham: University Press of America, 2001), all of which were available to Doherty, but which he appears not to have read. See further now Casey, *Jesus of Nazareth*, ch. 7.

Doherty in fact dedicates a lengthy chapter to an examination and testing of the arguments for the existence of Q.

More than this, however, is that Doherty also raises the arguments used against Q, especially those of Mark Goodacre, and argues them point by point detail before concluding with his reasons for explaining why he believes Q is still the most economical explanation for the "synoptic problem" …

No-one familiar with Doherty's work and reading Fisher's comments would ever suspect Doherty of being so thorough. Fisher is, indeed, bluntly making false assertions about Doherty's work even though she repeatedly insists she has read his discussion of Q thoroughly. (She seems to have entirely missed the one titled "The Nature and Existence of Q".)

Fisher's criticism that Doherty "takes Q for granted" is worrying on other grounds, too. Since Q is a central focus of her doctoral thesis, one has to wonder about the likely quality of the scholarship of the completed work.

Equally unfathomable is Fisher's contradiction of her points made in 9 and 10 by her point 8 – where she faults Doherty for using what is probably the most complex and detailed argument for Q of all, Kloppenborg.

So on one hand Doherty is accused of taking Q for granted, uncritically, despite an entire chapter by Doherty on the critical arguments for and against Q in which Doherty discusses Kloppenborg's arguments, and on the other hand she faults him for relying on one of the most comprehensive scholarly arguments ever produced for Q ("uncritically" — despite Doherty's detailed discussion of Kloppenborg in comparison with other views and his own independent contributions).[51]

All this illustrates yet again that Blogger Godfrey has no idea as to what genuinely critical scholarship is. All Doherty's criticisms of Goodacre are taken uncritically from Kloppenborg. No scholarship is independent just because a discussion is relatively long, as Doherty's book certainly is. Doherty does not discuss Kloppenborg in comparison with most other views, and he did not make any 'independent contributions'. In particular, he did not discuss any of the long tradition of scholarship which has examined evidence for Aramaic sources behind parts of the double tradition, which is not consistent either with all the Double Tradition being a single Greek document (Kloppenborg) or all due to Luke's use of Matthew (Goodacre). Doherty left all this out because Kloppenborg left it out, and Doherty is uncritically reliant on Kloppenborg. Blogger Godfrey did not notice because he evidently does not possess the necessary academic

---

[51] http://vridar.wordpress.com/2010/05/27/how-and-why-scholars-fail-to-rebut-earl-doherty/ [last accessed 14 May 2013].

background and is annoyed with Stephanie Fisher for pointing out the gaps in his knowledge. I noted above the relatively recent work of Black, Barrett and myself, none of which Blogger Godfrey appears to take into account.[52] He has simply followed Doherty because he likes his results.

Conclusions

In this chapter, I have surveyed arguments which cast doubt on the existence of Jesus as a historical figure because of what the Gospels, or 'Q', do not say. All of them ignore the fact that the Gospels were written in a high context situation, in which everything did not have to be repeated all the time. The first arguments were due to false ideas about what the Gospels should have said. In particular, they were not modern biographies, so it has been quite wrong of some mythicists to claim that Jesus cannot have been a historical figure because no one even remembered what he looked like. The Gospels were not intended to transmit that kind of information at all. As they stand, they fall within the rather broad parameters of ancient 'Lives' of people, which were often not interested in describing their physical appearance either.

The remaining arguments were due to Doherty's determination to believe in 'Q'. This is quite ironical, since this is a mythical document which has never existed, and Doherty used it as a plank for asserting that Jesus was a mythical being who never existed. At no point does Doherty even consider the possibility that the Double Tradition might be a number of different sources, not one of which was ever intended to transmit the main points of Jesus' ministry. The arguments which I considered first, in section 3, all arose from Doherty's determination not to believe the view of Goodacre and others, that *all* the so-called 'Q' material was due to Luke copying Matthew, which indeed it surely was not. To exclude this possibility, Doherty argued that Luke did not know Matthew's Gospel at all, which is not plausible. What is remarkable about Doherty's arguments is that they are virtually fundamentalist Christian arguments. He presupposes that, if Luke knew Matthew, he would have loved it all so much that he would have copied far more of it than Goodacre and others suppose, and even that he would have harmonized Matthew's account with his own, as fundamentalists do. These arguments are completely unconvincing.

In section 4, I considered a different group of arguments. All presuppose the existence not just of a finished document 'Q', but also of two important

---

[52] See pp. 117–18, 118nn. 11–12, noting Casey, *Aramaic Approach to Q*, with p. 000n. 12, referring to C. K. Barrett, 'Q: A Re-examination', *ExpT* 54 (1942–3), pp. 320–3; M. Black, 'The Aramaic Dimension in Q with Notes on Luke 17.22 and Matthew 24.26 (Luke 17.23)', *JSNT* 40 (1990), pp. 33–41.

layers, Q1 and Q2, and of an editor who could and would behave like a modern novelist, and write whatever he wanted. Thus Doherty argued that Q1 hardly contained anything specifically Jewish. This is not true, and Doherty found it significant only because he presupposed the separate existence of Q1. Otherwise, there is no reason why someone should not, for example, have selected wisdom-type sayings from the teaching of Jesus and transmitted them separately. This was exacerbated by misinterpretation of some sayings, ignoring among other things the Aramaic background of some of them. Doherty also tried to give Q1 a Gentile setting, and then found significance e.g. in the absence of circumcision. He was then unable to account for the differences between Q1 and Q2, all of which are parasitic upon the artificial isolation of these 'layers'. His arguments about John the Baptist are not only unconvincing in themselves, but presuppose completely creative editing of the 'Q' material, a model produced by Doherty.

I therefore conclude that all the arguments of the mythicists considered in this chapter are completely unconvincing. They depend on their complete inability to understand either the Gospels as they stand, or the sources from which they were formed.

In the next chapter, I consider arguments based on what is not said in the epistles, especially those of Paul.

5

What is not in the Epistles, especially those of Paul

Introduction

I have noted that one of the major arguments of mythicists is that, if there had been a historical Jesus, various things would have been written in New Testament documents, and since they are not found there, Jesus cannot have existed. The traditional form of this argument, associated especially with G. A. Wells, is that the Pauline epistles do not contain enough, or any, material about the historical Jesus. This has recently been carried much further by Doherty, who has also proposed some new interpretations of what Paul *really* meant in passages where he is normally thought to have been referring to the historical figure of Jesus, and has commented on what is not found in other New Testament epistles.[1] The purpose of this chapter is to discuss what is *not*, and what mythicists *allege* is not, found in the epistles, especially those of Paul. I discuss what Paul really said and meant in Chapter 6, though there is naturally some unavoidable overlap between these two chapters.

Two major mistakes underlie all the mythicists' arguments. One is the date of the synoptic Gospels, which they all date much too late, as we saw in Chapters 2 and 3. Normally, historians regard their oldest available sources as the most reliable, because they usually are, whereas later sources are more prone to suffer from story-telling and social memory, the rewriting of sources in the interest of the community to which a writer belongs. Moreover, we have seen that this is generally the case with the Gospels themselves. The oldest, the Gospel of Mark, is the most reliable of all. Sources recoverable from the Gospels of Matthew and Luke, especially parts of the Double Tradition, generally known as 'Q', are equally old and reliable. All three synoptic Gospels also include secondary material, and Matthew and Luke can be seen at work altering their main single

---

[1]Doherty, *Jesus: Neither God Nor Man.*

source, the Gospel of Mark. Later Gospels, however, beginning with those attributed to John and to Thomas, contain hardly any new and accurate historical material, and suffer to a massive degree from social memory. Much later Gospels, such as those of Judas and of Mary, contain hardly any historically accurate material at all, and were deliberately written in the interests of the falsehoods of social subgroups.

Building on their ludicrously late date of the synoptic Gospels, mythicists proceed to argue that the Pauline epistles are our earliest sources for the Life and Teaching of Jesus. This leads to their second and third major mistakes: they do not understand the *genre* of the epistles, nor do they understand any high context culture or situation. Paul's epistles were written to churches of committed Christians, to deal with problems which arose in those (mostly Gentile) churches: they were not in any sense lives of Jesus, as the synoptic Gospels may be considered to be, falling as they do within the parameters of *ancient* lives, though not of modern biographies. This is one basic reason why Paul had to discuss questions such as whether Gentile men should be circumcised, for this was a major problem in those mostly Gentile churches in which Gentiles had been converted to a form of Judaism, a religion which required the circumcision of boys, so that all normal Jewish men were circumcised, as were proselytes.

This is also one basic reason why Paul says so little about the life and teaching of Jesus, as is the fact that early Christianity was more or less a high context culture. To some extent, his Gentile Christians had been taught about Jesus already, so he could take such knowledge for granted. He therefore had no reason to mention places such as Nazareth, or the site of the crucifixion, nor to remind his congregations that Jesus was crucified on earth recently. Of these points, only the *fact* of Jesus' crucifixion was significant enough to be mentioned in the epistles, since Paul was convinced that, in the light of the sacrificial death of Christ, Gentiles *must not* undertake circumcision and thereby undertake to keep the whole of the Jewish law. Thus Jesus' death and Resurrection were of central importance, and did have to be mentioned repeatedly. All these converts would certainly know the obvious fact that Jesus was crucified on earth recently, and they are likely to have known that he was crucified outside the walls of Jerusalem. How many of them knew that he was born in Nazareth we have no idea, and it is most improbable that any of them knew exactly where he was crucified, since the site appears to have been unknown. Such matters were of no importance to followers of Paul in the early church. Nor do we know how many of them knew the story of the empty tomb. It was a secondary development, and it is a reasonable interpretation of Paul's comments on the Resurrection that he did not believe in it either.[2]

---

[2] Cf. Casey, *Jesus of Nazareth*, ch. 12.

At this point, mythicists take abundant advantage of the regrettable fact that conventional, as well as hopelessly conservative, scholars do not fully understand why Paul says so little about the historical Jesus. There is an extremely widespread assumption that somehow Paul *ought* to have behaved like much later Christians, and for this (largely unnoticed) reason he somehow *should* have relied on the authority of Jesus' teaching when he in fact relied on his own authority as an apostle sent out by God himself when he saw the risen Lord on the Damascus road. Thus he makes abundant reference to Jesus' death and Resurrection, the main points which in his view permitted the salvation of Gentiles without them having to observe the Jewish Law. He does also refer to Jesus' birth of David's line (Rom. 1.3–4), and to his being born 'of woman, born under the Law' (Gal. 4.4). This makes it quite clear that Jesus was not a mythical figure like the deities of the mystery religions. Paul also cited the authority of Jesus for his unusual prohibition of divorce, and distinguished it carefully from his own opinions, that it is better to remain unmarried, but better to get married if that's the only way to control your sexuality, and he reapplied Jesus' teaching to the situation of married couples one of whom was a believer, and the other not (1 Cor. 7.8–16). When he expounded moral instructions in his most systematic epistle, however, he did not refer to the teaching of Jesus at all (Rom. 12–14). Why should he? He believed that he was an apostle, sent out by God to convert Gentiles to a form of Judaism in which they did not have to observe aspects of Torah such as circumcision and the dietary laws. Most of Jesus' ethical teaching was in accordance with the Torah, with some additions designed to help Jews in Galilee to relate properly to each other.[3] Paul had no need to quote details of this teaching in Rom. 12–14. He did not of course know later developments of it!

At this point, the practical difficulties of writing in the ancient world are also important. As we have seen, people like Tertius had to dip a stylus into a revolting black substance which we dignify with the name of 'ink', and scrawl with it on a piece of papyrus. This was a slow and difficult process, which would further ensure that he did not write anything unnecessary.

What Paul does not say

One of the central mistakes is repeated by Acharya from a 1909 lecture by Mangasarian: 'Is it conceivable that a preacher of Jesus could go throughout the world to convert people to the teachings of Jesus, as Paul did, without ever quoting a single one of his sayings?'[4] This is not what Paul did at all.

---

[3] Cf. Casey, *Jesus of Nazareth*, ch. 8.
[4] Acharya, *Christ Conspiracy*, pp. 32–3, quoting M. M. Mangasarian's 1909 lecture 'The Jesus of Paul', with no date and only a reference to *The Truth about Jesus* at www.infidels.org [last

He went through most of the Greek diaspora, not 'throughout the world', to convert people to 'my Gospel' (Rom. 2.16), not to 'the teachings of Jesus'. The centre of Paul's Gospel was that, through Christ's death and Resurrection, Gentiles could be justified by faith, and thus saved without taking on the observance of the Jewish Law. There was nothing about that in 'the teachings of Jesus'. Hence it was possible for the Galatians to be misled into observing a different Gospel (Gal. 1.6–12). Hence also Paul commented that 'the Gospel preached by me is not according to man, for I did not receive it nor was I taught it by man, but through revelation of Jesus Christ' (Gal. 1.12–13).

It was three years later that Paul went up to Jerusalem to talk to Cephas, and during the fortnight he stayed there, he saw none of the other apostles except for Jesus' brother Jacob (Gal. 1.18–19). It was no less than *fourteen* years before he went up to Jerusalem with Barnabas and Titus, and 'I laid before them the Gospel which I preach among the nations' (Gal. 2.2). There were what Paul calls 'false brethren' who wanted the Gentile Titus to be circumcised, but Paul did not give in to them (Gal. 2.3–5). Then 'those of repute added nothing to me' (Gal. 2.6). How could they? They preached the teachings of Jesus, plus baptism in his name, his Resurrection and other such developments, but they had nothing to add to Paul's Gospel *to Gentiles*, about which the teachings of Jesus said nothing. They accepted it as a Gospel to Gentiles, so Paul came to an agreement with 'Jacob and Cephas and John, those reputed to be pillars…that we to the Gentiles, but they to the circumcision' (Gal. 2. 9). Their preaching will have been centred on the teaching of Jesus, as Paul's could not be, because the historical Jesus did not anticipate Paul's Law-free Gospel to the Gentiles.

Wells notes that Paul mentions Jesus' descent from David, and comments that 'There are many centuries between Paul and David, and Paul gives no indication in which of them Jesus' earthly life fell.'[5] Why should he? Paul wrote in a high context situation, in which well known points did not have to be constantly repeated. Everyone interested in Jesus knew that he had been crucified recently, including all Paul's converts, who did not need tedious letters read to them by Christians who could explain anything like this to anyone new who was not familiar with the story.

Wells then quotes the radical but, in this instance, conventional German Christian scholar Bornkamm, recording 'the "astonishing" fact that Paul "nowhere speaks of the Rabbi from Nazareth, the prophet and miracle-worker who ate with tax collectors and sinners, or of his Sermon on the Mount, his parables of the Kingdom of God, and his encounters with

---

accessed 14 May 2013], the only place where I used to be able to find it. The whole collection of essays has now been reprinted more than once. My copy is *The Truth About Jesus, Is He A Myth?*, published by Kessinger Legacy Reprints (Massachusetts: Whitefish, 2010). This has a number of imperfections, including instructions for illustrations, but no actual illustrations.
[5]Wells, *Did Jesus Exist?*, p. 18.

Pharisees and scribes. His letters do not even mention the Lord's Prayer".'[6] This is a mixture of many things dear to modern Christians, and underlines the fact that Bornkamm belonged to a low context culture, which caused him to expect all these points to be repeated in occasional epistles to congregations who knew most of these points perfectly well, though they had probably not heard of the Sermon on the Mount, which was composed by Matthew, and they may not have been keen on everything else in Bornkamm's list.

Moreover, the Sermon on the Mount, composed by Matthew, not delivered by Jesus, will certainly not have been available to Paul or his converts early in his ministry. If it ever came to his notice, a quite unknown factor, he will obviously not have liked some of it any more than Luke did. For example, I have noted Mt. 5.18-20:

> Amen I'm telling you, until heaven and earth pass away, not one iota or hook will pass away from the Law, until all things are fulfilled. [19]*Therefore*, whoever undoes one of the least of these commandments and teaches people thus, shall be called least in the kingdom of the heavens. But whoever does and teaches (them), he shall be called great in the kingdom of the heavens. [20]For I'm telling you, unless your righteousness exceeds that of the scribes and Pharisees, you will *certainly not enter* the kingdom of the heavens.

Where does that leave Paul? At v. 19, he at least gets into the kingdom, but he will be least when he gets there, because the whole of his mission to the Gentiles was completely contrary to the will of God as expounded in what is here supposed to be the teaching of Jesus. Moreover, it is at least a reasonable interpretation of vv. 18 and 20 that neither he nor his converts would get there at all. Why ever should Paul repeat material of this kind in his epistles, if he had ever heard of it? His opponents, however, necessarily unaware of its domestication in later Gentile Christianity, could have made capital of it.

The other points are somewhat different from each other, and here the *genre* of the epistles is important again. Paul believed that salvation for Gentiles was due to the death and Resurrection of the Lord Jesus Christ. His converts will have known, what he did say, that Jesus was 'born of woman, born under Law' (Gal. 4.4). That he came from Nazareth, and that he was addressed as 'rabbi', would be known to those of them familiar with a narrative account of the historic ministry, but it was of no particular importance for their salvation, and Paul had no reason to mention it in

---

[6]Wells, *Did Jesus Exist?*, pp. 18–19, citing without complete details G. Bornkamm, *Paul* (1969. Trans. D. M. G. Stalker, 1971. London: Hodder & Stoughton and New York: Harper & Row), p. 110.

epistles written about particular problems in Gentile churches, nor in his systematic presentation of his Gospel (Romans). For the same reason, the fact that Jesus was called a 'prophet' during the historic ministry was of no importance.

It was of central importance to Paul that 'I will not presume to speak of what Christ did not achieve through me for the obedience of nations, by word and deed, in power of signs and wonders, and in power of the Spirit...' (Rom. 15.18–19). These were what many people call 'miracles',[7] and they were the miracles of the risen Christ performed for the salvation of the Gentiles, and accordingly far more important to Paul than the healing ministry of the historical Jesus. Moreover, similar deeds were found among the Corinthian Christians, together with features such as prophecy and speaking in tongues (1 Cor. 12.9–10, 28–31). Moreover, he subsequently reminded them, referring to himself, that 'the signs of an apostle were done among you amid every endurance, with signs and wonders and mighty works' (2 Cor. 12.12). Paul nowhere lists his own signs and wonders and mighty works; why should he list those of the historical Jesus, which would be perfectly well known in the churches anyway? Moreover, despite his severe criticisms of the Corinthians' behaviour, he knew that they did what were regarded as remarkable deeds of the same kind. By these standards, the historical Jesus' ministry of exorcism and healing was not as remarkable as conservative Christians think it was, and it is they whom mythicists follow, because they used to be conservative Christians themselves. Moreover, the *genre* of the epistles is again important at this point. Paul would have needed a *particular* reason to mention this aspect of Jesus' historic ministry in Galilee, and I cannot see that the situation of the epistles gave him one.

Wells quotes next from Bornkamm that Jesus 'ate with tax collectors and sinners'. So he did, but why should Paul write about it? His main concern about people eating together was that Jewish and Gentile Christians should eat together, and he found grave fault with Cephas because he did so normally, but when men from Jacob the brother of Jesus came to Antioch, 'he withdrew and separated himself, fearing those of circumcision, and the rest of the Jews play-acted with him, so that even Barnabas was carried away with their play-acting' (Gal. 2.12–13). This is not merely unfair to Peter and Barnabas, who naturally wanted to eat with people they knew but did not see much of at the time, some indeed probably from the ministry of Jesus. It also shows that, unless he had a good and particular reason, Paul would not want to mention that the historical Jesus ate with tax collectors and sinners. On the contrary, he would be likely to be reminded that they were all Jewish, and that Jesus ate with them to bring them back to the

---

[7]On the problems involved in the use of this term, and relevant narratives in the Gospels, cf. Casey, *Jesus of Nazareth*, ch. 7.

observance of the Torah, which is not what Paul's mission to Gentiles needed at all.

Wells' quotation from Bornkamm continues with 'his parables of the Kingdom of God, and his encounters with Pharisees and scribes'. The parables of the kingdom caused a lot of trouble for Mark, who was followed in this matter by the other synoptic evangelists (Mk 4.10–12/Mt. 13.10–15/Lk. 8.9–10). Paul would have needed a very particular reason to repeat any of them, and it should not be surprising that he did not have one. If someone read this part of Mark's Gospel at a church meeting, a lot of explanation would surely have been necessary. As for 'his encounters with Pharisees and scribes', it is difficult to imagine anything more dysfunctional. Why ever should Paul use his epistles to Gentile Christians with problems in their churches to discuss points like this?

Lastly from Wells' quotation of Bornkamm, 'His letters do not even mention the Lord's Prayer'. Wells adds his own gloss on Paul to this: 'Indeed his statement that "We do not even know how to pray as we ought" (Rom. 8:26) implies his ignorance of this prayer which the gospel Jesus introduces with the words, "Pray like this".' There are two important points wrong with this. Firstly, the Lord's Prayer did not have the iconic status in Pauline Christianity which it had in subsequent Christian history. Wells' 'Pray like this' is his own bowdlerized version of Mt. 6.9a/Lk. 11.1–2, two different attempts by the evangelists to introduce the single translation of the prayer transmitted to them, and neither introduction was from Jesus.[8] Secondly, Wells' common misinterpretation of a small part of Rom. 8.26 misrepresents the context. Paul was discussing the situation of people's complete helplessness before God, except that God's own Spirit intercedes for us with sighs too deep for words. This situation would not be met by saying a formalized prayer without the intercession of the Spirit. That some of the Church Fathers saw a problem here illustrates how iconic the status of the Lord's Prayer became, and the extraordinary extent to which mythicists depend on traditional Christianity.

Wells then proceeds to elaborate, stressing certain particular omissions: 'Paul...does not mention any of the miracles Jesus is supposed to have worked, nor does he ascribe to Jesus any of his gospel ethical teachings... These omissions are particularly significant, for ethical teachings are prominent in Paul's epistles, and Jesus' biography, as we know it from the gospels, consists almost exclusively of miracles and teachings.' On Jesus' ethical teachings, Wells elaborates further, noting that 'Paul gives them on his own authority', and 'characteristically appeals not to any words of Jesus, but to passages from the OT'.[9] This again presupposes the extraordinary extent to which mythicists rely on traditional Christianity, and do

---

[8] On this prayer, cf. Casey, *Jesus of Nazareth*, pp. 226–33.
[9] Wells, *Did Jesus Exist?*, p. 19.

not understand the extent to which, at the time of the Pauline mission, what we call 'Christianity' was a form of Judaism. In Judaism, what we call the 'Old Testament' was Holy Scripture, just as much as the Bible is among Christians now, and in the Greek world, authoritative teaching was typically ancient. That Paul should treat traditional Scriptures like this was natural, and was supposed to be decisive. We have also seen that Paul was completely confident in his own authority as an apostle sent out by the risen Christ to convert the Gentiles. These two authorities were therefore quite sufficient, and Paul's continual appeal to them underlines the fact that he was writing epistles, not a life of Jesus.

Wells offers a quite inadequate discussion of the main exception, Jesus' unique prohibition of divorce, for which Paul therefore did appeal to his teaching. Wells does not offer any proper discussion of Mark 10.2–9 at all, and this is Jesus' authentic teaching on divorce, which Paul reapplied.[10] Instead, he compares it with Mark 10.11–12, which all critical scholars know is secondary.[11] Moreover, in one book, he does so under the title 'Paul's Failure to Corroborate the Gospels', which illustrates again his massive dependence on a very conservative view of Gospel traditions, and the way in which he ignores genuinely critical scholarship. His comments do show that Mk 10.11–12 is not authentic for something like the reason he gives: 'Jesus could not, as Mark alleges, have told a Palestinian audience that a wife should not seek divorce, since in Palestine only men were allowed to do so.'[12] This was true of observant Jews, wherever they lived, though not of Gentiles in Palestine. It has nothing to do with Jesus' unique teaching in Mk 10.2–9, which begins with opponents asking him whether it was lawful for a man to divorce his wife, which became a live issue during the historic ministry because Jesus prohibited divorce. It is also the reason why Mark has a separate introduction for vv. 10–12 at Mk 10.10. Wells then takes over from unnamed scholars the notion that this was originally 'a directive given by some Christian prophet speaking in the name of the risen one'. There is, however, no reason to attribute v. 11–12 to a prophet rather than anyone else, and as an explanation of Mark 10.2–9 it would be completely unmotivated.

Wells makes numerous mistakes of this kind. To give one more example, he declares that Paul could not 'have known anything of Jesus' instruction to baptize men everywhere (Mt. 28:19); otherwise he could not have declared that "Christ did not send me to baptize" (1 Cor. 1.17)'.[13] This is another extraordinary collection of comments. It has one thing right, one thing well known to critical scholars. Paul did not know, or did not believe, Mt. 28.19. Wells' reason for this is, however, quite unconvincing,

---

[10] Cf. now Casey, *Jesus of Nazareth*, pp. 295–8.
[11] Wells, *Did Jesus Exist?*, pp. 27–8; *Historical Evidence for Jesus*, pp. 23–4.
[12] Wells, *Historical Evidence for Jesus*, p. 23.
[13] Wells, *Did Jesus Exist?*, p. 19.

and when we get the reasons straight, we shall see another reason to believe that the Gospels are not inerrant, but this in no way casts doubt on the existence of the historical Jesus. Mt. 28.19 is part of Jesus' speech to the Eleven in Matthew's only proper Resurrection appearance. It contains the important information that 'some doubted' (Mt. 28.17), which can only be there because the lack of faith of some of the Eleven was so well known that Matthew could not leave it out. The instruction to which Wells refers is 'Go therefore and make disciples of all the nations, baptising them in the name of the Father and the Son and the Holy Spirit, teaching them to keep everything which I have commanded you...' (Mt. 28.19–20). How many of them did this? None at all! Eight of them are never heard of again, except in the opening chapters of Acts, which have all of them in Jerusalem, which is unsupported Luke and hardly reliable (the extraordinary stories about Philip at Acts 8.5–13, 26–40 are more likely to be about Philip the deacon, cf. Acts 6.1–6, 8.4–8, 21.8). Moreover, of the inner circle of three, only Peter is known on the basis of reliable information to have got very far away from Jerusalem. And the decisive evidence really is that of Paul, but not the bit which Wells quotes here. As we have seen, at a meeting in Jerusalem some years after his conversion, Paul came to an agreement with 'Jacob and Cephas and John, those reputed to be pillars...that we to the Gentiles, but they to the circumcision' (Gal. 2.9). This is Jacob, brother of Jesus, and two of the inner circle both in the historic ministry and in the Jerusalem church: they evidently did not experience what Matthew reported either. [14]

It follows that Matthew's Gospel is not inerrant, and that his Resurrection story is not literally true. What has this to with whether Jesus of Nazareth was a historical figure? Nothing at all. And this is a central mistake made by mythicists. They do not seem to realize that showing that some aspects of the Gospels, or of even later Christian tradition, are not literally true, has nothing to do with whether there was a historical figure of Jesus of Nazareth. And this now after years of critical scholarship, which has demonstrated beyond reasonable doubt that the synoptic Gospels contain both accurate and secondary traditions, and one task of critical scholars should be to distinguish between the two.

Paul's comment at 1 Cor. 1.17 is quite different, and Wells has misinterpreted it. Baptism was central to the Pauline mission. Paul offers a dramatic interpretation of this in his most systematic epistle:

Or do you not know that as many of us as were baptized into Christ Jesus, were baptized into his death? So we were buried to him through baptism into his death, so that as Christ rose from the dead through the glory of the Father, so also we might walk in newness of life... So you

---

[14] Cf. further now Casey, *Jesus of Nazareth*, pp. 479–81.

too consider yourselves dead to sin, but living for God in Christ Jesus. (Rom. 6.3–4, 11, but see the whole chapter)

Paul did not mean otherwise at 1 Cor. 1.17, which Wells has taken out of context. Paul portrays the Corinthian church as split into factions, some following him, others Apollos, others Cephas, with others claiming to follow Christ (1 Cor. 1.12). This is what led him to be thankful that he personally baptized very few of them, and to say that God did not send him personally to conduct baptisms but to preach the Gospel. This would have been perfectly consistent with the Eleven being sent out to '…make disciples of all the nations, baptising them…', if only that had been what they did.

Doherty inherited this tradition and carried it much further, and in the process he unintentionally clarified the assumptions which it requires. I noted above his foundational comment firstly on the epistles: 'important fundamentals of doctrine and background, which almost two millennia of Christian tradition would lead us to expect, are entirely missing.'[15] As I commented before: 'This is clean contrary to the nature of historical research. The last thing we should expect to find in first-century documents is the deposit of centuries of later Christian tradition, and later developments should not "lead us to expect" anything of the kind.'[16]

One of Doherty's most extraordinary examples is 'Calvary'. For example, he makes up a fictional conversation between Paul and his converts, which is in effect a caricature of the view that Paul was not really interested in the historical Jesus. It includes a comment from the fictional 'Julia', who says how Paul had been to Jerusalem and 'could stand on the very spot where Jesus was crucified'. He has Paul reply: 'My dear lady, I've never been to Calvary…it's only a little hill after all.' Again, on the text of Gal. 4.4f, which is important for establishing that Paul knew perfectly well that Jesus was a historical not a mythical figure, he suggests that Paul somehow should have said: 'God sent his son to die on Calvary and rise from the tomb.'[17]

The English term 'Calvary' is virtually a transliteration of the Latin calvaria, and would therefore not have been used by Paul either in conversation with his Greek-speaking converts or in a Greek epistle. The Latin calvaria meant 'skull', so Doherty has Paul say in effect, partly in the wrong language, 'I've never been to Skull', and supposes that he should have written, again partly in the wrong language, 'God sent his son to die on Skull and rise from the tomb'. The Latin calvaria is first recorded as used as a translation of Golgotha by the Latin father Tertullian (*Against Marcion*, III, 198). Our oldest source says that they – probably a whole cohort – 'took

---

[15] Doherty, *Jesus: Neither God Nor Man*, p. 15.
[16] See p. 111.
[17] Doherty, *Jesus: Neither God Nor Man*, pp. 664, 198; cf. further pp. 194–200 below.

Jesus to the Golgotha place, which is in translation, "place of skull"' (Mk 15.22). An Aramaic word of the approximate form *gōlgōlthā* meant 'skull'. The idea of it being 'a little hill' is not known until the Bordeaux pilgrim imagined it was the place she visited in 333 CE, so this would not be known to Paul either. It is likely to have been called 'the *gōlgōlthā* place' because it was strewn with the skulls of executed people.[18] Why should Paul want to visit such a revolting place? If he went at the wrong time, such as Passover, he might well find not only a site of previous executions, but people screaming in pain as they were crucified too. Pilgrimages to such sites, and the idea they were sacred, appear to date from the time of Constantine onwards, when people were no longer crucified there.

This has nothing to do with the salvation of Gentiles as a result of the Pauline mission. Doherty has altogether misrepresented Paul's whole life world by imposing much later Christianity on him. We shall see this is important in Chapter 6, when we consider his attempt to interpret what Paul really meant in his comments about Jesus. We shall find that, here too, he completely misrepresents Paul's life-world, imposing another quite different life-world on him. Moreover, what he seeks to impose on Paul is the conservative Christianity to which he used to belong, and which he has never quite managed to leave.

Another astonishing example is Doherty imagining that Paul should have behaved like much later Christians seeking relics! At this point, we must recall that Doherty, unlike many mythicists, was not brought up as a fundamentalist Protestant, but as a conservative Catholic, who presumably adored relics in customarily ineducable Catholic ways.[19] After once again announcing 'Most astonishing of all, there is not a hint of pilgrimage to Calvary itself', he asks:

> What about the relics? Jesus' clothes, the things he used in his everyday life, the things he touched?... If the Gospel accounts have any basis *we would expect* to find mention of all sorts of relics, *genuine or fake*: cups from the Last Supper, nails bearing Jesus' flesh, thorns from the bloody crown, the centurion's spear, pieces of cloth from the garments gambled for by the soldiers at the foot of the cross – indeed, just as we find a host of relics all through *the Middle Ages*...[20]

This is an extraordinary muddle which has just one point right: relics were characteristic of Christian piety *much later*. Otherwise, it seeks to impose upon Pauline Christianity the mediaeval Catholic religion which Doherty is supposed to have left.

---

[18] Cf. now Casey, *Jesus of Nazareth*, pp. 445–6.
[19] See pp. 25–7 above.
[20] Doherty, *Jesus: Neither God Nor Man*, pp. 80, 82 (my italics).

There are two main points to be made in response to Doherty's next uncomprehending comments, which confuse them. He cannot understand why relics of Jesus, pilgrimages to the Holy Land, and shrines there did not begin until the fourth century, and he declares: 'The total absence of such things in the first hundred years of Christian correspondence is perhaps the single strongest argument for regarding the entire Gospel account of Jesus' life and death as nothing but literary fabrication.'[21] Firstly, Doherty does not understand early Christian piety, which had no need of shrines or relics at all. This is partly because of his principle of understanding it in terms of later tradition, which did. Moreover, like many traditional Christians, he has no idea that at the time of Paul and the synoptic Gospels what we call Christianity was a form of Judaism, not a separate religion.

Secondly, Doherty ignores the political situation. Until the fourth century, Christians were members of a persecuted religion, and neither major pilgrimages nor the foundation of shrines and churches in Israel were practical. In the fourth century, however, the emperor Constantine made Christianity an officially permissible religion in the Roman Empire. Then his mother, the empress Helena, made the first major Christian pilgrimage to the Holy Land, where she founded the first churches and shrines. It was she who guessed at what have become the traditional sites of both Golgotha and of Jesus' tomb, and it was her son the emperor Constantine who ordered the building of the Church of the Holy Sepulchre over both of them. The finding of the true cross, complete with nails and miraculous powers, which would have been of no interest to the apostle Paul, was attributed to her as well, though in that story it is difficult to tell where truth ends and imaginative storytelling begins.

These are but examples of Doherty's complete failure to understand early Christianity. His interpretation of it in terms of later Christianity is shown again when he notes the importance of Jewish dietary laws. At the hand of a regrettable mistranslation of Rom. 14.14, he notes the perfectly true fact that Paul did not regard any food as inherently unclean, and comments that: 'If ever there were a moment when one would expect Paul to seize on Jesus' own declared position for support, this is it. His silence can only indicate that he is truly ignorant of such traditions as those in Mark 7:14–23...'[22]

This is completely misleading. The story which ends at Mark 7.14–23 begins with a perfectly accurate account of a dispute between Jesus and 'the Pharisees and some of the scribes who came from Jerusalem' (Mk 7.1). They noticed that Jesus' disciples ate food without washing their hands (Mk 7.2), and asked Jesus 'Why do your disciples not walk according to the tradition of the elders, but eat bread with profane hands?' (Mk 7.5). This

---

[21] Doherty, *Jesus: Neither God Nor Man*, p. 82.
[22] Doherty, *Jesus: Neither God Nor Man*, p. 29.

makes it quite clear that the subject of the dispute was eating food without washing one's hands, a non-biblical custom which Jesus and his disciples did not observe. Doherty has accordingly left the main point out, by simply referring to Mark 7.14–23. Jesus' response was quite explosive. He let fly with a quotation of Isa. 29.13, and proceeded to accuse these orthodox Jews of *replacing* the commandment of God with their own tradition, and declaring that they violated the fifth commandment with their vows to the Temple (Mk 7.6–13).

All this makes perfect sense in terms of the original dispute about the non-biblical custom of washing one's hands before meals, but there is a lengthy Gentile Christian tradition which has followed Mark's Gentile Christian gloss which Doherty quotes, 'cleansing all foods' (Mk 7.19). This tradition has claimed that Jesus himself abandoned Jewish food laws, which he did not do.[23] Mark 7.14 introduces comments on the dispute attributed to Jesus. Gentile Christians have loved to follow the gloss 'cleansing all foods' at Mk 7.19, and imagine that Jesus dropped Jewish food laws. The chances of him doing any such thing were, however, negligible. The ministry was conducted almost entirely among Jews, and in places like Capernaum non-kosher food will not have been available. Jesus therefore had no motivation for dropping the food laws. Secondly, the basic food laws are biblical, so Jesus had a decisive reason for keeping them. It follows, thirdly, that if Jesus had dropped the food laws, he would have had unusual and important reasons which he could not have failed to give, and that there would be an explicit dispute about it more ferocious than that about small details of sabbath observance. Fourthly, Simeon the Rock would not have needed a vision to persuade him to eat Gentile food, and Luke would not have presented him as making the significant point that he had not previously eaten anything common or unclean (Acts 10.9–16, esp. 10.14). It follows that the words 'cleansing all foods' (Mk 7.19) are the centre of Mark's rewriting of the tradition. From a grammatical point of view, they are an obvious gloss on words attributed to Jesus. Moreover, this comment satisfies an important need of the early church, which really did need to drop Jewish food laws, because of the success of the Gentile mission. The actual saying which is interpreted like this is Mk 7.15:

There is nothing outside a man going into him which can make him unclean, but the (things which) come out of a man are what make the man unclean.

---

[23] See now Casey, *Jesus of Nazareth*, pp. 326–31, an explanation which should be comprehensible to the general reader, referring to the more complex scholarship of Crossley, *Date of Mark's Gospel*, pp. 183–205, 'Dating Mark Legally (II): Mark 7.1–23'; Y. Furstenburg, 'Defilement Penetrating the Body: A New Understanding of Contamination in Mark 7.15', *NTS* 54 (2008), pp. 176–200, both with bibliography. Crossley's discussion would have been available to Doherty, but it is a work which he shows no sign of having read.

Mark has Jesus explain this saying to the disciples 'in the house away from the crowd' in response to their asking him about 'the parable' (Mk 7.17). Jesus' explanation consists of a lengthy list of sins including adultery, theft and deceit, which come out of a man and defile him (Mk 7.18–23). If Jesus intended Mk 7.15 to mean that, he would surely not have called the crowd together in order to say Mk 7.15 to them without any such explanation, for they would not have had a hope of understanding him. He would rather have taught the crowd in terms which they could understand, a task for which vv. 21–3, with the extensive list of sins, are perfectly well adapted, provided only that this is what Jesus really meant. We must therefore infer that, like the obvious gloss in 7.19, 'cleansing all foods', the explanation of Mk 7.15 with a list of sins is part of Mark's rewriting for the early church. Jesus' criticism of the disciples' lack of understanding in needing an explanation (Mk 7.18) should also be interpreted as part of Mark's rejection of Jewish food and purity laws, when the successful Gentile mission needed them to be rejected. This fits well with Mark's criticisms of the disciples elsewhere.

At the same time, given that Mark believed his own explanation of what Mk 7.15 meant, he is most unlikely to have invented it as a single saying directed at the crowd. We must infer that Mk 7.15 was transmitted to him as part of Jesus' public teaching. Moreover, the repetition of the two halves of the verse at the end of 7.18 and in 7.20 is very like 7.15 but with some variation at a verbal level: '... everything from outside going into a man cannot make him unclean' (7.18); ... 'what comes out from a man, that makes the man unclean' (7.20). The version in Mk 7.18 has the particularly idiomatic Aramaic (or Hebrew) negative, 'everything ... not', rather than 'nothing'. We must infer that Mark used, or more probably made, two translations of the same Aramaic original, that in Mk 7.15 being slightly more idiomatic Greek.

For the original interpretation of Jesus' saying, we must turn to Jewish purity law. From this perspective, the second half of the saying is the easier to interpret: '...what comes out of a man, that makes the man unclean' (Mk 7.20). From the perspective of Jewish purity law, things coming out of people do make them unclean: the Bible specifies bodily discharge (Lev. 15.2–5), semen (Lev. 15.16–18), menstrual blood (Lev. 15.19–24), and any other discharge of blood from a woman (Lev. 15.25–30). Jesus is bound to have believed this, because these commands are biblical and unambiguous. The first part of the saying makes perfect sense in the original context of the first part of this dispute, referring to the unnecessary nature of washing to remove uncleanness from people's hands: '... everything from outside going into a man cannot make him unclean' (Mk 7.18). This is one reason why we should infer that unclean food was so remote from Jesus' environment that he did not have it in mind. Matthew's editing shows that he thought that handwashing was one main point, for he concludes his account of this dispute: 'but eating with unwashed hands does not defile the man' (Mt. 15.20). In this respect, Matthew was right.

It is probable, but somewhat uncertain, that Paul knew the original tradition of Jesus' dispute with scribes and Pharisees. Peter and the inner circle of the Jerusalem church certainly did, because they were there at the time. Paul knew that Jesus was 'born under the Law' (Gal. 4.4). It will not have occurred to him that Jesus abandoned Jewish food laws. Had he suggested this, his opponents would have had a field day. If he knew Mark 7.14–23, which he may well have done, he will have known that it was not literally true, as would the inner circle of the Jerusalem church, and his opponents. He could not possibly have used it, in Romans 14 or anywhere else.

Finally, it will be noted that my discussion depends on the points established in Chapter 3. There is real information about the historical Jesus available from the synoptic Gospels, which enables critical scholars to sort out to a significant degree which traditions are true and which are secondary development. This enables us to locate Jesus in his original Jewish environment. Doherty chooses not to address these issues himself or to take into account existing scholarship. Consequently, he has no hope of seeing how the Pauline epistles may or may not relate to it, either when they do, as for example with the issue of divorce, or when they do not, as with the issue of unclean foods.

What other Epistles do not say

Doherty puts forward similar arguments concerning what is absent from other New Testament documents, and these suffer from the same faults as his comments on the epistles of Paul.

For example, Doherty says of Jesus' mother: 'non-Gospel writings before Ignatius have nothing to say about Mary; her name is never mentioned'.[24] This is inaccurate: Luke mentions 'Mary the mother of Jesus' present at Acts 1.14. It is difficult to check up on the accuracy of this, but it is certainly there. Doherty especially comments that: 'The author of 1 Peter fails to offer Mary as a model in 3:1–6 when he is advising women to be chaste, submissive in their behaviour, and reverent like those who "fixed their hopes on (God)." Instead, he offers the biblical figure of Sarah.' This has two of the major faults which I have noted in his comments on what is absent from Paul. Firstly, later Mariolatry had not yet developed, so the author of 1 Peter did not have a significant reason to mention Jesus' mother Mary, whose behaviour may not have been well known to his audiences. Doherty has imagined Paul should have said this in the first century CE because it

---

[24] Doherty, *Jesus: Neither God Nor Man*, p. 58.

is what he was brought up to believe in the Catholic faith centuries later. Secondly, what we call the Old Testament was regarded as Holy Scripture, so the author naturally felt that the biblical figure of the major matriarch Sarah was a suitable role model for women in general.

Again, the author of the epistle to the Hebrews refers clearly to Jesus' prayer in the garden of Gethsemane and subsequent suffering:

...who in the days of his flesh offered up prayers and supplications with strong crying and tears to him who was able to save him from death. And being heard because of his godly fear, although he was Son, he learnt obedience from what he suffered, and being perfected... (Heb. 5.7–9)

It should be obvious that 'in the days of his flesh', used of someone who had been pre-existent, but who was now faced with death, and who after his death rose from the dead and was appointed a high priest after the order of Melchizedek, 'refers to Jesus' earthly life with its human weakness'.[25] Doherty, however, is determined to exclude all references to Jesus' earthly existence from the epistles. He therefore manipulates the meaning in accordance with his gross misinterpretations of the word 'flesh', which I confront in the next chapter.[26] Thus he interprets it of 'the spiritual flesh of his visit to the lower realm',[27] by which Doherty does not mean the earth, which he is determined to exclude, but a spiritual realm below the moon, where Jesus sacrificed himself in a spiritual crucifixion.

Doherty then denies that there can be any reference to a historical event on the ground that '"offering up prayers and supplications" is drawn from Ps. 116.1, which uses the same words (in the LXX version), while "loud cries and tears" [Doherty's ET of part of Heb. 5.7] is an enlargement on Psalm 22.24 "when I cried to him, he heard me" (again in the LXX wording)'.[28] Everything is wrong with this. In the first place, the LXX references are both spurious: neither reference is close enough to the wording of Hebrews for us to posit deliberate usage. Secondly, if such a biblically oriented writer as the author of the epistle to the Hebrews did use biblical language to describe an event, it would never be sufficient to show that the event did not occur.

Doherty then declares that 'Dependence on Gethsemane is also dubious since the Gospel scene is almost certainly Mark's literary invention...' Doherty offers no evidence of this. There is of course a regrettable American tradition of working like this on Mark's Gospel, using literary means to

[25] R. McL. Wilson, *Hebrews* (New Century Bible Commentary. Basingstoke: Marshall, Morgan & Scott, 1987), p. 98.
[26] See pp. 177–200.
[27] Doherty, *Jesus: Neither God Nor Man*, p. 175.
[28] Doherty, *Jesus: Neither God Nor Man*, p. 227.

turn anything consistent and coherent into Markan invention.[29] This is a particularly bad example, because if the story is not literally true, it is difficult to see why followers of Jesus should invent it. This is especially the case with Jesus' prayer, which may easily be read as showing that he was reluctant to die, which is not what his followers who believed in the atoning value of his death would need, unless it were true.

Without giving any references, Doherty then follows a long tradition of regrettable scholarship in declaring that 'The chances of such a scene forming in oral tradition are next to impossible, since it involves words and actions ascribed to Jesus which were not heard or witnessed by anyone.'[30] Comments of this kind are usually based on the fact that the inner circle of disciples went to sleep, but they assume that they did so with quite extraordinary speed. We should rather interpret the Markan narrative with care. Mark says that Jesus told the disciples when they got to Gethsemane: 'sit here while I pray' (Mk 14.32). Then he took Peter and Jacob and John with him, and when he began to be in extreme distress, he told them: '...remain here and watch. And going forward a little way, he fell to the ground and prayed...' (Mk 14.34–5). The witness of Hebrews, that he 'offered up prayers and supplications with strong crying and tears' does no more than say explicitly what would be obvious at the time, because that is how Jews in distress prayed – as far as we know, silent prayer had not been invented. Thus Peter and Jacob and John, only a 'little' way away, were in a perfect position to hear any intelligible prayers that he offered up. Mark then gives a very brief account of his prayer, including a quotation: Jesus 'prayed that if it were possible, the hour might pass from him. And he said, 'Abba (father), all things are possible for you – take this cup away from me. But not what I will, but what you (will)' (Mk 14.35–6). This is very short, and the inner group of three would hardly go to sleep too soon to hear that much. At the same time, they will not have been used to staying awake long after dark, and they had drunk more wine than usual because of Passover. Eventually, therefore, they did go to sleep. When Jesus remonstrated with the leader of the Twelve, he said: 'Simeon, you're sleeping! Did you not have the strength to watch for one hour?' (Mk 14.37). We should not take 'one hour' too literally, but we should take it seriously. They went to sleep eventually, not too soon to hear anything of Jesus' prayers.

It follows from this that Doherty's attempt to show that the author of Hebrews was not properly aware of the historical Jesus should not be regarded as successful.

---

[29] E.g. Kelber, *Passion*, pp. 41–60.
[30] Doherty, *Jesus: Neither God Nor Man*, p. 228.

Conclusions

In this chapter, I have considered what mythicists make of what they say is not mentioned in the epistles, mostly those of Paul. I have found three major mistakes underlying their arguments. One is their unacceptably late dating of the synoptic Gospels. This enables them to suppose that the Pauline epistles are our earliest sources for the life and teaching of Jesus. This leads to their second major mistake: they treat the epistles as if they were written to convey information about the life and teaching of Jesus, which they were not. Most of the Pauline epistles were written to deal with specific problems in (mostly Gentile) churches: Romans was written to present a systematic account of Paul's law-free Gospel to the Gentiles. Consequently, Paul had little reason to mention most of Jesus' life and teaching, which his churches would know from oral tradition and, by the time that he wrote most of his epistles, the Gospel of Mark.

Underlying all this is the third point. Mythicists are totally unaware that the epistles were written in a high context situation, while they themselves belong to a low context culture. This is why they constantly have unrealistic expectations of what Paul and other authors of epistles should have written.

These points, taken together, entail that the conclusions drawn from the absence of information about Jesus in the epistles are almost entirely false. I drew particular attention to the work of Doherty, because he openly and clearly lays bare an assumption of the mythicists' arguments, one which is in fact entailed by, but unnoticed in, more conventional scholarship: 'important fundamentals of doctrine and background, which almost two millennia of Christian tradition would lead us to expect, are entirely missing.'[31] The mythicists' arguments are partly dependent on Paul holding beliefs which had not yet been thought of. I noted for example Doherty's view that Paul should have visited 'a little hill' called 'Calvary'. In Paul's time the site of Jesus' crucifixion was naturally not referred to by him with the Latin term 'Calvary', nor was it believed to be a little hill. Again, I noted dependence on Gentile Christian interpretation of, for example, Jesus' view of Jewish food laws, which he upheld.

Finally, I noted that sometimes the mythicists deny references in the epistles to events in the life of Jesus when they are patently there. I discussed a clear example of this at Heb. 5.7-9. This leads us naturally into the next chapter, where I consider the drastic misinterpretation of many passages in the epistles by mythicists.

---

[31] Doherty, *Jesus: Neither God Nor Man*, p. 15.

6

What is written in the Epistles, especially those of Paul

Introduction

In the previous chapter, I discussed several things that Paul does not say. Mythicists make much of the fact that he does not mention many significant aspects of the life and teaching of Jesus. I noted that his epistles are occasional letters written to his converts. They therefore deal with immediate problems, such as whether Gentiles should undertake circumcision when they converted to what we call Christianity, which was then a form of Judaism. The epistles are not lives of Jesus, and they therefore do not discuss many aspects of Jesus' life and teaching, which they could assume were known in the churches. They were also written in a high context situation, which was homogeneous enough for people not to have to repeat everything all the time, whereas American and many other scholars belong to a low context culture, which gives them quite unrealistic expectations of what the authors of the epistles ought to have written.

Imagining that Paul did not believe anything about Jesus that he does not say in these epistles also entails creating absolute havoc with his life, as well as misinterpreting those passages in which he really does discuss aspects of the life and teaching of Jesus. The purpose of this chapter is to discuss first of all Paul's life, especially as it is misrepresented by mythicists. Secondly, I deal with those passages in which Paul does mention some aspects of Jesus' life and teaching, especially his birth and death.

The life of Paul of Tarsus

Paul was born in the Greek city of Tarsus, in Asia Minor, at roughly the same time as Jesus was born in Nazareth – we do not know the exact date. He was born of the people of Israel, 'of the tribe of Benjamin' (Phil. 3.5), so he was originally called Saul, as he is called in the early chapters of

Acts. He was 'circumcised on the eighth day...a Hebrew from Hebrews' (Phil. 3.5), so his parents were Aramaic-speaking Jews, and observant at least when they could be. He was also a Roman citizen, as we know from Acts. To be born both a Jew and a Roman citizen, this far east and as early as this, his mother, or both his grandmothers, must have been slaves, and his father, or both his grandfathers, must either have been slaves too, or they must have served in the auxiliary legions, in which case they could be granted Roman citizenship when they retired from active service. Hence Paul's Roman name, Paul, and the fact that Luke lets slip that Saul was also called Paul just when he encountered the proconsul Sergius Paulus, governor of Cyprus (Acts 13.9). Sergius Paulus was a distinguished member of the Roman gens Pauli, to a member of whom one or more members of Paul's family had been enslaved. This explains Paul's Graeco-Roman name. None of this is known to mythicists, for the highly regrettable reason that it is hardly known to conventional scholarship either. I have seen it properly presented only in a 1994 article by the classicist Peter van Minnen, which New Testament scholars have generally ignored.[1]

There is a tradition, recorded by the Church Father Jerome, that Paul's parents came from Gischala, which is in Galilee. This tradition has them taken with Paul to Tarsus (Jerome, *Commentary on Philemon*, at vss. 23–4). The tradition is plausible, but it is very late in date, and not altogether consistent (cf. Jer. *De Vir. Ill.*5), so we cannot rely on it. If it should be right, it would mean that Paul's parents were both slaves of a member of the gens Pauli in Tarsus, not that his father or grandfather were legionaries. It would also mean that Paul was circumcised on the eighth day, and called Saul, before his parents were enslaved.

Be that as it may, Paul's family background explains his shifting and changing identity: 'I became to the Jews as a Jew...to those without law as without law' (1 Cor. 9. 20–1). Given that 'law' in this context must refer to the Jewish Law, and that 'those without law' are Gentiles, this was the permanent situation of both slaves and legionaries. Jewish slaves would starve if they did not eat the food available in their owners' homes, and men who volunteered to serve in the legions would have to eat Gentile food and fight on the sabbath. At the same time, Jewish slaves could observe the Law most of the time when they had been set free, and legionaries could observe the Law at home too. This also explains Paul's comments at Rom. 7.14–25, which has nothing to do with Paul's own existential situation, and everything to do with his family background. It sets out the position of Jewish people who wished to be observant but who were overcome by sinful behaviour. Jewish slaves, legionaries, freedmen and freedwomen were in this situation all the time.

---

[1] P. van Minnen, 'Paul the Roman citizen', *JSNT* 56 (1994), pp. 43–52.

Misrepresenting Paul's life

At a quite unscholarly level, the simplest way to dispose of Paul's evidence about Jesus is perhaps to argue that Paul did not exist either. Acharya argues this.[2] Her first argument entails the overliteral interpretation of Acts which mythicists have inherited from the most conservative Christians. She quotes Acts 26.4 (without giving the reference), part of a speech in which Paul says that his manner of life from his youth 'is *known by all the Jews*' (her italics). From a literary perspective, this is appropriate in the speech which Luke puts in his mouth. Acharya, however, imagines that it entails that Josephus and others should have mentioned the surprisingly large force which Luke says was sent to Caesarea to bring Paul before the governor Felix (Acts 23.23–4, for which she does not give the reference either). In the real world, we cannot check up on the size of this force, and if Luke is accurate, that would still not give Josephus a reason to discuss such a minor incident.

This is another version of the mythicists' common argument that, if New Testament stories were true, a variety of other authors would repeat them. Acharya's second example of this kind is to point out that Gallio, proconsul of Achaia when Paul was brought briefly before his tribunal (Acts 18.12–22, for which she does not give the reference either), was the brother of Seneca, who does not mention 'Paul or the wonder-working Christ'.[3] But the incident of Paul being brought before Gallio was hardly significant enough for him to have mentioned it to Seneca when he saw him again, and Seneca was a Stoic philosopher who was most unlikely to be impressed by more stories of 'wonder-working'.

Acharya then refers to the three accounts of Paul's conversion in Acts, describing them as 'different (and apocryphal) accounts'.[4] She appears to have made the assumption, common among mythicists, that anything not demonstrably inerrant is wholly false. Paul's conversion, or call, is not in the least implausible and is required to understand a number of features of his epistles. Barrett comments much more sensibly on these three accounts:

> The agreements are much more important than the disagreements…In essentials the three Acts narratives agree with one another, and with the evidence of the epistles…Luke probably thought that in ch. 9 he was supplying the basic facts in as striking a manner as possible. The account

---

[2] Acharya, *Christ Conspiracy*, pp. 173–7.
[3] Acharya, *Christ Conspiracy*, p. 173, quoting another book by a mythicist, L. M. Graham, *Deceptions and Myths of the Bible* (Secaucus: Citadel, 1975), p. 292. It is difficult to find out anything much about Graham. Someone of this name is said to have been an American who lived 1903–34: it has also been alleged that the name is a pseudonym.
[4] Acharya, *Christ Conspiracy*, p. 173.

in ch. 22 is adapted to the Jewish audience to which it is addressed...In ch. 26...there are clear signs that Luke is abbreviating his narrative...[5]

In short, Luke was an *ancient* historian, not a conscious author of inerrant Scripture.

The remainder of Acharya's argument is based on extremely wayward comparison with Apollonius of Tyana. Apollonius lived in the first century CE, but it is extremely difficult to find accurate information about him because what information we might have had about him has been quite overlaid by a book about him written by Philostratus, and by subsequent controversies firstly in the ancient world, and continuing into modern times. Philostratus was an Athenian sophist who lived c. 170–247 CE, and he wrote a life of Apollonius at the request of the empress Julia Domna. While he had access to some information supposed to have come from Philostratus' companion Damis, his account is in general wildly legendary. Some stories are comparable to stories about Jesus, perhaps because that is where Philostratus got them from, and his work was used in anti-Christian material already at the time, and consequently attacked by Church fathers. It has been controversial ever since, but it is clear from sober scholarship that it cannot be relied upon except for a few very basic points.

There is no excuse for Acharya to continue with the bizarre description of Apollonius as 'the Nazarene', which he was not. She gives no references for this gross product of anti-Christian tradition. I have particularly noted two books. The first is by J. M. Roberts in 1892, and its subtitle indicates the unreality of its contents: *Ancient Voices from the Spirit Realms Disclose the Most Startling Revelations, Proving Christianity to be of Heathen Origin*.[6] Roberts was a spiritualist, and he declares that Philostratus personally appeared to him and revealed the 'true' story that Apollonius the Nazarene was the original figure behind false Christian stories about both Jesus and St Paul. Accordingly this was Roberts' fantasy world, not historical research! The second book is a 1964 work, *Apollonius of Tyana the Nazarene*, by R. W. Bernard, who was born as Walter Siegmeister into a family of Russian Jews in New York.[7] Bernard also wrote *The Hollow Earth: the Greatest Geographical Discovery in History Made by Admiral Richard E. Byrd in the Mysterious Lane Beyond the Poles – the True Origin of Flying Saucers*.[8] This book is dedicated 'To the Future Explorers of the

[5]Barrett, *Acts*, pp. 441, 443, 444, 445.
[6]J. M. Roberts, *Antiquity Unveiled: Ancient Voices from the Spirit Realms Disclose the Most Startling Revelations, Proving Christianity to be of Heathen Origin* (Philadelphia: Oriental, 1892. 2nd edn, 1894), pp. 16–47.
[7]R. W. Bernard, *Apollonius of Tyana the Nazarene* (New York: Fieldcrest, 1964).
[8]R. W. Bernard, *The Hollow Earth: the Greatest Geographical Discovery in History Made by Admiral Richard E. Byrd in the Mysterious Lane Beyond the Poles – the True Origin of Flying Saucers* (New York: Fieldcrest, 1964).

New World that exists beyond North and South Poles in the hollow interior of the Earth'. Bernard argued that there is an enormous land from which the Eskimos originated, and where an advanced civilization exists now. It is they who travel in flying saucers. I hope this makes clear the total lack of any sense of reality characteristic of people who produce and repeat material about Apollonius the Nazarene.

Acharya uses this tradition to play games with names, a habit of mythicists which we shall have to confront at length in Chapter 7, when we consider attempts to argue that Jesus Christ is to be found in ancient Egypt and elsewhere. She says: 'it has been claimed that "historica"' details later added to the gospel version of the mythos were taken from the life of Apollonius the Nazarene', without any proper reference to Roberts, Bernard, or anyone of that ilk. She adds that: 'In this theory, Apollonius was also called "Apollos," or "Paulus" in Latin.'[9] This had indeed been claimed before, but it is quite false.

Acharya then claims close similarities between the stories of Apollonius and Paul. As with the parallelomania which we shall have to confront in the next chapter, these comparisons have major faults. For example, she notes that, according to Philostratus, 'Apollonius "acquired from the Arabians a knowledge of the language of animals", an interesting story considering that Paul claims in Galatians that he made a three-year visit to Arabia...'[10] It should be obvious that the story of Apollonius learning the language of animals is not literally true, and that this is not what Paul went to Arabia for either. It was a large place, and it is quite ludicrous to suppose that because there are stories of two different people going there in quite different circumstances, they must be the same person really. It is a pity for us that Paul does not say a lot about why he went. The obvious reasons are to meditate on the Scriptures and God's will for him following his conversion, for which purpose there is nothing wrong with the conjecture that he went to Sinai, which he describes as in Arabia (Gal. 4.25).[11] He may then have tried to convert Aramaic-speaking Jews and Nabateans in Arabia.[12] Paul says that he returned to Damascus, and that it was after three years that he went up to Jerusalem to see Cephas, stayed for fifteen days and otherwise the only apostle he saw was Jacob, the brother of the Lord.

In a different passage in a different epistle, Paul says that 'in Damascus the ethnarch of Aretas the king was guarding the city to seize me, and I was let down through a window in a basket through the wall and escaped from his hands' (2 Cor. 11.32–3). This was obviously Aretas IV, king of the Nabateans, and this puts Paul's escape before 40 CE at the latest, which fits everything else we know about the chronology of his life. Paul must

---

[9] Acharya, *Christ Conspiracy*, p. 173.
[10] Acharya, *Christ Conspiracy*, p. 174.
[11] N. T. Wright, 'Paul, Arabia, and Elijah (Galatians 1:17)', *JBL* 115 (1996), pp. 683–92.
[12] M. Hengel, 'Paul in Arabia', *BBR* 12 (2002), pp. 47–66.

have done something to cause this trouble, and the most obvious thing for him to have done was to preach the Gospel among the Nabateans. This has nothing to do with the quite different story of Apollonius acquiring knowledge of the language of animals from the Arabians.

Acharya further claims that Paul's visit to Arabia 'or the east, also corresponds to the claim that Apollonius went to the east, where he gathered various books, including those containing the story of Krishna'.[13] This is based on the fact that Philostratus devoted two and a half of the eight books of his *Life of Apollonius* (1.19–3.58) to the description of a journey of Apollonius to India. This has nothing whatever to do with Paul going to Arabia or anywhere else.

I hope it is clear from these examples that Acharya's arguments have no connection with historical reality.

Freke and Gandy claim that Paul was a Gnostic.[14] Their discussion is one-sided and shows no understanding of Paul at all. After lots of mostly unconvincing arguments connecting Paul with Gnosticism they almost relent in their conclusions, commenting that 'Paul is neither anti-Gnostic or pro-Gnostic, because in his day the great schism between Gnostics and Literalists had yet to occur.'[15] This is almost true. Its only problem is their description of 'Literalists', which seems to have more to do with their past lives as fundamentalists, than with the Church Fathers. One of the most important points was made in 1934 by Bauer, who demonstrated beyond reasonable doubt that the ecclesiastical ideas of orthodoxy and heresy were not available at the time of St Paul. There were furious disputes, especially over Paul's mission to the Gentiles, but in these disputes, neither side could successfully appeal to authoritarian Christian orthodoxy, and get away with having their opponents dismissed by labelling them heretics.[16]

Freke and Gandy begin by claiming: 'Traditionally, Paul is viewed as a bastion of orthodoxy and a crusader against the heretical Gnostics.'[17] As usual, they give no references, and appear to be firing at the conservative Christians whom they used to be, rather than at genuinely critical scholars. Among notable scholars, I have found only strange comments by Elaine Pagels, one of the few scholars to whom they eventually refer. She declares; 'Whoever knows contemporary New Testament scholarship knows Paul as the opponent of gnostic heresy', and adds references to the regrettable German scholar Schmithals that Paul 'writes his letters…to attack

---

[13] Acharya, *Christ Conspiracy,* p. 174.

[14] Freke and Gandy, *Jesus Mysteries,* pp. 195–215.

[15] Freke and Gandy, *Jesus Mysteries,* p. 214.

[16] W. Bauer, *Orthodoxy and Heresy in Earliest Christianity* (1934. Trans. from the 2nd edn, with appendices by G. Strecker, by a team ed. R. A. Kraft and G. Kroedel. Philadelphia: Fortress, 1971. Rep. Mifflintown: Sigler, 1996).

[17] Freke and Gandy, *Jesus Mysteries,* p. 195.

gnosticism'.[18] As far as I am aware, that is not the view of normal Pauline scholars, and it has no merit, because of the reasons given by Bauer, and widely accepted ever since. Schmithals was a German soldier in the second half of the Second World War. He remained in Germany throughout his life, and wrote from a very conservative perspective. This gave him some following on the Christian right.[19]

Freke and Gandy make the perfectly true and important point that many Gnostics thought very highly of Paul. For example, Clement of Alexandria alleges that 'Valentinus was a hearer of Theudas. And he was the pupil of Paul' (*Strom.* 7.17). Such a claim would not be made by Clement unless it was believed to be true, but we cannot check up on it, and Valentinus wrote too late to be regarded as a reliable source for Paul himself. Freke and Gandy then refer to very late texts, *The Prayer of the Apostle Paul*, *The Apocalypse of Paul*, and *The Ascent of Paul*.[20] *The Prayer of the Apostle Paul* is a very short Coptic text from Nag Hammadi which cannot be dated earlier than the second half of the second century, and which cannot reasonably be said to have any connection with the ministry of the historical Paul.[21] *The Apocalypse of Paul* is another short Coptic text, also found at Nag Hammadi, and which cannot be dated before the second half of the second century.[22] It tells a story of Paul's ascent through the heavens, and it too has nothing to do with the historical Paul. It should not be confused with the Greek *Apocalypse of Paul*, which is a quite different and equally apocryphal document. *The Ascent of Paul* is known only from a report by the fourth-century Church Father Epiphanius, unless it was in fact the Coptic *Apocalypse of Paul*.

Freke and Gandy next refer to *The Acts of Paul*, commenting that this document 'describes Paul travelling with a woman called Thecla – a woman who conducted baptisms!' *The Acts of Paul*, which includes *The Acts of Paul and Thecla*, which were written by a presbyter c. 170 CE, has a complex textual history, and only *The Acts of Paul and Thecla* has been given a proper critical edition, though there is a sound English translation of all this work, which includes also *3 Corinthians*, and *The Epistle*

---

[18] E. Pagels, *The Gnostic Paul: Gnostic Exegesis of the Pauline Letters* (Philadelphia: Fortress, 1975), p. 1. I have used the 1992 reprint by Continuum (London and New York).

[19] An informative article is now available in the German version of Wikipedia. The English translation obtainable online is poor. A conservative Christian assessment of his work is provided by P. B. Boshoff, 'Walter Schmithals: His contribution to the theological and historical interpretation of the New Testament', *HTS* 67 (2011), with bibliography. Boshoff also wrote *History and Theology: Walter Schmithals on the unity of the New Testament* (Princeton Theological Monographs 47. San Jose: Pickwick, 2001).

[20] Freke and Gandy, *Jesus Mysteries*, p. 196.

[21] For an introduction and translation, see Robinson et al., *Nag Hammadi Library in English*, pp. 27–9.

[22] For an introduction and translation, see Robinson et al., *Nag Hammadi Library in English*, pp. 256–9.

of the Corinthians to Paul.[23] It was first condemned by Tertullian, who commented:

> ...if certain Acts of Paul, which are falsely so named, claim the example of Thecla for allowing women to teach and to baptize, let men know that in Asia the presbyter who compiled that document, thinking to add of his own to Paul's reputation, was found out, and though he professed he had done it for love of Paul, was deposed from his position. How could we believe that Paul should give a female power to teach and to baptize, when he did not allow a woman even to learn by her own right? Let them keep silence, he says, and ask their husbands at home. (*On Baptism* 17)

This work was nonetheless popular in parts of the ancient church, because it entertained people so much, and many Christians did not object to women as Tertullian did. It has, however, no connection with the historical Paul.

After noting correctly that Paul wrote epistles in Greek, and that his ministry was to churches in pagan cities, Freke and Gandy offer a selection of evidence in their attempt to push Paul's epistles into a Gnostic and even pagan frame of reference. For example, they say that 'Paul frequently uses terms and phrases from the Pagan Mysteries.'[24] Their first example is *pneuma,* 'spirit', which occurs over 350 times in the Septuagint, the Bible of the Greek-speaking churches, beginning with 'spirit of God was borne above the water' (Gen. 1.2). Other examples include a prophecy of a future Davidic king, 'And spirit of God will rest upon him, spirit of wisdom and understanding, spirit of counsel and strength, spirit of knowledge (*gnōseōs*) and piety, spirit of fear of God will fill him' (Isa. 11.2). This has nothing to do with pagan mysteries.

Another of their examples is *sophia,* 'wisdom'. This is also common in the LXX, especially in the wisdom literature. There we find for example that 'Beginning of wisdom [is] fear of LORD' (Prov. 1.7). A very elaborate picture of her is given in Sirach, where she gives a speech in 'assembly of Highest', and declares 'I came out of mouth of Highest and covered earth like mist. I dwelt in the heights, and my throne [was] in a pillar of cloud' (Sir. 24.2, 3–4). Then 'the creator of all' ordered her, 'dwell in Jacob, and let your inheritance be in Israel' (Sir. 24.8). After she has said more about herself, the author comments: 'All these [things] [are] book of covenant of God Most High, Law which Moses commanded as inheritance for assemblies of Jacob' (Sir. 24.23). This is different from the myth of 1 Enoch 42, where Wisdom came down to earth to live among the sons of men, but

---

[23] J. W. Barrier, *The Acts of Paul and Thecla: A Critical Introduction and Commentary* (WUNT 2, 270. Tübingen: Mohr Siebeck, 2009); Hennecke and Schneemelcher, *New Testament Apocrypha*, vol. I, pp. 213–70.
[24] Freke and Gandy, *Jesus Mysteries*, p. 199.

found nowhere to stay, so she returned to heaven and took her seat among the angels (1 En. 42.2). In the hellenized Wisdom of Solomon, Wisdom is again completely central, and even more elevated. Here we learn that 'a multitude of wise [people] is salvation of world, and a prudent king is steadiness of a people' (Wsd. 6.24). This comes after he has declared, 'Now what wisdom is, and how she came into being, I will tell, and I will not conceal mysteries from you...' (Wsd. 6.22). All this is the real cultural background of Paul, on the basis of which he preached the Gospel to Gentiles: he did not preach mystery religions to them.

Freke and Gandy further claim that 'Paul even calls himself a "Steward of the Mysteries of God", which is the technical name for a priest in the Mysteries of Serapis.'[25] This is the wrong cultural background again, and an inaccurate quotation. What Paul really says is: 'Thus let a man consider us as servants of Christ and stewards of mysteries of God', and he explains that 'what is required in stewards is that one be found trustworthy' (1 Cor. 4.1–2). He does not mention Serapis, as he would need to do if he suddenly intended to introduce anything so pagan.

They add a reference to Paul cutting his hair at Cenchreae, 'for he had a vow', without proper reference to Acts 18.18, where this is said. They declare that this is 'a curious report', which it is only because we are not supplied with more details. They further declare that it is 'not in accordance with Jewish Law, which states that hair is only to be shorn in Jerusalem'.[26] They give no reference for this, and I know of none. It was the case for a *specifically Nazirite* vow (Num. 6.18 as universally interpreted), which this therefore will not have been. They then announce that 'near Cenchreae, however, was a temple of Isis where Greek sailors cut their hair and dedicated it to the goddess as "Stella Maris", in hope of a safe crossing'. There certainly was a temple of Isis at Cenchreae. It is much more important that Paul would not have done this as a vow to Isis, because he was not a worshipper of Isis. If this was an established custom, there was nothing to stop Paul joining in it without dedicating a vow to Isis, not least because he *already* had a vow (Acts 18.18). Jewish people were perfectly entitled to make vows to God, as long as they kept them (Num. 30.2), so this shows Paul being carefully observant before he set off for Jerusalem.

Freke and Gandy further propose that the phrase 'face to face' at 1 Cor. 13.12 'is a ritual formula of the Pagan Mysteries'.[27] They ignore all the biblical examples of this normal Greek expression, as for example Gen. 32.31, where Jacob says, 'I have seen God face to face', and Deut. 34.10, where it is said that 'there rose up no more a prophet like Moses, whom

[25] Freke and Gandy, *Jesus Mysteries*, p. 199.
[26] Freke and Gandy, *Jesus Mysteries*, p. 367n. 40.
[27] Freke and Gandy, *Jesus Mysteries*, p. 200.

the Lord knew him face to face'. The LXX and normal everyday Greek are the real cultural background of Paul's comments.

Freke and Gandy then go for supposedly Gnostic comments by Paul, which they misrepresent in a similar way. They begin by claiming that 'The genuine Paul preaches the Gnostic doctrine of Illusionism, claiming that Jesus came not as a person, but in the "likeness" of human flesh.' They cannot quote any direct evidence of him preaching 'the Gnostic doctrine of Illusionism' or claiming that Jesus 'came not as a person'. For Jesus coming only 'in the "likeness" of human flesh', they begin with Rom. 8.3, which they translate conventionally as 'God sent his own Son in the likeness of *sinful* flesh' (my italics).[28] Here it is the *sinful* which is the main point of his use of the term 'likeness'. As Paul put it at 2 Cor. 5.21, 'Him who did not know sin [i.e. Christ], He [i.e. God] made sin on our behalf, so that we might become God's righteousness in him.' This has nothing to do with illusionism, or Jesus not being a man. On the contrary, it is, in Paul's view, because Jesus was a sinless man who *died* an atoning death that Gentile Christians can be redeemed through him.

Freke and Gandy next refer to Phil. 2.7, which they quote simply as 'bearing the human likeness'. This is from the so-called Philippians hymn, which is part of Paul's epistle to the Philippians, which he probably wrote with Timothy's help c. 62 CE from Rome. It is the first document in which Jesus is clearly pre-existent. It is important that this belief took some thirty years to develop, and that in two respects it fits into the more general patterns of the development of messianic and intermediary figures in Second Temple Judaism.[29] First, some of these figures were also believed to be pre-existent. Secondly, this piece is a midrash on the story of Adam. Adam was created in the image and likeness of God (*eikōn* Gen. 1.26, 27; *homoiōsis* Gen. 1.26): he did consider being on a level with God something to be grasped, for he tried to obtain it by eating of the tree of life (cf. Gen. 3.5, 22); he did not empty himself, but was punished by God for his sin, being made to work the ground and to be subject to death. It was also believed that God would highly exalt man with all the glory of Adam. This may be explicit (cf. CD III, 20; 1QS IV, 23; 1QH XVII, 15), or it may take the form of the glorification of the righteous (cf. e.g. Dan 12.3; Wsd. 3.1–9; 4.16; 5.1, 15ff; 2 Bar 51). These contrasts are so basic and extensive that they can hardly have been absent from the mind of the author of this piece.

With this in mind, we must consider some details. 'In the form of God' indicates a high status, but not necessarily full deity. The words 'form' (*morphē*) and 'image' (*eikōn*) overlap to a large extent, and there were two reasons why the author should not use 'image' at this point. First,

---

[28] Freke and Gandy, *Jesus Mysteries*, p. 201, with supporting quotations at p. 368n. 54.
[29] Cf. Casey, *From Jewish Prophet to Gentile God*, pp. 78–96, 112–17.

many Jews believed that man did not lose the image of God at the fall of Adam – hence Paul's description of a man as the 'image' (*eikōn*) and 'glory' (*doxa*) of God (1 Cor. 11.7). Secondly, 'form' is more suitable for drawing the contrast with Jesus 'taking the form of a slave' during his earthly life. Further, the form of God included his glory, the visible radiance of light that could be seen at a theophany. It is obvious that man does not possess this (cf. Rom. 3.23; 3 Bar. 4.16; Apc. Mos. 21.6). The 'form of God' was therefore something that Adam could be thought to have lost, and Jesus could be thought to have laid aside when he 'took the form of a slave'. 'Being on a level with God' (*isa theō*) indicates high status, but not full deity. The term *isa* overlaps in meaning with *k*, 'like', used at Gen. 3.5, 22, where Adam became 'like' God when he obtained knowledge of good and evil (LXX *hōs*, 'as', 'like').

All this is the real reason why this piece describes Jesus in his earthly life as 'becoming in the form (*homoiōma*) of men', and proceeds 'and being found in appearance (*schēma*) as a man'. This does not mean that he was not really a man, as is further shown by the way this piece continues: 'he humbled himself, becoming obedient unto death', which is characteristic of people, not of gods, and precisely what Gnostics denied of Jesus: 'but the death of [a] cross', which was universally recognized as the most appalling form of death imposed by the Roman imperial power.

Freke and Gandy pass to Rom. 1.9–14 and 1 Cor. 2.9. They misrepresent Rom. 1.9–14, partly at the hand of Pagels, who was openly and clearly discussing Gnostic exegesis, not what Paul meant or how the Romans would have understood him.[30] This is why she translated *charisma...pneumatikon* with the conventional English for a Gnostic term, 'pneumatic charisma', rather than 'spiritual gift', which much better represents what Paul meant and what the Romans will have understood. They translate part of Paul's text and comment: 'In his Letter to the Romans Paul writes: "I long to see you, so that I may share with you a certain Pneumatic charisma", of which he says, "I would not have you remain ignorant." If Paul wants to urgently share something with his correspondents, why doesn't he write it in his letter?'

To understand what Paul meant, we need first of all a more accurate translation. After saying that he always mentions the Roman Christians in his prayers, Paul continues,

> asking if by any means now at last I may succeed by the will of God in coming to you.[11] For I long to see you, that I may impart to you some spiritual gift so that you may be strengthened, [12]that is, to be encouraged among you through each other's faith, yours and mine. [13]For I do not

---

[30] Freke and Gandy, *Jesus Mysteries*, p. 201, misusing Pagels, *Gnostic Paul*, p. 15, referred to at p. 368n. 58, with p. 404.

want you to be unaware, brethren, that I have often planned to come to you, and I have been prevented until now, so that I might have some fruit among you too, just as among the rest of the Gentiles. (Rom. 1.10–13)

It should be obvious that what Paul does not want the Romans to remain ignorant of is not some secret spiritual gift, but his long-term plans to come to visit them, as a continuation of his mission to the Gentiles. The spiritual gift is indefinite for a quite different reason. As Cranfield put it: 'There is an intentional indefiniteness..., due to the fact that he has not yet learned by personal encounter what blessing they particularly stand in need of.' Similarly Dunn: 'What Paul has in mind here is not specified, nor could he be sure how God would bring his grace to expression in him.'[31] Moreover, unlike Freke and Gandy, Cranfield and Dunn note Paul's careful definition, indeed almost correction, of himself in v. 12, which makes clear that this is a process of mutual encouragement, not simply of Paul passing on something to the Romans. Like Paul's mission to the Gentiles in general, this would not be in any way secret or Gnostic.

Freke and Gandy's discussion of 1 Cor. 2.9 is equally misleading. The text may be translated as follows:

But as it is written, 'What eye did not see and ear did not hear, and did not go up into the heart of a man, what God prepared for those who love him.'

They comment on this only from a Gnostic perspective, declaring that 'Initiated readers would undoubtedly recognize these words as a Mystery formula pronounced at the time of initiation. The vow of secrecy undertaken by the followers of the Gnostic sage Justinus incorporated these words...' They refer to Hippolytus recording the oath of secrecy in this group, but they do not note that it is longer than this and omits the words 'as it is written'.[32]

The quotation is problematic for a quite different reason. It should obviously come from the Old Testament, but a precise parallel is not to be found there. The nearest is LXX Isa. 64.3 (for Hebrew Bible Isa. 64.4), which may reasonably be translated:

From of old we did not hear, nor did our eyes see a god beside you, and your works which you will perform for those who wait for mercy.

This is obviously not the same, though such use is perhaps implied by Clement of Rome, and more than one possible explanation for this has been suggested. It has been suggested that Paul combined Isa. 64.4 with Isa.

---

[31] Cranfield, *Romans*, p. 201, vol. 1, p. 79; Dunn, *Romans*, vol. 1, p. 30.
[32] Freke and Gandy, *Jesus Mysteries*, pp. 201–2.

65.17, but this is not precise enough to help much. It has been suggested that he knew a different text. Recent work on the Dead Sea Scrolls makes this suggestion not foolish, but it is very conjectural. Origen thought that the quotation came from the *Apocalypse of Elijah* (*On Matthew*, at Mt. 5.29). Origen was learned enough for this to be our best guess, given the unfortunate fact that the *Apocalypse of Elijah* has not survived.[33] Alternatively, it has been noted that similar sayings are very widespread in the early church, not just among Gnostics. Freke and Gandy note Gospel of Thomas, saying 17: Jesus said, 'I will give you what no eye has seen, what no ear has heard, what no hand has touched, and (what) has not arisen in the heart of man.' It is not probable that the Gospel of Thomas would take it from Paul. The large number of approximate parallels[34] suggests that Paul may have quoted from memory, intending to quote Isaiah, but actually remembering a similar proverb.

The importance of all this is that it simply shows how biased Freke and Gandy are to suggest that Paul's own interpretation of this had anything to do with Gnosticism.

They continue with translations which attempt to push what Paul says in a Gnostic direction. For example, they misquote part of Phil. 1.9, commenting: 'He offers a prayer "that your love may more and more be bursting with Gnosis".'[35] What Paul really wrote may reasonably be translated as follows:

And this I pray, that your love may abound yet more and more in knowledge [*epignōsis*, not *Gnōsis*] and all discernment, [10]so that you may approve what is vital so that you may be pure and blameless for the day of Christ, [11]being filled with the fruit of righteousness through Jesus Christ, to the glory and praise of God. (Phil. 1.9–11)

This concludes Paul and Timothy's opening thanksgiving for the faith of all members of the church in Philippi, not for a select group of Pneumatics. Like v. 6, it looks forward to the final judgement (the day of Christ), as Gnostics did not. The part of knowledge in faith does not make it Gnostic, any more than, for example, 'He who seeks the Lord will find knowledge (*gnōsis*) with righteousness' (Prov. 16.5 LXX).

Freke and Gandy do manage to notice that 'In 1 Corinthians Paul seems to diminish the importance of Gnosis, claiming "Gnosis puffs up".'[36] This is a partial quotation from 1 Cor. 8.1, which is about people in the

---

[33]For scholarly discussion, see especially Thiselton, *First Epistle to the Corinthians*, pp. 248–52.
[34]For lists of parallels, see especially DeConick, *Original Gospel of Thomas*, pp. 100–1; Plisch, *Gospel of Thomas*, pp. 72–4.
[35]Freke and Gandy, *Jesus Mysteries*, p. 203, with the reference at p. 368n. 67.
[36]Freke and Gandy, *Jesus Mysteries*, p. 368n. 67.

Corinthian church who were eating food which had been sacrificed to idols. They evidently claimed as part of their justification that 'we all have knowledge', and they may reasonably be described as 'proto-Gnostics'. Paul begins his criticism of them, 'Knowledge (*Gnōsis*) puffs up, but love builds up' (1 Cor. 8.1), and he is very critical of them. Freke and Gandy seek to sidestep this criticism by referring to Clement: 'But Clement explains that this is not to be understood as "swollen up" but means in fact "to entertain great and true sentiments," *see Stromata*, 68. To the Gnostics, including Clement, the Gnosis was the Pneumatic initiation of the holy breath or spirit.'[37] Clement does say this at *Strom.* Bk. I, ch. 16, but it is completely impossible as reasonable exegesis of 1 Cor. 8.1. It rather shows what Freke and Gandy are doing. They have decided on irrational commitment to Gnostic exegesis of Paul, regardless of what he meant when he wrote.

Freke and Gandy follow Gnostic exegesis so much that they virtually accuse Paul of believing in two Gods! The section in which they do this is quaintly called 'PAUL A.D.JEHOVAH'.[38] While Jehovah is a regrettably common version of God's name in English, Freke and Gandy do not seem to have realized that it is entirely secondary. It consists of the original consonants of God's name YHWH, with Y transcribed as J and W transcribed as V, with the vowels of *Adōnai*, 'Lord'. When Jewish people came to believe that God's name should not normally be pronounced, they called him *Adōnai*. It is this which was translated into Greek as *kurios*, which also meant 'Lord'. It should therefore be obvious that Paul did not say anything about Jehovah, though he had a lot to say about God.

Freke and Gandy comment as follows:

Paul claims that the Law is the product of the "mediator". What does he mean by calling Jehovah, supposedly the one God and lord of all, a "mediator"? If so, a mediator between what and what? The Gnostics claimed that Paul is teaching the Gnostic doctrine that Jehovah is the "demiurge", a lesser god who mediates between the ineffable supreme God and creation. Paul certainly does not regard Jehovah as the true God, for he continues: "The mediator is not one, God is one."

For this, they refer to Gal. 3.19–20 and for Gnostic exegesis only to Pagels, who was discussing gnostic exegesis, not what Paul meant.[39] This is extraordinarily uncomprehending and indeed quite malicious exegesis of Gal. 3.19–20, which may reasonably be translated as follows:

---

[37] Freke and Gandy, *Jesus Mysteries*, pp. 368–9n. 67.

[38] Freke and Gandy, *Jesus Mysteries*, pp. 209–10.

[39] Freke and Gandy, *Jesus Mysteries*, pp. 209–10, with p. 370n. 107 and 404.

> Why then the Law? It was added because of transgressions, until the seed
> should come for whom the promise was made, ordained through angels
> by the hand of a mediator. Now a mediator is not of one, but God is one.

It should be obvious that this means that the Law was ordained by God
through angels by the hand of Moses. God is accompanied by angels when
he descends to give the Law to Moses already at LXX Deut. 33.2, 'on his
right angels with him', and this is repeated in late Jewish tradition. In the
book of Jubilees, written in Hebrew c. 166–5 BCE, the Lord himself appears
to Moses on mount Sinai, as in the Hebrew Bible. However, he commands
the angel of the presence: 'Write for Moses from the first creation until
my sanctuary is built in their midst forever and ever' (Jub. 1.27). Thus
'the angel of the presence...took the tablets' (Jub. 1.29) and 'spoke to
Moses by the word of the LORD, saying, "write the whole account of the
creation..."' (Jub. 2.1). This is the cultural background to Paul's view that
'the Law was ordained through angels', a view which Luke also attributes
to an equally hellenized Jew, Stephen (Acts 7.53).

It was the universal Jewish view that, when God gave the Law to the
people of Israel, the mediator was Moses. For example, at Exod. 19.19, the
people of Israel, having seen the thunder and lightning and the mountain
of Sinai smoking stood far off, and said to Moses: 'You speak to us, and let
not God speak to us, lest we die.' Moses mediates consistently between God
and the people of Israel in this sense. This was well known to everyone,
which is why Paul did not need to say that the mediator was Moses, not
God, or that he mediated between God and the people of Israel. Freke and
Gandy seem to me to have misrepresented Paul and Judaism completely.

Another way of completely misrepresenting Paul's life is to misrepresent
his relationship with the Jerusalem church. There have been two attempts
to do this by mythicists that I feel bound to discuss. One is by Leidner,
who portrays him as completely subservient to them, and the other is by
Doherty, who imagines that they shared all the beliefs which Doherty
attributes to him.

In *The Fabrication of the Christ Myth*, the Jewish author Leidner, who
claims no more than to be 'an educated layman', portrays Paul as subservient to the Jerusalem church in terms drawn from the modern Christian
mission field. For example, after repeating selected quotations from early
radical scholarship to pour scorn on everything in the narrative of Acts,
Leidner omits the evidence of Paul himself that Jacob and Cephas and
John 'gave the right hand of fellowship to me and Barnabas, that we to
the Gentiles, but they to the circumcision' (Gal. 2.9). He refers to Acts 15
alone for 'permission' granted by 'the Jerusalem leaders' 'to preach to the
gentiles that they could join the church, but were free from observance of
the Mosaic law'. Leidner then simply declares: 'The overall evidence shows
that Paul never got this grant, that he faced hostility from the "Judaizers"
at every turn, and that quite probably he was expelled and excommunicated

from the Jerusalem church.'[40] The only truth in this is that Paul really did face a lot of hostility from people reasonably described as 'Judaizers'. The notion that he 'was expelled and excommunicated from the Jerusalem church', to which he did not belong, is a piece of creative fiction by Leidner.

Leidner next refers to Paul's first visit to Jerusalem three years after his conversion, when he went to stay with Cephas for 15 days, and saw Jesus' brother Jacob too (Gal. 1.18–19). Leidner's comments on this are, however, another piece of his creative fiction. He says that 'The simplest explanation for this meeting with the top sect leadership was that this was Paul's initiation, along with a study course in sect doctrine. Leaving Jerusalem, where he had been ordained a missionary after his study course with James, Paul took up his career as an emissary of the Jerusalem sect.'[41] This creative fiction by Leidner is contrary to the straightforward evidence of our primary sources, and the notion that Paul was 'ordained' to a 'career' is anachronistic. Leidner then has him as 'an itinerant missionary', which is true, 'far down in the ranks of the sect' and 'hard put to get a speaking engagement'. This is more creative fiction, and the notion that what he was trying to get was 'a speaking engagement' is anachronistic too.

In his subsequent discussion, Leidner lays down Jewish rules which are quite alien to anyone with a shifting and changing identity, which Leidner refuses to recognize in Paul. For example, 'We can be sure that in these two weeks in the home of Peter, and in the grim formidable presence of James, the young Paul', who must have been about the same age as Peter and Jacob, c. 35–40, which was not 'young' in the ancient world at all, 'observed each of the six hundred and thirteen rules of the Law'. These rules do not seem to have been counted as early as this, and do not include the additions which Paul will have observed as a Pharisee before his conversion. Moreover, while Paul accepted that Jews observed the whole Law, it is simply strange to say that he observed 'each of the 613 rules'. For example, he would not have needed to observe Lev. 14.10, which requires a cleansed leper to offer a sacrifice of two lambs; nor could he observe the rules for the chief priest at Lev. 21.10–15, since he wasn't one; nor will he have needed to observe Deut. 22.29, requiring a man to marry an unbetrothed virgin whom he has violated, since he did not violate an unbetrothed virgin.

Leidner adds to what Paul did, 'along with prayer, fasting and ablutions, and with total orthodoxy…Whatever he would say in later years, it is obvious from this episode that he was orthodox at this time.'[42] It is obvious to Leidner only because he has a fixed and unchangeable Jewish identity, and consequently cannot contemplate Paul's shifting and changing identity. Paul will have behaved as an observant Jew when he

---

[40] Leidner, *Fabrication of the Christ Myth*, p. 49.
[41] Leidner, *Fabrication of the Christ Myth*, p. 63.
[42] Leidner, *Fabrication of the Christ Myth*, p. 123.

was with Cephas and James. He was already behaving as he wrote down later: 'I became to the Jews as a Jew...to those without Law as without Law' (1 Cor. 9. 20–21). It is also difficult to see quite what Leidner means by 'orthodox', a term which is anachronistic when applied to this period, unless it is carefully defined. I did offer a careful discussion especially for the interpretation of the Jesus movement, its opponents, and the emergence of Christianity from Judaism in 1991, but Leidner does not refer to this.[43]

Leidner does refer later to the important incident when Paul went with Barnabas and Titus to visit the Jerusalem church (Gal. 2.1–10). However, he dates it much too late. Since he does not believe in the historical Jesus, nor in the narrative of Acts, he has no reason to follow the conventional dates for Paul's conversion, so that leaves him with no time from which to date the three- and fourteen-year intervals in Gal. 1–2. Given Paul's support for Gentile converts not having to observe Jewish Law, Leidner says of Paul that 'He was no longer a devout Jew but was now numbered with the apostates...'[44] This is entirely due to Leidner's fixed and unchangeable Jewish identity, on account of which he cannot contemplate Paul's shifting and changing identity. On that basis, Leidner makes the extraordinarily arbitrary declaration: 'The inference forced on us is that it was the catastrophic event of the fall of Jerusalem and the destruction of the Temple that had changed Paul. Therefore the chronology has to fit that.'[45] He proceeds to create his own story about that visit. Never mind that a strong Christian tradition has Paul martyred in Rome under Nero c. 65 CE, or that this fits with the narrative of Acts, which stops after his arrival there. These sources are Christian, and that is sufficient reason for Leidner to put them on one side. No one interested in historical research should follow him. Thus he ends up with Paul, Cephas who seems to have been put to death at about the same time as Paul, and Jacob who was martyred in 62 CE (Jos. *Ant.* XX, 199–203), all in Jerusalem c. 74 CE!

One other piece of falsehood by Leidner must be mentioned. On his visit to Jerusalem c. 48 CE, now dated by Leidner c. 74 CE, Paul took with him Barnabas and Titus. He comments on people whom he calls 'false brethren' who wanted Titus to be circumcised, 'to whom we did not yield in submission for a moment' (Gal. 2.4–5). Leidner ignores all recent scholarship, and follows Johannes Weiss in 1914, in arguing that the oldest reading omitted the word *oude*, so that it meant that Paul and Titus did give way and Titus was circumcised. Leidner calls the normal text 'a major forgery', and announces that 'Paul never did get his apostleship, his gospel and his independence ratified in Jerusalem.' He then comments on Paul's

---

[43] Casey, *From Jewish Prophet to Gentile God*, pp. 17–20.
[44] Leidner, *Fabrication of the Christ Myth*, pp. 123–4.
[45] Leidner, *Fabrication of the Christ Myth*, p. 124.

further comments, 'Paul is falsifying the story', and 'Word of Paul's activities got back to Jerusalem, and he was now considered a lapsed heretic'.[46]

It is now generally recognized that Weiss was mistaken. Moreover, his mistake is no excuse for Leidner's creative fiction. The omission of *oude* is almost confined to Western mss in Latin, and the *only* Greek ms to do the same is the western Codex Claromontanus of the sixth century CE. The description of the omission of *oude* as the 'oldest' reading is accordingly quite misleading. It is a *western* reading which originated in *Latin*, and it makes nonsense of Paul's whole argument. As Betz put it: 'it seems clear that the variant readings are secondary and that the reading of Nestle-Aland is to be preferred...these theological tendencies show that variant reading to be secondary.'[47]

I hope it is clear from this discussion that, like Acharya and Doherty, Leidner has no sense of historical reality.

Doherty makes equal but almost opposite nonsense of Paul's mission by imagining that the Jerusalem church agreed with the beliefs which Doherty attributes to him. He begins his book with falsehood: 'Once upon a time, someone wrote a story about a man who was God...Later generations gave this storyteller the name of "Mark"...'[48] Stephanie made the basic and important point that 'Mark doesn't! John does'. Blogger Godfrey, one of the bloggers whom Doherty regards as his constituency because he imagines that they have the freedom of the internet to have supposedly 'open minds',[49] commented that she 'borders on a dishonest representation of Doherty by her omission of the words..."Once upon a time"'.[50] This illustrates the way that Blogger Godfrey has not lost his fundamentalist attitudes, and treats unscholarly people who reach the conclusions he wants as if they had written Holy Scripture, which should be quoted complete as well as verbatim. The first main point is that this is a completely misleading opening, and that it was not Mark who did this, but the Fourth Gospel. Moreover, Doherty used to believe this because he was a conservative Catholic, and Blogger Godfrey used to believe it as a member of the Worldwide Church of God.

The second main point is that Doherty proceeds to attribute similar views to Paul and other early Christians, at the hand of his principle that

---

[46]Leidner, *Fabrication of the Christ Myth*, pp. 126–9.

[47]H. D. Betz, *Galatians: A Commentary on Paul's Letter to the Churches in Galatia*, (Hermeneia. Philadelphia: Fortress, p. 91), referring without sufficiently careful reference to B. M. Metzger (ed.), *A Textual Commentary on the New Testament* (London: UBS, 1971), pp. 591–2.

[48]Doherty, *Jesus: Neither God Nor Man*, p. 1.

[49]See pp. 3–4 above, citing Doherty, *Jesus: Neither God Nor Man*, pp. vii, viii, referring back to http://jesuspuzzle.humanists.net/Critiquesrefut1.htm and to Doherty, *Jesus Puzzle* [last accessed 7 February 2013].

[50]http://vridar.wordpress.com/2010/05/27/how-and-why-scholars-fail-to-rebut-earl-doherty/ [last accessed 14 May 2013].

the epistles should be understood in the light of much later Christian Tradition. For example, he has 'the Jerusalem tradition' believe Christ was 'a divinity who is not identified with a recent historical man', the letters of Paul and others 'start with the *divine* Christ', and the Jesus preached by the early Christians 'is a part of the very Godhead itself', even though he notes that Paul 'fails to provide any defense of the elevation of Jesus of Nazareth to divinity'.[51] None of this is justified either by careful exegesis of the Pauline letters, nor by proper evidence that early members of the Jerusalem church believed things written down in the Pauline epistles years after either of Paul's first two visits to Jerusalem, nor by proper consideration of the secondary literature to the development of New Testament Christology. For example, it is now several years since I used identity theory to explain this development, taking the almost conventional view that the full deity of Jesus is first found in the Johannine literature, and arguing that this is to be explained by that community's Gentile self-identification, which involved a serious conflict with the Jewish community.[52] Doherty does not discuss any scholarship of this kind.

This leaves Doherty with a quite unrealistic and genuinely insoluble problem. He comments: 'Yet we are to believe not only that Jews were led to identify a crucified criminal with the ancient God of Abraham, but that they went about the empire and practically overnight converted huge numbers of other Jews to the same outrageous – and thoroughly blasphemous – proposition.'[53] None of this happened. Doherty does not say who tells us to believe this. One is simply left to imagine that he got it from the hopelessly conservative Catholic faith to which he used to belong: it certainly is not the view of critical scholars. Again, since 'Paul did not invent the Christ cult', and 'the evidence in Paul clearly implies that the Jerusalem group thought as he did on the question of Jesus' divinity…it must have been thriving even in Jerusalem'. Moreover, 'Who, then, in the very heart of Israel, had turned Jesus into a cosmic deity and attached Hellenistic mythologies to him as soon as he was laid in the grave?'[54] All this is quite spurious. It is due to overinterpreting selected sentences from the Pauline epistles which had not been written at the time of Paul's second visit to Jerusalem, and simply imagining that the Jerusalem group shared the beliefs which Doherty has taken from later Christian tradition and wrongfully attributed to Paul.

The last serious distortion of Paul's life in the work of mythicists is to imagine that he did not know any of Jesus' relatives nor anyone else from the historic ministry either. Paul in fact says that on his first visit to Jerusalem he went and stayed with Cephas and saw also Jacob the brother of the Lord (Gal. 1.18–19). Again, at 1 Cor. 9.5, Paul refers to 'the rest of

---

[51] Doherty, *Jesus: Neither God Nor Man*, pp. 16, 19, 21, 22.
[52] Casey, *From Jewish Prophet to Gentile God*.
[53] Doherty, *Jesus: Neither God Nor Man*, p. 22.
[54] Doherty, *Jesus: Neither God Nor Man*, p. 23.

the apostles', i.e. other than himself and Barnabas, and 'the brothers of the Lord and Cephas'. It follows that he knew Jesus' brother Jacob, and at least knew *of* other brothers. Mythicists argue that 'brothers' does not mean 'natural brothers' but 'brethren' in the much wider sense of 'other believers'. At this point, it is again important that mythicists used to be conservative Christians: they did not believe that Jesus had natural brothers because they believed in the perpetual virginity of the Blessed Virgin Mary, a doctrine not known before the second century CE. They still do not believe that Jesus had natural brothers, but mythicists at this level are just like the fundamentalists whom they used to be – they have beliefs in accordance with their convictions, and if they have to replace the reasons for them, they go ahead and replace them with different ones.

There is no doubt that the Greek word 'brother (*adelphos*)' can refer to a colleague in a reasonably close-knit organization, as well as the sense of referring to other sons of the same parents. It is not, however, likely to be what it means in either of these passages. At Gal. 1.19, it is important that mythicists have already taken steps to argue that the Gospels should not be taken into account in interpreting the epistles, whereas in real life Paul's audiences will have known that Jesus had siblings who included Jacob (Mk 6.3).[55] Doherty, noting the perfectly correct fact that at Phil 1.14, believers are described as 'brothers *in* the Lord', announces that 'brethren in/of the Lord' were interchangeable, which was simply not the case.[56] Then he makes the convenient suggestion that the word the (*ton*) might not have been in the earliest mss, though there is no evidence of its omission. He then declares, 'I once asked if Paul had the word *ton* written in big caps', because Doherty fails to acknowledge that all mss at this date were written in large capital letters – small letters had not yet been invented.[57] This illustrates very well that, years after treating the text of the New Testament as inerrant, mythicists treat it as something they can always alter when they feel like it, in accordance with their predilections and in total contempt for anything recognizable as principles of reasonable textual criticism.

Doherty's discussion of what was possible in Greek, and of what we should call the generic use of the Greek article, seems to me confused and unconvincing. He first declares that 'there was no way to specify "*a* brother of the Lord" except by simply leaving out the definite article'.[58] Paul could, however, have done this. Secondly, he could have written *adelphos tis tou kuriou*, 'a brother of the Lord'. Thirdly, he could have written *heis tōn adelphōn tou kuriou*, 'one of the brothers of the Lord'. Paul had, however, no reason to write any of these things. Jacob was a common name in a culture which had no equivalent of our surnames, and Paul had this very

---

[55] Cf. pp. 110, 113, 136, 138, 141, 143, 155 above.
[56] Doherty, *Jesus: Neither God Nor Man*, p. 60.
[57] Doherty, *Jesus: Neither God Nor Man*, p. 62.
[58] Doherty, *Jesus: Neither God Nor Man*, p. 62.

simple way of saying which Jacob he met, in a high culture context in which further explanation was not necessary. After his inadequate discussion of the Greek article, which should have said simply that it is generic more often than e.g. the English definite article 'the', Doherty is left without a reason for Paul's description of Jacob as 'the brother of the Lord'. He ends up suggesting that it may have originated 'as an interpolation or a marginal gloss'. All this is caused by anti-historical convictions that Paul could not have referred to Jesus' brother Jacob, as he did. It is also based on an arbitrary view of New Testament textual criticism, which is hopelessly out of date.

Mythicists also have to dispose somehow of Cephas/Peter, who was the leader of the Twelve during the historic ministry. Freke and Gandy first of all suggest that Cephas was not the same person as Peter. Their first argument is that 'Paul...does not equate Cephas and Peter as one and the same person.'[59] He had no need to do this literally, because he could take it for granted. As Freke and Gandy say themselves, 'Cephas' means 'rock' in Aramaic', whereas 'Peter' means 'rock' in Greek. It is evident from Paul's epistles that 'Cephas' was in normal use among Greek-speaking members of the churches, and that he did not need to explain who this person was, as was natural when he wrote to believers familiar with stories of Jesus' ministry, in a high context situation. Turning him into two different people makes nonsense of the only passage where Paul in fact uses 'Peter'. He says of his second trip to Jerusalem after his conversion/call, when he went to see 'the men of repute (*hoi dokountes*)' (Gal. 2.2), that 'the men of repute (*hoi dokountes*)' (Gal. 2.6), 'seeing that I was entrusted with the Gospel of the uncircumcision as Peter (was entrusted with that) of the circumcision,[8] for he who empowered Peter with apostleship of the circumcision empowered me too (with apostleship) to the Gentiles,[9] and knowing the grace given to me, Jacob and Cephas and John, those reputed (*hoi dokountes*) to be "pillars", gave me and Barnabas the right (hand) of fellowship, that we to the Gentiles, but they to the circumcision' (Gal. 2.7–9). It should be obvious from this that Peter = Cephas.

Freke and Gandy's second argument depends on a strange list in a late second-century document often known as the *Epistle of the Apostles,* which they call an 'early Christian scripture'. This document has no title, and is not really an Epistle. It became known to scholars in the late nineteenth century, following the discovery of some leaves of a Coptic version, written in the fourth or fifth century, in 1895. A longer version survives in Ethiopic, the earliest known mss of which date from the eighteenth century. It is not mentioned by any early Christian writer. There is no excuse for calling this 'an early Christian scripture'. It has a list of the Twelve, with Peter third in the list and Cephas last, which happens otherwise only in the *Apostolic*

---

[59] Freke and Gandy, *Jesus Mysteries,* p. 187.

Church Order, from the late third or fourth century. That Freke and Gandy should take this seriously as an early historical source demonstrates again their total lack of concern for the date of documents, and their lack of historical sense. All it means is that a very late Christian source was written by someone who was ignorant and did not know Aramaic.

Freke and Gandy's third argument is that 'there is nothing in Paul's letters to suggest that the Cephas he meets in Jerusalem and Antioch is the Peter of the Gospels who personally knew Jesus. In fact quite the opposite'.[60] This is based on Paul's comments beginning at Gal. 2.11: 'But when Cephas came to Antioch I opposed him to his face, because he stood condemned.' They do not understand that this was because when men from Jacob came down from Jerusalem, Cephas, Barnabas and 'the rest of the Jews' stopped eating with Gentiles and ate with the men from Jacob instead. Freke and Gandy allege that Paul calls Cephas a hypocrite, which he does not. He says that 'the rest of the Jews play-acted (*sunupekrithēsan*) with him, so that even Barnabas was carried away with their play-acting (*hupokrisei*)' (Gal. 2.13). Both these words are difficult to translate. They derive from acting on stage. The noun *hupokritēs*, from which we get the English 'hypocrite', meant 'actor', though all the related Greek words were also used of insincere behaviour, especially in the political field. It is of central importance that Paul accuses all the Jewish Christians of Antioch, including his co-worker Barnabas, and he does so because he thought their behaviour would damage the preaching of the Gospel of salvation for Gentiles without their having to take on observance of Jewish Law. They are not likely to have agreed with him. Paul mentions Cephas particularly, because he was one of the leading 'men of repute (*hoi dokountes*)' in the Jerusalem church.

As often, Freke and Gandy then make up their own story about what Paul would have said if Cephas was 'the Peter of the Gospels who personally knew Jesus'. They comment: 'Yet Paul does not bring up the fact that, if Cephas is the Peter of the Gospels, he must have known that Jesus ate and drank with sinners and prostitutes and defended himself against the criticism that he was violating Jewish Laws', citing Mk 2.15–17.[61] This misses the point completely. If Paul had said anything on these lines, he would have lost the argument. Cephas and other Jewish Christians could easily have pointed out that Jesus was observant, and ate with tax collectors and sinners (not prostitutes in particular, as far as we know) to call upon them to repent and bring them back to basic observances: 'I came not to call righteous (people) but sinners' (Mk 2.17), correctly glossed 'to repentance' (Lk. 5.32). Freke and Gandy add: 'if he is the Peter of the gospels, why doesn't Paul throw in his face the fact that he had fallen asleep in the garden of Gethsemane, and denied the Lord three times with

---

[60] Freke and Gandy, *Jesus Mysteries*, p. 188.
[61] Freke and Gandy, *Jesus Mysteries*, p. 188, with p. 363n. 130.

curses, and had even been compared to Satan by Jesus himself?' (citing Mk 8.33).[62] This is completely unrealistic too. Paul was not mindlessly slagging off Cephas, and throwing at him everything he could find. If he had done this, he would have lost the argument completely too, because most people would have sided with the leader of the Twelve who had become one of the leading 'men of repute (*hoi dokountes*)' in the Jerusalem church. Paul was trying to defend his Gospel of salvation for Gentiles who did not have to observe the Jewish Law, so he criticized Cephas, Barnabas and all the Jewish Christians in Antioch for what he imagined they had done wrong, not for the sake of it.

Doherty adds an argument from 1 Cor. 9.1. Paul's opponents in Corinth seem to have challenged his apostleship, and his response includes: 'Am I not an apostle? Have I not seen Jesus our Lord?' This is an obvious reference to his conversion/call on the Damascus road, when Paul believed that the risen Christ sent him out to preach the Gospel to the Gentiles. Doherty argues that 'this implies that his type of seeing...is the same as that of the apostles to whom he is comparing himself'.[63] This argument is simply an arbitrary invention by Doherty. It was central to Paul's mission to the Gentiles that his call was *different* from the mission of apostles who were sent out during the historic ministry, or who were sent out by the churches.

What Paul does say about the historical Jesus

We have seen that mythicists make a lot of what Paul does not say about the historical Jesus. We have seen that they are seriously at fault both in dating the synoptic Gospels too late, and thus imagining that people in the Pauline churches did not know *any* Gospel stories, and in misrepresenting the genre of the Pauline and other epistles. They are not lives of Jesus. They are occasional letters, mostly written to largely Gentile churches which Paul had founded, and they were written in a high context culture. Consequently, they mention the historical Jesus only when Paul found aspects of his ministry both important for his mission to the Gentiles and relevant for the immediate problems which he discusses. Mythicists do their utmost to dispose of these relatively few references with strange exegesis and allegations of interpolations. I therefore discuss all these references in this section, beginning with Jesus' birth.

Paul discusses Jesus' birth in two important passages. One is Gal. 4.4, where he says that 'God sent his son, born of woman, born under Law...' This means that Jesus' mother gave birth to him, and that he was born as a Jew. It is not necessarily inconsistent with his pre-existence or the virgin

---

[62] Freke and Gandy, *Jesus Mysteries*, p. 188, with p. 363n. 133.
[63] Doherty, *Jesus: Neither God Nor Man*, p. 42.

174 JESUS: EVIDENCE AND ARGUMENT OR MYTHICIST MYTHS?

birth, but it does not require either of them. Jesus' pre-existence is not found with certainty until Phil. 2.6–8, which was probably written c. 62 CE. There is no sign of the virgin birth in Paul's epistles, and the first stories of it may not have been written when he wrote Galatians either, so he and his congregations may really not have believed in it. The other reference is at the beginning of Paul's most systematic epistle, written to the Romans in preparation for his first visit to them. There, in what appears to be a pre-Pauline formulation, he refers to God's son as 'born of David's seed according to flesh, [4]appointed son of God in power according to Spirit of holiness from resurrection of dead, Jesus Christ our Lord...' (Rom. 1.3–4). This also makes clear Jesus' human birth.

Doherty spends a whole chapter trying to dispose of the evidence of Gal. 4.4.[64] He begins with 'God sent his Son'. He notes that God is also said to have sent angels, personified Wisdom (citing Wsd. Sol. 9.10), and the Holy Spirit. He turns to Gal. 4.6, where Paul says that 'God sent the spirit of his son into our hearts, crying "Abba, Father".'[65] In a lengthy meandering argument in between, he declares that the subject of 'to redeem those under the Law, so that we might receive sonship' (Gal. 4.5) is God, *not* Jesus. Then he concludes that, since what he calls 'the purchase', where I have translated 'to redeem', takes place in Paul's time, the time of faith, which is more or less true, 'the sending [sc. of the son] ought to take place at the same time as the purchase'. This is arbitrary in itself, and quite inconsistent with Paul's theology. Paul believed that believers are 'justified through his [sc. God's] grace through the redemption which is in Christ Jesus, whom God set forth as a sacrifice through faith in his blood...'(Rom. 3.24–5). This is why God sent his son, and there had to be a gap between God sending him and faith in the atoning value of his death because he had to live a human life so that he could die. This also makes Doherty's dogmatic differentiation between God and Jesus in the subject of 'to redeem' at Gal. 4.5 unjustified, since the redemption could be thought of as carried out by God, who sent Jesus to die, or by Jesus, who willingly underwent his atoning death. These are no more than two slightly different ways of looking at the same event, in which both God and Jesus were obviously central.

Doherty's next argument is also quite confused. 'What has happened in this process is not that the *acts* of Jesus have just taken place, but the *effects* of them have just come into play, through their revelation and their acceptance by believers.' Translating part of Gal. 4.5 freely as 'purchase[d] freedom for the subjects of the Law', he comments: 'It has not been the death and resurrection which are the immediate cause of that freedom, and so the "God sent his son" in verse 4 should imply no reference to a

---

[64] Doherty, *Jesus: Neither God Nor Man*, pp. 197–212, ch. 15, '"Born of Woman"?'
[65] Doherty, *Jesus: Neither God Nor Man*, pp. 197–9.

life which contained such events.'[66] In fact it was Jesus' atoning death and Resurrection which were central to Paul's Gospel of salvation for Gentiles.

Nor should we forget how soon the spread of the Gospel began. In Romans 16, Paul sends greetings to many believers including Andronicus and Junia, whom he describes as 'my kinsmen and fellow-prisoners, who are outstanding among the apostles, who were also in Christ before me' (Rom. 16.7). Paul was converted/called within a year or two of Jesus' death; it follows that these are two outstanding apostles who were converted/called even earlier. That Paul describes them as '*in Christ* before me' is likely to mean that they preached the Gospel to Gentiles before he did. This would be natural for Jews in Rome or anywhere else in the diaspora. Many Jewish people believed that in the last days Gentiles would be converted, and the many Godfearers, Gentiles who were attached to synagogues throughout the diaspora, were not usually expected to be observant – indeed their existence depended on them not being generally observant, otherwise they would have been proselytes. When Paul preached throughout the diaspora, he always began in a new city in the synagogue, where he would convert a few Jews and far more Godfearers, who would then foster the spread of the Gospel by the normal process of networking.

It is unfortunate at this point that Paul does not tell us *why* he persecuted the church when he was still a Pharisee. It is noteworthy, however, that there is no record of him persecuting the followers of Jesus in Galilee, where his followers were observant and not hellenized. He first turns up agreeing to someone being persecuted at the death of Stephen, who was overtly a Hellenist (Acts 7.58, cf. 6.1–6). Only then is he found taking part in the persecution of the church in Jerusalem. After that, Luke says that he went and asked for letters from the high priest to the synagogues in Damascus, so that he could find people 'of the Way' and bring them bound to Jerusalem (Acts 9.1–2). Damascus had a flourishing Jewish community, with many hellenized Godfearers attached to it, with female proselytes. Paul himself says simply that he was 'according to Law Pharisee, according to zeal persecuting the church, according to the righteousness in Law become blameless' (Phil. 3.5–6).

It is therefore an entirely reasonably hypothesis that hellenization was central to Paul's persecution of followers of Jesus, and that this was also a central factor in his conversion/call.

Be that as it may, it should be obvious that there was no significant gap between the death and Resurrection of Jesus, and the preaching of the Gospel in his name.

Doherty further argues that 'born of woman, born under Law' (Gal. 4.4) is unnecessary for Paul's argument.[67] It is essential for Paul's argument,

---

[66] Doherty, *Jesus: Neither God Nor Man*, pp. 200–1.
[67] Doherty, *Jesus: Neither God Nor Man*, pp. 203–4.

but it is exactly what Doherty is determined not to believe. That Jesus was 'born of woman' ensures that he was a human being who could die his atoning death, and quite different from the deities of the mystery religions, of which both Paul and his converts would have some awareness. That he spent his life 'under Law' referred to the fact that he was an observant Jew, who could fulfil the prophecies made by God to his chosen people in what we call the Old Testament, and essential to his being able to redeem those under the Law, part of Paul's faith which was perfectly consistent with all this being in accordance with the overall purposes of God.

Doherty then misinterprets a few comments on this passage by Burton in his commentary on Galatians published in 1920, and fails to acknowledge subsequent scholarship.[68] His basic objection is that Paul should not have used the word *ginomai*. But as Burton said, this is unambiguous in its context precisely because Paul qualifies it with 'of a woman'. That other words for human birth were normal is quite irrelevant, because *ginomai* was normal too. For example, at Iliad V, 548, 'of Diocles were born (*egenesthēn*) twin sons'. At Hdt. VII, 11, Xerxes tells Artabanus that if he fails to punish the Athenians, he should not be 'born (*gegonōs*) of Darius, son of Hystaspes, son of Arsames' followed by more of his lineage. At PFlor 382, 38, the author refers to 'the son born (*genomenos*) of me'. At Wsd. Sol. 7.1–5, 'Solomon' describes himself as a 'mortal man', and says that he 'was fashioned in (my) mother's womb (to be) flesh (*sarx*)'. He continues, 'And when I was born *(genomenos)*, I drew in the common air and fell on the ground...' (Wsd. 7.3). Nothing could be clearer than this passage! This normal classical and Hellenistic usage continued after the New Testament period. This usage was entirely natural because birth is the way in which human beings come into existence.

Doherty then resorts to a desperate measure all too common among mythicists, and suggests that the phrase he cannot cope with is an interpolation. He first of all relies on a hypothetical reconstruction of the text of Galatians used by Marcion. For textual criticism, reports of Marcion are hopelessly unreliable, and the proposed reconstruction is based on the *Latin* text of Tertullian, writing at the beginning of the *third* century. This is not a reliable witness to what Paul wrote! Doherty then abuses some general comments on the text of the New Testament by Ehrman, who was partly concerned to refute the American fundamentalists by whom he is still surrounded. In the process, Doherty draws attention to the variant reading *gennōmenon*, and he imagines that this very late alteration, for which he does not give the proper attestation, is somehow evidence that other orthodox scribes interpolated the whole phrase, which it is not.[69]

---

[68] E. D Burton, *A Critical and Exegetical Commentary on the Epistle to the Galatians* (ICC 48. Edinburgh: T&T Clark International, 1921), pp. 218–9.
[69] Doherty, *Jesus: Neither God Nor Man*, pp. 207–11, misusing B. D. Ehrman, *The Orthodox Corruption of Scripture* (Oxford: Oxford University Press, 1993).

Doherty concludes with an argument that Paul would never have written that Christ was 'born under the Law'.[70] This is based on overliteral interpretation of selected quotations from Paul, a procedure all too familiar from the work of American fundamentalists. He begins with Rom. 3.20: 'from works of Law all flesh shall not be justified before him [i.e. God], for through Law knowledge of sin'. He uses this, with Rom. 7.7, 21 to argue that Gal. 4.4 would entail that Christ was 'subject to the Law', which it does, 'and therefore a prey to its impediments', by which from the following discussion Doherty appears to mean hopelessly sinful. All this is because Doherty cannot see that Paul presents Christ as an observant Jew because as a matter of well-known recent historical fact he was, and because from Paul's point of view Christ had to be an observant Jew in order to fulfil God's promises to humankind, which were made to his chosen people. Hence Paul appeals to the Corinthians, 'we beg for Christ's sake, be reconciled to God. [21]He [i.e. God] made him who did not know sin [i.e. Christ] sin for our sake, so that we might become God's righteousness in him' (2. Cor. 5.20–1). Again, 'Christ redeemed us from the curse of the Law, becoming a curse for us, for it is written "Cursed be everyone who is hanged on a tree" [Deut. 21.23 LXX],[14]so that the blessing of Abraham might come in Christ Jesus to the Gentiles, so that we might receive through faith the promise of the Spirit' (Gal. 3.13–14).

I have noted that the other important passage in which Paul refers to Jesus' birth is Rom. 1.3–4, where he refers to 'his son who was born of David's seed according to flesh, [4]appointed son of God in power according to Spirit of holiness from resurrection of dead, Jesus Christ our Lord...' Doherty begins his discussion with misleading comments on Paul's opening verses:

Paul, slave of Christ Jesus, called apostle set apart for Gospel of God, [2]which He promised beforehand through his prophets in holy scriptures, [3]concerning his son who was born of David's seed...

Doherty comments: 'God in scripture had looked ahead – *not to Jesus, but to the gospel that told of him.*'[71]

This is a ludicrous division of Paul's comments into two parts. Of course Paul believed that God in Scripture foretold the Gospel of God: what is quite ludicrous is that this is supposed to mean that he did *not* look forward to 'his son who was born of David's seed', as Paul so clearly says that he did. Doherty then announces what *we* would expect, which again has nothing to do with Paul: 'We would expect Paul to say that God had announced information beforehand about *Jesus*, not about his own gospel.'

---

[70] Doherty, *Jesus: Neither God Nor Man*, pp. 211–12.
[71] Doherty, *Jesus: Neither God Nor Man*, p. 88 (his italics).

Never mind that Jesus was central to Paul's Gospel. Doherty seems to be absolutely incapable of understanding that the centre of Paul's Gospel was salvation for Gentiles, and that the life, death and Resurrection of Jesus were central to that. His expectations are based entirely on his former being as a hopelessly conservative Catholic, and his membership of a low context culture.

Doherty then misinterprets Kingsley Barrett, who translated *kata sarka* somewhat freely as 'in the sphere of the flesh', to make clear that 'Paul does not mean that on a fleshly (human) judgement Jesus was a descendant of David, but that in the realm denoted by the word flesh (humanity) he was truly a descendant of David.'[72] It should be obvious that this is indeed what Paul meant. By the time Doherty has finished with it, however, it is not supposed to mean anything of the kind. He turns it into an event which took place entirely '*in the spirit world*', like the *contrasting* "'appointed son of God in power according to the Spirit of holiness from the resurrection of the dead'. No one who meant what Doherty says would write 'born of David's seed according to flesh'.

It has been correctly noted that there are not many references to the teaching of the historical Jesus in the epistles. This is because they are not lives of Jesus, but occasional letters to the churches, mostly about particular problems in them, all written in a high context situation, in which everything members believed did not have to be constantly repeated. The obvious exceptions are 1 Cor. 7.10–11 and 11.23–5. The first of these passages concerns divorce. As we have seen, Jesus' prohibition of divorce was almost unique, and required him to explain why divorce was allowed in the Torah (Mk 10.2–9).[73] This is why Paul refers to his teaching, even as he clearly applies it to the new situation required by the conversion of some Gentiles without the conversion of their married partners. He comments:

> I instruct those who are married, not I but the Lord, a woman is not to be separated from her husband – [11]but if she is separated, let her remain unmarried or be reconciled to her husband – and a man is not to divorce his wife. [12]I, not the Lord, tell the others, if a brother [i.e. a church member] has an unbelieving wife and she is willing to live with him, let him not divorce her. [13]And if a woman has an unbelieving husband and he is willing to live with her, let her not divorce her husband. (1 Cor. 7.10–13)

Here Paul begins with Jesus' teaching prohibiting divorce (7.10–11). He could not cite any other authoritative source for this, because it was not

---

[72] Barrett, *Romans*, p. 18.
[73] See p. 140 above.

the view of the Torah, and consequently not the view of the rabbis, and thus not part of traditional Jewish teaching which Paul normally takes for granted in the moral teachings in his letters. I have not noted much discussion of this passage in the work of mythicists. Doherty puts this passage with a small number of others, and announces that 'Prophets like Paul...made pronouncements which came, as they imagined it, directly from the spiritual Christ in heaven. Paul is passing on to his readers directives and promises he has received through revelation.' In a footnote, he refers only to the scholarship of Bultmann, Kelber and Mack, ignoring the fact that only Kelber really goes as far as to say that 'these sayings could have come from Jesus, but could just as well have been prophetically functioning sayings of the risen Lord', and omitting Kelber's completely inadequate reason, 'Since Q itself does not differentiate between the earthly Jesus and the post-resurrectional Christ...'. Doherty then concludes, following a quotation from Bultmann which is not about this saying at all: 'This common type of rationalization, that the early Church did not differentiate between the words of the Risen Lord and the teachings of Jesus on earth, simply masks the fact that the idea of the latter nowhere appears in the early record.'[74]

This leaves Doherty with no proper explanation of the origin of the saying attributed to Jesus at 1 Cor. 7.10–11. It makes no sense as a saying of a Christian prophet. If Jesus was not responsible for the prohibition of divorce, no Christian prophet in the diaspora would have dared to invent such disruptive teaching, and had he done so somewhere like the church at Corinth, he would not have got much of a reception from Corinthian Christians. If Paul had originated such teaching, which he was not likely to do because it was contradictory to the Jewish traditions which Paul normally drew on for his ethical teaching, he would have attributed it to himself and not to the Lord. Jesus of Nazareth, however, was an original teacher within the prophetic tradition, and this teaching fits perfectly into his efforts to foster good relationships among the Jews of first-century Galilee.[75]

Mythicists' comments on 1 Cor. 11.23–5 have been much more extensive, and contain so many mistakes that it is difficult to enumerate them all in a brief compass. Wells makes most of the major traditional mistakes, but I concentrate on refuting Doherty, because, unlike Wells, he is in a position to have read the most recent discussions.[76] The passage may reasonably be translated as follows:

---

[74] Doherty, *Jesus: Neither God Nor Man*, p. 30, with p. 716n. 15, with a partial quotation from Kelber, *Oral and Written Gospel*, p. 206, and misleading citations of Bultmann, *History of the Synoptic Tradition*, p. 127 (ignoring his comments on this passage on pp. 49–50), and of Mack, *Myth of Innocence*, p. 87n. 7.
[75] See now Casey, *Jesus of Nazareth*, pp. 295–8.
[76] Wells, *Did Jesus Exist?*, pp. 25–7; Doherty, *Jesus: Neither God Nor Man*, pp. 48–9.

For I received (*parelabon*) from the Lord, what I also handed on to you, that the Lord Jesus, in the night in which he was betrayed/handed over, took bread [24]and after giving thanks broke (it) and said, 'This is my body which is for you. Do this in remembrance of me. [25]Likewise also the cup after they had dined, saying, 'This cup is the new covenant in my blood. Do this, as often as you drink (it), in remembrance of me.' [26]For as often as you eat this bread and drink the cup, you proclaim the Lord's death until he comes.

Doherty begins by announcing that 'Since *paralambanō* elsewhere meant "received through revelation", and since Paul speaks generally about his doctrine as coming through this channel – and since the words plainly say so – this passage should mean that Paul has received this information through a direct revelation from the Lord Jesus himself.' Everything is wrong with this, beginning with Doherty's misunderstanding of how Jewish people discussed the transmission of their traditions from the fountainheads of those traditions. He gives no examples of his contention that '*paralambanō* elsewhere meant "received through revelation"', so I cannot respond directly to passages which he may have had in mind.

Almost all New Testament examples refer to receiving traditions transmitted by human beings, though this was of course believed to be a means of revelation. For example, at Gal. 1.9, Paul tells the Galatians: 'As we have said before, I also now say again, if anyone preaches to you a gospel contrary to what you received, let him be anathema!' It is obvious from the context that the Galatians received the Gospel from Paul, and he is telling them that they should not receive a different gospel preached to them by any other human beings. It should be equally obvious that this tradition of good news through human beings was believed to be divinely inspired, so it was a form of revelation. The same view of the transmission of traditions is given with the verb *paralambanō* at Mk 7.4; 1 Cor. 15.1; Phil. 4.9; 1 Thess. 2.13; 4.1, and 2 Thess. 3.6. The only exception known to me in the New Testament follows almost straight on from Gal. 1.9. At Gal. 1.12, Paul says of the Gospel preached by himself to the Gentiles: 'For I did not receive it from man, nor was I taught (it), but (I received it) through revelation of Jesus Christ.' This is clearly presented as an exception, and an exception which we know to have been essential to Paul's life, so we should not announce without further ado that he meant this wherever else he discusses his reception of a tradition.

What is of central importance is that, as I pointed out in 1998, in accordance with a long line of scholarship which was available to Wells, much expanded in the light of recent work following the discovery of the Dead Sea Scrolls, which was not available to Wells but was available to Doherty, both 'received' and 'handed on', were 'normal terms for the transmission of traditions. He [i.e. Paul] claims to have received the tradition *apo tou kuriou*,[i.e. from the Lord], thereby naming the fountainhead of the tradition, in accordance with normal Jewish custom.'[77] The most dramatic example is the rabbinical custom of describing oral traditions, which are not found in the written text of the Hebrew Bible, as *Halakha LeMoshe MiSinai*, literally 'legal judgement (given) to Moses from Sinai'. There is a particularly entertaining story of God sending Moses incognito to Rabbi Aqiba's academy, where he listened to halakhic debates:

> Not being able to follow their arguments he was ill at ease, but when they came to a certain subject and the disciples said to the master 'Whence do you know it?' and the latter replied 'It is a law given to Moses at Sinai' he was comforted. (b. Menahot 29b)

Paul's term 'received' corresponds to the rabbinical Hebrew *qbl*, and 'handed on' corresponds to the rabbinical Hebrew *msr*, both of which Paul will have been familiar with from the days when he sat at the feet of Gamaliel. Both Paul's Greek words are likewise used of the transmission and reception of Greek philosophical traditions, and of the transmission of traditions in the mystery religions. It should therefore be obvious that Paul received this tradition directly from human beings who passed it on to him. When he preached to the Corinthians c. 54 CE, he naturally handed it on to them.

However, Jewish people normally and ordinarily rewrote traditions in accordance with the needs of their communities, and this is what Paul did, as I showed by comparing his tradition carefully with that of Mark.[78] Doherty simply ignores this. The first main point is that Mark's account fits perfectly into its setting in first-century Aramaic-speaking Judaism. In particular, when Mark's Aramaic source is correctly interpreted, it makes perfect sense as an account of a Passover meal, at which Jesus did not institute the later Christian Eucharist. Christian members of a Hellenistic cult would have no motivation for inventing this Jewish setting, nor for using Aramaic idioms in so doing. Nor would they have any motivation for altering Paul's account of Jesus' institution of the Eucharist, omitting 'Do this in remembrance of me' (1 Cor. 11.23), and the 'new covenant', and any indication of repeating the occasion.

The second main point is that Paul had every reason to rewrite the tradition to control riotous Corinthian meals. He does not mention Passover, so that he can apply his instructions to 'the Lord's Supper', the communal meal in the Corinthian meetings, and he adds 'do this in remembrance of me' for the same reason. The word over the cup is now placed

---

[77] Casey, *Aramaic Sources of Mark's Gospel*, pp. 248, referring back to Casey, *Is John's Gospel True*, ch. 8, for more extensive discussion of Jewish authorship habits.

[78] See Casey, *Aramaic Sources of Mark's Gospel*, pp. 219–52 for detailed scholarly discussion, including a reconstruction of Mark's Aramaic source, and for a summary in English for the general reader, *Jesus of Nazareth*, pp. 429–37.

after the meal, so the Corinthians will not start to drink until after they have finished eating. They will therefore be much less likely to get drunk, especially not while some of them are still hungry. 'This is my blood' has been seriously altered. It was quite safe for Jesus, who so interpreted a cup of wine, which was generally known as 'the blood of the grape', when the interpretation of the elements of the Passover meal was his responsibility. He did so after the common cup had been passed around. There was therefore no danger that anyone would feel they had drunk blood. Paul has, however, dispensed with the Passover imagery, and the cultural context of the Eucharist, which ensures that Gentile Christians who take part in Eucharists do not feel they drink blood either, had not yet been established. It was therefore very sensible and responsible of him to write instead: 'This cup is the new covenant in my blood.' He added: 'Do this as often as you drink, in remembrance of me.' His rewriting was thus perfectly adapted to the needs of the Corinthian community, as he saw them.

There are also several references to Jesus' death in Paul's epistles, because he regarded it as central to the salvation of the Gentiles without their having to take on observance of Jewish Law. The most unusual is 1 Cor. 5.7: 'Christ our Passover was sacrificed.' I know of no significant discussion of this by a mythicist. It makes no sense apart from Jesus' death, nor does it make good sense as the belief of a Hellenistic cult. It makes excellent sense as the product of a community who knew that Jesus died at Passover, and that he interpreted the bread and wine at that meal as his body and blood, thereby looking forward to his sacrificial and atoning death.

Another general reference is at 1 Thess. 2.14–16. Here Paul compliments the Thessalonians for imitating the churches of God in Judaea, for they suffered the same things from their compatriots as they did from 'the Jews/ Judaeans, [15]who killed both the Lord Jesus and the prophets...' Doherty resorts to one of the favourite tricks of mythicists, by announcing that this is an interpolation, thus disposing of very clear evidence that Jesus had been put to death in Judea recently.[79] This view was held in the nineteenth century, when a number of people tried to get critical scholarship off the ground. It was deliberately revived with Bauer in mind by the maverick British scholar Brandon in 1951.[80] It has since had something of a revival in the USA, beginning with an article by Pearson in 1971.[81] As well as wrongly attributing this view to Wayne Meeks, Doherty ignores all unfavourable scholarly responses, including the major attempts by Schlueter and Bell to argue the contrary.[82] I translate here 1 Thess. 2.13–16, to include all

---

[79] Doherty, *Jesus: Neither God Nor Man*, pp. 18, 657–9.

[80] S. G. F. Brandon, *The Fall of Jerusalem and the Christian Church* (London: SPCK, 1951. 2nd edn, 1957).

[81] B. A. Pearson, '1 Thessalonians 2:13–16: a Deutero-Pauline Interpolation', *HThR* 64 (1971), pp. 79–94.

[82] Doherty wrongly cites W. Meeks, *The First Urban Christians: The Social World of the*

the verses which have been regarded by one scholar or another as an interpolation:

> And for this reason we too give thanks to God unceasingly, because when you received the word of God which you heard from us you accepted (it) not (as a) word of men but, as it truly is, word of God which is at work among you believers. [14]For you became imitators, brethren, of the churches of God which are in Judaea in Christ Jesus, because you too suffered the same things from your own countrymen as they (suffered) from the Jews/Judaeans, [15]who killed both the Lord Jesus and the prophets and drove us out and do not please God and oppose all people [16]hindering us from speaking to the Gentiles so that they might be saved, to complete their sins at all times. But wrath has come upon them until the end/completely *(eis telos)*.

Doherty ignores both the conventions of ancient rhetoric, which Schlueter presented with exceptional clarity, and Paul's shifting and changing identity. His first point is to follow the regrettable tradition of referring the end of v. 16 to the fall of Jerusalem in 70 CE. This is hopelessly anachronistic. The Jews in Judaea had all sorts of problems before that. For example, in 49 CE, shortly before the most probable date for the authorship of 1 Thessalonians, there was the Passover of the Crush. Following an incident in view of which the procurator Cumanus sent for troops, Jewish people in the Temple took fright and fled, and some 20,000–30,000 died when they could not get out (Jos. *War* II, 223–7/*Ant.* XX, 106–112). Shortly afterwards, a number of other serious problems followed, with other incidents in which many Jews were killed (Jos. *War* II, 228–44/*Ant.* XX, 113–133). This was the situation in Judaea when Paul wrote 1 Thessalonians. His interpretation that 'the wrath has come upon them' was entirely reasonable for someone of his convictions, whether he meant 'until the End', which he believed was at hand (e.g. 1 Thess. 4.15–18), or 'completely' (two possible meanings of his Greek *eis telos*).

Two other major points must be borne in mind in interpreting Paul's comments. In dealing with the term *Ioudaioi* in the Fourth Gospel, it is important that it means 'Jews' rather than merely 'Judaeans' unless the context makes the more restricted meaning clear. Here, however, Paul has just referred to 'the churches of God which are in Judaea in Christ Jesus',

Apostle Paul (New Haven: Yale Univ., 1983), p. 9n. 117 as regarding this passage as an interpolation: in fact, Meeks, p. 227n. 117, correctly attributes this view to Pearson, and does not simply accept it, though he seems to think that some material has been interpolated. Among those whom Doherty does not mention, let alone refute their arguments, are C. J. Schlueter, *Filling up the Measure: Polemical Hyperbole in 1 Thessalonians 2:14–16* (JSNTSup98. Sheffield: JSOT, 1994); R. H. Bell, *The Irrevocable Call of God: An Inquiry into Paul's Theology of Israel* (WUNT 184. Tübingen: Mohr Siebeck, 2005), pp. 56–84.

and it is they who '(suffered) from the Jews/Judaeans'. This means that the more restricted meaning, 'Judaeans', might have been primarily in his mind. On the other hand, the Passover of the Crush was attended by Jews from all over the diaspora, and Paul and the Thessalonians will not have forgotten the circumstances in which Paul had to leave Thessalonica when he first preached there.

According to Luke, when Paul preached in the synagogue there, he persuaded some people, presumably Jews, 'and a large crowd of Godfearing Greeks and not a few of the leading women' (Acts 17.4), just what he would be aiming for. The result was a riot caused by members of the Jewish community, who dragged Jason and others before the politarchs, who took security from them and let them go. The brethren therefore at once sent Paul and Silvanus away by night to Beroea (Acts 17.10). There too they preached in the synagogue, and this time 'many' Jews believed, 'and not a few of the Greek women of good standing and men' (Acts 17.12). However, when the Jews in Thessalonica found out that Paul was preaching in Beroea, some of them pursued him there too, with the result that the brethren sent him away, and he was taken to Athens (Acts 17.13–15). This is the situation reflected at 1 Thess. 2.17–3.2:

> But we, brethren, being bereft of you for a short time, in person not in heart, were exceptionally zealous with great desire to see your face, because we wanted to come to you, I Paul again and again, and Satan thwarted us...we were willing to be left in Athens alone (pl.), and sent Timothy...

This is the situation in which Paul wrote 1 Thess. 2.13–16. The conventions of ancient rhetoric allowed him to be ruder than we might imagine appropriate, and his shifting and changing identity combined with this to allow him to let fly as he did elsewhere in his epistles. Perhaps the most outstanding (but certainly not the only) example is Phil. 3.2–3: 'Beware of the dogs, beware of the evil workers, beware of the mutilation (*katatomē*). ³For we are the circumcision (*peritomē*), who worship God in spirit and boast in Christ Jesus and do not trust in the flesh...' This is also directed, not at observant Jews who have not heard the Gospel, but at Christians who were trying to compel Gentile converts to be observant, in this case to undertake circumcision.

Doherty also comments briefly on Romans 11.[83] Romans 9–11 is a very important passage in a much later and more systematic epistle, in which Paul sought to come to terms with the position of the Jewish people in salvation history. From his perspective, the Jewish people were the chosen

---

[83] Doherty, *Jesus: Neither God Nor Man*, pp. 658–9.

people, to whom he belonged, to whom the promises of God were made, and to whom the Gospel was preached. Most of them, however, did not accept the Gospel. Paul expresses his great distress at this situation, and argues that all Israel will be saved after 'the fullness of the Gentiles comes in' (Rom. 11.25). This can be reconciled with 1 Thess. 2.16 by supposing that the wrath of God came upon them literally 'until the End'. It is not obvious that this is what Paul meant, because he had not written Rom. 9–11 when he wrote 1 Thess. 2.16, but it is an entirely reasonable part of an argument of cumulative weight that 1 Thess. 2.13–16 fits perfectly into Pauline theology in general, and should not be regarded as an interpolation.

I therefore conclude that Doherty's arguments are completely unconvincing, and determined by his need for his 'results'.

Paul's epistles are full of references to Jesus' death – for example: 'while we were still sinners, Christ died for us' (Rom. 5.8); 'we believe that Jesus died and rose' (1 Thess. 4.14); 'you proclaim the Lord's death until he comes' (1 Cor. 11.26). There are several explicit references to Jesus' crucifixion – for example: 'But we preach Christ crucified' (1 Cor. 1.23); 'Far be it from me to boast except in the cross of our Lord Jesus Christ' (Gal. 6.14). There is one explicit reference to Jesus' burial, in the pre-Pauline tradition at 1 Cor. 15.3–7: 'For I handed on to you at first, what I also received, that Christ died for our sins according to the scriptures, [4]and that he was buried, and that he was raised on the third day according to the scriptures, [5]and that he appeared to Cephas, then to the Twelve...'

There is far too much evidence of this kind for it to be simply disposed of, and the interpretations of it proposed by mythicists are quite extraordinary. Doherty is among those mythicists who seek to dispose of the evidence of 1 Cor. 15.3–7, which does clearly place Jesus' death on earth by saying he was 'buried', and clearly treats it as a recent event by mentioning people who are supposed to have seen Resurrection appearances, who include both people whom Paul had met (Cephas, Jacob etc.) and people of whom he says that some were still alive.

Doherty begins from overliteral interpretation of Gal. 1.11–12, in a manner worthy of a fundamentalist. Paul's whole epistle is *about* how he preached the Gospel according to which the Galatians, like other Gentile Christians, were freed from observance of the Jewish law by faith in Jesus Christ who died for their sins. He expresses great distress that the Galatians have changed to 'another Gospel' (Gal. 1.6), and that 'if anyone preaches to you other than what you received, let him be anathema' (Gal. 1.9). This is the important context in which Paul says:

> For I am making known to you, brethren, that the Gospel which was preached by me is not according to man, [12]for I did not receive it from man, nor was I taught (it), but (I received it) through revelation of Jesus Christ. (Gal. 1.11–12)

This is an obvious reference to Paul's visionary experience on the Damascus road, when he believed that he was sent out personally by Jesus Christ to convert the Gentiles. This is what he was not taught by man. This is also why Paul was so concerned to make the point that when God 'was pleased...to reveal his Son in me, so that I might proclaim the good news of him among the Gentiles' (Gal. 1.15–16), it was three years before he went to Jerusalem to visit Cephas and met also Jesus' brother Jacob. It is ludicrous to imagine that they did not tell him anything about Jesus. It was then fourteen years before he went up to Jerusalem again, and laid before 'those of repute' 'the Gospel which I preach among the Gentiles' (Gal. 2.2). Then, as we have seen, 'those of repute added nothing to me' (Gal. 2.6). In its context, this clearly means that they had nothing to add to Paul's Gospel *to Gentiles*, about which the teachings of Jesus said nothing.[84] They accepted it as a Gospel to Gentiles, so Paul came to an agreement with 'Jacob and Cephas and John, those reputed to be pillars...that we to the Gentiles, but they to the circumcision' (Gal. 2.9).

Doherty proposes that his overliteral interpretation of Gal.1.12–13 should control our interpretation of 1 Cor. 15.3–4. Hence he comments: 'Unless we assume that he is blatantly contradicting himself, logic dictates that Paul's "received" in 1 Corinthians 15:3 must mean "received through revelation."'[85] This is not 'logic', it is Doherty's total lack of sympathy for Paul's mission to the Gentiles, expressed further in his comment that Paul 'would hardly need to defend himself against deriving it [i.e. his Gospel] from Peter and James if *all* he were referring to was freedom from circumcision and the Law – something they were not likely to be advocating' (my italics).[86] Freedom from circumcision and the Law for Gentile Christians was the centre of Paul's Gospel and his whole life after his conversion/call, not some minor point. We may think that this is not what Peter and Jacob were likely to be advocating, as indeed it was not, but it is blindingly obvious from Paul's polemic in his epistle to the Galatians that some people were persuading some other people in Galatia of the opposite: that Gentile Christian converts should be circumcised and undertake observance of the whole Jewish Law, so that Paul needed to point out that 'those of repute' accepted his Law-free mission to the Gentiles. For all we know, some people in Galatia may have suggested otherwise, and Paul is likely to have suspected this. That is why Paul needed to make so vigorously the point that 'the Gospel which was preached by me is not according to man, [13]for I did not receive it from man, nor was I taught (it), but (I received it) through a revelation of Jesus Christ' (Gal. 1.12–13).

---

[84] See pp. 57, 59, 110, 134–8, 140, 143, 150, 172–3, 186, 244.
[85] Doherty, *Jesus: Neither God Nor Man*, p. 46.
[86] Doherty, *Jesus: Neither God Nor Man*, p. 718n. 21.

This has nothing to do with the introduction to the pre-Pauline tradition at 1 Cor. 15.3–7: 'For I handed on to you at first, what I also received, that...' As I pointed out in discussing 1 Cor. 11.23–5,

> ...both "received" and "handed on", were normal terms for the transmission of traditions... Paul's term 'received' corresponds to the rabbinical Hebrew *qbl*, and 'handed on' corresponds to the rabbinical Hebrew *msr*, both of which Paul will have been familiar with from the days when he sat at the feet of Gamaliel. Both Paul's Greek words are likewise used of the transmission and reception of Greek philosophical traditions, and of the transmission of traditions in the mystery religions.[87]

It should therefore be even more obvious in the case of 1 Cor. 15.3–7 that Paul received this tradition directly from human beings who passed it on to him, and that when he preached to the Corinthians c. 54 CE, he handed it on to them. This is accordingly straightforward evidence that Paul, earlier members of the churches, and the Corinthian community, knew perfectly well that Jesus' life and death had taken place recently, and that believers, including some people who knew him while he was alive, believed that he had risen from the dead. This is what Doherty and other mythicists do not wish to know.

Jesus' death by crucifixion was historically straightforward, in the sense that crucifixion was a very common penalty inflicted by Roman authorities on slaves and provincials. It was well known as a very cruel form of death. Cicero described crucifixion as 'that most cruel and disgusting penalty' (Cic. *Verr.* 2.5.165). He commented from the perspective of a distinguished Roman citizen:

> How grievous a thing it is to be disgraced by a public court; how grievous to suffer a fine, how grievous to suffer banishment; and yet in the midst of any such disaster we retain some degree of liberty. Even if we are threatened with death, we may die free men. But the executioner, the veiling of the head and the very word 'cross' should be far removed not only from the person of a Roman citizen but his thoughts, his eyes and his ears. For it is not only the actual occurrence of these things, but the very mention of them, that is unworthy of a Roman citizen and a free man. (*Rab. Perd.* 16)

It was a regrettably well-known Roman penalty in Israel. For example, after Herod the Great's death in 4 BCE, there were a lot of rebellious upsets in Israel, and Publius Quinctilius Varus, the Roman governor of Syria, brought three legions down to Israel. After sacking Sepphoris, he went on

---

[87] See p. 181.

to Jerusalem, where he crucified no less than 2,000 people (Jos. *War.* II, 75/ *Ant.* XVII, 295). It was blindingly obvious to everyone that these events took place on earth!

Following his arrest by Jewish authorities with whom he had been in serious conflict for some time, Jesus was handed over to the Roman governor, Pontius Pilatus, who condemned him to death by this standard penalty of crucifixion. The titulus on his cross said he was 'king of the Jews', Pilate's term for a bandit, and he was crucified between two other men whom Pilate also condemned to crucifixion as bandits. This is the story which would be well known in the Pauline churches, and which Doherty is determined to omit when considering how to interpret Paul's epistles. In its place, he has a story in which Jesus was mythically 'crucified' by evil powers in the sublunar realm.

For his alternative story, Doherty draws on ideas some of which are found in Neoplatonic texts which are to be dated from before the time of Paul. For example, Xenocrates (c. 396–314 BC) already divided the universe into the realm above the moon (the supralunar) and the realm below the moon (the sublunar), and he believed that the sublunar realm was occupied by daemons. Scholars generally consider the Middle Platonic period to have begun c. 90 BCE with the work of Antiochus of Ascalon (c. 125–68 BCE). Following Xenocrates, Antiochus also expressed a belief in daemons, which inhabit the sublunar realm (the supralunar realm being reserved for the divine celestial bodies). There is, however, no evidence that such ideas were known in Judaism, the main source of Paul's ideas, nor that they were widespread enough to be generally known to his Gentile converts. Accordingly, it is of central importance that at this point Doherty completely alters one of his major points of method. Having argued up to this point that Paul did not believe anything that he does not mention, he imagines that he could take for granted this mythical realm and the quite unparalleled notion of a spiritual crucifixion up there, without mentioning anything of the kind.

In Judaism, demons lived in the underworld. At Job 7.9, 'Just as a cloud dissipates and vanishes, those who go down to Sheol will not come back.' This is where people were supposed to go after death. In due course, this developed into the idea of the punishment of the wicked under the earth. For example, in 1 Enoch 22, Enoch sees a place where the spirits of the dead have been separated, and one place 'was fashioned for the spirits of the sinners ...set apart... for the great day of judgement'. Likewise, as for the sons of God who mated with the daughters of men, 'it has been ordered to bind you in bonds in the earth for all the days of eternity' (1 En. 14.5). So 'evil spirits shall come forth from their bodies', and 'evil spirits they shall be called upon the earth' (1 En. 15.9). It would have taken a lot to move this into Neoplatonic notions of daemons in the sublunar regions, and the texts which Doherty cites for this are mostly very late in date, and not clearly Jewish.

Doherty proposes that 'Paul's Christ Jesus was an entirely supernatural figure, crucified in the lower heavens at the hands of the demon spirits'.[88] For this purpose, he uses the most conservative Christian ideas of Christ's divine nature, in which he was brought up to believe, and is supposed to have dropped. He begins from the so-called Philippians hymn, first found in an epistle probably written c. 62 CE, which Doherty interprets in the light of later Christian tradition. He describes Jesus in this hymn as 'a divine being who "shared in God's very nature"'.[89] Despite his quotation marks, Doherty provides no reference. It is very close to some translations of Phil. 2.6 which I have seen. For example, NIV has 'being in very nature God'. As we have seen, however, the text simply says 'being in the form of God', and this should be understood in the light of this piece's Adam Christology. I commented for example:

> 'In the form of God' indicates a high status, but not necessarily full deity. The words 'form' (*morphē*) and 'image' (*eikōn*) overlap to a large extent, and there were two reasons why the author should not use 'image' at this point. First, many Jews believed that man did not lose the image of God at the fall of Adam – hence Paul's description of a man as the 'image' (*eikōn*) and 'glory' (*doxa*) of God (1 Cor. 11.7). Secondly, 'form' is more suitable for drawing the contrast with Jesus 'taking the form of a slave' during his earthly life. Further, the form of God included his glory, the visible radiance of light that could be seen at a theophany. It is obvious that man does not possess this (cf. Rom. 3.23; 3 Bar. 4.16; Apc. Mos. 21.6). The 'form of God' was therefore something that Adam could be thought to have lost, and Jesus could be thought to have laid aside when he 'took the form of a slave'.[90]

Doherty, however, uses his interpretation of Phil. 2.6–11 to turn Jesus into 'this self-sacrificing deity (who operates in the celestial spheres, not on earth)'.[91]

Doherty then turns to the question of who killed Jesus. He first of all reminds his readers that he has removed 1 Thess. 2.15–16 as an interpolation, a necessary step in his argument, but one which he has not justified.[92] He then turns to 1 Cor. 2.6–8. It is clear from Paul's arguments in this chapter as a whole that some members of the church in Corinth considered themselves wise, and made significant use of the term 'wisdom'. Paul disputed this. In so doing, he claimed that 'my word and my kerygma (were) not in persuasive (words) of wisdom, but by a demonstration of

---

[88] Doherty, *Jesus: Neither God Nor Man*, p. 101.
[89] Doherty, *Jesus: Neither God Nor Man*, p. 103.
[90] See pp. 160–1.
[91] Doherty, *Jesus: Neither God Nor Man*, pp. 104.
[92] See pp. 160–1.

spirit and power, [5]so that your faith might not be in men's wisdom but in God's power' (1 Cor. 2.4–5). This is essential to understanding why Paul should continue with 1 Cor. 2.6–8:

> But we speak wisdom among the mature, but wisdom neither of this age nor of the rulers of this age/world who are being done away with. [7]But we speak the wisdom of God hidden in a mystery, which God foresaw before the ages for our glory, [8]which none of the rulers of this world/age knew. For if they had known, they would not have crucified the Lord of glory.

This makes it quite clear that Paul rejected the so-called wisdom of the Corinthians on the ground that it belonged to this world, whereas he preached salvation history, which included the crucifixion of Jesus. In subsequent verses, Paul associates his message with the Spirit, and maintains the contrast with human wisdom. For example, he comments that 'we speak not in words taught by human wisdom but in words (taught) by the Spirit' (1 Cor. 2.13). This whole context is necessary for understanding 1 Cor. 2.6–8, and Paul's comments are sufficiently unusual to have led to suggestions that Paul did not write 1 Cor. 2.6–16.[93] Doherty does not, however, discuss the possibility that *this* is an interpolation. It is too important for him to let it go!

Doherty proposes that *archontes*, the Greek word conventionally translated 'rulers' above is 'a technical term for the spirit forces, the "powers and authorities" who rule the lowest level of the heavenly world...'[94] He offers no evidence for it being a 'technical term', and I know of none. Moreover, he did manage to notice that 'In both pagan and Jewish parlance, the word *archontes* could be used to refer to earthly rulers and those in authority (as in Romans 13:3).' There is massive evidence for this, and this evidence shows clearly that it is not a 'technical term' for powers and authorities who 'rule the lowest level of the heavenly world'. Doherty might have noted particularly 'the rulers (*archontes*) of the Gentiles' (Mt. 20.25); Pilate gathering together 'the chief priests and the rulers (*archontas*) and the people' (Lk. 23.13); 'the rulers (*archontes*)' mocking Jesus when he was being crucified (Lk. 23.35); Cleopas and an unnamed follower of Jesus telling him, as yet unrecognized after his Resurrection, that 'the chief priests and our rulers (*archontes*) handed him over to the death sentence and crucified him' (Lk. 24.20); Peter addressing the people and referring to them putting Jesus to death, saying, 'I know that you acted in ignorance, as did

---

[93] Cf. e.g. M. Widmann, '1 Kor 2:6–16: Ein Einspruch gegen Paulus', ZNW 70 (1979), pp. 44–53; W. O. Walker, '1 Cor. 2:6–16: A Non-Pauline Interpretation?', JSNT 47 (1992), pp. 75–94; and the comprehensive discussion of the passage in Thiselton, *First Epistle to the Corinthians*.
[94] Doherty, *Jesus: Neither God Nor Man*, p. 104.

also your rulers (*archontas*)' (Acts 3.17); when 'their rulers (*archontas*) and elders and scribes were gathered in Jerusalem', including Caiaphas, Peter addressed them 'rulers (*archontes*) of the people and elders' (Acts 4.5, 6, 8); Peter and others applying to Jesus' death part of Ps. 2, including 'the kings of the earth appeared, and the rulers (*archontes*) gathered together against the Lord and against his anointed', which they decoded as 'there really were gathered together in this city against your holy servant Jesus whom you anointed Herod and Pontius Pilate' (Acts 4. 26–7); and Paul preaching that 'those who live in Jerusalem and their rulers (*archontes*)', not realizing who he was and being ignorant of the scriptural prophecies of his death, 'asked Pilate to have him done away with' (Acts 13.27–8).

1 Cor. 2.6–8 is so unusual that it is not surprising that there has been more than one interpretation of 'the rulers (*archontes*) of this age/ world' from the patristic period onwards.[95] In view of evidence like that surveyed briefly above, the obvious view is that it means the chief priests, elders and scribes, who brought about Jesus' death, together with Pontius Pilate, who sentenced Jesus to crucifixion, and his Roman soldiers who carried out his sentence. This also fits in with Paul's overall apocalyptic world view, according to which the present age is coming to an end, and the Age to Come, inaugurated by Jesus' Resurrection, is at hand. This is what is meant by 'the rulers of this age/world...being done away with' (1 Cor. 2.6).

The major alternative view has been that 'the rulers (*archontes*) of this age/world' were heavenly or demonic powers. This is first known as the interpretation of Marcion, appears to have been the view of Origen (see especially his commentary on 1 Cor. 2.6), and it has been prominent among modern interpreters of Paul. Barrett is among fine scholars who take this view. He notes especially the background of this age and the Age to Come in Jewish apocalyptic, and adds that: 'Paul, like many of his contemporaries, conceived the present world-order to be under the control of supernatural beings, often represented by or identified with the planets, or other heavenly objects.'[96] This view is reasonable. It must be noted that Barrett does not make Doherty's mistake of announcing, without any supporting evidence, that *archontes* is 'a technical term for the spirit forces, the "powers and authorities" who rule the lowest level of the heavenly world...'[97] This is where Doherty is certainly wrong. This view has two major problems. One is the evidence noted in favour of the first view. The other is that '*none* of the rulers of this world knew'. This means that the devil himself did not know quite what he was up to, and it is reasonable to doubt whether this is what Paul really believed.

---

[95] For a brief scholarly survey, see e.g. Thiselton, *First Epistle to the Corinthians*, pp. 233–9.
[96] Barrett, *1 Corinthians*, p. 70.
[97] Doherty, *Jesus: Neither God Nor Man*, p. 104.

Thirdly, these two views are sometimes combined. This view is also logical. If the second view is at all feasible, which it must be considered to be, the rulers of this age up there were controlling the rulers of this age down here, and they would all be done away with soon. Moreover, this view may be thought to have the advantage of explaining why Paul did not explain who 'the rulers (*archontes*) of this age/world' were: he meant all of them! The main problems with this are the same as with the second view. Expressions such as 'the rulers (*archontes*) of this age/world' normally meant the people in charge of what was left of this age/world until God brought it to an end, and *none* of the rulers of this age/world would mean that the devil did not know quite what he was up to.

Finally, the reason for some degree of uncertainty is that Paul himself was chiefly concerned to tell the Corinthians to stop playing about with the temporary wisdom of this age/world and believe in the redemptive power of Jesus' death. If I am right to favour the first of the three views noted here, he will simply not have realized that he could be taken to mean the second or third view.

Doherty adds in favour of his view that 'the rather sweeping character of the phrase', which he translates simply as 'rulers of this age', 'is at odds with a view that *all* [my italics] Paul was referring to was the Roman procurator Pontius Pilate and possibly the Jewish High Priest Caiaphas as responsible for Jesus' crucifixion. They could hardly be styled "the rulers of this age".'[98] This is completely misleading, especially in reducing the 'rulers' to one man (given the wrong title!) and 'possibly' one more! From Paul's point of view, illustrated by the passages quoted above, the Roman *praefectus* Pontius Pilate and his troops represented the Romans who ruled the world, so from an apocalyptic perspective, they ruled this age which was fast approaching its end. The chief priests, scribes and elders, *led* by the High Priest Joseph Caiaphas, plus Herod Antipas etc., ruled Judaism and Israel in the last days which would shortly be over. From Paul's perspective, these two groups of people really were 'the rulers of this age', they were responsible for crucifying Jesus, and none of them knew the 'wisdom of God hidden in a mystery, which God foresaw before the ages' (1 Cor. 2.7).

Doherty turns next to Eph. 3.9–10. This epistle was not written by Paul, but by one of his followers, not earlier than the end of the first century, and more probably in the second. He does not use the word *ekklēsia*, 'assembly, church', for individual churches, as Paul did most of the time, but only for the one universal church, for the unity of which he was very concerned. He was writing for, and probably in, Asia Minor, and he was evidently concerned about differences among Christians in the area which eventually produced Marcion, whom the author may or may not have known. He knew and used Colossians a lot.

---

[98] Doherty, *Jesus: Neither God Nor Man*, p. 105.

At Eph. 3.9–12, pseudo-Paul explains his Gospel to the Gentiles like this:

to enlighten everyone as to what is the management of the mystery hidden from the ages in God who created everything, [10]so that the manifold wisdom of God might be known now to the authorities (*archais*) and powers in the heavenlies through the church, [11]according to the purpose of the ages which he carried out in Christ Jesus our Lord, [12]in whom we have boldness and access in confidence through faith in him.

Doherty's comments are a mixture of truth and bias. This time pseudo-Paul's 'authorities and powers' really are up there 'in the heavenlies'. It should be noted, however, that, to make his meaning clear, Pseudo-Paul had to specify this. Doherty adds:

This writer is consistent with general Pauline expression in allotting the task of revealing God's long-hidden mystery to the 'church', to men like himself, not to any recent historical Jesus. The last phrase of the quote refers to the workings of Christ in the higher spiritual world, his redeeming actions within God's eternal realm and time. In other words, the world of myth.[99]

The first part of this is true, and the rest of it is false. The real historical Jesus had nothing to do with how 'the Gentiles are co-heirs and belonging to the same body and sharing in the promise in Christ Jesus through the Gospel [7]of which I became a minister according to the gift of the grace of God given to me...' (Eph. 3.6–7). Neither Paul nor his immediate followers imagined that he had, either. That is no excuse for attributing to this author the notion that 'redemption through his blood' (Eph. 1.7), *after* which God 'raised him from the dead and sat (him) at his right hand in the heavenlies' (Eph. 1. 20), *all* took place *only* 'in the higher spiritual world'.

Doherty turns next to a regrettable translation of Col. 2.15, which was not written by Paul personally either, as it is not in his Greek style. However, it claims to be from Paul and Timothy when Paul was in prison, so it may well have been written by Timothy when Paul was in prison, leaving Paul to add his greeting at the end in his own hand (Col. 4.18).[100] It does not contain developments which would make that improbable. After a presentation of God's work in Christ, the author makes a somewhat metaphorical and perhaps even overblown declaration, which may reasonably be translated as follows:

---

[99] Doherty, *Jesus: Neither God Nor Man*, p. 105.
[100] J. D. G. Dunn, *The Epistles to the Colossians and to Philemon* (NIGCT. Grand Rapids Eerdmans and Carlisle: Paternoster, 1996), pp. 35–8.

And you, who were dead in transgressions and in the uncircumcision of your flesh, He [i.e. God] made you alive with him, forgiving us all transgressions. [14]Having obliterated the account against us with its requirements, which was against us, he removed it from among us, nailing it to the cross. [15]Having disarmed the authorities (*archas*) and powers, he openly disgraced them, triumphing over them. (Col. 2.13–15)

On the basis only of a regrettable translation of v. 15 alone, Doherty declares that this verse 'again places Jesus' crucifixion in a supernatural milieu, for it is difficult to see any historical scene on Calvary contained in this idea'.[101] Once again, we see here Doherty's assumption that Paul ought to have repeated Calvary if he believed that Jesus was crucified on earth. Calvary was, however, characteristic of much later Christian piety, to which Doherty used to belong. This passage is characteristic of the Christian piety best known from the Pauline epistles, in which the major importance of Jesus' crucifixion was that it led to the salvation of Gentiles, to which Timothy has added the defeat of supernatural powers. These comments embody also again Doherty's double standard, according to which Paul would have mentioned Jesus' crucifixion was on earth if he believed anything so obvious in a society where crucifixion was a common event, but did not need to mention that Jesus was crucified in the sublunar realms of the heavenlies, an otherwise unknown idea.

Doherty does eventually try to produce evidence which he imagines makes the crucifixion of Jesus in the sublunar realm plausible. The first document which he mentions in this context is *The Hypostasis of the Archons*, a Gnostic work of the third century CE, which survives only in one Coptic ms from Nag Hammadi, though it is often assumed to have been originally written in Greek.[102] This really does refer to Paul as 'the father of truth, the great apostle', and at 87, 24 it does refer to the rulers (*archontes*). Doherty uses it to claim that 'considering that the roots of Gnosticism go back before the establishment of an historical Jesus in the Gospels, we are once again witnessing an understanding of archontic rulers as spirit demons unassociated with any earthly princes, and thus a pointer to the older understanding in the time of Paul'.[103] This predating of selected parts of a text from the third century CE shows a total lack of historical sense. This document also has Adam created by 'the rulers (*archontes*)' (87, 25ff), and in typical late Gnostic fashion, it has the being who declared himself the one God be a blind being who was sinful, and it does not present the death of

---

[101] Doherty, *Jesus: Neither God Nor Man*, p. 105.
[102] For an English translation by Bentley Layton, with a very brief introduction by R. A. Bullard, see J. M. Robinson (general ed.) and Members of the Coptic Gnostic Library Project of the Institute for Antiquity and Christianity, Claremont, California, *The Nag Hammadi Library in English* (Leiden: Brill, 4th edn, 1996), pp. 161–9.
[103] Doherty, *Jesus: Neither God Nor Man*, p. 109.

Jesus at all. It should be obvious that this source is too late and unPauline to be used to interpret the historical Paul.

Doherty correctly notes that evil spirits come into their own in the apocrypha and pseudepigrapha. He correctly refers to 1 Enoch, which was written well before the time of Paul. Next he refers confidently to the '1st century Testament of Solomon'.[104] This is much too early a date. Schürer-Vermes-Millar, in a section primarily the responsibility of Vermes, note correctly that its 'complex textual history naturally makes it difficult to date'. There is, however, good reason to think that 'it was current in some form around A.D. 400'; further, 'the archetype of all the full versions (incorporating the demonology) cannot have been put together before the early third century A.D.'.[105] This means that it is quite ludicrous of Doherty to conclude on the basis of this evidence that 'by Paul's time they [i.e. the demons] have become vast powers that infest the heavens'.[106] There is no such idea in 1 Enoch, and the Testament of Solomon shows only that such ideas were believed by some people some 200 years after Paul's time.

In addition to the Testament of Solomon, Doherty turns to the *Questions of Ezra* (Recension B). This is an even later document. It survives only in Armenian. The earliest surviving ms is dated to 1208 CE. This has been labelled recension A, and Recension B is known only from the seventeenth century. Stone was unable to determine whether it was originally composed in Armenian, which would certainly mean a very late date, or translated into Armenian from another language.[107] It is not, however, known anywhere outside the Armenian church. It is evident that it was not written until centuries after Paul's life and death, so once again this is the wrong cultural background for understanding anything that Paul wrote or might have believed.

The next document to which Doherty turns is the *Ascension of Isaiah*. This is a composite work. In its present form it is a Christian work, which appears to have been written in Greek, only fragments of which survive. It utilised an older Jewish work, *The Martyrdom of Isaiah*, which was still known to Origen and the *Apostolic Constitutions*, but which has not survived except as used in the Christian *Ascension of Isaiah*. The whole text of this composite work survives only in Ethiopic. This translation was probably made sometime in the fourth to sixth centuries. The oldest ms is, however, from the fifteenth century. A similar textual tradition is found in the first Latin translation, which survives only in fragments. A different textual tradition is found in the second Latin translation and in the Slavonic version, which contain only chs 6–11, generally known as the *Vision of Isaiah*, so they attest to its independent existence. The second

---

[104] Doherty, *Jesus: Neither God Nor Man*, p. 109.
[105] Schürer-Vermes-Millar, vol. III.1, p. 373.
[106] Doherty, *Jesus: Neither God Nor Man*, p. 109.
[107] M. E. Stone, in Charlesworth (ed.), *Old Testament Pseudepigrapha*, vol. I, p. 592.

Latin translation was first published in 1522, on the basis of a ms which is no longer known. The Slavonic translation exists in two forms, of which the second is a shorter version of the first. The earliest ms of the first version dates from the twelfth century, and the translation was apparently made in the tenth or eleventh century.

It should be obvious from this that the date of anything resembling the text of what we can now read is difficult to determine. Knibb makes the entirely reasonable suggestion that the *Vision of Isaiah* 'comes from the second century CE', and gives correct reasons for disputing attempts to date it any earlier. Schürer-Vermes-Millar, in a section primarily the responsibility of Vermes, likewise suggest that 'the *Vision of Isaiah* belongs probably to the second century A.D.', while Charlesworth puts it 'around the end of the second century A.D.'.[108] This document too is therefore too late in date to form evidence of the cultural environment in which Paul wrote to his converts. Doherty, however, simply announces that a community wrote this 'vision' 'probably towards the end of the 1st century CE'.[109] There is no excuse for dating it so early, and it would still be too late for Paul, but Doherty could rely on an enthusiastic audience of bloggers!

When a New Testament scholar, Dr James F. McGrath, Clarence L. Goodwin Chair in New Testament Language and Literature at Butler University, Indianapolis, pointed out the importance of the *Ascension of Isaiah* for Doherty's argument and its late date, Blogger Godfrey accused him of not having read Doherty's book, and made the quite misleading claim that people 'may further be interested to be informed of Michael Knibb's case (*Old Testament Pseudepigrapha*, vol. 2, pp. 143–76) for the earlier Jewish work behind the Ascension being dated to the end of the first century – given the time needed for the Nero redivivus myth to gain traction.'[110] Knibb in fact says something like this only of the section 3.13–4.2, partly by way of pointing out that this Christian section is not as early as the original Jewish *Martyrdom of Isaiah*: he was not discussing the *Vision of Isaiah* which is so important to Doherty's argument, and which, as we have seen, Knibb dates in the second century CE.

'Roger', however, commented on Blogger Godfrey's blog: 'A verse from the Ascension of Isaiah (11:34 of the Latin and Slavonic versions) is quoted in 1 Corinthians 2:9. Modern scholars ignore this and claim instead that Paul just mangled a quote from Isaiah 64:4. The early biblical scholar Jerome, however, is explicit that Paul's quote is from the Ascension of Isaiah. In both 1 Cor. 2:9 and the Ascension of Isaiah 11:34 the quote

---

[108] M. A. Knibb, in Charlesworth (ed.), *Old Testament Pseudepigrapha*, vol. 2, pp. 149–50; Schürer-Vermes-Millar, vol. III.1, p. 338n. 8; Charlesworth, *Pseudepigrapha and Modern Research*, p. 125.

[109] Doherty, *Jesus: Neither God Nor Man*, p. 119.

[110] Vridar.wordpress.com 2011/01/09 [accessed 23 October 2013].

reads the same word for word.'[111] As is typical of blog commentators with an imperfect grasp of the subject under discussion, 'Roger' gives no references to the work of Jerome, who wrote in the fourth and early fifth centuries, and who did not say what 'Roger' claims. As we have seen, Origen thought that the quotation came from the *Apocalypse of Elijah* (*On Matthew*, at Mt. 5.29).[112] Jerome did not like this, because it would mean that Paul introduced something not from Scripture with 'as it is written'. So he traced the quotation to Isa. 64.3 in Hebrew, which is hardly convincing (Jer. *Epistle 57 to Pammachius* 9). In his commentary on Isa. 64.3, published c. 410 CE, noting that the quotation is *not* given word for word, he comments: 'Ascensio Isaiae et apocalypsis Eliae hoc habent testimonium' (Jerome, *Comm. in Iesaiam* 64:3). This may reasonably be translated: 'The *Ascension of Isaiah* and *the Apocalypse of Elijah* have this evidence.' This means that Jerome thought that these works quoted Paul, not the other way around! Modern scholars know this perfectly well: both passages of Jerome are quoted for example by Schürer-Vermes-Millar, who do not, however, misinterpret them![113] This is typical of ignorant bloggers, and of people who comment on their blogs. They accuse scholars of omissions and of ignorance, when it is they themselves who have misinterpreted what texts they have managed to take some note of. Finally, this 'quotation' is not found in the other versions, notably not in the Ethiopic, which is the most complete. Hence Knibb prints it in a footnote, quoting it from the Slavonic and Second Latin versions, rather than in his text.

Doherty begins by declaring that in the *Ascension of Isaiah* 'we can find corroboration for this picture of a divine Son who descends into the lower reaches of the heavens to be crucified by the demon spirits'.[114] Doherty has, however, formed this picture himself from two late documents and his own interpretations of selected New Testament pieces, so this is either decisive or his whole argument is in ruins. We have seen that he dates it too early, 'probably toward the end of the first century CE', which would still be too late for Paul to take its contents for granted. Doherty also says that many elements of the picture which he draws are revealing, 'not least for the picture they disclose of the *evolution* of thought about the descending Son and his role. That picture indicates that in its earlier strata, the Vision speaks of a divine Son who operates entirely in the supernatural realm.'[115] In fact this document hardly ever uses the term 'Son', but prefers the term 'Beloved', though it uses Lord quite a lot and does use Son, Jesus and Christ for him when he is down here.

---

[111] vridar.wordpress.com 2011/01/09, comment by Roger – 2011/01/13 at 2:58 p.m. [accessed 23 October 2013].
[112] See p. 163 above.
[113] Schürer-Vermes-Millar, vol. III.1, p. 340; vol. III.2, p. 801.
[114] Doherty, *Jesus: Neither God Nor Man*, p. 119.
[115] Doherty, *Jesus: Neither God Nor Man*, p. 119.

Moreover, it says:

The Lord will indeed descend into the world in the last days, who is to be called Christ after he has descended and become like you in form, and they will think that he is flesh and a man...[14]and they will lay their hands upon him and hang him on a tree [*Lat² Slav* 'and kill him'], not knowing who he is...[15]And when he has plundered the angel/prince of death, he will ascend on the third day... (9.13–15)

At 11.1, *Lat² Slav* have: 'And I saw one like a son of man, and he dwelt with men in the world, and they did not recognize him.' They do not then have 11.2–22, where the Ethiopic has bizarre but earthly details:

And after two months of days, while Joseph was in his house, and Mary his wife ...[8]Mary then looked with her eyes and saw a small infant, and she was astounded...[9]her womb was found as at first, before she had conceived...[12]the story about the infant was spread abroad in Bethlehem... [15]and they took him and went to Nazareth in Galilee...[17]And I saw (that) in Nazareth he sucked the breast like an infant, as was customary, that he might not be recognized. [18]And when he had grown up, he performed great signs and miracles in the land of Israel and (in) Jerusalem. [19]And after this, the adversary envied him and roused the children of Israel, who did not know who he was, against him. And they handed him to the king and crucified him and he descended to the angel who (is) in Sheol. [20]In Jerusalem, indeed, I saw how they crucified him on a tree, [21]and likewise (how) after the third day he rose and remained (many) days...[22]And I saw when he sent out the twelve disciples and ascended.

It will be evident that, despite its docetic Christology, this document does portray Jesus as living a life like a human being, living first in Nazareth, performing miracles in Israel, including Jerusalem, being crucified in Jerusalem, and rising on the third day. The same is true of 3.13–4.22. A lot of manipulation is required to dispose of all this evidence and get Jesus crucified by demon spirits in the sublunar region instead.

Doherty has three tricks. One is his favourite trick of imagining that the authors of this composite late document did not believe anything which they do not say explicitly in selected passages. For example, in ch. 10, God instructs 'my Lord Christ' to descend through the heavens. At 10.8, He says: 'You shall descend through the firmament and through the world as far as the angel who (is) in Sheol, but you shall not go as far as Perdition.' Doherty comments: 'One can assume that Sheol is located below the earth, giving us no mention of a stop on earth, let alone anything that must be done there.'[116] It is typical of Doherty that he does not here refer

---

[116] Doherty, *Jesus: Neither God Nor Man*, p. 120.

to 11.1–22, and, interpreting the text with gross literalism and omitting all we know about normal Christian documents, imagines that this is enough to show that the author(s) cannot have believed in Jesus' ministry on earth.

Doherty's second trick is to insert his conviction that people believed that Jesus was crucified in the heavens where the text says little or nothing. For example, Doherty comments on 9.14–16: 'This prophesied action takes place entirely in the heavens. "The god of that world – meaning Satan – stretches out his hand and they – Satan and his evil angels – hang the Son upon the tree, not knowing who he is."'[117] Here, as often, the devil is held responsible for an evil event. Crucifixions, however, took place on earth, as everyone knew, and there is nothing positive in this (or any other!) text to justify moving the crucifixion of Jesus up there. The subject of 'will lay their hands upon him and hang him upon a tree' (9.14) is obviously people who were there at the time, the conventional story which had been well known for centuries when this document was being compiled. There is no excuse for Doherty to invent the idea that this was really 'Satan and his evil angels' crucifying Jesus up there in the heavens.

Doherty's third trick is to treat this composite, badly written and badly preserved document as if it had been the completed and accurately transmitted work of one coherent author, until someone added the supposedly secondary additions which he wishes to dispose of. This applies to the above passage too, for it has not been consistently and properly preserved, like many passages from which most people have no need to create havoc. I have noted the variations in traditions at ch. 11.

Doherty further devotes a whole chapter to failing to understand Paul's view of 'flesh' (*sarx*), under the ludicrous title 'Dancing with Katie Sarka Under the Moon'.[118] 'Katie Sarka' is his bowdlerization of the Greek expression *kata sarka* 'according to (the) flesh', and 'Under the Moon' is Doherty's idea that Jesus was crucified in the sublunar regions, rather than on earth like everyone else, even though no primary source points out this difference. He announces that 'the use of the term "flesh"' (*sarx*)... 'seems to be unique to Christian writers'.[119] It is not unique to Christian writers, and Doherty's idea that it is appears to be entirely dependent on his selection for consideration 'non-Christian documents' which 'speak about spiritual entities and humans acting in heavenly realms'.[120] Of course there is no such use of 'flesh' in non-Christian documents, but this is because Christian belief in anything like the incarnation of the historical Jesus was unique: it is not simply due to the usage of the Greek word *sarx*, which appears unique only because none of these other beings were historical figures, as the historical Jesus was.

---

[117] Doherty, *Jesus: Neither God Nor Man*, p. 121.
[118] Doherty, *Jesus: Neither God Nor Man*, p. 157.
[119] Doherty, *Jesus: Neither God Nor Man*, p. 157.
[120] Doherty, *Jesus: Neither God Nor Man*, p. 157.

For example, Paul comments that 'flesh and blood cannot inherit the kingdom of God' (1 Cor. 15.50), reflecting the widespread Jewish usage of 'flesh and blood' to mean human beings as we are here on earth. Again, he uses 'all flesh (*sarx*)' with a negative to mean no one, as for example at Rom. 3.20, where no one is justified before God by works of the Law: similarly, at Dan. 2.11, we read of the gods, whose dwelling is not with any person (*sarkos*).

Paul's view of Jesus was, however, genuinely different from his view of other human beings, and, equally, different from anyone's view of pagan deities, and this is the real reason why his use of the term 'flesh' with reference to Jesus is different in detail from the use of this term elsewhere: he had some new things to say. In particular, he believed that after he 'died' and 'was buried', Jesus 'rose on the third day' (1 Cor. 15.3–4), and 'is on the right [hand] of God' (Rom. 8.34, cf. Col. 3.1). During his life on earth, Paul believed that he 'did not know sin' (2 Cor. 5.21). Paul also came to believe that, before his life on earth, Jesus was 'in [the] form of God' (Phil. 2.6). This story is quite different from the story of the life of any other human being or deity, and that is the real reason why Paul wrote many things about Jesus in which he says different things about his flesh from what had been said about any being previously. Doherty concealed this from himself, and anyone who believes him, by dismissing most of these comments as 'interpolations' and misinterpreting the rest.

Hence, 'God sent his Son in likeness of flesh of sin' (Rom. 8.3), not because his flesh was in any way unreal: everyone knew that he died a revolting death when he was crucified; he was sent 'in likeness of flesh of sin' because Paul believed he was pre-existent and sinless. Again, Paul says of God's son, 'Christ Jesus our Lord', that he was born of the seed of David 'according to flesh'. It would not normally be necessary to say that, but Paul was about to say that he 'was appointed son of God in power according to the spirit of holiness from the resurrection of the dead', the unique belief which made 'according to flesh' a necessary qualification of his being born of the seed of David (Rom. 1.3–4). Again, he dismisses people who knew the historical Jesus by commenting: 'so we no longer know anyone according to flesh: and if we knew Christ according to flesh, but now we no longer know [him like this]'.

I hope this is sufficient to make clear that Doherty has completely misinterpreted Paul. He has made the major unscholarly mistake of imagining that Paul could not have believed what Doherty does not believe.

It is clear from all these comments that Doherty has completely misinterpreted Paul in accordance with what he does and does not wish to believe. It is therefore not surprising that his argument has failed to persuade any serious scholars.

Conclusions

In this chapter I have discussed some examples of what I consider to be unacceptable pseudo-scholarship. I began with what little we know about Paul's early life. He was born Jewish, round about the same time of Jesus, circumcised with Aramaic-speaking parents, but in a seriously assimilating environment, which was due to his parents being enslaved to members of the gens Pauli, which is how he came to be called Paul as well as Saul. This is how he came to be observant among Jews, while converting Gentiles to what we call Christianity while arguing that they should not be made observant at all. Mythicists have argued that he did not exist, or that he was a Gnostic, or that he was totally subservient to the Jerusalem church but later expelled from it, and considered a 'lapsed heretic' when he met there in 74 CE, or that he always believed that Jesus was fully divine, that he did not know Peter or any members of Jesus' family, and/or that he did not believe that Jesus lived on earth, but was thought to have been crucified in the sublunar regions, and that scholars are completely ignorant of the main primary sources. None of these views have anything to recommend them. They simply show the extraordinary extent to which anti-Christian views have produced uncritical and unscholarly results.

7

It all happened before, in Egypt, India, or wherever you fancy, but there was nowhere for it to happen in Israel

Introduction

It is extraordinary that mythicists claim that many events in the life of Jesus have happened somewhere else before, and that none of his teachings were original. It is even more extraordinary that they have claimed on this basis that he never existed as a historical figure. I propose that two main problems are that their claims that the events happened before are partly false, and partly based on vague similarities. Thirdly, their ideas of what is supposed to have happened during Jesus' life are based on their previous lives as fundamentalists rather than on critical scholarship. For example, they have produced spurious parallels to Jesus being born of a virgin on 25 December, which he was not: many Christians, however, including fundamentalists, believe that he was. The parallels to his teachings are also exaggerated in the same ways, but an even more fundamental problem is the whole idea that if anyone's teachings are not wholly original, they did not exist. If consistently followed through, that would dispose of the existence of most teachers!

As far as I can tell, the most profound problem underlying all these faults is opposition to very conservative forms of Christianity, which hold that Jesus was completely unique. Moreover, most mythicists are not merely former Christians, as I am myself, but former Christian fundamentalists. This is what appears to have given them their profound need to dispose of Jesus' existence altogether.

Parallelomania and falsehood

Claims of this kind are all based on supposed parallels between the life and teaching of Jesus on the one hand, and events and teachings attributed to other people on the other. Many of these parallels are based on events which did not happen anywhere, many are based on seeing similarities where differences are more important, and genuine similarities, especially in Jesus' teaching, show only that he was not absolutely unique, which of course he was not, not that he did not exist.

The term 'parallelomania' is derived from a classic article by Samuel Sandmel.[1] He defined 'parallelomania' as 'that extravagance among scholars which first overdoes the supposed similarity in passages and then proceeds to describe source and derivation as if implying literary connection flowing in an inevitable or predetermined direction'.[2] Mythicists have not merely ignored Sandmel's warning, they have perpetrated even more serious examples than the ones he criticized.

I begin with Jesus' name, which is an excellent example of the ludicrous word games which mythicists play. It is well known to all sober scholars that the English name Jesus is derived via the Latin Iesus from the Greek *Iēsous*. This was the conventional Greek rendering of the Hebrew and Aramaic name *Yēshua'* or *Yᵉhōshua'*, which has come into English more directly as 'Joshua', the important character in the Hebrew Bible after whom Jesus was named. Consequently, *Iēsous* is used several times in the Septuagint, the Greek translation of what we usually call the Old Testament, and there are no less than *twenty different* men called *Iēsous* mentioned by the Jewish historian Josephus, writing in Greek. There are accordingly no serious problems with this straightforward Jewish name, which is neither unique nor mythical nor derived from outside Judaism.

Mythicists have, however, played word games to derive him from an alien deity, generally from Egypt. For this purpose, they have normally used out-of-date pseudo-scholarship, which had no merit when it was written. For example, Harpur claims that 'there was a Jesus in Egyptian lore many thousands of years ago. His name was Iusu, or Iusa, according to Gerald Massey, and that means "the coming divine Son who heals or saves".'[3] As usual, Harpur does not make scholarly reference to any primary sources from Egypt. This is important, because his claim about Iusu, or Iusa, has not been supported by any modern Egyptologist, Massey never was a competent Egyptologist, and he is now more than a century out of date.

---

[1] S. Sandmel, 'Parallelomania', *JBL* 81 (1962), pp. 1–13.
[2] Sandmel, 'Parallelomania', p. 1.
[3] Harpur, *Pagan Christ*, p. 5, with p. 219n. 1, which does not even have a proper reference to the work of Massey. He refers instead to Kuhn, *Who is this King of Glory?*, p. 264, who made incompetent use of Massey's incompetent work, e.g. G. Massey, *A Book of the Beginnings* (London: Williams & Norgate, 1881), vol. II, p. 108.

Acharya plays a different word game. She managed to notice that Jesus was a normal Jewish name, and the same as what we normally call Joshua. She, however, announces that this also comes from IES, supposedly an anagram of Dionysus, and she quotes Jacolliot in 1870 declaring that 'all these names of Jesus, Jeosuah, Josias, Josue derive from two Sanscrit words Zeus and Jezeus...'[4] This claim is false, and it is irresponsible of Acharya to repeat it without reference to primary sources or to any criticism.[5] Jacolliot was a French barrister who worked in India. He had a wild imagination, and nothing he wrote should ever be believed without being carefully checked.

In English, Jesus is generally known as Jesus Christ. It is well known to all sober scholars that Christ is the English form of the Greek *Christos*, which means 'anointed'. Consequently, *Christos* is also used many times in the Septuagint, generally of the king of Israel or their high priest, both of whom were anointed. For example, at Lev. 4.5, the Lord instructs Moses as to what 'the anointed priest (*ho hiereus ho christos*)' should do. At 1 Kgdms 26.23, David says he refused to allow an attack on Saul on the ground that he is 'Anointed of [the] Lord (*Christon kuriou*)'. The range of usage is a little wider than this, partly because the Lord can metaphorically anoint anyone for an important task. At Isa. 45.1, Isaiah declares, 'Thus saith the Lord God to my anointed (*tō̧ Christō̧ mou*) Cyrus', indicating that the Lord God determined that Cyrus has an important task to perform. Accordingly, all proper scholars are also aware that, however difficult are the problems in understanding historically how the term Christ came to be applied to Jesus, it is a perfectly Jewish term which originally meant 'anointed'.[6]

Mythicists, however, having been indoctrinated to imagine that Jesus Christ was perfectly unique, have now searched the world to find any parallel anywhere, and come up with more word games. For example, Harpur comments:

> Significantly, both Massey and Kuhn – and other authorities – testify that the surface of the coffin lid of the mummified Osiris (every deceased person was referred to as the Osiris) constituted the table of the Egyptian's cult's Last Supper or Eucharist. It was the board on which the mortuary meals were served. The coffin bore the hieroglyphic equivalent for KRST. Massey connects KRST with the Greek word *Christos*, messiah, or Christ. He says, 'Say what you will or believe what you may,

---

[4]Acharya, *Christ Conspiracy*, p. 256, with p. 263n. 2, referring to L. Jacolliot, *The Bible in India*, p. 301, as if it were published by Sun Books in 1992: it was translated by 'R. G.' and published in London by Hotten, in 1870.
[5]Cf e.g. already E. A. Reed, *Hindu Literature: Or the Ancient books of India* (Chicago: Griggs, 1891), p. 386.
[6]For an attempt to solve these difficult problems, see Casey, *Jesus of Nazareth*, pp. 392–8.

there is no other origin for Christ the anointed than "Horus the Karast", or "anointed son of God the Father".'

Nonetheless, he notes correctly that 'Modern Egyptologists dispute this', which was already true when he wrote it, and instead of giving a good reason for following a scholar who wrote before the advent of modern critical scholarship and is now considered out of date, Harpur quotes his authority as if it were decisive and in a manner which is not dissimilar to a fundamentalist Christian quoting Scripture.[7] Furthermore, the description of Massey and Kuhn as 'authorities' is ridiculous.

Ward Gasque consulted a number of modern Egyptologists, and found that the Egyptian KRST is the word for "burial", so it is a very appropriate word to turn up on Egyptian coffins, and has no connection whatever with the Jewish and Christian term 'Christ'.[8]

Other mythicists have found Christ in all sorts of other places. For example, Acharya claims that, when Cicero went to Greece, he found the term 'Christ' on lots of inscriptions. She does not quote a single inscription, however, but simply refers back (without apparently even knowing the name of the author) to a book published in 1842.[9] Here, however, Logan Mitchell, an author about whom I can find out little else except his authorship of this book, simply asks: 'Did not Cicero, when he travelled to Greece, find inscriptions on monuments to many Christs?' He does not, however, answer his question by quoting any evidence. This was incompetent in 1842: to repeat it without any evidence in 2004, as Acharya did, was irresponsible too.

Acharya also joins the lengthy and incompetent tradition that Christ is the same as the Indian Krishna. She declares that his name is sometimes spelt Christna in English, and Acharya quotes a Hindu writer giving a Bengali form Christo.[10] Such views are part of an ineducable tradition of exaggerating contacts between Christianity and Hinduism, which produced these supposed forms of the name Krishna.

---

[7]Harpur, *Pagan Christ*, p. 101, with p. 224n. 6, again without any proper detailed reference to the work of Massey: see the comments of Massey, *Ancient Egypt*, pp. 186–248. The quotation is from p. 219.

[8]hnn.us/articles/6641.html [accessed 23 October 2013].

[9]Acharya, *Suns of God*, p. 467, with p. 494n. 73 and p. 570, referring without the author's name to L. Mitchell (under the pseudonym of Hypatia), *The Christian Mythology Unveiled* (London, privately printed, 1842), p. 148: it is p. 149 in my copy, which was reprinted by Kessinger (n.d.), and attributed to Mitchell Logan. I have taken the name Logan Mitchell, and the pseudonym Hypatia, from the catalogues of major libraries, because, whenever I have been able to check up on them properly, they are consistently of a very high standard, and better than Kessinger. There are other recent reprints.

[10]Acharya, *Suns of God*, p. 158, with p. 166nn. 31–2, referring to S. S. Giri, *Kriya: Finding the True Path* (San Diego: Sanskrit Classics, 1991), p. 22, which is as biased as any fantastic religious book one can ask for.

These regrettable mistakes appear to have two basic causes. One is the fundamentalism from which mythicists have emerged, which requires uncritical adherence to a version of the Christian faith which exaggerated the uniqueness of Jesus Christ, with no respect for dates or for the Jewish culture of the historical Jesus. After leaving such a version of the Christian faith, they are determined not to believe that Jesus was unusual, and they still have no respect for dates or for the Jewish culture of the historical Jesus. The second basic cause is linguistic incompetence. Mythicists do not seem to realize how common are similarities between different words in different languages, which merely look alike. Porter has an obvious example, when he points out that the French poisson, which means 'fish', has nothing to do with the English poison![11] The main point is that examples are legion, and may be taken from umpteen languages. For example, the German für means 'for': it has nothing to do with being furry. The French for 'for' is 'pour': it has nothing to do with pouring liquids. The Hebrew bath is a measurement of liquids, in the region of 40 litres: it has nothing to do with a decent person keeping clean by having a bath. The Aramaic hākāh means 'here'. It has nothing to do with the haka, a traditional Maori dance now performed by the All Blacks before each of their rugger games. The Greek alla means 'but': it has nothing to do with the Arabic Allah, which means 'God'. Apparently identical words may also have quite different meanings in the same language. If one of our students says he is going into 'banking', I do not expect him to spend his life causing aircraft to turn corners. If I am walking beside a river with a friend who says she would like to sit 'on the bank', I do not imagine that she wants to go back into town and sit on the roof of NatWest.

Such incompetent word games were played on a large scale by A. B. Kuhn (1880–1963). For example, he commented on the 'stable', which he found in the 'Christian legend' which he imagined 'held true enough to story of Jesus' birth to retain the ancient allegory of the birth of Christos in a stable', a view for which he did not find it necessary to quote any ancient primary source. He suggested that the 'stable' is to be read as 'stability' or 'stabilization'. 'The Christ is born in the stable, or stabilized relation between body and soul.'[12] Neither the Gospel of Matthew or Luke, which have no stable, nor any other ancient sources, were written in English, so this pun and Kuhn's interpretation of it are ludicrous beyond belief. Again, he comments that:

A fact of etymology that seems to have eluded scholarly recognition is that this little article the is basically the designation of deity, equivalent to God itself. El, Hebrew for 'God', is the Spanish masculine singular

---

[11] Porter, Unmasking the Pagan Christ, p. 38.
[12] Kuhn, Rebirth for Christianity, p. 209.

word for *the*, as in *el sombrero*, 'the hat'. The English *the* is the whole stem for the Greek word for 'God', *theos*.'[13]

In my opinion, this 'argument' displays total contempt for language, logic, culture and scholarship. It is blindingly obvious to all sane people that the English word 'the' is the definite article in English, and this is not in any way altered by the fact that *el* in Spanish is also the definite article, whereas *El* in Hebrew and other Semitic languages is a term for 'God', or the chief God. Nor is the Greek *theos* in any way relevant for interpreting the English word 'the'.

Kuhn's view of 'the' alphabet was discussed at greater length in *The Esoteric Structure of the Alphabet*.[14] It begins with an extraordinary statement of faith in the wisdom of ancient Sages 'embodied in tomes of a vast body of literature' which has been hopelessly misinterpreted 'with an intellectual befuddlement that approaches the status of a universal dementia for some two millenia'. This is never supported with proper evidence and argument, and belongs to the theosophy to which Kuhn adhered. He then proceeds to declare that this was encoded in *the* alphabet 'to safeguard precious cosmic and anthropogenic truth from desecration by the "rabble"'. Why they should do this is never explained, and Kuhn proceeds as if there were only *one* alphabet, which he treats conveniently as if it were English, into which occasional words such as the Hebrew *El* and Greek *theos* are transliterated.

Given the above it is not hard to see why Kuhn is generally ignored by competent modern scholars.[15] That Harpur and Acharya cannot see through him, and have invented the idea that his work has been suppressed, further exposes the flaws in their own methods.

I turn next to Jesus' birth. The treatment of this by mythicists is an excellent example of everything going wrong. Firstly, it ignores critical scholarship altogether. Critical scholars have known for years, and have written repeatedly in readily available books, that Jesus was not born of a virgin, and that his birth was not generally dated on 25 December until the fourth century CE. When I summarized for the general reader the reasons for not believing in the stories of his virgin birth, I was able to quote the distinguished Catholic theologian Hans Küng: 'today of course it is admitted even by Catholic exegetes that these stories are a collection

---

[13] Kuhn, *Rebirth for Christianity*, p. 22.

[14] A. B. Kuhn, *The Esoteric Structure of the Alphabet*. I have used a Kessinger reprint, perhaps of 1993, and have not been able to find proper details of the original. It is said in an online library catalogue to have been printed in Elizabeth, NJ, as early as 1900, by Academy Press, but I have not been able to confirm this either.

[15] For competent scholarly work on the origins and developments of alphabets, see, e.g. F. Coulmas, *The Writing Systems of the World* (Oxford: Blackwell, 1989); P. T. Daniels and W. Bright (eds), *The World's Writing Systems* (Oxford: Oxford University Press, 1996).

of largely uncertain, mutually contradictory, and strongly legendary and ultimately theologically motivated narratives, with a character of their own'. Then I cited several works of critical scholarship, including the standard summary for the general reader by the Protestant scholar Freed.[16] Mythicists ignore all this completely, and search for 'parallels' in other deities being born of a virgin on 25 December.

Secondly, most of the parallels which they come up with are inaccurate, and involve stretching the word 'virgin' intolerably. In normal English, this term means a woman who has had no sex, and this is what both Matthew and Luke meant when they told their entertaining and inaccurate tales. If applied to a deity who produced a child, it ought to mean that she gave birth without having sex. Harpur simply declares that Zoroaster was 'born in innocence and of a virgin birth from a ray of divine reason (Logos)',[17] but gives no reference to any primary source that his readers might use to verify what he has said. This statement proves seriously misleading, however, because sources about Zoroaster were not written down until the ninth century CE onwards, and survive in even later mss, by which time they may be contaminated by Christianity rather than the other way round, and they are stunningly difficult to read.

The normal tradition about Zarathushtra, dating back to the Avestas, is that when his mother Dughdova gave birth to him, he laughed, whereas babies normally cry. His father was Pourushaspa, and this much is already found in the Gathas. For example, Mary Boyce, arguably the world's leading authority on Zoroastrianism, translates part of Denkard 7 ch. 2 as follows.[18] Here the person called in the West Zoroaster, is not called Zarathushtra, but Zardusht.

(41) And Purushasp drove the cows back; and Purushasp said to Dugdov: Dugdov!...Milk these two cows...(42)...And the bodily substance of Zardusht was in the milk...(46)... Thus Zardusht's fravahr and his bodily substance came together. (47) And it is revealed that after the hom and the milk had been mixed together and consecrated to Ohrmazd, Purushasp and Dugdov drank them. And thus the Glory, fravahr and bodily substance of Zardusht were united in his parents. (48) Then the pair...lay together, desiring a son. (52) And that man was conceived who was the just Zardusht.

---

[16] Casey, *Jesus of Nazareth*, pp. 145–58, including a quotation of H. Küng, *On Being a Christian* (1974. Trans. E. Quinn. New York: Doubleday and London: Collins, 1976–7), p. 451, and citing works including E. D. Freed, *The Stories of Jesus' Birth: A Critical Introduction* (Sheffield: Sheffield Academic, 2001).
[17] Harpur, *Pagan Christ*, p. 34.
[18] M. Boyce (ed. and trans.), *Textual Sources for the Study of Zoroastrianism* (Textual Sources for the Study of Religion, J. R. Hinnells (ed.). Chicago: University of Chicago Press, 1984).

Despite the strange and rather miraculous events surrounding his birth, it should be obvious from this that Zarathushtra was believed to have been born after his parents had sexual intercourse, not when his mother was still a virgin.

More miracles follow in Denkard 7, 3, which begins as follows, again in Boyce's translation:

> (1) About the miracles made manifest after the birth of the most fortunate of beings until his coming to consultation with Ohrmazd. (2–3) This is revealed, that he laughed at birth, (3) at which Purushasp said: 'O Dugdov! This man-child saw the coming of glory and the coming of blessedness, when he laughed at his birth...'

This is normal Zoroastrian tradition. Boyce comments on the Gathas: 'For their interpretation not only years of specialised linguistic study are needed, but also a sound knowledge of the later holy texts, and of the forms of worship. Such competence is rarely united in a single scholar...' She comments on the literary tradition found in them:

> ...they are the only examples of this tradition to survive in Iran; and this literary isolation, together with their great antiquity, means that they contain many words of unknown or uncertain meaning, and have baffling complexities of grammar and syntax. All this, added to their depth and originality of thought, makes them extraordinarily difficult to translate. Only a few verses can be understood in a wholly unambiguous way...[19]

This demonstrates the flaws in Harpur's argument in appearing to quote a text without giving the reference, without saying which translation he used, and without any reference to general Zoroastrian tradition.[20]

Various writers have also suggested between them that Mithras was born of a virgin on 25 December in a cave, attended by shepherds. For example, Acharya, despite apparently being aware that Mithras was produced from a rock, nonetheless repeats the Haarlem atheist Jackson declaring in 1941 that 'Mithra, a Persian sun-god, was virgin born, in a cave, on 25 December. His earliest worshippers were shepherds...'; then Drews declaring c. 1910 that the Goddess (Acharya does not say he was referring to Mary=Maya=Maia) 'appears among the Persians as the "virgin" mother of Mithras'; then Berry

---

[19] Boyce, *Textual Sources for the Study of Zoroastrianism*, Foreward, p. 1.
[20] General information about Zoroastrianism was always available to Harpur and others: e.g. M. Boyce, *Zoroastrians. Their Religious Beliefs and Practices* (London: Routledge & Kegan Paul, 1979; London: Routledge, rev edn, 2001); an introduction for the general reader is now provided by J. Rose, *Zoroastrianism. An Introduction* (I. B. Tauris Introductions to Religion. London and New York: I. B. Tauris & Co Ltd., 2011).

c. 1955 or so declaring that 'Mithras was supposed to have been born of a virgin, the birth being witnessed by only a few shepherds'; then Carpenter in 1921 announcing that 'The Saviour Mithra too, was born of a Virgin' – and he adds that 'Mithra's prototype, the Indian Mitra, *was* born of a female, Aditi, "the mother of the Gods", the inviolable or *virgin* dawn.'[21]

Here all the most important points are false. John Hinnells, a genuinely expert modern scholar, described the story in 1971 as we may see it in Mithraic iconography, in which it is clear, as literary sources confirm, that Mithra was produced from a rock: Mithra, 'wearing his Phrygian cap, issues forth from the rocky mass. As yet, only his bare torso is visible. In each hand he raises aloft a lighted torch, and, as an unusual detail, red flames shoot out all around him from the *petra genetrix*.'[22] This is the Roman version, the only source for the so-called 'shepherds'. It is not, however, clear that the representation of them intended them to be shepherds at all, and they assisted the birth, they did not witness it. Aditi was not a virgin in any normal sense either, and it should be obvious that referring to dawn as 'the inviolable or *virgin* dawn' does not turn anyone or anything into a woman, whether human or divine, who gives birth to a child without having sex beforehand.

It follows that these parallels are not even relevant to understanding the secondary birth stories of Matthew and Luke, still less the real birth of the historical Jesus, probably in Nazareth.

Acharya noticed the late date of the whole idea that Jesus was born on 25 December.

She also managed to notice that Jesus' birth was dated by various people in the ancient world on other days. Despite quoting a seemingly unreliable website, she also noticed that Clement of Alexandria noted that several different dates had been put forward. She does not explore the spurious basis of every single suggestion, and concludes without any justification from these late sources:

> The discrepancies in Jesus's birthday indicate his non-historical nature. The idea that the followers of an 'historical' Jesus would have no clue as to when he was born is ridiculous, particularly in consideration of how significant birthdays were to Jewish mothers.[23]

---

[21] Acharya, *Suns of God*, p. 133, referring to J. G. Jackson, *Pagan Origins of the Christ Myth* (originally published New York: Truth Seekers, 1941), without proper page reference; A. Drews, *The Christ Myth* (Amherst: Prometheus, 1998), p. 116, not noting that this is a much earlier work, e.g. trans. from the 3rd edn by C. Delisle Burns (London: Fisher Unwin, 1910); G. Berry, *Religions of the World* (New York: Barnes & Noble, 1955), p. 56; E. Carpenter, *Pagan and Christian Creeds* (Health Research, 1975, but noting the earlier publication date of 1921).
[22] J. R. Hinnells in J. R. Hinnells (ed.), *Mithraic Studies: Proceedings of the First International Congress of Mithraic Studies* (2 vols. Manchester: Manchester University Press, 1975), vol. 1, p. 173.
[23] Acharya, *Suns of God*, p. 232.

This shows Acharya's total lack of historical sense. These pseudo-calculations in Egypt almost 200 years after Jesus' birth show only that his birth date was not known miles from Israel long after his life and death. They do not mean that his birth date was unknown to his mother! Once again, it is important that we do not have a modern biography of him. Neither his mother nor other members of his family wrote about him. Moreover, while the Gospels fit within the rather broad parameters of ancient lives, they are unusual precisely in being Gospels, which were intended to repeat aspects of Jesus' life and teaching which the Gospel writers considered important for salvation. The date of Jesus' birth was quite irrelevant to this, and that is one reason why they do not mention it or anything else of that kind. We should also note that there is no evidence that birthdays were considered particularly important in first-century Galilee. For all we know, Jesus' brother Jacob, Peter and the sons of Zebedee really had no interest in the date of Jesus' birth.

As a different kind of argument, Acharya quotes Remsburg in 1909, concerning Philo's supposed presence: 'He was living in or near Jerusalem when Christ's miraculous birth and the Herodian massacre occurred.' She also has Jesus appear in 'Philo's homeland'.[24] She uses the fact that Philo does not mention him as showing that none of the story is true. But Philo lived in Alexandria, not in Jerusalem, so this is not even enough to demonstrate the obvious point that the birth narratives of Matthew and Luke are not literally true. It illustrates yet again Acharya's dependence on out-of-date scholarship which was not considered to be of good quality even at the time it was written.

Acharya further argues that Jesus was not a carpenter. She begins by going through the massive number of lives supposedly lived by Buddha, taking the number 8,000 from Bell in 1790, and a massive list including 'carpenter' and 'mason' from Hardy in 1853.[25] This is not part of normative Buddhist tradition, and Acharya might have noted that carpenters were essential people in real life throughout the ancient world, so the Buddha being incarnate once as one is quite irrelevant to whether Jesus was a carpenter in Nazareth.

Secondly, Acharya cites, without any proper reference, Origen writing in *Contra Celsum* that Jesus is not called a carpenter in any of the Gospels then current in the churches. This is in fact Origen in *Contra Celsum* VI, 36, saying of Celsus:

---

[24] Acharya, *Suns of God*, p. 379, quoting without proper reference J. E. Remsburg, *The Christ: a critical review and analysis of the evidences of his existence* (New York: Truth Seeker, 1909), and p. 380.

[25] Acharya, *Suns of God*, p. 298, quoting J. Bell, *Bell's New Pantheon* (London: Bell, 1790), vol. 1, p. 316; and R. S. Hardy, *A Manual of Buddhism* (India: Chowkhamba Sanskrit Series, 1967), pp. 100, 376, not noting that this was originally published in 1853 (London: Partridge & Oakley, 2nd edn, 1880).

He next makes fun of the (things) concerning the tree, assailing it on two grounds, saying it is introduced because of this, either because our teacher was nailed to a cross, or because he was a carpenter by trade. He does not notice that the tree of life is mentioned in the writings of Moses, but he does not see that nowhere in the Gospels current in the churches is Jesus himself recorded as a carpenter.

This is a mistake by Origen in Alexandria in the third century CE, and it is not difficult to see how this mistake arose. Jesus is correctly called a carpenter in the authentic, but not altogether complimentary account of his visit to his home town of Nazareth when he was conducting his ministry centred in Capernaum. The inhabitants commented: 'Is not this the carpenter, the son of Mary and brother of Jacob and Joses and Judah and Simeon? And are not his sisters here with us? And they were offended at him' (Mk 6.3). This is the correct text, which will have been known to Celsus. Being a carpenter was, however, to ply a very ordinary trade, as Celsus and Origen both knew. Matthew therefore, while reproducing the incident, changed this to: 'Is not this the son of the carpenter?' (Mt. 13.55). Luke rewrote the incident completely, and John did not reproduce the incident at all.

Matthew was the most read Gospel in the early church, and there is a pronounced tendency for manuscripts of Mark to assimilate to Matthew, even when they do not have a particular reason, as they did here. Hence, some manuscripts of Mark assimilate to Matthew here. The most important is the very fragmentary Alexandrian ms P[45], which was written in the third century CE. Just enough of it survives to make clear that it was assimilated to Matthew, and read 'the son of the carpenter'. Later Alexandrian manuscripts rightly did not do this. Origen should have known better than to follow this inferior reading, but this is the point where we should all realize that, however learned he was for his time, he was not a modern scholar, let alone a modern textual critic. He was stuck because of Celsus' criticisms, and followed an inferior reading in Mark because it was what Matthew wrote, and it fitted in with what he needed to believe.

Acharya concludes that 'the occupation of Jesus as a carpenter was an interpolated afterthought'.[26] This points to a lack of competence in textual criticism, and a misunderstanding of either Jewish culture, or the culture of Celsus and Origen.

I turn next to Jesus' baptism by John the Baptist, a major event early in his life as a Jewish prophet. This baptism was a distinctively Jewish ceremony. As Mark put it: 'John came baptising in the desert and preaching a baptism of repentance for forgiveness of sins' (Mk 1.4). Josephus, writing later, felt it necessary to be very careful; he interpreted John to mean that

---

[26] Acharya, *Suns of God*, p. 299.

the Jews 'must not use it [i.e. baptism] to gain pardon for some sins, but for the consecration of the body, because the soul had already been consecrated by righteousness' (*Ant.* XVIII, 117). This cannot be paralleled all over the ancient world. All kinds of washing *were*, however, common. This difference is what mythicists ignore, so that they can pretend that Jesus' baptism by John was not distinctive, which they use to argue that it was not historical, which is basically not a valid argument either.

Harpur declares that Horus was baptized in the River Eridanus (or Arutana) by the Egyptian John the Baptist Anup, who was also later beheaded.[27] As usual, he gives no proper references to Egyptian sources. Murdock (=Acharya) goes much further. She comments that the comparison 'between Anup and John has been extrapolated for a variety of reasons', and adds that '"Christian" terminology has been utilized to describe what was found in the ancient Egyptian texts and monuments, as well as elsewhere around the Roman empire during the era.'[28] This is important, because it is central to the way in which most of the so-called parallels to the life and teaching of Jesus have been manufactured by mythicists. In real life, Horus was not thought to have been baptized by Anup/Inpu, who was supposed to have been a jackal-headed Egyptian deity, not a Jewish man, and Inpu was not beheaded either.

Murdock correctly notes some of the different ways in which Anup/Anpu has been transliterated, being usually known in English as Anubis, which comes directly from Latin and indirectly via Latin from Greek. She also correctly notes that Anubis was well known in the Graeco-Roman world. She asks: 'Who replaced Anubis within the Christian mythos and ritual?' She answers her own question: 'A scientific analysis reveals John the Baptist to represent the most likely candidate.'[29] This is the wrong question, because it *assumes* that Christianity is so secondary that it *must* have had a replacement for Anubis. In fact it did not, and Murdock's so-called analysis is neither 'scientific' nor historical nor culturally accurate. In particular, Inpu was portrayed with the head of a dog, probably a jackal, but black, because these animals scavenged on the edges of graveyards, and he was also thought to be in charge of the burial of the dead, until this task was taken by Osiris. John the Baptist had neither any such appearance, nor any such task.

Murdock then plays another word game, noting that *An*up has two letters in common with the Greek form of John's name 'Iōannēs, which she spells out conveniently as Io-*An*-nes. The Greek word 'Iōannēs originated as an attempt to find a suitable Greek form for rendering the Hebrew name Yōḥanān and similar forms. It is not common in the LXX, where

---

[27] Harpur, *Pagan Christ*, p. 93.
[28] Murdock, *Christ in Egypt*, p. 233.
[29] Murdock, *Christ in Egypt*, p. 235.

there are also other transliterations, such as '*Iōanan* and '*Iōannan,* both of which were fixed forms. It became sufficiently common in rendering Jewish names of the form *Yōḥanān* and the like for there to be ten other men called '*Iōannēs* in Josephus, including a high priest and the famous John son of Levi, of Gischala, a significant figure in the Roman war. There is accordingly no connection between the names Anup/Inpu and '*Iōannēs.*

Murdock further suggests that 'as the jackal-headed God, Anubis ranks as "one crying in the wilderness", as those animals notoriously do...'[30] This is almost comically inaccurate. Anubis was supposed to be an Egyptian God, not an average jackal, and Murdock gives no evidence that anyone imagined he spent his time crying in a wilderness! John is said to have fulfilled Isaiah's prophecy of 'a voice of one crying in the wilderness' (Isa. 40.3 at Mk 1.3) because early Christians found that an appropriate comment on his ministry, not because they had any interest in Anubis or imagined that John the Baptist was like a jackal. This is another completely misleading description of an Egyptian deity in quite inappropriate Jewish/Christian terms, and it has no historical or cultural value.[31]

Murdock then quotes the perfectly respectable, though now somewhat dated, scholarship of Budge, who noted that John the Baptist was portrayed as the 'ferryman of the dead' in dependence on Egyptian material, citing the *Encomium on John the Baptist.* Murdock, however, quite fails to mention that this is an Egyptian work written some *half a millennium after* the time of John the Baptist! Egyptian Christians of that period really did borrow Egyptian material, but this has nothing whatever to do with early Christianity. It illustrates beautifully the well-established fact, known to all critical scholars, that *late* Christian sources have more and more accretions from all over the place. This should be significant for people deciding whether they should be Christians, and which Christian beliefs they should hold if they do become Christians. It is totally irrelevant to the existence of historical figures such as Jesus and John the Baptist, and for historical research into their lives, which should be primarily concerned with the earliest sources.

Murdock then proceeds to pre-Christian use of the Greek words *baptō* and *baptizō.* They both meant 'dip', but not in any meaningful sense 'baptize', as Murdock alleges. She quotes a passage of Nicander, which is about pickling vegetables, and has nothing to do with baptism, to which it is accordingly irrelevant. She even discusses 'the act of baptizing the vegetable' which is as ridiculous as any 'parallel' I have come across.[32]

---

[30] Murdock, *Christ in Egypt*, p. 240.
[31] For brief and completely sober accounts of Inpu/Anubis for the general reader, see, e.g. D. M. Dexey, 'Anubis', in D. B. Redford (ed.), *The Ancient Gods Speak: A Guide to Egyptian Religion* (New York: Oxford University Press, 2002), pp. 21–2; G. Hart (ed.), *The Routledge Dictionary of Egyptian Gods and Goddesses* (London: Routledge, 2005), pp. 25–8.
[32] Murdock, *Christ in Egypt*, p. 245n. 2.

Then, as now, people did not *baptize* vegetables, but they did wash, boil, and immerse them! Nicander was really discussing boiling vegetables and then immersing them in vinegar, to do what we call 'pickle' them. This is a striking example of the inappropriate use of Christian terminology to describe all sorts of things, in spurious attempts to make them sound more alike.

Murdock continues to use the term 'baptize' in this culturally inappropriate way of Egyptian myths, and ends by associating John the Baptist with Aquarius. She quotes Hardwicke in 1884 announcing that

> ...his nativity is fixed by the Catholic church at June 24th, at the first moment of which day *Aquarius* rose above the horizon...At midnight on Aug. 28th and 29th *Aquarius* was seen at Alexandria above the southern horizon, travelling along the ecliptic with his head above the equator, as though it had been cut off.[33]

In the first place, this date 'fixed by the Catholic church' is very late, and probably parasitic on the incorrect date of the birth of Jesus on 25 December. I have noted it fixed by the Council of Agde in 506 CE! This means that it is centuries too late to be taken into account in assessing the historicity of John the Baptist. What is even more central is that what might or might not be seen of Aquarius on 28 and 29 August has nothing to do with the regrettably normal penalty of chopping people's heads off, let alone the chopping off of John the Baptist's head in the fortress of Machaerus.

I turn next to the Twelve, who were an important group during the historic ministry of Jesus, but not during the period of the early church. Jesus chose the Twelve to symbolize the twelve tribes of Israel. Mythicists, however, seek to replace this obvious fact of history by claiming umpteen parallels which basically centre on the twelve signs of the Zodiac, which, like Jesus' Twelve, were always regarded as twelve in number.

The twelve signs of the Zodiac were perfectly well known in Israel. For example, Josephus says that the twelve loaves of the Shewbread in the Temple in Jerusalem represented 'the circle of the Zodiac and the year' (*War* V, 217). In describing the extraordinary veil of the Temple, he says that on it was portrayed 'a whole view of the universe', and he added 'except for the signs of the Zodiac' (*War* V, 214), to avoid an obviously possible misunderstanding. In describing the high priest's extraordinary vestments, he made the true point that on the front of his ephod, a sort of tunic, there were twelve stones on each of which was written one of the names of the mythical heads of the twelve tribes (*War*, V, 233–4). Nonetheless, in describing Moses' provision of this garment, he also commented, 'whether

---

[33] Murdock, *Christ in Egypt*, p. 253, quoting W. W. Hardwicke, *The Popular Faith Unveiled* (London: the Author, 1884), p. 195.

one would like to think of the months, or the like number of the stars which the Greeks call the circle of the Zodiac, he would not be mistaken' (Jos. *Ant.* III, 186). There is also some evidence of horoscopes at Qumran, where the hopelessly fragmentary 4Q318 indicates the passage of the moon through the signs of the Zodiac, and predicts terror and affliction brought by strangers if it thunders in Gemini.

There is, however, no trace of the Signs of the Zodiac in the Gospels. There is some important information about the Twelve. Mark says that Jesus 'made Twelve so that they might be with him, and so that he might send them out to preach and to have power to cast out demons' (Mk 3.14–15). This corresponds to the two central points of his ministry. Jesus' preaching and teaching ministry was directed at Israel as a whole, so it is logical that he should send his closest followers out to carry on that ministry. That there should be 12 of them corresponds naturally to the twelve tribes of Israel. The account of the Twelve during the ministry bears out this summary. They turn up with him at various points, including his final Passover (Mk 14.17, 20).

Some significant information may be gleaned from Mt. 19.28/Lk. 22.30. Some of the opening part of it has been removed through the editing of the evangelists, but Luke's version has 'you will eat and drink at my table', and Luke had little reason to edit this in. If Jesus really said something longer on these lines, Matthew and Luke might both have reason to replace it with what we now read. It would also make an excellent occasion for the Twelve to sit on twelve thrones, and for all of them to drink new wine. What Jesus said must therefore have included this: '... you will eat and drink at my table ... you will sit on thrones judging the twelve tribes of Israel'. This is quite extraordinary: the Twelve will judge Israel. Not Abel, not Abraham, not Moses, but the Twelve.

Another saying refers to the same occasion. Luke has clearly edited his version, so I mostly follow the Matthaean version as being nearer to what Jesus said, but I restore Jesus' characteristic term 'kingdom of God' for Matthew's characteristic 'kingdom of heaven', and I keep Luke's 'you' for Matthew's 'the sons of the kingdom':

> Many will come from east and west and recline with Abraham and Isaac and Jacob in the kingdom of God, but you will be cast into outer darkness: there will be weeping and gnashing of teeth (Mt. 8.11–12/Lk. 13.28–9).

The background to this saying is the normal Jewish expectation of the restoration of Israel in the last times. As Second Isaiah said in the name of the Lord, 'Do not fear, for I have redeemed you ... I will bring your seed from the East, and from the West I will gather you' (Isa. 43.1, 5). Those who came from the East would naturally include the lost ten tribes, so the Twelve would have all twelve tribes to judge when they sat on their thrones.

There is no connection between the Twelve in the Gospels and the signs of the Zodiac, and the supposed mythical parallels are very forced. For example, Acharya (=Murdock) claims that the Twelve were 'not "real people" but represent the twelve signs of the zodiac', and for this supposed 'solar myth' she announces, without citing any primary sources, let alone dating them, 'King Arthur and his 12 Knights; "Balder and his twelve judges; Odysseus and his Twelve Companions; Romulus and his Twelve Shepherds"; as well as Jacob and his 12 sons, et al.' Instead of primary sources, Acharya quotes the novelist Robert von Ranke Graves, who, in total contempt for historical research practised by his ancestor von Ranke, was espousing the idea of the Beth-Luis-Nion alphabet, which was so called because B.L.N. 'are the radical consonants of Belin the Celtic God of the solar year'. Graves did this not to produce a mythical group of twelve, but examples of the thirteen consonants with mythical groups of thirteen. Graves cited no primary sources either, and his numbers are not confirmed by other sources, which are, however, no more reliable than he is. For example, Higgins in 1833 produced 17 letters in this alphabet.[34] Graves goes back to slightly earlier Irish sources, but the whole idea that any of this might be early enough to have influenced early Christianity is quite beyond belief. Graves also has another figure, the 'Danish Hrolf and his twelve Berserks'.[35]

Of these groups, King Arthur was a legendary figure supposed to have lived centuries after the time of Jesus. The earliest source known to me in which he has twelve knights is that of Wace, in *Roman de Brut*, dated in 1155 CE, and it is a reasonable hypothesis that the number 12 is taken from Jesus' Twelve apostles, not least because other sources have different, and indeed much larger numbers.[36]

Balder was a Norse deity of the second millennium CE. He too was therefore not part of a 'solar myth' which could have influenced the Gospels. As far as I have been able to determine, it was his father Odin who was supposed to have presided over twelve judges in Gladsheim, a hall in Asgard, where they presided over the affairs of Asgard. While there is some evidence of mediaeval cross-fertilization in the stories of Jesus and

[34] Higgins, *Anacalypsis*, p. 9, with p. 11, referring back to G. Higgins, *The Celtic Druids* (London: Hunter, 1827–9).
[35] Acharya, *Suns of God*, p. 469, with p. 495n. 84, citing no primary sources but only the novelist Robert von Ranke Graves. This is on p. 196 of R. Graves, *The White Goddess* (G. Lindop (ed.). Manchester: Carcanet, 4th edn, 1997. Faber 7 Faber, 1999), which is readily available; the original edition was published in 1948 (London: Faber & Faber).
[36] For Wace, see J. E. Weiss, *Wace's Roman de Brut: a history of the British* (Exeter: University of Exeter Press, 1999, rev edn, 2002, 2003). More generally, see, e.g. C. Dean, *Arthur of England: English Attitudes to King Arthur and the Knights of the Round Table in the Middle Ages and the Renaissance* (Toronto: University of Toronto Press, 1987); R. Barber, *Myths and Legends of the British Isles* (Woodbridge: Boydell, 1999); M. Ashley, *A Brief History of King Arthur* (London: Robinson, 2010).

of Norse mythology, reading any of this back into myths which could have influenced the Gospels is hopelessly contrary to history and culture.[37]

Twelve companions are not important in stories of Odysseus as they are in stories of Jesus. He did take 'the twelve best of (my) companions' (*Od.* IX, 195), when he headed for the cave of the Cyclops, leaving the rest of his crew behind. The Cyclops tore two of them limb from limb and ate them, and so on. This is just one incident in the *Odyssey,* and it has nothing whatever to do with a myth of people or deities having twelve companions, let alone with the Gospels.

Romulus, the legendary founder of Rome, did not generally have twelve shepherds about him, as Jesus had the Twelve during the ministry. According to the dominant version of the myth of the foundation of Rome, Romulus and his twin brother Remus were suckled by a she-wolf. They were found by a shepherd Faustulus, who brought them up with his twelve sons. At least his story is older than the Gospels, but it was not sufficient to form a 'solar myth' which could explain the origin of the Twelve.[38]

Harpur obviously heads again for Egypt, but he simply comments that, in one of his roles, Horus 'was "a fisher of men with twelve followers"', with quotation marks but no reference to any primary source in which we might find the quotation.[39] Murdock (=Acharya) tries to do better, and reveals the hopeless lack of evidence for any such thing. She comments, for example: 'Various of these groupings of a dozen towing the sun boat could be deemed the "Twelve Rowers in the Boat with Horus", or the "Twelve Sailors in the Ship or Ra". It is not much of a leap from these particular aquatic terms to the "Twelve Fishers of Men with Jesus", (Mt. 4.18–22; Mk 1.16–20)...'[40] That 'various of these groups' 'could be deemed' means in Acharya-speak that this is not what primary sources actually say. Nor are there 'Twelve Fishers of Men with Jesus' in Matthew, Mark or anywhere else in the New Testament! In the original and perfectly true story, Jesus said 'I will make you fishers of men' to a grand total of two disciples, Simeon and his brother Andrew, who are clearly described as fishermen (Mk 1.16–17). Jacob and John the sons of Zebedee, who became, with Simeon the Rock, two of the inner group of three of the Twelve, are also described in such a way as to make clear that they were fishermen too (Mk 1.19–20). More of the Twelve may possibly have been fishermen. We have, however, no good reason to believe that, and it is not particularly probable in view of the variety of

---

[37] Cf. e.g. J. Lindow, *Murder and Vengeance Among the Gods: Baldr in Scandinavian Mythology* (Helsinki Suomalainen tiedeakatemia, Academia Scientiarum Fennica, 1997).
[38] Cf. e.g. T. J. Cornell, *The Beginnings of Rome: Italy and Rome from the Bronze Age to the Punic Wars (c. 1000–264 BC)* (London: Routledge, 1995); M. Beard, J. North, and S. Price, *Religions of Rome,* vol. 1, *A History* (Cambridge: Cambridge University Press, 1998).
[39] Harpur, *Pagan Christ,* p. 6, cf. pp. 86–7.
[40] Murdock, *Christ in Egypt,* p. 276, with n. 8, citing no primary sources but only Kuhn, p. 208, not even specifying which book!

occupations necessary to keep life going in Galilee. All of the Twelve were certainly not fishermen, since Matthew was a tax collector (Mt. 10.3).

This is a prime example of contempt for our primary sources and their culture, combined with inaccurate conjectures. The synoptic Gospels are set in Israel, where the story of the twelve tribes was endemic, known to everyone, and referred to in the Gospels, as we have seen.[41] The rather small number of references to fishing and fishermen make excellent sense in this setting too, because fishing was a major aspect of practical and mundane daily life round the lake of Galilee. The 'mythical' parallels strained for by mythicists, however, are not generally convincing. This illustrates beautifully the nature of the work of mythicists. They are not scholars, and they do not believe in evidence and argument any more now than they did when they had fundamentalist Christian convictions. They just have different convictions to be attached to.

I do not propose to discuss extensively the teaching of Jesus. Critical scholars do not claim that his teaching was entirely original, and I have argued elsewhere that he recreated Judaism from a prophetic perspective.[42] This means that a lot of his teaching, though fresh to his audiences, was not original. For example, in a major incident during his last visit to Jerusalem, a scribe asked Jesus which was the most important commandment of all, and Jesus responded with a summary of love of God and love of one's neighbour (Mk 12.28–34).[43] He began with the opening of the *Shema‘*, written at Deut. 6.4–5: 'Hear Israel, the Lord our God, the Lord is One. And you shall love the Lord your God with all your heart and with all your being and with all your might.' With the love of the one God firmly stated as the first duty of faithful Jews, Jesus went to Lev. 19.18 for another central commandment: 'You shall love your neighbour as yourself.'

The scribe greatly approved of Jesus' selection of two central commandments. He began with a summary quotation which picks up Deut. 6.4 and continued in terms reminiscent of Deut. 4.35 and Isa. 45.21: 'For good, rabbi, you have truly said that "He is one and there is none beside him".' From a cultural point of view, this is the most perfectly Jewish response that one can imagine. The scribe continued with the transcending importance of these two commandments even over against the cultic centre in which he and Jesus stood together, a few days before they would observe the feast of Passover: 'And to love Him with all one's heart and all one's mind and all one's strength, and to love one's neighbour as oneself, is more than all the burnt offerings and sacrifices.' Jesus expressed his approval with one of his favourite terms, which was central to Judaism, not original to him: 'You are

---

[41] See pp. 214–17.
[42] Casey, *Jesus of Nazareth*.
[43] For more detailed discussion for the general reader, see Casey, *Jesus of Nazareth*, pp. 284–6.

not far from the kingship of God' (Mk 12.34). This locates Jesus where the Jesus of history really belonged, within Judaism.

Mythicists, however, make the same sort of false claims about the secondary nature of his teaching that we have seen in their comments on his life. For example, Acharya claims Horus was supposed to have delivered a Sermon on the Mount in Egypt.[44] However, critical scholars have known for years that Jesus did not deliver the Sermon on the Mount: it was compiled by Matthew the evangelist, and includes sayings of Jesus as well as a great deal of secondary material. Moreover, there is no primary evidence that Horus delivered a sermon on a mount at all. Matthew was influenced by Moses, not by Horus. I have noted Matthew's Jesus saying,

> ...whoever undoes one of the least of these commandments and teaches people thus, shall be called least in the kingdom of the heavens. But whoever does and teaches [them], he shall be called great in the kingdom of the heavens.[20] For I'm telling you, unless your righteousness exceeds that of the scribes and Pharisees, you will certainly not enter the kingdom of the heavens. (Mt. 5.19–20)

This is secondary, but it is perfectly Jewish, and looking for 'parallels' to it attributed to Horus is neither relevant nor fruitful.

A supposedly scholarly attempt to cast doubt on the historicity of the teaching of Jesus is an extraordinary book by the Old Testament 'scholar' Thomas L. Thompson, *The Messiah Myth*, published in 2005.[45] It demonstrates lack of knowledge of first-century Judaism and of New Testament scholarship, and has remarkably little to say about Jesus. Thompson begins with very dogmatic comments on the canonical Gospels as 'four variants of a legend-filled, highly stereotyped "biography"', supposedly written 'many decades after the date ascribed to their stories'.[46] He does not justify these comments. His account of the history of scholarship includes the assertion that Schweitzer's 'mistaken prophet is historical primarily because he does not mirror the Christianity of Schweitzer's time. But the *assumption* [my italics] that this mistaken prophet of the apocalypse is a figure appropriate to first-century Judaism is itself without evidence.'[47] This is a ludicrous comment on the work of Weiss and Schweitzer, and does not

---

[44] Acharya, *Christ Conspiracy*, p. 226, with p. 234n. 41, citing G. R. S. Mead, *Did Jesus Live 100 BC?* (Health Research, 1965), not noting that this is a reprint of a book published in London by the Theosophical Publishing Society in 1903, and without any page reference. She adds supporting comments from J. M. Robertson (also 1903, but given as 1966), Carpenter (1920, but given as 1975), Potter (1958) and Massey (1887, but given as 1985).

[45] T. L. Thompson, *The Messiah Myth. The Near Eastern Roots of JESUS and DAVID* (New York: Basic Books, 2005; rep. London: Pimlico, 2007).

[46] Thompson, *Messiah Myth*, p. 3.

[47] Thompson, *Messiah Myth*, p. 6.

take proper account of more recent work, which has securely located Jesus in first-century Judaism.[48] This view is based on careful study of the primary sources for first-century Judaism, as well as the synoptic Gospels, and if something is wrong with it, Thompson should have illustrated his counter-argument with scholarly discussion of the sources.

Thompson continues by suggesting that if Jesus were mistaken about the coming of the kingdom, 'Mark – let alone a presumably much later John writing his Gospel – would have known about the failure of Jesus' messianism. They would have found it as unacceptable as Schweitzer did.'[49] This shows a total lack of understanding of Mark, first-century Judaism, and the Fourth Gospel. Mark did not believe that Jesus was a failed Messiah at all! On the contrary, he believed that Jesus' prophecies that the kingdom of God was at hand (cf. Mk 1.15; 9.1; 14.25; Mt. 6.10/ Lk. 11.2 etc.) would shortly be fulfilled when he returned in triumph on the clouds of heaven (Mk 13.26, 30; 14.62 etc.). We know that he did not, but Mark did not know that he would not. On the contrary, he followed the normal habit of people in first-century Judaism, and imagined that when the kingdom had not come quite as soon as expected, it would nonetheless come shortly. That did *not* make Jesus a failed Messiah! The authors of the Fourth Gospel completely rewrote history in accordance with the needs of the social memory of their community, as I pointed out in a 1996 book which was also available to Thompson.[50] He does not discuss any scholarship of this kind either.

Thompson moves on to the Westar Jesus seminar, and some of his comments on it are equally extraordinary. For example, he declares that 'Biblical Scholars outside the United States find the seminar's conclusions consistently conservative.'[51] For this extremely general statement, he offers not one jot of evidence! The mind boggles to imagine what he has read, and who he has been talking to. Among direct criticisms of the American Jesus Seminar for its arbitrary and radical, not conservative, work examples include, from England, Dunn in 2003, so a work which might have been available to Thompson, and the contents of which were abundantly discussed at the SNTS Jesus seminar and informally at SNTS, both *before* and after it was published. Dunn also notes the earlier criticism

---

[48] Cf. A. Schweitzer, *The Quest of the Historical Jesus: First Complete Edition* (1906. 2nd edn, 1913. 2nd ET J. Bowden et al. ed. and trans. London: SCM, 2000); J. Weiss, *Jesus' Proclamation of the Kingdom of God* (1892. Trans., ed. and with introduction by R. H. Hiers and D. L. Holland. London: SCM and Philadelphia: Fortress, 1971); and, outstanding among many recent books which were available to Thompson, and which he could therefore have discussed, Dale C. Allison, *Jesus of Nazareth: Millenarian Prophet* (Minneapolis: Fortress, 1998); B. D. Ehrman, *Jesus: Apocalyptic Prophet of the New Millennium* (Oxford: Oxford University Press, 1999).
[49] Thompson, *Messiah Myth*, p. 7.
[50] Casey, *Is John's Gospel True?*
[51] Thompson, *Messiah Myth*, pp. 10–11.

of Tuckett in 1999, which was more obviously available to Thompson.[52] Graham Stanton, who came from New Zealand and was president of SNTS in 1996–7, so after Thompson came to Europe, as well as editor of *New Testament Studies* for several years, was severely critical of the seminar in a standard work published in 2001, so this was also available to Thompson.[53] In the same volume, Teresa Okure, Professor of New Testament at the Catholic Institute of West Africa at Port Harcourt, in her native Nigeria, objects to 'opponents' of Christianity who 'vilify, or at best "secularise" Jesus in art, films and scholarship, seeing in him no more than a human being. To many Christian observers, a notable example of the latter is the so-called "Jesus seminar" started in 1985 by Robert Funk...'[54]

Various other works have little or nothing to say about the American Jesus Seminar, but clearly take a more conservative view of Jesus than it did. These include, from Germany, Gnilka, *Jesus of Nazareth: Message and History* (1993. ET 1997); from South America, Sobrino, *Jesus the liberator* (ET 1994), and from France, Schlosser, *Jésus de Nazareth* (1999, 2nd edn, 2002).[55] I do not wish to *commend* all these works. It is rather that they make nonsense of Thompson's declaration that 'Biblical Scholars outside the United States find the seminar's conclusions consistently conservative',[56] and show that this comment is false. Moreover, Thompson was a supposedly established Old Testament scholar when he came to Europe in 1993, and joined what was then a reputable academic department in Copenhagen which had significant international contacts. It must have taken him some time to write *The Messiah Myth* (2005). Why did he not ensure that he went to academic meetings of New Testament scholars, including the annual meetings of SNTS, which I attended throughout this period without ever coming across him? Then he might have obtained a more accurate view of what New Testament scholars outside the United States really think. Or does his use of the term 'Biblical Scholars' really mean that he prefers talking to sceptical Old Testament scholars who agree with him?

---

[52] Dunn, *Jesus Remembered*, pp. 58–65, citing inter alia C. M. Tuckett, 'The Historical Jesus, Crossan and Methodology', in S. Maser and E. Schlarb (eds), *Text und Geschichte. Facetten theologischen Arbeitens aus dem Freundes- und Schülerkreis: Dieter Lührmann zum 60. Geburtstag* (Marburger theologische Studien 50. Marburg: Elwert, 1999), pp. 257–79.

[53] G. N. Stanton, 'Message and Miracles', in M. Bockmuehl (ed.), *The Cambridge Companion to JESUS* (Cambridge: Cambridge University Press, 2001), pp. 56–71, at 64–5.

[54] T. Okure, 'The global Jesus', in Bockmuehl (ed.), *Cambridge Companion to JESUS*, pp. 237–49; I quote from p. 244.

[55] J. Sobrino, *Jesus the liberator: a historical-theological reading of Jesus of Nazareth* (1991. Trans. P. Burns and F. McDonagh. Tunbridge Wells: Burns & Oates, 1994); J. Gnilka, *Jesus of Nazareth: Message and History* (1993. Trans. S. S. Schatzmann. Peabody: Hendrickson, 1997); J. Schlosser, *Jésus de Nazareth* (Paris: Noesis, 1999; 2nd edn, Agnès Viénot Éditions, 2002) – there is no ET.

[56] Thompson, *Messiah Myth*, pp. 10–11.

Thompson is known to have attended the European Seminar in Historical Methodology at the European Association of Biblical Studies. While this is by no means a group of scholars who agree with each other, it is a closed group which does not contain any New Testament scholars. It was therefore not a place where he could encounter New Testament scholars. He could of course have gone to other meetings and held informal discussions with New Testament scholars, but his comments appear to show that he has not done anything of the kind.

The bulk of Thompson's book is devoted to discussion of what he calls 'tropes'. Much of this has nothing to do with Jesus at all, let alone the historical Jesus. For example ch. 5, 'The Myth of the Good King', ch. 6, 'The Myth of the Conquering Holy Warrior', ch. 8, 'Holy War', ch. 9, 'Good King, Bad King', and ch. 10, 'The Figure of David in Story and Song' hardly mention Jesus at all. Those chapters that do mention Jesus are pitted with mistakes. Some comments appear to presuppose traditional Catholic belief in the priority of Matthew, though Thompson now appears simply to prefer Matthew rather than believe it was literally earlier. For example, Thompson's discussion of the 'Cleansing of the Temple' depends on Mt. 21.10–17, so that the story 'closes on a cryptic scene of healing the lame and the blind [who] have come to Jesus (Mt 21.14) in obvious imitation of Isaiah's foreigner and eunuch'.[57] He does not explain why Mark's account is significantly different, nor why it contains so many Aramaisms.

I have already criticized Thompson in a brief article in *Bible and Interpretation*, in which I pointed out that he is not a competent New Testament scholar.[58] In the (pretty appalling) debate which followed, he claimed that he does not believe in the priority of Matthew. He appears not to 'believe' in the priority of Matthew simply because he has given up faith-based scholarship altogether.

Other comments presuppose even later parts of the Gospels, or still later Christian belief. For example, Thompson declares that Jesus 'is the servant of God and the good shepherd'.[59] But Jesus is 'the good shepherd' only at John 10.11 in the New Testament, and he is not 'the servant of God' in the New Testament at all.

These tricks make it easier to imagine that Jesus was a mythical figure, because the later the sources used, the more mythical parallels can be found. They have nothing to do with the historical Jesus, whom Thompson rejects.

Other mistakes are more mundane. For example, Thompson declares that Mark 7 'presents a discourse about hygiene', and contains 'a

---

[57] Thompson, *Messiah Myth*, p. 80.
[58] P. M. Casey, 'Is Not This an Incompetent New Testament Scholar? A Response to Thomas L. Thompson', *Bible and Interpretation*, http://www.bibleinterp.com/opeds/cas368006.shtml [last accessed 14 May 2013].
[59] Thompson, *Messiah Myth*, p. 108.

caricature of "the tradition of the elders".[60] This reads modern culture
back into the environment of Jesus. We know that we should wash our
hands before meals and after going to the toilet as a matter of hygiene,
but nothing like this was known in first-century Judaism. This much
was well known in scholarship which was available to Thompson. In
standard works about this passage available to him, Taylor (1952)
discussed 'the practice of ritual washing', and Hooker (1990) correctly
headed her discussion 'A dispute about purity'.[61] Neither of them was
ignorant enough to treat the dispute as a matter of hygiene, and an Old
Testament scholar familiar with the book of Leviticus should have known
at least that much, and have had more understanding of 'the tradition of
the elders'. The passage has of course been difficult to sort out because
of the Christian prejudices applied to it, and because of the problems
posed by the paucity of primary source material, so that the most recent
scholarship is needed to make complete sense of it, but that is no excuse
for Thompson's mistakes.[62]

Jesus does turn up in ch. 7, 'The Myth of the Dying and Rising God'. This
also draws on late elements in the Gospels, and *presupposes* that anything
which draws on old tradition cannot have been part of the ministry of
the historical Jesus. It cannot be said to *demonstrate* anything. Thompson
begins with *Matthew's* version of Jesus' words at the Last Supper. He
does not explain why Matthew has Jesus recline (only?) with the Twelve,
rather than come with them, which he surely did (Mt. 26.20/Mk 14.17);
why accordingly Jesus does not say in Matthew that his betrayer would
be 'one of the Twelve' (Mk 14.20), a shocking fact which makes sense
only if more people than the Twelve were present, as one would expect at
Passover unless there were a very strong reason for him to do otherwise,
which we would expect to be explained because it would be a significant
divergence from normal Jewish custom: the follow-on from this, when
Mark supposedly omitted Judas asking Jesus whether he was the one who
would betray him, with Jesus answering 'You said [so]' (Mt. 26.25 only, cf.
Jn 13.26–30); why Mark took the trouble to have Jesus interpret the cup
only *after* everyone had drunk from it, when Matthew had not said this; or
why Mark supposedly altered 'the kingdom of my Father' (Mt. 26.29) to
'the kingdom of God' (Mk 14.25), when Matthew altering Mark is again
so much easier to explain. All these points support the priority of Mark.
I argued as early as 1998 that Mark's narrative is based on a very early,

---

[60] Thompson, *Messiah Myth*, p. 69.
[61] Taylor, *Mark*, p 335–6; Hooker, *Mark*, p. 172.
[62] These problems were finally sorted out by Crossley and Furstenburg: Crossley, *Date of Mark's Gospel*, pp. 183–205, 'Dating Mark Legally (II): Mark 7.1–23'; Y. Furstenburg, 'Defilement Penetrating the Body: A New Understanding of Contamination in Mark 7.15', *NTS* 54 (2008), pp. 176–200, both with bibliography; and for a summary for the general reader, see Casey, *Jesus of Nazareth*, pp. 326–31.

abbreviated but authentic, Aramaic account of this event.[63] Thompson does the same with this as with all respectable New Testament scholarship: he leaves it out.

Thompson also omits every indication that Jesus expected the coming of the kingdom soon. For example, he does not discuss Jesus' plea to the inner group of three in Gethsemane 'that you may not enter into trial' (Mk 14.38/Mt. 26.41). Instead, he declares that Matthew 'reiterates the songs of Thutmosis III and Ramses IV'.[64] This artificially removes Jesus from his historical environment and places him where Thompson likes instead. He does not explain how Matthew might have known the 'songs of Thutmosis III and Ramses IV', nor does he quote any of them, to the point where it is not clear what Matthew is supposed to have drawn from them. He also declares that the 'metaphor of "new wine" draws on the biblical tradition of royal ideology...'[65] Does he not know that new wine was a real substance which real people drank when they could afford it, and that everyone who could drank wine at Passover? The next section is about 'Dionysus, Baal and Tammuz', and, like most of the book, it has precious little to do with Jesus. The final section of the chapter is headed 'Metaphors of Resurrection and Eternal Life', and, like most of this book, it has nothing much to do with Jesus either.

In short, this is the most incompetent book by a professional scholar that I have ever read. It is not a serious improvement on the works of Doherty and Murdock, instead illustrating the pitfalls which await professional scholars who step outside their 'field of study'. It does so because, like other mythicists, Thompson has not followed evidence and argument. Having begun as a Catholic who followed the convictions fed him by the church, he has been converted to a different set of convictions.

Thompson has now published a collection of essays, which he has edited with an undergraduate student, Thomas Verenna, who was also an American Catholic.[66] I propose to discuss two of the essays here. The opening essay, 'Introduction', is attributed to both of them. In it, they make nonsense of the quest of the historical Jesus, by including every known falsehood in their list. For example, they include 'a cynic sage', and 'a Pharisee', at the hand of the grossly biased Westar Jesus seminar, and the equally biased Jewish maverick Hyam Maccoby.[67] No pseudo-scholarship of that kind could possibly show that Jesus was not a historical prophet and teacher, whose teaching had some apocalyptic elements, and who deliberately headed for martyrdom in Jerusalem.

---

[63] Casey, *Aramaic Sources of Mark's Gospel.*

[64] Thompson, *Messiah Myth*, p. 199.

[65] Thompson, *Messiah Myth*, p. 199.

[66] T. L. Thompson and T. S. Verenna, *'Is This Not the Carpenter?' The Question of the Historicity of the Figure of Jesus* (Sheffield: Equinox, 2012).

[67] Thompson and Verenna, *'Not the Carpenter?'*, pp. 9–10, with nn. 17, 26, and lots of others.

I also take issue with Thompson's own essay, 'Psalm 72 and Mark 1:12–13: Mythic Evocation in Narratives of the Good King'.[68] First, in Mark's account, unlike that of Matthew, this is simply the end of the story of Jesus' baptism by John the Baptist, which Thompson hardly discusses. He treats it as a story told by Mark, and assumes that it was not a historical event, whereas it was a major event in the life of the historical Jesus.[69] Once again, Thompson prefers the story told by Matthew, and this time Luke's even more expanded and rewritten narrative as well. Here he finds two of his biographical 'tropes'. The first is supposed to have 'historical roots in ancient Egypt's royal ideology and specifically witnessed in celebratory proclamations of the accession to the throne by Pharaohs Merneptah and Ramses IV'. This time he quotes from Pritchard's *Ancient Near Eastern Texts*, which shows that it has no proper connections with the Gospels. Thompson announces that it is 'implied by the proclamation of the "good news" and found in narratives, especially healing and feeding stories'. His second trope is taken from 'ancient Near Eastern royal ideology', and ignores the fact that Jesus was not a king.

Thompson turns next to Job 29, which again has only the most general points in common with the Gospels. Then he finally gets to Psalm 72, but his discussion does not explain why he chose this particular Psalm, most of which has nothing to do with Jesus. He labels Ps. 72.1–4 'the good news', but this phrase is not found in the psalm. Inappropriate items include 'slaying the dragon', Thompson's interpretation of the king crushing the oppressor (vs 4) and his enemies licking the dust (vs 9), and the kings of Sheba and Seba bringing him gifts.

I turn now to the final events in Jesus' life. As is well known, he went up to Jerusalem, fully intending to die, an event which he helped to precipitate by doing what is often called 'Cleansing the Temple'. On the day before this, he walked to Jerusalem from Jericho and rode for the last two miles on a donkey. Freke and Gandy discuss the mythical associations of riding on a donkey and people waving palm branches, especially in supposed parallels from Dionysus and mystery religions.[70] The branches are not said to be palms in the synoptic Gospels. Palm trees were, however, ubiquitous in the real daily lives of ordinary people going from Jericho to Jerusalem, and donkeys were ubiquitous as pack animals and for riding on throughout the ancient Near East. Once again, Freke and Gandy are selective in appealing to mundane items turning up in myths and ignoring their presence in ordinary daily life, especially daily life in the right place at the right time.

The next day, Jesus 'cleansed the Temple', and thereby precipitated the final action against him, which led to his crucifixion. He was, however,

---

[68] Thompson and Verenna, *'Not the Carpenter?'*, pp. 185–201.
[69] For a summary for the general reader, see Casey, *Jesus of Nazareth*, pp. 173–83.
[70] Freke and Gandy, *Jesus Mysteries*, pp. 53–4.

determined to celebrate his final Passover with his disciples first, and took great pains to ensure that he did so.[71] Mythicists follow the Christian traditions to which they used to belong: they take precious little notice of the Jewish Passover, and imagine that Jesus instituted the Eucharist, which is not mentioned in Mark or Matthew, nor during the Passion narrative of John. They then find the Eucharist all over the ancient world by the simple expedient of describing meals with bread and wine, or the eating of a deity (which Jesus was not), as 'Eucharists'.

For example, Acharya comments that: 'The Eucharist, or the sharing of the god's blood and body, has been a sacred ritual within many ancient mystery religions, and the line ascribed to Jesus, "This is my blood you drink, this is my body you eat," is a standard part of the theophagic (god-eating) ritual.'[72] This completely misrepresents both Jesus and Judaism. The last thing he would ever have said is 'this is my blood you drink', because of the Jewish taboo on drinking blood, and Acharya's placing this comment in inverted commas highlights its lack of verifiable authenticity. Moreover, Jesus was not regarded as God during his historic ministry, so this was not part of a 'theophagic... ritual', so what Acharya has not altogether quite invented is also dependent on much later Christian sources.

Acharya further states that: 'The Christian form of the Eucharist is highly similar to the ritual as practised as part of the Eleusinian mysteries, in detail...' As far as we can tell from our meagre sources, this is simply false.[73] It is, moreover, irrelevant, as Jesus celebrated the Jewish Passover, not the later Christian Eucharist. Acharya claims that: 'The Eleusinian Eucharist honored both Ceres, goddess of wheat, and Bacchus/Dionysus, god of the vine.' The Eleusinian mysteries were in fact centred on the story of Persephone, known as *Korē*, the maiden, who was the daughter of Demeter, who was in due course identified with Ceres.[74] According to the main story in the *Homeric Hymns*, Persephone, daughter of Demeter and Zeus, was carried off by Hades, god of the underworld, and brother of Zeus, with Zeus's consent. This event was witnessed by the goddess Hecate, and her screams were heard by *Helios*, the sun. Demeter spent nine days searching the earth for her daughter before Hecate and Helios told her what had happened.

Demeter was so annoyed with Zeus that she left Mount Olympus and wandered the earth. She went to Eleusis, and after trouble there, she

---

[71] For a summary account for the general reader, see now Casey, *Jesus of Nazareth*, pp. 429–37.

[72] Acharya, *Christ Conspiracy*, p. 200, without any references.

[73] See now H. Bowden, *Mystery Cults in the Ancient World* (London: Thames & Hudson, 2010).

[74] An intelligible and up to date account is given by Bowden, *Mystery Cults in the Ancient World*, esp. ch. 1, 'The Eleusinian Mysteries'; cf. esp. also ch. 5, 'Dionysus', and pp. 206–11 on the (much exaggerated) connections between Christianity and mystery cults.

demanded that the people of Eleusis build her a temple, promising rites for them to perform to soften her anger. She then stopped grain from growing across the earth. Zeus appealed to Demeter to return to Olympus, which she agreed to do only if Persephone was returned to her. Zeus sent Hermes, the messenger of the Gods, to ask Hades to release her. Hades did release her, but only after he had given her a pomegranate seed to eat. When Persephone was reunited with her mother, Demeter explained that, because she had eaten food in the underworld, she would have to spend a third of each year there. Zeus sent Rhea (his own mother and that of Demeter) to placate Demeter, she was reconciled with the gods and let the grain grow again.

Demeter then taught the rites of the mysteries to the rulers of Eleusis, and the whole earth bloomed again! Bowden correctly makes the obvious point: 'At the heart of the myth is an explanation of the cyclical nature of agriculture…'[75]

There are other sources in which Dionysus is closely associated with Demeter. What I have not found, however, is evidence of anything that could reasonably be described as 'the Eleusinian Eucharist'. Once again, Acharya is guilty of describing pagan material in Christian terminology to make them sound more alike. Bowden notes that the tradition, which she in fact follows, owes much to Protestant polemicists arguing that the 'primitive Christianity' of the early church was corrupted by the incorporation of rites and doctrines drawn from non-Christian mystery cults, as well as to critics of Christianity as a whole.[76] Acharya's hopelessly late dating of the Gospels, and omission of the Jewish Passover, also enables her to assume that baptism was an initiation rite, a very basic parallel to mystery religions having initiation rites. The Jewish Passover, however, had no initiation rites. It was celebrated by all observant Jews. Jesus did not baptize. When Christianity was emerging from Judaism, baptism was an entrance ceremony open to anyone who chose to join this emerging sect, which was then a form of Judaism. Followers of Jesus at this time also ate common meals without any need for prolonged initiation. What lies behind all this is that Acharya was once committed to a ludicrously conservative form of Christianity, in which Jesus was completely unique, and Christianity was supposed to be a completely unique religion with inerrant Scriptures. Christians were initiated by means of baptism and confirmation. Acharya's ignorance of relevant historical research is equally evident in her present arguments. She has simply altered the perspective of ignorance from which she writes.

After his final Passover with his disciples, Jesus went to the garden of Gethsemane and waited to be betrayed and arrested, and after interrogation

---

[75] Bowden, *Mystery Cults in the Ancient World*, p. 28.
[76] Bowden, *Mystery Cults in the Ancient World*, p. 207.

by the high priest and his council he was sent to Pilate, who crucified him as a bandit, with two other bandits. The argument that Jesus cannot have been crucified because so many mythical beings were said to have been crucified is dependent on the most incompetent 'parallels' that I have ever seen assembled. It is well known that crucifixion was not only the cruellest of punishments inflicted by the Roman imperial power, it was also extremely common in real life in this world. Attempts to provide 'parallels' from myths, however, suffer very badly from describing as 'crucifixion' all sorts of things which have precious little in common with this penalty.

For example, Carrier claims that the Sumerian goddess Inanna, whom he describes as 'the Babylonian Ishtar', 'was stripped naked and crucified, yet rose again'. He describes this as 'the center of a major Sumerian sacred story, preserved in clay tablets dating over a thousand years before Christ'.[77] This is completely misleading. Inanna was a vegetation goddess, which is the basic reason why she was said to have died, descended to the underworld,[78] and come back again. This was a symbol, in story mode, for the obvious fact that vegetation dies, and comes to life again some months later. This is the central reason why there are lots of ancient stories about more or less dying and rising deities. Moreover, people told masses of stories on this major theme, and many of the stories are quite different from each other, as well as different from anything in real life, and consequently they are not all about vegetation.

The Sumerian story of Inanna is older than Carrier claims. In it, when Inanna had descended to the underworld and was stripped of all her clothing,

Inanna was turned into a corpse,
A piece of rotting meat,
And was hung from a hook on the wall.[79]

It should be obvious that this has nothing to do with the Roman penalty of crucifixion.

Moreover, after a few pages, Carrier goes back on himself, though not without repeating his major mistake. He comments: 'Holding has tried to protest that Inanna wasn't really crucified. But being humiliated by being stripped naked, killed and nailed up in shame amounts to the same thing to any reasonable observer.'[80] In the context of discussing the historicity of Jesus of Nazareth, it is not the same thing at all. Jesus suffered the Roman

---

[77] R. Carrier, *Not the Impossible Faith: Why Christianity Didn't Need a Miracle to Succeed* (Lulu, 2009), p. 17.
[78] For translation and commentary, see D. Wolkstein and S. N. Kramer, *Inanna. Queen of Heaven and Earth. Her Stories and Hymns from Sumer.* (New York: Harper & Row, 1983).
[79] Wolkstein and Kramer, *Inanna*, p. 60.
[80] Carrier, *Not the Impossible Faith*, p. 19.

penalty of crucifixion, and Inanna, a goddess worshipped in Sumer two millennia previously, did not. Thus Jesus was nailed to a cross so that he would die, whereas Inanna was 'hung from a hook on the wall', as large joints of meat were and still are.

On the previous page, Carrier has a caveat of which he should have taken much more notice: 'my point is not that the Christians got the idea of a crucified god from early Inanna cult…I always caution strongly against overzealous attempts to link Christianity with prior religions.'[81] It is regrettable that he did not take this advice to heart himself.

Among the many features of the story which have nothing to do with later Christianity is Ninshubur going around to one deity after another. When Inanna had not returned after three days and three nights, Ninshubur went to the temple of Enlil, who refused to help. Ninshubur cried to Enlil, and subsequently to Nanna and then Enki: 'do not let your daughter be put to death in the underworld'.[82] This indicates how careful we should be about saying that Inanna had died at all, as Jesus certainly did when he was crucified by Roman soldiers outside Jerusalem in this earthly world.

Enki brought forth dirt from under his fingernail, and fashioned a *kurgarra* and a *galatur*, both creatures who were neither male nor female. After a lengthy debate with Erishkigal, 'the Queen of the Underworld', who 'was moaning with the cries of a woman about to give birth', in which they turned down other offers from her, they said: 'We wish only for the corpse which hangs from the hook on the wall.' When this was granted to them,

The *kurgarra* sprinkled the food of life on the corpse.
The *galatur* sprinkled the water of life on the corpse,
Inanna arose… [83]

Inanna was about to ascend from the underworld when all sorts of things went wrong, with the *galla*, the demons of the underworld, trying to prevent her. When Ninshubur met her, the *galla* said they would take Ninshubur in place of Inanna, an offer which she refused. There were similar incidents with her sons Shara and Lulal. It was different when they got to her husband Dumuzi, who, unlike Ninshubur, had done nothing to get her out of the underworld:

Inanna fastened on Dumuzi the eye of death.
She spoke against him the word of wrath.
She uttered against him the cry of guilt:
'Take him! Take Dumuzi away!'[84]

---

[81] Carrier, *Not the Impossible Faith*, p. 18.
[82] Wolkstein and Kramer, *Inanna*, p. 61.
[83] Wolkstein and Kramer, *Inanna*, p. 67.
[84] Wolkstein and Kramer, *Inanna*, p. 71.

The *galla* seized Dumuzi and beat him, and a number of adventures followed, after which Inanna sought for him, and when she found him, she took him by the hand and declared,

> You will go to the underworld
> Half the year.
> Your sister, since she has asked,
> Will go the other half.[85]

This reflects the climate in Sumer, where, for example, Dumuzi's sister 'Geshtinanna "root-stock of the grapevine" reigns over the wine whose grapes and figs are harvested from the Sumerian earth each autumn; while Dumuzi, in his aspect of Damu, the power in the growing grain, reigns over the beer, whose barley grows in the earth the other six months of the year, to be harvested in the spring.'[86]

I hope this is sufficient to make absolutely clear that the stories of the death of Jesus, much of which are literally true, and of his Resurrection, have nothing whatever to do with stories of the Sumerian goddess Inanna, and for similar reasons, nothing to do with creatures who have been loosely labelled by modern scholars as 'dying and rising' deities.[87]

Acharya produces the story that Krishna was shot with an arrow that pinned him to a tree, which killed him. She first comments correctly: 'The orthodox depiction of Krishna's death relates that he was shot in the foot by a hunter's arrow while under a tree.'[88] It should be obvious that this too has nothing to do with the Roman penalty of crucifixion. Acharya then turns to hopelessly out-of-date secondary literature which has abundantly biased descriptions. For example, she turns again to Jacolliot in 1876, this time with a story in which there were several arrows, and Krishna was suspended in the branches of a tree. This ends up with 'the pinning of the god to a tree using multiple nails'.[89] Jesus was not thought to be a god when he was put to death, though the idea that he was fully God was central to Acharya's religion. There is no excuse for describing arrows as 'nails', nor for imagining that Jesus' death by the Roman penalty of crucifixion for criminals, especially slaves and provincials, was a repetition of a story about Krishna.

Again relying on out-of-date scholarship, Acharya announces that the

---

[85] Wolkstein and Kramer, *Inanna*, p. 89.

[86] Wolkstein and Kramer, *Inanna*, p. 168.

[87] For a brief account of the stories of Inanna seen properly in their Sumerian cultural background, see Wolkstein and Kramer, *Inanna*, pp. 115–73.

[88] Acharya, *Suns of God*, p. 241, without any references to primary sources.

[89] Acharya, *Suns of God*, p. 241, with p. 286n. 1, referring to L. Jacolliot, *The Bible in India: Hindoo Origin of Hebrew and Christian Revelation* pp. 253–4, 574, this time as if it were published in 1876: it was translated by 'R.G.' and published in London by Hotten, in 1870.

Egyptian *ankh* is really a cross.[90] It was not a Roman cross or a Christian crucifix. It was, however, known to the Church Fathers and others as the *crux ansata*, because it has in common with both that it has a stem and a crossbar, and at the top a loop into which you can fit a human face if you feel like it. And that is all. Acharya also imagines that Barnabas asserted that 'the brazen serpent of Moses was set up as a cross'. However, she gives no reference, and I cannot find one.[91] Several Fathers regarded the brazen serpent as a *type* of Christ (cf. Jn 3.14–15), but that is not what Acharya says. Acharya further declares that 'Moses himself makes the sign of the cross at Exodus 17:12, when he was on a hilltop with Aaron and Hur.'[92] Now that she has actually given a reference for a change, it is easier to demonstrate that her comments are false. In this piece of Jewish fiction, we are told that, in a battle between Israel and Amalek, 'it came to pass, whenever Moses raised his hand, Israel prevailed, and whenever his hand rested, Amalek prevailed' (Exod. 17.11). In accordance with the logic of this weird tale, it follows naturally that 'Moses' hands grew heavy', so 'Aaron and Hur held up his hands' (Exod. 17.12). What has this to do with the Roman penalty of crucifixion, or the even later Christian habit of making the sign of the cross? Nothing whatever!

Acharya also turns to one of Homer's stories about Odysseus. In Odyssey Book XII Circe warns Odysseus about the dangers he will face at sea. One of these is the Sirens. In the adventure of the Argonauts, Jason and his men faced the danger of the Sirens with the help of the singing of Orpheus. Odysseus has no Orpheus to drown out the lovely voices, so he orders his men to stuff their ears with wax and tie him to a mast so he can't escape, but can still hear them singing (Homer *Od.* XII, 36–110, 165–200). It should be obvious that this has nothing to do with the Roman penalty of crucifixion either.

Acharya further argues that the Passion narrative is not only secondary, but there was not enough time for it to happen, and, with no references at all, except a vague one to Kuhn, Harpur makes the same claim.[93] Acharya repeats the claim that 'Jesus is made to pray three times while his disciples are asleep...' We have seen that this claim is quite false. The inner group of three disciples had to hear only a very short prayer, which they will have heard perfectly well *before* they went to sleep.[94] She then claims that: 'The whole gospel story purports to take place over a period of a few weeks, and the entire "life of Jesus" represents about 50 hours total.' This is complete nonsense, so unrelated to the story of the Gospels that one hardly knows what to say. Are we really supposed to imagine that the Passion took place

[90] Acharya, *Suns of God*, p. 254, without any references to primary sources.
[91] Acharya, *Suns of God*, p. 254, without any references to primary sources.
[92] Acharya, *Suns of God*, p. 254.
[93] Acharya, *Christ Conspiracy*, pp. 204–5; Harpur, *Pagan Christ*, pp. 146–7.
[94] See pp. 148–9; Casey, *Jesus of Nazareth*, pp. 438–9.

within 50 hours of Jesus' baptism by John the Baptist, with the migratory ministry round Galilee fitted in between times? It is not even long enough for Jesus to walk back to Galilee and then walk to Jerusalem for the final events! The Gospels are written within the form of the ancient *bios*, or life; as we have seen, they do not have a proper chronological outline, and from our point of view they are short.[95] This is very regrettable for us, but it does not entail this gross falsehood.

Acharya then turns to J. M. Robertson, an atheist who left school in 1869 at the age of 13, and who later wrote in an anti-Christian manner. She quotes him commenting that 'The fact that the whole judicial process took place in the middle of the night shows its unhistorical character.' Really? Does everything always happen in the daytime? Joseph Caiaphas, as high priest, could do what he liked in his own house at night, and the result, which has already been written up in Mark, was probably not what we would recognize as a 'judicial process'.[96] Roman governors started work first thing in the morning, which is why that was when the chief priests, elders and scribes handed Jesus over to Pilate (Mk 15.1), not 'in the middle of the night'.

Acharya then turns to Carpenter, a gay anti-Christian socialist (1844–1929) with apparently no relevant qualifications, who wrote in 1920:

> If anyone will read, for instance, in the four Gospels, the events of the night preceding the crucifixion and reckon the time which they would necessarily have taken to enact…he will see – as has often been pointed out – that the whole story is physically impossible.[97]

Carpenter's list of what is supposed to have happened includes Luke's story of Jesus being sent by Pilate to Herod and then back again (Lk. 23.6–12). This need not have taken as long as Carpenter liked to imagine, but it is written completely in Luke's style and, like much of the proceedings before Pilate, it is historically not altogether plausible. Carpenter then has 'the preparation of a Cross', as if that would have taken a long time too. In fact, the Romans simply had to produce a crossbeam, and they are likely to have had plenty of them available, because they expected to crucify more people. Carpenter next has 'the long and painful journey to Golgotha'. The journey was certainly painful for Jesus, but given he was supposed to have been crucified three hours after he was taken before Pilate, it was not too long to have taken place.

Acharya turns next to Dujardin (1861–1949), who wrote in 1927; she quotes from an abbreviated translation published in 1938. Dujardin was

[95] See p. 110; Casey, *Jesus of Nazareth*, pp. 184–5.
[96] Cf. Casey, *Jesus of Nazareth*, pp. 440–3.
[97] E. Carpenter, *Pagan and Christian Creeds*, quoted by Acharya as published by Health Research in 1975, but originally published in London by Allen & Unwin, 1920.

a symbolist writer and journalist, who was equally prejudiced against Christianity. The part which Acharya chose to quote reads as follows:

The improbabilities of the accounts in the gospels are transparent... let us only note that Jesus is arrested, arraigned before two courts, and executed in the space of a few hours. The Jewish tribunal sits in the middle of the night, and this very night is the night of a religious feast, an absurdity which of itself proves how far the writer was from the events and place about which he wrote. No custom is respected: the Sabbath for instance, is again and again violated, and Jewish law and custom are ignored. As for Pilate, he is an inconceivable caricature of a Roman magistrate.

This presupposes a very literal but not very accurate understanding of the Gospel accounts. The only true part is the last sentence: we should not believe the story of the trial before Pilate, when none of the disciples were there. Jesus was not 'arraigned before two courts'. He was interrogated by the high priest and his accomplices in the evening, and condemned by the Roman governor the following morning. That the night was 'the night of a religious feast' indicates an emergency, not an impossibility. The sabbath did not come until Jesus was (almost?) buried, so it was not repeatedly violated. Jewish law and custom were mostly followed, not ignored at all.

We must therefore conclude that Acharya has simply selected anti-Christian people who are hopelessly out of date. Her comments have nothing to recommend them.

Places

Another approach is to argue that none of the places where Jesus lived and worked existed.[98] For example, Zindler has argued that Nazareth, Capernaum and other places significant in Jesus' life did not exist.[99] Nazareth and Capernaum are examples of quite different kinds. Nazareth was a very insignificant village, which explains Zindler's first point, that it is not mentioned in various ancient sources, including the basic Jewish sources, the Old Testament, Josephus and the Talmud. Given also that later building in the immediate area includes the modern town of 60,000 people,

---

[98] Part of the following discussion was published in Casey, *Jesus of Nazareth*, pp. 128–32.
[99] F. R. Zindler, 'Where Jesus Never Walked', *American Atheist* 36 (1996–7), pp. 33–42, which I accessed at http://www.atheists.org in December 2009, and therefore cite by the page numbers of my printout. Cf. Zindler, *Jesus the Jews Never Knew*, pp. 1–2, 4, 72, which makes some of the same points more briefly.

the absence of recoverable archaeological remains would not have been significant, had it been the case.

Zindler's second point is to make fun of Lk. 4.29–30, and of pilgrim traditions based on it. This is Luke's rewritten version of Jesus' visit to Nazareth, an accurate account of which is given at Mk 6.1–6 (cf. Mt. 13.53–8). According to Luke only, the inhabitants threw Jesus out and 'led him to the brow of the hill on which their city was built' (Lk. 4.29). Zindler uses this to argue that Nazareth did not exist, but critical scholars know that 'There is no site corresponding to the description in Luke 4.29' and that 'Luke expands Mark … *thirdly* by a redactional rounding off of the event …'.[100] Moreover, late pilgrim traditions are hopelessly inaccurate. Accordingly, Zindler's comments do not cast doubt on the existence of Nazareth or the accuracy of Mk 6.1–6, and illustrate again that he repeatedly ignores serious scholarship, and prefers to attack the piety of ignorant Christians, one of whom he used to be.

Zindler proceeds to make fun of Franciscan excavations and of pious veneration of the supposed site of the Annunciation. There are genuine problems with pious excavators, as all critical scholars know, and most critical scholars do not believe in the stories of Jesus' birth, so there was indeed no site of the Annunciation.[101] It does not follow that there was no Nazareth.

A more thorough attempt to demonstrate that Nazareth did not exist at the time of Jesus has recently been made by Salm.[102] Salm got one point right: late pilgrim traditions, which believed Lk. 4.29 and accordingly assumed that there was a brow of a hill on which Nazareth was built, caused problems with the location of the site. This situation was made worse by the pious assumptions of early excavators, who interpreted what they found in accordance with what church traditions led them to believe should be there.[103] This does mean that the *precise* location of the settlement at the time of Jesus is somewhat uncertain. Moreover, absolutely precise information about the date of some finds is not always available, not least because some finds, such as shards and lamps, can be difficult to date with precision. However, there does not seem to be any serious doubt among competent investigators that some finds are of sufficiently early date, and that these include a vineyard with walls and a tower, which show that there was some sort of settlement, and shards which are said to date from the Herodian period. Salm himself imagines that, when the settlement was restarted after 70 CE, it was on the

---

[100] Respectively, Rousseau and Arav, *Jesus and His World*, p. 214; G. Lüdemann, *Jesus after 2000 Years* (Trans. J. Bowden. London: SCM, 2000), p. 283.

[101] On the birth stories, see now Casey, *Jesus of Nazareth*, pp. 145–51.

[102] R. Salm, *The Myth of Nazareth: The Invented Town of Jesus* (Cranford, NJ: American Atheist Press, 2008).

[103] See especially the proper critical study of J. E. Taylor, *Christians and the Holy Places: The Myth of Jewish-Christian Origins* (Oxford: Clarendon, 1993), pp. 221–67.

Nazareth valley floor. He comments: 'One obvious lacuna in the archaeological record is that the Nazareth valley floor has never been excavated ...
is now heavily built over and will in all likelihood never be excavated.'[104]
This is a main point. Its significance is that some absence of archaeological
evidence is not evidence of the absence of Nazareth.

This underlines the importance of the literary evidence, which Salm
handles extremely poorly, having no relevant scholarly qualifications in this
area. He begins with the *Protevangelium of James*, which was written in
the second half of the second century, and which consists of late inaccurate
storytelling.[105] Its stories presuppose that Joseph and Mary lived in Judaea
before the birth of Jesus, as Matthew seems to have believed (Mt. 2.19–23).
Salm, however, misinterprets this to mean that the 'hometown' *of Jesus* was
in Judaea, whereas this document is not about the life of Jesus, and does
not even mention *his* hometown. Salm next misinterprets a passage of the
Christian writer Julius Africanus (c. 200 CE) quoted by Eusebius, claiming
that he describes Nazara and Cochaba as 'villages of Judea' and quoting
an antiquated American translation to this effect. Julius in fact described
them as Jewish villages (*kōmōn Ioudaikōn*, Eus. *H.E.* I, 7, 14), so he meant
Nazareth in Galilee, an interpretation which Salm describes merely as
'conceivable'.[106]

Salm proceeds to the *History of Joseph the Carpenter*, an even later
legendary work, not written before the *fourth* century.[107] According to
Salm, this text 'locates Nazareth in Judea and within walking distance of
the temple'.[108] This is not true. It says that, after Herod's death, Joseph,
Mary and Salome, obviously with Jesus, 'returned into the land of Israel,
and lived in a city of Galilee which is called Nazareth' (*HJC* 9, cf. Mt.
2.19–23). When Joseph was near death at the age of 111, 'he rose up and
went to Jerusalem' (*HJC* 12). After praying in the Temple, 'he returned to
his own house in the city of Nazareth' (*HJC* 14). When he died, Jesus and
Mary 'rent their clothes and wept. And indeed, the inhabitants of Nazareth
and of Galilee, having heard of their lamentation, flocked to them, and
wept from the third hour even to the ninth' (*HJC* 24–5). It should be
obvious that this text locates Nazareth in Galilee, and the brevity of its
spurious account of Joseph's final visit to the Temple at the ludicrous age of
111should not be taken to indicate otherwise.

None of the other texts cited by Salm puts Nazareth in Judaea either. The
whole idea has been invented by Salm, and is based on his misinterpretation

---

[104] Salm, *Myth of Nazareth*, p. 289, cf. 225–6.
[105] For an ET, see E. Hennecke and W. Schneemelcher, *New Testament Apocrypha* (Trans.
R. McL. Wilson. Philadelphia: Westminster, 1963), vol. 1, pp. 404–17.
[106] Salm, *Myth of Nazareth*, pp. 295–6.
[107] I quote from the ET of A. Walker, in A. Roberts and J. Donaldson, *Ante-Nicene Christian
Library*, vol. XVI (Edinburgh: T&T Clark, 1870), pp. 62–77.
[108] Salm, *Myth of Nazareth*, p. 296.

of texts which are too late to establish anything for the time of Jesus. It is also extraordinary that, after his comments on the archaeology of the real Nazareth in Galilee, Salm shows no concern about the absence of archaeological evidence of the existence of his invented Nazareth supposedly in Judaea. Salm's conviction that Nazareth did not exist at the time of Jesus is obviously contrary to the evidence of Mk 1.9, 'Jesus came from Nazaret of Galilee'. In accordance with his conviction, Salm declares that 'the word *Nazaret* ... is the interpolation of a later hand'.[109] While a few manuscripts read *Nazarat*, and many read the more conventional *Nazareth*, no ancient manuscripts omit this word, but atheists Price and Zindler remove inconvenient evidence in this arbitrary way too.[110]

Salm's attempt to support this by the obvious fact that Mark treats Capernaum as Jesus' home *during the ministry* is quite wrong, and his citation of Mk 6.3 in support of his notion that Jesus' family resided in Capernaum makes nonsense of Mk 6.1–6. Here Jesus returns to his 'home town (*patris*)', and his reception by the inhabitants, who know his family and him as a carpenter, is not consistent with this place being the centre of his ministry.[111]

Salm proceeds to get in a muddle over the different forms of the name Nazareth, but he demonstrates only that he does not understand place names in Israel or the problems which arise from transliterating words from Aramaic and/or Hebrew into Greek. For example, he imagines that Mark's four examples of the adjective 'Nazarene' applied to Jesus must mean something other than 'from Nazareth', apparently because he has removed 'Nazaret' from Mk 1.9, leaving no references to it in Mark. He then discusses the form 'Nazara', found for example at Mt. 4.13, which Salm oddly assumes is from 'Q', apparently because the same *form* 'Nazara' is also found in the otherwise quite different Lk. 4.16. Salm declares that this cannot be Nazareth in Galilee, because it 'did not exist before 70 CE, when the putative "Q" document was compiled', so '*Nazara* in "Q" must refer to some other place'.[112] He proceeds to locate it as the site which he has invented in Judaea, with no evidence to support his view. Accordingly, I consider Salm's work to have no value at all. His archaeological comments about Nazareth in Galilee are too strict, his work on texts is incompetent and destructive, and there is no archaeological or other evidence of Nazareth in Judaea.

Capernaum is quite different from Nazareth.[113] It was a town on the

---

[109] Salm, *Myth of Nazareth*, p. 300.
[110] Casey, *Jesus of Nazareth*, pp. 35–6, 41–3.
[111] Cf. Casey, *Jesus of Nazareth*, pp. 143–4.
[112] Salm, *Myth of Nazareth*, pp. 300–1.
[113] Cf. Rousseau and Arav, *Jesus and His World*, pp. 39–47, with bibliography; J. D. Crossan and J. L. Reed, *Excavating Jesus: Beneath the Stones, behind the Texts* (London: SPCK and San Francisco: HarperSanFrancisco, rev. edn, 2001), pp. 118–35.

shore of the Lake of Galilee which seems to have been the major centre of Jesus' ministry. If there were no remains of it, that would be a serious matter, but it has been successfully excavated at a site known as Tell Ḥum. Zindler dismisses the two occurrences of Capernaum in Josephus in order to claim that Capernaum is unknown outside the Gospels before the end of the first century.[114] In fact, however, Josephus says how he was injured and taken to a village called *Kepharnōkon* (*Life* 403–4 ms P, *Kapharnōmōn* ms W, other variants), which Zindler is quite sure is a different place from the Gospel town *Kapharnaoum*. Zindler takes no account of either differences in pronunciation or differences in transliteration of the Semitic *kphr nḥm* into Greek, which are sufficient to account for this. Moreover, Taricheae, to which Josephus was taken next, is the later name of Magdala, which was genuinely nearby.

Zindler points out that the Gospels are not precise about exactly where near a shore of the sea of Galilee Capernaum was located. This is true, but it does not mean that anything is wrong with its identification with Tell Ḥum, which fits all the Gospel evidence perfectly. Zindler makes a lot of the absence of the site of Capernaum in Christian tradition for 'several centuries'. In fact, however, Capernaum became very well known before the end of the reign of Constantine (306–37 CE), when a church was built there, the earliest date at which this was possible. Zindler pours scorn on Franciscan excavation of the site. This was indeed faulty, but doubts about the identification of Peter's house should not lead us to undervalue the fact that the kind of house in which Peter would have lived has been found. Zindler declares that 'finding the remains of a first-century synagogue is a prerequisite for establishing any site as a candidate for the biblical Capernaum'. [115] There are two reasons why this is wrong. First, we do not know that the synagogue which Jesus attended was a sufficiently distinctive site for its remains to be identifiable as such. Secondly, a later synagogue covered the most promising site, so decisive excavation is most unlikely. This does not show that the site was not a first-century synagogue, let alone that the whole place is not Capernaum. Zindler does not say anything about what he thinks the site at Tell Ḥum was, which is of central importance because it is so perfectly suitable for having been Capernaum, and it was certainly there at the time.

Zindler then casts doubt on the existence of various other places. He does not seem to realize that all he has really done is to cast doubt on his previous commitment to the inerrancy of Scripture, not on the existence of Jesus. His criteria are quite remote from those which should be used in historical and cultural research into first-century Galilee. First, he supposes that small villages and even hamlets in Galilee did not exist if they are not

---

[114] Zindler, 'Where Jesus Never Walked', p. 6.
[115] Zindler, 'Where Jesus Never Walked', p. 9.

mentioned in the Bible, or in Josephus. But the Bible was finished long before the time of Jesus, so it does not mention small villages and hamlets in Galilee which existed in the first century CE, nor even all those in Judaea. Moreover, Josephus says that there were 204 'cities and villages' in Galilee (*Life*, 235), which shows that he did not mention most of them. Therefore, the fact that he does not mention any particular village or hamlet does not mean that it did not exist, let alone that no one went there, let alone that anyone reported to have gone to such a place did not exist.

Secondly, as we have already seen in the case of Capernaum, Zindler's knowledge of the way Semitic names were transliterated into Greek, and thence into English, is unreliable. He produces complete havoc with the name of Mary Magdalene, who was so called because she came from Magdala. Magdala was located at or near the present village of Migdal on the western shore of the Lake of Galilee, some three or more miles north of Tiberias. Its Aramaic name was Migdal Nunya (or Nunaya), 'Tower of Fish' (b. *Pes.* 46). Josephus calls it by its later Greek name *Taricheae*, which means 'salted fish'.[116] A first-century mosaic found there shows a boat with one mast, a square sail and three oars on each side. An actual boat found on the north-western shore of the lake was in use at the time of Jesus.[117] It is 27 feet long, had a shallow draft and sat low in the water, so it would be easy to pull nets full of fish into it, but it could fill quickly with water in a storm. There are recent reports of a first-century synagogue being found there too. It is said to have been 'discovered in 2009 during a salvage dig conducted by Dr. Dina Avshalom-Gorni of the Israel Antiquities Authority at the location of a new hotel at Migdal Beach, the site of ancient Magdala'.[118]

In place of this obvious origin for the name Mary Magdalene Zindler makes up the idea that it was derived from 'the' Egyptian town of Migdol, presumably referring (without any reference) to Exod. 14.2. This is not remotely plausible, and Zindler's replacement of everything we know about Magdala with this is purely destructive fiction.

Thirdly, Zindler uses any evidence, well known to genuine critical scholars, that the Bible and its manuscript tradition is not inerrant, as if it were evidence that everything in the Bible is wrong and therefore that Jesus did not exist. The last step is the worst of all, since no problems about

---

[116] On Magdala, see briefly Rousseau and Arav, *Jesus and His World*, pp. 189–90; and at greater length, J. Schaberg, *The Resurrection of Mary Magdalene: Legends, Apocrypha, and the Christian Testament* (London and New York: Continuum, 2002), pp. 47–64; J. Schaberg, with M. Johnson-Debaufre, *Mary Magdalene Understood* (London and New York: Continuum, 2006), pp. 17–31.
[117] For a brief discussion including both boats, see Rousseau and Arav, *Jesus and His World*, pp. 25–30.
[118] E.g. Wikipedia, s.v. 'Migdal Synagogue'. I am not aware of a proper published report, and Wikipedia cannot be regarded as an adequate academic source, not even when supported by other online sources of a similar kind. I have not found more recent sources which were of more practical help.

where anyone has been, especially in the ancient world, can show that such a person did not exist. For example, Zindler pours scorn on the report that Jesus went to Dalmanutha (Mk 8.10), replaced in Matthew's account with Magadan (Mt. 15.39). This is at the end of the story of the feeding of the 4,000, which is an obvious midrash, whose historicity critical scholars do not believe in.[119] We really do not know where Jesus is supposed to have gone at the end of that untrue story: the whole idea that Jesus did not exist does not follow from this at all.

Zindler makes a complete mess of Bethany. This was a small place, east of Jerusalem. Jesus stayed there, during his final visit to Jerusalem (Mk 11.11; 14.3). This is a reliable report.[120] The Temple Scroll from Qumran says: 'You shall make three places, to the East of the city, separate from each other, to which shall come the lepers and... (11Q XLVI, 17–18)'. This is how it came about that Jesus had dinner 'in the house of Simon the leper', when an anonymous woman anointed him with expensive ointment and he looked forward to his forthcoming death (Mk 14.3–9). When he was walking from Jericho on his final journey to Jerusalem, he sent two of his disciples there for the donkey on which he rode into Jerusalem (Mk 11.1–11). It has probably been excavated, but all operations of this kind have been upset by later Christian belief in the resurrection of Lazarus, which has naturally led them to seek for his tomb and venerate what they found.[121]

It is very regrettable that the Fourth Gospel, the latest and most inaccurate of the four Gospels in the New Testament,[122] says that 'These things,' including a lot of obviously secondary material, 'took place in Bethany beyond the Jordan, where John was baptising' (Jn 1.28). Origen was the first person known to have looked for this place. He failed to find it.[123] Zindler, however, identified the two places, which is ridiculous, and he makes the consequently foolish announcement that 'Bethany must lie on both sides of the Jordan at once.'[124] The Gospel attributed to John is quite secondary enough without attributing further confusion to it . This is the final piece of evidence in my argument that Zindler is not a serious scholar and that his contribution to our knowledge of early Christianity is worthless.

[119] The most important scholarship concerns the feeding of the 5,000 (Mk 6.30–44). See especially R. D. Aus, *Feeding the Five Thousand: Studies in the Judaic Background of Mark 6.30–44 par. and John 6.1–15* (Lanham: University Press of America, 2010).
[120] Casey, *Jesus of Nazareth*, pp. 308, 410.
[121] Cf. Rousseau and Arav, *Jesus and His World*, pp. 15–16, with some bibliography.
[122] The evidence of this is set out at some length for the general reader in Casey, *Is John's Gospel True?*
[123] Barrett, *John*, p. 175.
[124] Zindler, 'Where Jesus Never Walked', p. 10.

Conclusions

In this chapter, I have surveyed nothing but mistakes. I began with supposed parallels to the Life and Teaching of Jesus. Many of these have nothing to do with the historical Jesus, many others are quite spurious. Those that have some substance show only that the Gospels are not inerrant, and Jesus was not perfectly unique. They also show that, long after Jesus' death, Christians really did borrow some beliefs and some iconography from other religions. Finally, mythicists have argued that various places in the Gospels did not exist at the time of Jesus. These claims are almost uniformly false.

8

Conclusions

The most important result of this book is that the whole idea that Jesus of Nazareth did not exist as a historical figure is verifiably false. Moreover, it has not been produced by anyone or anything with any reasonable relationship to critical scholarship. It belongs in the fantasy lives of people who used to be fundamentalist Christians. They did not believe in critical scholarship then, and they do not do so now. I cannot find any evidence that any of them have adequate professional qualifications.

In the opening chapter, I surveyed the people who have done this 'work'. I pointed out that, as far as I can see, none of them has proper qualifications in New Testament Studies from a decent university. This is a necessary factor in enabling them to ignore critical scholarship, and to pour scorn on critical scholars when they notice them. When possible, I also documented their background in fundamentalist Christianity, and their 'conversions' to atheism, when anything like a change of mind controlled by evidence and argument was beyond them.

Some of them claim to have elementary qualifications in modern history. In Chapters 2 and 3 I showed how this distorted their comments on such main points as the attestation of the historical Jesus. In particular, I pointed out that he came from a primarily oral culture in first-century Galilee, from which literary attestation is hardly to be expected. Archaeological evidence should be handled with great care, and too much should not be expected of that either. Mythicists also make up stories in which New Testament scholars have no historical qualifications at all, and are completely ignorant of historical research. I pointed out that this is creative fiction: some of us began our education with topics including ancient history, and spent our lives doing historical research. I am not the only one to have taught ancient history too.

In Chapter 2, I gave some details of the date and nature of the synoptic Gospels, and in Chapter 3 I amplified this greatly. The two most important points are that Mark and Matthew should be dated long before the fall of Jerusalem in 70 CE, that Mark is full of Semitisms which indicate his use of Aramaic sources, and both Matthew and Luke include some such passages too. Mythicists ignore both points: they do not learn Aramaic, so that they cannot see the evidence of the use of Aramaic sources, and they do not read the major works of secondary literature.

For example, in a perfectly plausible narrative in which Jesus healed a sick woman whom some people imagined was dead, he said *Talitha qum*, 'girl get up', using the form of *qum* which is not gender-specific, as was reasonable in Galilee at the time. Again, at Mk 14.25, the most difficult and therefore most certain reading has Jesus say 'we shall not add to drink', a natural Aramaic idiom for 'we shall not drink again'. The main point is that there are masses of such examples, properly documented from primary sources in learned secondary literature, and that mythicists require us to ignore them all, because they do not fit in with their fantasy world.

One of the major arguments surveyed in Chapters 4 to 6 concerns not what the primary sources say, but what is absent from them. There is a widespread assumption that the epistles of Paul and others are somehow really sources for Jesus, and would therefore have been sources for the historical Jesus if he had existed, from which mythicists conclude that he did not exist. I argued that this is completely wrong from beginning to end. For example, Paul, the most important writer of epistles, wrote to churches where he had converted people to his view that Gentiles did not need to undertake circumcision and other works of the Jewish Law to be saved. For this purpose, he did not need to refer to the teaching of Jesus, for this did not mention this matter. He referred to the teaching of Jesus only when he needed to do so. He therefore refers repeatedly to the death and Resurrection of Jesus, which were fundamental to his conviction that Gentiles did not have to keep the Law to be saved. Mythicists have, however, invented all kinds of spurious reasons for imagining that Paul did not really write such passages. None of their arguments should be accepted, and they frequently manifest another major fault of the arguments of mythicists, namely dependence on pseudo-scholarship which was incompetent when it was written, and is now hopelessly out of date.

Another major point is the arguments of Doherty for imagining that Paul really meant all kinds of things which have not previously occurred to properly qualified Pauline scholars but which fit into his arguments. In Doherty's fantasy world, Paul, and lots of people in his environment, really believed that Jesus was spiritually crucified in the sublunar realms. I pointed out that this is based on a small number of documents which are too late, mostly much too late, in date, and which do not belong to the environment of early Christianity at all. The quality of Doherty's argumentation is poor, and reflects his lack of qualifications in New Testament Studies.

In the final chapter, I considered the arguments that Jesus' teaching was in no way original, because of parallels in ancient Egypt, India, and all over the place. Of course Jesus' teaching was not wholly original, but that is not a valid argument against his existence. Moreover, most of the 'parallels' adduced are not valid. Likewise, it has been well known to critical scholars that the stories of his birth are not literally true. Most of the parallels adduced are, however, completely spurious. For example, Horus was not generally supposed to have been born on 25 December either.

I therefore conclude that the mythicist arguments are completely spurious from beginning to end. They have been mainly put forward by incompetent and unqualified people. Most of them are former fundamentalist Christians who were not properly aware of critical scholarship then, and after conversion to atheism, are not properly aware of critical scholarship now. They frequently confuse any New Testament scholarship with Christian fundamentalism.

The mythicist view should therefore be regarded as verifiably false from beginning to end.

Appendix: Latinisms

Introduction

It is well known to scholars that there are a number of Latinisms in Mark's Gospel, provided that we describe Latin loanwords as 'Latinisms'. Some of us are not given to doing this, especially not in elementary work, because it can mislead students beginning study and general readers, as it appears to have misled Blogger Godfrey and his commentators. Some of the older Christian scholarship used 'Latinisms' to form an argument of cumulative weight in favour of the traditional Christian view that Mark's Gospel was written in Rome. This view was then used to support the Christian tradition that Mark heard Peter preach, and his Gospel is therefore perfectly reliable. Only very conservative Christians believed this. The best scholarship in favour of this Gospel being written in Rome was generally considered to be reasonable, but not decisive.

Latin was closely related to Greek, and spoken throughout the Roman Empire, and a number of loanwords, such as *dēnarion* and *legiōn*, were items for which there were no reasonable alternatives. Some of the more idiomatic Latinisms had been in use in Greek for some considerable time. There are very few of these, which is what I meant when I wrote, in refuting Riley's attempt to revive the priority of Matthew and the secondary nature of Mark, that his notion that Mark had 'to interpolate an unnecessary Latinism when he hardly has any others' is quite unconvincing. I was not discussing Latin loanwords, and this should have been obvious in its context in a book written for scholars.[1]

Blogger Godfrey's proposal

Blogger Godfrey, however, in a blog entitled with his customary politesse, *Roll over Maurice Casey: Latin, not Aramaic, explains Mark's bad Greek*, not only drew attention to a certain proportion of these 'Latinisms', which would have been reasonable, but also declared that they nullified the evidence of Aramaic influence on Mark.[2] This is quite incompetent, which

---

[1] Casey, *Aramaic Sources of Mark's Gospel*, p. 144.
[2] http://vridar.wordpress.com/2010/12/06/roll-over-maurice-casey-latin-not-aramaic-explains-marks-bad-greek/ [last accessed 14 May 2013].

is why it had not previously been suggested. Nor is Greek which contains Latin loanwords for Roman objects 'bad' Greek, any more than we speak 'bad' English when we say we went to a restaurant. The purpose of this appendix is to note Mark's Latinisms, including loanwords, to put them in their cultural context, and to point out that they in no way undermine the importance of Mark's Aramaisms, which Blogger Godfrey appears determined to ignore.

Blogger Godfrey does not refer to any learned scholarship, but to an elementary piece from a Canadian Christian college, formerly Atlantic Baptist College, then (1996) Atlantic Baptist University, now named Crandall University, which has no outstanding New Testament scholars on its staff. This is yet another piece of evidence that Blogger Godfrey is quite incapable of leaving his fundamentalist Christian background behind, in spite of his conversion to an equally dogmatic form of atheism. The list of Latinisms provided by Crandall University includes loanwords, by which standard it is incomplete, but otherwise satisfactory. They are all included in the more extensive list provided by Gundry in his standard conservative commentary.[3]

Blogger Godfrey does not mention that the Introduction from which he quotes also argues that Mark's first language was Aramaic. After briefly surveying the evidence of Mark's Semitisms, which scholars have dealt with in infinitely more detail, it comments:

From the above data, one can infer that the author's first language was not Greek, and he did not have a Hellenistic education, so that he did not have enough facility in Greek to write in a highly literary style. The Semitic features of the Gospel of Mark probably indicate that the mother tongue of the author was a Semitic language (probably Aramaic), which is consistent with his being a Palestinian Jew.

It further suggested,

From the vividness of description of the Gospel of Mark, it seems that the author was an eyewitness or have [sic!] had access to eyewitness accounts.

After considering the evidence of Papias,[4] it further commented:

One can conclude that the author was John Mark, who used the apostle Peter as his source for his gospel. He did not concern himself, however,

---

[3]R. H. Gundry, *Mark: A Commentary on His Apology for the Cross* (Grand Rapids: Eerdmans, 1993), pp. 1043–5.
[4]On Papias, see pp. 50, 81–4, 80 above: Casey, *Jesus of Nazareth*, pp. 65–8, 86–9.

with chronological accuracy, and so did not attempt to arrange Peter's teaching 'in order'.

How trustworthy is this tradition in your judgement?

It seems trustworthy, because it is an old tradition quoted by a usually reliable anthologist and it agrees with the internal evidence.

This piece did not suggest that Mark's Latin loanwords negated the evidence of his Semitisms in any way. It rather argued in traditional fashion that it was evidence that Mark was written in Rome for people who did not understand Aramaic, and that it is a very reliable witness which depended on the reminiscences of the apostle Peter. The author commented, for example:

The presence of Latinisms and Latin translations of Greek words in the Gospel of Mark implies that the intended readers were Latin speakers, even though they could read or at least understand Greek. Latin speakers would have been found most readily in Italy, although not exclusively.

It will be noted that here the author distinguishes between 'Latinisms' and 'Latin translations of Greek words', a careful distinction which should help people not to be misled. He concluded the whole piece:

If Papias is correct, Mark's purpose seems to have been to preserve Peter's eyewitness testimony and depository of traditions about Jesus for the Roman church.

I hope this is enough to show that Blogger Godfrey's quotations from a conservative Christian website were designed to mislead people, whether or not he misled himself first.

'Latinisms'

A normal list of 'Latinisms' in the widest sense in New Testament Greek was given in the standard grammar of Blass-Debrunner-Funk, which expressed views which were standard because they were soundly based in the excellent scholarship for their times available to the authors when they wrote. Their comments included the following, with bibliography available to them when they wrote:

A vulgar idiom is normally more susceptible to foreign influences;

consequently loanwords in the NT, too, are an index of its relation to the popular language.

In this connection the question of *Semitisms* is uppermost ... (1) Many expressions which a Greek would not have used were bound to creep into a faithful written translation of a Semitic original. Such *translation Semitisms* include (a) those universally recognized for the LXX and accordingly those in quotations in the NT; (b) those to be expected in the NT books which probably rest on an Aramaic original (parts of the Synoptics and Rev)... *Latinisms* are not so strongly represented in the NT as the Semitic element ...[5]

Their examples of Latin loanwords naturally include *legiōn* and *dēnarion*; their examples of Latin suffixes added to Greek words include *Hērōdianoi*; they also note that 'Phraseological Latinisms are scarce and used mostly in connection with Roman authorities and the like.' This is what I meant when I referred in a book for scholars to Mark having so few Latinisms, a comment which properly qualified scholars were not likely to misunderstand, as unqualified bloggers have done. Their examples include *to hikanon poiein* (Mk 15.15) = satisfacere, from the account of Pilate releasing Barabbas; and *tithenai ta gonata* = genua ponere (Mk 15.19), from the account of Roman soldiers mocking Jesus. There is no suggestion here that Mark's Latinisms in any way undermine the importance of his Semitisms, which they could not possibly do. Moreover, in many cases, including both of these, the expressions occur in Greek elsewhere, so it is not always clear that they would be perceived as Latinisms when they were spoken. In these two cases, however, it is likely that Mark's informants were Latin-speaking, even if they spoke to Mark in Greek, so it would be natural for their Greek to include more Latinisms than the language of most speakers of Greek.

If loanwords are included, there are of course lots of Latinisms in Aramaic (and Hebrew) texts too. They are for Roman objects, and naturally include *dīnr* for denarius (e.g. Tg Ps-J Exod. 30.13; p. Keth. 7, 9/8 (31d)) and *lgyōn* for legion (e.g. Tg. Ps-J Num. 13.1; Tg Ezek. 30.9). Loanwords for items of currency have been ubiquitous in most languages for centuries, and still are. For example, in English we always talk about the 'yen' when we discuss Japanese currency, and, before the Euro took over, we always used to talk about the 'franc' for French currency and the Deutschmark or Mark for German currency. This was and is very sensible of us, since it is easy to get used to and understand, whereas anything else could be confusing. It does not mean that we speak 'bad' English!

---

[5] *A Greek Grammar of the New Testament and other Early Christian Literature*, F. BLASS A.D.A. DEBRUNNER *A Translation and Revision of the ninth-tenth German edition incorporating supplementary notes of A. Debrunner*, by ROBERT W. FUNK (Cambridge: Cambridge University Press and Chicago: University of Chicago Press, 1961), pp. 3–6.

Blogger Carr

The discussion on Blogger Godfrey's blog accused me of all kinds of mistakes and malpractice. All of them seem to me to stem from a combination of ignorance and prejudice. Most of them are not worth repeating, but one or two must be refuted with quotations of what I really wrote, because they wrongfully accuse me of gross incompetence and prejudice. An outstanding example, as so often, is provided by Blogger Carr:

Casey, of course, knows perfectly well that there are Latin loan words in 'Mark'.
Naturally, he is a True Biblical Scholar so does not inform his readers that there are any Latin loan words in 'Mark'.
As it would detract from the idea that there were Aramaic sources for Greek, detectable by the bad Greek, Casey does not even mention the prescence [sic!] of Latin loan words.
A real scholar mentions facts which might seem to other scholars to put his work into question, and attempts to answer those questions.
This is what I am used to when I see scientists writing. I naively took it for granted that all scholars in all fields had the same sorts of standards as the lowliest scientific researcher into the memory of mice.
I now have entered a world where True Bible Scholars simply ignore whatever does not fit their ideas.[6]

Everything is wrong with this. It is not true that I did not even mention the presence of Latin loanwords. I discussed the ones which I thought were of genuine historical significance, and I gave a significant amount of Roman background to some of these, where I thought this was of historical significance. I therefore discussed legiōn, Hērōdianoi, denarius, and centurion. So, in discussing the story usually known as the 'Gadarene swine', I commented:

The first aspect of the story that is untypical of Jesus, but widespread in stories of exorcism, is that, even after making an effort to order the unclean spirit out of the man (Mk 5.8), Jesus has to ask it its name (Mk 5.9). This is narratively convenient so that the storyteller can tell us its name is 'Legion, for we are many', the first indication that the storyteller was disenchanted with Roman legions. The second feature untypical of Jesus, but widespread in stories of exorcism, is that Jesus sends the demons out in such a way that they visibly enter something else, so they

---

[6]http://vridar.wordpress.com/2010/12/06/roll-over-maurice-casey-latin-not-aramaic-explains-marks-bad-greek/ Comment by Steven Carr – 2010/12/06 at 9.27 p.m. [last accessed 14 May 2013].

can be seen to have gone out. What they are sent into is a 'large herd of pigs'; indeed somewhat belatedly the storyteller entertains us with the information that there were about 2,000 of them! (Mk 5.11–13). Pigs were notoriously unclean animals, because Gentiles kept them and ate pork, as Jews did not. From a Jewish perspective, therefore, pigs were especially suitable animals for unclean spirits to be sent into. The existence of a herd of 2,000 pigs, though not strictly miraculous, is not something that would ever happen in real life; it is part of a story told to entertain people, and enable them to marvel at Jesus' ability to defeat the powers of evil with the power of God.

At this point, we can be more precise about the 'Legion'. The author had in mind the tenth legion, Legio Decem Fretensis, which had a boar as one of its symbols. It was stationed in the province of Syria, firstly at Cyrrhus, so it was the northernmost of the Syrian legions, and then from 18 CE onwards in the client kingdom of Commagene, which was annexed to Syria. The otherwise powerless storyteller has made great fun of a legion. The effect of Jesus sending the demons into 2,000 pigs is equally entertaining: 'the herd rushed down the steep bank into the sea ... and drowned in the sea' (Mk 5.13). This effectively gets the demons back into the underworld where they belong, for the story assumes they go down to the Abyss. It also dumps a legion where many Jews would have loved to see the Roman legions go. But the storyteller, a Jewish Christian entertaining Christians miles away, where he knew about Decem Fretensis, was regrettably unconcerned about the geography of the Decapolis. Whether this took place in the country of the Gerasenes (the original text of Mark) or the Gadarenes (some manuscripts which were influenced by Matthew) is the difference between whether the pigs had to run 33 miles, or just 6 miles, to get to the lake of Galilee! The storyteller was not concerned either to think about pigs which can swim.

This is a wonderful tale, which should not be taken literally.[7]

Again, I offered a considerable discussion of *Hērōdianoi*.

In form it is a Latinism, on the analogy of Caesariani, which meant 'followers of Caesar', and 'Tiberiani', which meant 'followers of Tiberius'. The most famous word of this kind is the later Christiani, our word 'Christian'. This was coined in the Latin-speaking business community of Antioch to mean 'followers of Christ' (cf. Acts 11.26). The Latin Herodiani accordingly meant 'followers of Herod'. The word will not have changed since the days of Antipas' father, Herod the Great. It will have been used in Mark's Aramaic source because this was what they were actually called, and there was no straightforward Aramaic alternative. Mark therefore simply took it over into his Greek translation.

---

[7]Casey, *Jesus of Nazareth*, pp. 242–3.

We have also seen that Herod the Great and Herod Antipas both had strong Roman connections. Herod the Great's buildings with Graeco-Roman names included the fortress of Antonia in the Temple complex at Jerusalem, called after Mark Antony, and the city of Caesarea. He also renamed the rebuilt Samaria as Sebaste, after the Greek form of Augustus, and he named two fortresses Herodium, after himself. This is just the sort of person who would produce Herodiani on the analogy of Caesariani. We have also seen that Herod the Great sent his son Antipas to be educated in Rome for several of his teenage years. When Herod Archelaus died, Antipas took over the dynastic name of Herod, and he used it on coins and inscriptions. We have also seen that his Greek cities with Roman names included Tiberias, his new capital, after the emperor Tiberius, and Livias, later Julias, after Augustus's wife. This is just the sort of person to maintain the description of his supporters as Herodiani. This is precisely the situation required for speakers of Aramaic to use the Latin term Herodiani.[8]

This not only discusses the Latinism *Hērōdianoi*: it puts it in its cultural context, and explains both how Aramaic speakers came to use it, and how Mark came to use it too.

I offered some further observations when discussing Mark's use of *dēnarion* (Mk 12.15). Here, however, I was more concerned with the historical situation in which Jesus himself used the term 'denarius' in Aramaic (though apart from the consonants *dnr* we cannot know exactly what form he used). I did not draw attention to it being a Latin loanword because I thought all general readers would be aware that we all use loanwords for foreign currencies, and I did explain that a denarius was a Roman coin. I did not imagine that this would be commented on by people like Blogger Carr who show every sign of not having really read it.

I commented on Jesus' teaching in the Temple:

The first dispute (Mk 12.13–17) shows that the alliance between some of the Pharisees and the Herodians was active in Jerusalem. They came to ask him whether tribute should be paid to the Roman emperor or not (Mk 12.13–14). This was a hot political issue. If Jesus gave too submissively an affirmative answer, he might lose support from faithful Jews who believed in his preaching about the kingdom of God. If he said 'no', they might get him on a charge of sedition or the like before the Roman governor, a merely political offence which he had no interest in committing. Hence he told them to bring him a denarius, a Roman coin which they possessed and he did not.

This is a much sharper point than it may appear at first sight. Roman

---

[8] Casey, *Jesus of Nazareth*, p. 341.

denarii were not in general use in Israel at that time. The Herodians, however, were supporters of Herod Antipas, and/or other highly Romanized Herods, so Jesus could rely on them having some Roman denarii, even in the Temple. Moreover, those Pharisees who were allied with the Herodians were at least prepared to co-operate with them, and they had already taken counsel with them to get Herod Antipas to put Jesus to death (Mk 3.6). Jesus got them to point out the image and inscription of the emperor on the denarius. It is almost certain that the Herodians would have the current denarii which were in widespread circulation in the Roman Empire as a whole, the second set minted by the reigning emperor Tiberius, in very large numbers. On one side (the obverse), every such denarius had Tiberius' laurel-crowned head and the inscription 'TI CAESAR DIVI AVG F AVGVSTVS', 'Tiberius Caesar Augustus, son of the deified Augustus'. On the other side (the reverse) was a seated female figure, perhaps Livia as Pax (Peace), and the end of Tiberius' inscription, 'PONTIF[EX] MAXIM[VS]', the Roman version of 'High Priest', the religious position of the Roman emperor, much worse than Joseph Caiaphas, whatever one thought of him.

This idolatrous coin violated Jewish Law, and these Pharisees and Herodians had brought it into the Temple. In response to them, Jesus gave his famous judgement: 'Give to Caesar what is Caesar's, and to God what is God's' (Mk 12.17). This is shockingly clever. They can go and give the emperor's coins back to him if they like, for at one level they belonged to an idolatrous empire, not to God's chosen people. It was however their responsibility not to forget that 'the earth is the LORD's, and its fullness' (Ps. 24.1), including the metal from which idolaters had made the images on the coins which Pharisees did not need to use, and which Herodians possessed because they were supporters of a client king of Rome.[9]

Here I explained the Roman background to an incident in the life of Jesus. It should be obvious that Mark could not be unaware of this when he repeated the story.

Finally, I had less to say about the word 'centurion', and here too my comments concentrated on the historical significance of what Mark had to say. For example, I commented on Pilate sending for 'the centurion' when he heard of Jesus' death:

According to Mark, Pilate was surprised that Jesus was already dead, and sent for 'the centurion', who confirmed that Jesus was indeed already dead (Mk 15.44–5). From Mark's point of view, Pilate and the centurion were the best witnesses that Jesus was dead, because they

---

[9]Casey, *Jesus of Nazareth*, pp. 422–3.

were the authoritative outsiders responsible for his death. Some people would therefore be motivated to produce this story. On the other hand, this story was not retained by either Matthew or Luke. Many people lasted much longer than six hours on a Roman cross, even after being scourged, and people were occasionally taken down and revived. Matthew and Luke may not have liked Pilate's surprise that Jesus was dead, as it might encourage people to believe that the centurion was wrong, and Jesus survived crucifixion for a time, rather than being raised from the dead. It is accordingly more probable that the story thus far is literally true.

Moreover, we have seen that Simon of Cyrene was pressed into service to carry Jesus' crossbeam (Mk 15.21). The traditional explanation of this unusual feature of a crucifixion, that Jesus was too weak to carry the crossbeam, is the only reasonable one. It is therefore entirely probable that Jesus died on the cross unusually quickly, in six hours. Pilate will have been concerned that Jesus should not survive, and he may not altogether have trusted Joseph of Arimathea because of his apparent haste. He may perhaps also have been aware of Joseph's traditional Jewish piety, 'expecting the kingdom of God', which had no place for the Roman Empire in it. The centurion also coheres very well with supposing that a whole cohort attended the crucifixion of three men regarded by Pilate as dangerous leaders who might be rescued by armed followers. Hence Pilate felt it safe, as well as necessary, to send for the senior centurion personally: this would give him the opinion of a responsible experienced battle-hardened soldier who knew from much experience the difference between a wounded man and a corpse, and it would leave the victims guarded by an armed cohort, perhaps still led by a tribune assisted by five centurions. Hence also Mark's perfectly correct information that Mary Magdalene and some other women watched from a distance (Mk 15.40). They will not have been able to approach nearer, and had any of the men joined them, they would have been liable to suffer the same fate as Jesus, or to have been summarily, or slowly and cruelly, dispatched, as pleased their captors.[10]

This too presupposes that Mark related a lot of correct information about Roman customs, some of it centred on the word 'centurion'. This has nothing to do with the evidence of interference from Aramaic in other parts of Mark, nor with his use of Aramaic sources. There are no such signs in this passage, which may well have been transmitted to him in Greek, perhaps orally.

Blogger Carr's comments on scholarly practice are irrelevant too, apart

---

[10] Casey, *Jesus of Nazareth*, p. 450.

from his crude and misleading use of the term 'bad' Greek. The idea that Mark's Latinisms, understood broadly to include his Latin loanwords, somehow negate the evidence of his use of Aramaic sources is not a theory put forward by decent scholars: it is a mistake by Blogger Godfrey. Learned articles on the memory of mice or anything else do not discuss the outpourings of incompetent bloggers. Nor can they discuss anything suggested after their articles were published: Blogger Godfrey's notion that 'Latin, not Aramaic, explains Mark's bad Greek' was not available to me when I wrote, because, as far as I know, no one else had been incompetent and foolish enough to suggest it.

What I really did not do was to discuss every one of Mark's Latin loanwords, such as *modios* (Mk 4.21), 'measure', in a collection of pithy sayings, or *speculator* (Mk 6.27), 'guard' or even 'executioner', in the untrue story of John the Baptist's death. I did not do this because it would not lead anywhere significant beyond the obvious fact that Mark's Gospel was written somewhere outside Israel in the Roman Empire.

It should be obvious that this has nothing to do with Aramaic idioms such as 'we shall not add to drink' (Mk 14.25), part of the evidence that Mark was translating an Aramaic source in his account of Jesus' final Passover with his disciples;[11] nor with my solution to the traditional problem posed by Mark appearing to say that Jesus 'was angry' when he healed or pronounced clean a man who was suffering from a skin disease. Here I suggested that Mark's *orgistheis*, which normally means 'be angry' in monoglot Greek,

is perfectly comprehensible as a literal and unrevised translation of an Aramaic source which gave a perfectly accurate albeit very brief account of an incident which really took place. The Aramaic source will have read *regaz*. This word often does mean 'be angry', which is why Mark translated it with *orgistheis*. But the Aramaic *regaz* has a wider range of meaning than 'be angry', including 'tremble' and 'be deeply moved'. Accordingly, Mark did not mean that Jesus was angry. He was suffering from interference, the influence of one of his languages on another. All bilinguals suffer from interference, especially when they are translating, because the word which causes the interference is in the text which they are translating. In Mark's mind, the Greek word for being angry (*orgistheis*) also meant 'tremble' or 'be deeply moved', because this was the range of meaning of the normally equivalent Aramaic word in front of him.[12]

---

[11] Casey, *Jesus of Nazareth*, p. 435.
[12] Casey, *Jesus of Nazareth*, p. 63.

No arguments of this kind can possibly be affected by the fact that Mark uses some Latin loanwords elsewhere.

Blogger Godfrey again

Blogger Godfrey has made many comments which draw into question his knowledge and understanding of first-century Jewish culture. This time, he has shown equal ignorance and lack of sympathy for first-century culture in the Roman Empire. For example, he misrepresents my view as follows:

> Mark was not fully competent in either Aramaic or Greek.
> He was reading an Aramaic word on a wax tablet, and the letters were small, and one of the letters was not clearly legible.
> Casey does not say this, but his argument also depends on Mark not ever having heard this story orally, but knowing nothing about it apart from what he was reading on a small wax tablet. And this was within five or so years of Christ's death that Mark was unaware of hearing the story – if he had heard it he would have been able to understand the common Aramaic word immediately.[13]

First, I have never suggested that Mark was not fully competent in Aramaic or Greek. Godfrey's misrepresentation of me is entirely due to his total lack of understanding of bilingual translators, and of the conditions under which Mark had to work. Mark was fully competent in Aramaic, and his Greek suffers from interference, not from incompetence, a view which suggests that Godfrey is still expecting Scripture to be inerrant. Secondly, I did not suggest that the letters were small: small letters had not yet been invented. Godfrey's comment also suggests that the difficulty over one letter is due to the illegibility of a wax tablet; anyone familiar with the LXX will know that *resh* and *daleth* and other things can easily be confused when written on papyrus. The underlying problem is really the difficulty of writing, and consequently reading, in the ancient world, even by the relatively small proportion of the population who could read, and the even smaller number who could write.

Thirdly, I did not say that my argument depends on Mark not ever having heard this story orally, because it does not depend on that at all, nor do I believe it. Of course Mark will have heard the story orally, perhaps in more than one somewhat gossipy form. What Blogger Godfrey appears unable to even contemplate is that Mark had an unimpeachably accurate Aramaic source written by an eyewitness of the ministry, whether Matthew

---

[13] http://vridar.wordpress.com/2010/12/06/roll-over-maurice-casey-latin-not-aramaic-explains-marks-bad-greek/ [last accessed 14 May 2013].

the apostle and tax collector or someone we do not know of. This is why he preferred it as his source, and sought to translate it as accurately as he could, suffering from the interference normal among bilingual translators. Of course Mark understood the common Aramaic word immediately, but he understood it as bilingual translators are liable to.

Another of Godfrey's comments totally out of synch with ancient culture is the following:

> With half the disciples from well-to-do businesses and such a wealthy coterie of women financial backers they would not need to resort to wax tablets at all. Unless the Pharisees had Pilate freeze their bank accounts after the crucifixion.[14]

The problem here is not just the gross exaggeration of the wealth of some of Jesus' followers, or the anachronistic idea that there were 'bank accounts' and that Pilate could 'freeze' them. The nearest things there were to 'bank accounts' were deposits in the Temple, which only much richer people than any of Jesus' followers could afford to make. Pilate would have got into terrible trouble if he interfered with them – he caused enough trouble by using Temple treasury funds, not private ones, to build an aqueduct for the benefit of Jerusalem (Jos. *War* II, 175–7). Any Pharisees wanting to do anything about such deposits would obviously go to the chief priests, especially the chief priest in charge of the treasury, not to the Roman governor.

What is even more remote from the first-century Roman Empire is the notion that such wealth as was available at that time would somehow remove the use of wax tablets, which were a normal part of recording things then, not least among tax collectors. Quintilian comments on authors preparing their work: 'It is best to write on wax (ceris), in which it's easiest to delete, though weak sight may prefer parchment (membrarum)' (X, 3, 30). He goes on to say that writing with 'ink' is much more tedious. This was true, and explains why Matthew the apostle and tax collector, who would be experienced in writing and keeping records on wax tablets because of his job, wrote brief accounts of incidents from Jesus' life and some of his teaching on wax tablets. Others may have done the same. In theory, they could have gone to far more trouble and written on single sheets of papyrus, but they had no good reason to do so. Whole works were written with 'ink' on papyrus, to try to ensure that they lasted.

---

[14] http://vridar.wordpress.com/2010/12/06/roll-over-maurice-casey-latin-not-aramaic-explains-marks-bad-greek/ Comment by Neil Godfrey – 2010/12/07 at 9:27 p.m. [last accessed 14 May 2013].

Conclusions

This appendix is a catalogue of confident and incompetent mistakes, much fuelled by anti-Christian and anti-scholarly prejudices. Scholars have long since established that Mark's native tongue was Aramaic, and that he used Aramaic sources when writing his Gospel. I have added a lot of new work, because I had the Aramaic Dead Sea Scrolls available to me, as scholars such as Meyer, Wellhausen and Black did not. None of this can possibly be undermined by the fact that Mark has a number of Latin loanwords, as well as a very small number of idiomatic Latin expressions.

INDEX